To Ray X n.

THE HISTORY OF SELBY
From the Earliest Times to the year 2000

By

Patricia Scott

BLACKTHORN PRESS

Blackthorn Press, Blackthorn House
Middleton Rd, Pickering YO18 8AL
United Kingdom

www.blackthornpress.com

ISBN 0 9546300 3 3

Printed and bound by Antony Rowe Ltd, Eastbourne

ILLUSTRATION CREDITS

The publisher and author are grateful to the following for help with
providing illustrations: Fred Harland 1899-1990 by permission of Mrs E
C Fenteman, Yorkshire Archaeological Society, Selby Times, York City
Archives, Yorkshire Evening Press.

INTRODUCTION

In the year 1800, *"The History of Selby, Ancient and Modern"*, was published by James Mountain, watchmaker and bookseller in Wide Street. This first book on the town was followed by the only full-scale history of Selby and its abbey. *"The History and Antiquities of Selby"* was written in 1867 by W. Wilberforce Morrell who was born in Bank House, Selby and became a well-known historian.

What qualification had I, apart from enthusiasm and a love of local history, to fulfill Morrell's wish that, in the future, another writer might have a more up-to-date history of Selby published? Maybe it is that I, like Morrell, have had many historical articles printed in the *'Selby Times'* newspaper. I have enlarged on what was written by Morrell in the 1860s, concentrating mainly on the social aspects of the history of Selby, and, especially during the days of the monastery. What is known and can now be discovered of the town's past is increasing almost by the week for documentary evidence, such as court and parish records, officials' accounts, census returns and archaeological finds, are now accessible in libraries and record offices. The use of these records from the past accounts for the varied spellings of certain names or places in the book.

I discovered when writing this history book that it could not be achieved without help and advice from numerous people. I wish to thank the staff of the following institutions for their assistance in my research: Selby, York, Goole and Leeds libraries, J.B.Morrell library York University, Brynmor Jones Library Hull University, British Lending Library Wetherby, Borthwick Institute York, English Heritage York, National Monuments Record Centre Swindon, York City Archives, York Museum, York Archaeological Trust for Excavation and Research Ltd., MAP Archaeological Consultancy Ltd. Malton, Yorkshire Archaeological Society, Leeds, North Yorkshire County Council Planning and Countryside Unit and N.Y.C.C. Records Office, Ask Oxford OUP, Selby Inland Drainage Board and Selby Town Hall.

It is impossible to name all the persons who have, in some way, generously given me their time or the benefit of their knowledge. I am especially indebted to Mike Barratt of Selby District Council, Charles and Rose Bryce, John Goodchild and David and June Thornton. Lastly, but mostly, I am indebted to Ann Challenger for access to the notes and books of her late aunt, Miss A.W.Richardson; to Ian Neale for translating the numerous Latin documents; Mike Graham for painstakingly checking every page; and my husband, Alan, whose loyal support has sustained me to the completion of this social history of Selby and the surrounding district.

Patricia Scott

A NOTE ON WEIGHTS, MEASURES AND MONEY

The weights, measures and monetary values used in this book are the ones contemporaries used. These may be summarised as:

Money:

4 farthings	=	1d (penny)
12d (pence)	=	1s (shilling)
1s	=	5p
20s (shillings)	=	£1 (pound)
21s (shillings)	=	1 guinea

Weight:

16oz (ounces)	=	1lb (pound)
1lb	=	0.45 kilograms
14lb (pounds)	=	1 stone
1 stone	=	6.35 kilograms
2 stones	=	1qr (quarter)
1qr	=	12.70 kilograms
4qr (quarters)	=	1cwt (hundredweight)
1cwt	=	50.80 kilograms
20cwt	=	1 ton
1 ton	=	1.02 tonnes

Volume:

2 pints	=	1 quart
1 quart	=	1.14 litres
4 quarts	=	1 gallon
1 gallon	=	4.55 litres
2 gallons	=	1 peck
1 peck	=	9.09 litres
4 pecks	=	1 bushel
1 bushel	=	36.40 litres
8 bushels	=	1qr (quarter)
1 quarter	=	2.91 hectolitres

Distance:

12in (inches)	=	1ft (foot)
1ft	=	0.305 metres
3ft (feet)	=	1yd (yard)
1yd	=	0.91 metres
22yds (yards)	=	1 chain
1 chain	=	20.12 metres
10 chains	=	1 furlong
1 furlong	=	201.17 metres
8 furlongs	=	1 mile
1 mile	=	1.61 kilometres

Area:

30¼ sq yds	=	1 perch
1 perch	=	25.29 sq metres

40 perches = 1 rood = 1210 sq yds = 1011.56 sq metres
4 roods = 1 acre = 4840 sq yds = 0.405 hectares

Prepared by Stephen Harrison

CONTENTS

ILLUSTRATIONS

Following page 73

1. Iron Age burial site complete with chariot found during excavation for the Al (M) motorway.
2. Selby Abbey showing The Crescent and New Street.
3. Temple Manor Nursing Home showing 13th. century doorway of Preceptory of Knights Templar and the later octagonal tower.
4. Tomb of Sir Hugh Pickworth in Selby Abbey, early 14th. century.
5. Selby cross returned from the park to the Market Place in 1986.
6. Half-timbered houses on Gowthorpe demolished in 1935 and replaced by hoardings.

Following page 182

7. Hull to Selby Railway Bridge spanning the Ouse. The line was opened 1st July, 1840.
8. Primitive Methodist Chapel built in 1862, Selby Town Hall since 1992.
9. Rifle Armoury and Drill Shed of the 38th. West York Rifle Volunteers opened in 1865, now commercial premises.
10. A late 19th. century view of Messrs. Moss, Rimmington & Co.'s Mills, looking south from New Lane.
11. Demolition of the Abbey Tythe Barn c1896.
12. Selby Local Board Offices rebuilt c1890s, now a Public House.
13. Part of Selby Union Workhouse added in 1892, now used by Social Services.
14. Ernest and Percy, brothers of William H. Whisker, with their hawking cart, early 20th. century.
15. Gas lighting in Selby Market Place in Edwardian times.
16. Selby's wooden toll bridge before its replacement by a steel one in 1971.
17. Last toll paid on Selby Toll Bridge on the 19th. September, 1991.
18. Selby Abbey 2004.

MAPS

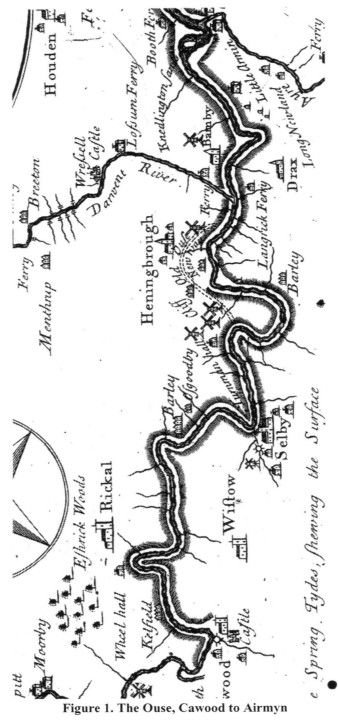

Figure 1. The Ouse, Cawood to Airmyn

CHAPTER 1

SETTING THE SCENE

In the year 2002 amateur archaeologists discovered a site of great historical interest on the coast of East Anglia. Artefacts found there, which included flint hand axes and animal bones bearing the marks of tools, signified to the professionals that primitive man had been present in England some 200,000 years earlier than had previously been believed. The examination of teeth and bones found at Boxgrove in East Sussex in 1993 and 1995 had already suggested to scientists that early man had first inhabited this country 500,000 years ago. Current evidence indicates that it was not until Europe was in the grip of the last of the Ice Ages that man inhabited the area later to be known as Yorkshire. This was near the end of the Palaeolithic Age, a period stretching from the first emergence of man to the retreat of the ice sheets that had covered vast areas of the Earth. More discoveries or future excavations may push back the dates when it is believed that man first settled in Yorkshire or made his home in Selby.

The most recent of over 15 glacial periods, lasted 60,000 years and ended around 10,000 years ago. It had been during the latter stages of this Ice Age that many of the features in Yorkshire had been formed and the terrain where Selby is today had probably been so inhospitable as to be of no interest to the first hunting and foraging bands from Europe. During the last expansion of glaciers over the Earth, the North of England, Snowdonia and the Highlands of Scotland had been covered by thick sheets of ice. It has been estimated that in some glacial periods the surface of the ice had risen above the summit of Ingleborough, in the Dales. When the ice at last loosened its hold on the land, glaciers moved slowly down the slopes eroding the landscape in their paths. Most of these rivers of ice moved at a rate of between 3 to 300 metres per year. Their huge force was powerful enough to gouge out masses of the bedrock, to scrape and split asunder rock surfaces and to pulverise the loosened pieces into small particles. The glaciers carried the boulders, gravel and sand and other debris with them and as the ice melted these materials were deposited along their way. The weight of the ice sheets, a mile thick in places, left deep depressions and long gullies which were later filled by the waters flowing down the mountain sides to form lakes and rivers.

The geographical region now known as the Vale of York was once covered by an ice-dammed lake which spread clays, sand and gravel over the land. The subsequent movement of these materials by the melting ice and the numerous waterways spreading over the land, plus the tidal flooding of the southern part of the Vale, eventually produced an area made up of sandy heaths, peaty carr land and extensive forests. Snaith, seven miles south of Selby, developed on a narrow semicircular ridge of clay and sandstone that divided the marshes and ings of Birkin, Haddlesey, Carlton and Drax, from the Carrs of Pollington and the watery districts of Balne. The shrinking of the last ice sheets created other hummocks of clay topped with gravels. Two of these ridges stretch across the Vale of York and are known today as the York and Escrick Transverse

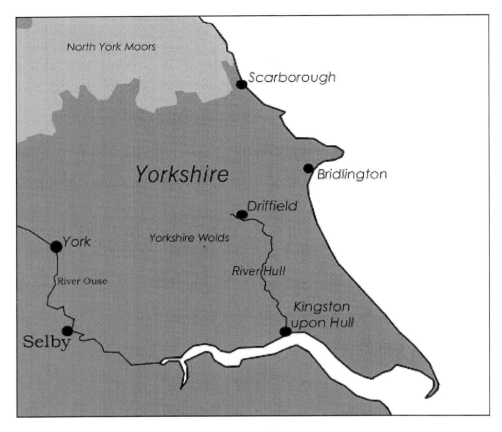

Figure 2.
Selby: location map

Moraines. Other deposits left by the ice formed the mounds now known as Hambleton Hough and Brayton Barff. The superabundance of water also turned the Vale and the East Anglian Fens into the largest waterlogged expanses in the country. Askham Bog, today a Yorkshire Wildlife Trust Nature Reserve, is a rare example of one of these ancient fens. Numerous plants not found in the surrounding area flourish there because the debris left by the glaciers of the last Ice Age has kept the soil alkaline. There is still some disagreement amongst experts concerning how far the ice actually reached in this area. To help to find some possible answers to this question a British Geological Survey team came to Selby in September 2002 to bore holes through the old lake bed and to survey the coal-bearing rocks around the Selby pit complex. The results of their work are yet to be published but the consensus is that the ice came down as far as Escrick. It also moved down the North Sea as far as the Norfolk Coast blocking off the Humber. The ice pushed into the lake carrying the silt and clay further than other debris; these sediments were eventually covered by sand washed in when the water was able to drain away.

The Ice Ages were interspersed by long periods known as Interglacials when the weather was milder and many animals roamed the land. Glaciation destroyed much of the evidence of life in Yorkshire but some scientifically valuable sediment has been preserved in limestone caves. New dating techniques were used in Victoria Cave, near Settle, to confirm that large mammals such as the narrow-nosed rhinoceros and hippopotamus had roamed in that area during the last climatic phase of the Ice Age. Bones, teeth and antlers discovered in the cave in the 1870s and later in 1937 were re-examined. The bones were identified as belonging to the numerous animals that had either sought out the caves for shelter or been dragged there as part of a predator's meal. The creatures that had inhabited Yorkshire during the Interglacials included the brown bear, spotted hyena, lion, straight tusked elephant, rhinoceros, hippopotamus, giant deer and giant ox or bison. When the last Ice Age brought the severest of arctic conditions they disappeared, to be replaced by the woolly mammoth, the woolly rhinoceros and the wild ox. Remains of these enormous animals have been found in areas across Yorkshire but not in the vicinity of Selby. Britain at that time was part of the Continental land mass which made it possible for hunters to cross from Europe into eastern England. It was around 10,000 years ago as the ice cap continued to shrink that a succession of hunters from North Germany and Jutland crossed the land bridge into Yorkshire in pursuit of the cold climate animals that lived along the edges of the ice. They travelled along the high ridges and moraines of Yorkshire carefully avoiding the marshy, murky swamps of the lowlands. During the following 5000 years as the climate slowly improved and the land became clothed in a rich, natural vegetation, a succession of people came to Yorkshire.

The First Arrivals

The first arrivals in Yorkshire towards the end of the Palaeolithic stage were people of the Old and then Later Middle Stone Age so called because of their use of stone tools. They survived in a sub-arctic climate by hunting the mammoth and the giant deer. They also fished for food and gathered wild fruits. Recently the thighbone of a female who had lived during the Middle Stone Age or, Mesolithic Age, was found in a gravel pit at Staythorpe, near Newark in Nottinghamshire. This rare find was made around the year 2002 by Glyn Davies, archaeologist at Sheffield University. Tests carried out on the bone by other scientists at Bradford confirmed that roughly 7,700 years ago people of the Middle Stone Age lived almost exclusively on meat. Indeed it was reported that the levels of nitrogen and carbon found in the bone suggested that the lady had been eating almost as much meat as a wolf! The nearest evidence of the presence of Stone Age people in the Selby area is a stone axe hammer, found at Sherburn-in-Elmet and believed to have been from the Mesolithic. A long period of time passed during which the people of the Palaeolithic Age died out and changes occurred in the physical geography of Western Europe. The North Sea basin was flooded and the English Channel formed, separating what is now known as the British Isles, from the continent. Wetter weather conditions prevailed and dense forests of alder and oak plus much lush vegetation covered great expanses of the land.

The next arrivals made great advances in the cultural development of the Yorkshire region. They reached the area from the Mediterranean around 6000 years ago. These immigrants of the New Stone Age, or Neolithic period had learnt how to produce their own food, a most important advance for it allowed people to settle in one place if they so wished. During the next thousand years or so, forests were felled and villages were formed. The inhabitants learnt how to tame wild animals such as the auroch, ancestor of the domestic cattle, for milk products and meat. They ploughed the land and grew crops of wheat and barley. They led a hard life doing everything by hand as they struggled to survive in the worsening weather conditions. There is no tangible evidence that any of these farmers settled in the area where Selby lies today but several finds in the vicinity of the town show that hunters or travellers did use routes through the thick, dark forests or found safe pathways across the soggy terrain of the southern lowlands of Yorkshire. In 1960, a finely polished stone adze, or hatchet, from the Neolithic Period was turned up by Alan Lewis of Sand Pit Farm whilst hoeing amongst a crop of young sugar beet plants. The field he had been working in was near Cat Babbleton, a short distance from Selby, and sited on a low ridge of glacial moraine across which the Camblesforth to Selby road now passes. An even more finely polished axe was picked up from amongst the gravel that was being graded in the Rainbow Sand and Tile Company's plant at Pollington. The gravel had been excavated from a quarry on the ridge of another glacial moraine between the River Aire and the River Went. Both artefacts were removed to the York Museum. Neolithic polished axes were also discovered in the wider area around Selby at Church Fenton, Escrick, Skipwith and Wheldrake; a flint knife was unearthed at Kirk Smeaton. There is no evidence of any artefacts from that era being found where Selby town stands today.

From Beaker People to Iron Age

The Early Neolithic settlers buried or cremated their dead in long or round barrows. The Later Neolithic people who had arrived in Yorkshire roughly 4000 years ago came to be known as the Beaker People from their habit of burying fine pottery beakers with their dead. These newcomers entered Yorkshire by the Humber estuary then spread across the Yorkshire Wolds or used the high ground to reach the Pennines. Over 150 examples of beakers from that period have been uncovered in the Yorkshire area. Those found nearest to Selby were in two Burial Mounds discovered in an area originally known as Ferry Fryston, near to the River Aire. The first excavations had been carried out there during the 19th. century. In 1962, "rescue excavations" were carried out on the mounds during the building of Ferrybridge 'C' Power Station. In the earlier digs on Mound One, Canon W. Greenwell, a "barrow enthusiast", had uncovered cremations, skeletons and several artefacts. These included a beaker- earliest of the samples found; a copper or bronze awl, 1.05 inches long, a food vessel and two collared urns. The more recent excavations, supervised by A. L. Pacitto, concentrated on the second mound. Here, although the ground had suffered from agricultural activities the team discovered an undisturbed crouched inhumation in an oval gravel pit. The body lay on its left side with a notched flint dagger behind the pelvis. The dagger, which may have previously been attached to a belt, was a very neatly flaked one with a pale blue patina with three notches on each side of the haft. The skeleton belonged to a middle-aged male who had suffered from poor teeth and severe spinal arthritis. Fourteen years later a survey made over the area of Ferrybridge on behalf of the Aerial Archaeology Committee revealed the position of a henge. A henge was a type of ritual monument peculiar to the British Isles and generally associated with the Beaker People. They normally consisted of circular areas of up to 500 metres across edged by ditches with the banks usually made outside them. Some had burial pits and circles of stone or timber uprights. The construction at Ferrybridge 100 metres in diameter, had a ditch and an external bank with two entrances in it placed opposite to each other. The archaeologists classed the feature as a Class II Henge because it had had two gaps made in its earthworks not one.

In addition to the Bronze Age burial mounds found near Ferrybridge other artefacts believed to be from that period were discovered in the Vale of York. Socketed axes and palstaves were found at Ulleskelf. One of these palstaves, a form of axe with side flanges, was made of bronze and had flanges of an unusually ornamental character believed to be in the Etruscan and Italian style. Other palstaves were also unearthed at Howden and Fulford.

The Late Neolithic period is also known as the Bronze Age because the smiths who had already worked with gold and silver had also learnt how to alloy copper from Ireland with Cornish tin to make a much tougher material known as bronze. Trading practices were developed during a long peaceful period. The copper and gold from Ireland had been brought along a trade route that began at the Ribble and then crossed Yorkshire via the Aire and Wharfedale Gaps and the York Moraines. Goods were also carried over the seas to and from Scandinavia.

The tranquil era that had been enjoyed by the Neolithic groups was disrupted as it became more difficult to build up good supplies of food. By the Late Bronze Age farms that had once been isolated from each other now had their fields abutting on one another as the settlers struggled to raise enough crops. Unrest had begun to develop amongst the communities as each strived to protect their precious grain stores from marauders. Around 750 BC, Celtic farmers began to infiltrate into Britain bringing with them weapons and tools made of iron. The climate which had continued to be cold and wet had had a serious effect on the Celtic communities living in Europe where they faced serious problems caused by the frequent flooding of their lands, poor harvests and an ever increasing population. These war-like tribes had fought amongst themselves for territory and spread out over Europe before crossing the Channel in search of land in Britain. About 250 BC one tribe, known as the Parisi, migrated from Belgium and occupied Holderness and parts of the Yorkshire Wolds. A great number of Beaker people were conquered by the Brigantes, a more aggressive group from Gaul. The arrival of these bellicose invaders caused more Britons to not only protect their homesteads with ditches and fences but to erect formidable forts on many of the hilltops.

By the first century AD. various tribal groups of Brigantes controlled most of Northern Britain from their central strongholds in West Yorkshire. The chiefs of the tribes, in what became known as the Iron Age, had absolute rule over their followers and the native bronze-making peasantry. They introduced the use of iron for many things because it was in plentiful supply. The Celtic aristocracy kept its own customs, and, despite their war-like demeanour encouraged and supported all forms of skilled craftsmanship. Some of them congregated in settlements that would become towns such as Aldborough. Most, however, were farmers who dwelt in circular huts with protective stockades built around their fields.

The river system that today collects up to four-fifths of the precipitation on Yorkshire and carries it into the Humber and then out into the North Sea was in place by this time. Many of the names of the rivers are derived from Celtic words which include Aire, Calder, Wharfe, Nidd and Ouse. An example of how these waters were navigated was unearthed in 1985 by a group of men who had been carrying out drainage work on the banks of the River Foulness, at Hasholme, near Holme-upon-Spalding Moor. Enclosed in a bed of clay under two metres of earth they discovered a log boat of the kind used by the Celtic tribes to travel along the waterways. This rare find is now housed in the Transport and Archaeology Museum in Hull. It is impossible to say precisely when the banks of the River Ouse were formed or when areas of land in the southern part of the Vale of York emerged from the marshes and mudflats to become of use to prospective settlers however in AD 2001 when English Heritage carried out a National Mapping Programme in the area, 1,300 undiscovered earthworks and historic features were revealed. Signs of ancient settlements had always been easier to identify on ridges and high places but consistent cultivation of the lowlands had made it appear, on the ground, as if there had been few features to find there. The growing of crops, however, has greatly contributed to the quality of the modern practice of carrying out research using aerial photographs. It was discovered that any former Iron Age or Roman ditches containing soil that was more moist than the surrounding earth caused the crops growing above these earthworks to stand taller or appear as a different shade on an aerial photograph. One of the earthworks revealed in the mapping programme carried out in 2001 lay not more than four miles from Selby. It confirmed the presence of a possible Iron Age or Roman site on Skipwith Common. Signs of this had first been discovered on old World War II aerial photographs and others taken during the floods of 1999/2000. An archaeological dig that took place two years later uncovered evidence that pointed to the possibility of some form of Iron Age activity in the town of Selby itself. Early in March, 2003, the York Archaeological Trust carried out an evaluation on land near to the premises of the General Freight Company, situated at the eastern end of Ousegate. Two sherds were found at the bottom of one of the excavated trenches which clearly suggested they may be prehistoric. The pieces, which appeared to have lain there undisturbed since the vessel from which they came had been broken, were found in a feature of uncertain function aligned north-south. This is the first evidence to hint at the presence of Iron Age man in Selby.

Nine months after the find in Selby a rare and nationally significant discovery near Ferrybridge caused archaeologists to question their beliefs regarding Iron Age tribal boundaries. A two-horse chariot, complete with the skeleton of a 30 to 40 year old man and his spear, was unearthed in an Iron Age burial site during excavations for the route of the new A1 motorway. Ferrybridge had always been thought to be the territory of the Brigantes but it was the Parisi who, although they mostly interred their dead in cemeteries, ceremoniously buried important people with a chariot or cart. This burial at Ferrybridge is especially important for two reasons. It is the only English example of a chariot buried intact, others found had been dismantled and the wheels laid flat. The burial is also special because, apart from one found at Newbridge, near Edinburgh, the 18 others uncovered are all around Wetwang in East Yorkshire, believed to be one of the centres of the Parisi tribes. Further investigations of the sherds found at Selby may confirm if it was the Brigantes or the Parisi who visited or dwelt in the town.

Roman Finds

Most of the artefacts already referred to in this chapter were found in a wide area around Selby. It was not until the 1990s that archaeological digs and the use of aerial photography provided evidence to show that the next invaders of Britain did utilize the land in and close to the place now known as Selby. About the time of the first Celtic settlements in Britain, Rome had just been a district of little significance in central Italy. It was from there, however, that the next invaders of this island eventually came. Rome was surrounded by enemies and the continuous struggle to keep their independence made the Romans both tough and resilient in adversity and skilful in warfare. As the centuries passed they used these skills to extend their boundaries until gradually the whole of Italy came under their control. By 60 BC the Romans, then a world power, advanced to the shores of the Channel. Five years later, the Proconsul of Gaul, Gaius Julius Caesar turned his attention to the land across the water. He knew that Britain was inhabited by tribesmen of the same Celtic stock that had confronted the Romans in Gaul, Germany and Spain and that they had given shelter to refugees fleeing from the wrath of his armies. The general opinion in the Roman Empire was that Britain, an island of undefined size, was a source of mineral wealth and was inhabited by barbarians. Caesar foresaw no difficulty in invading the land and subjugating its tribes to the rule of Rome. However, plagued by the vagaries of the Channel tides and the inclement weather and, finally, by the expertise of the Celts at chariot warfare, the Proconsul made little inroad into the hinterland on his first landing in Britain. The Romans retreated to the Continent for the winter. When he returned the following year Caesar had increased the number of his ships, his legions and his cavalry. This time he was successful in subduing some of the Celtic tribes in the south of the country. After acquiring several hostages and fixing some annual tributes Caesar returned home to pursue his path of power which eventually led to his assassination in 44 BC. No other Roman force crossed the Channel during the next ninety-seven years.

Changes, however, did take place amongst the Celtic tribes as they realised the benefits they would gain from trading with the Romans. British chiefs vied for Roman support which brought them luxuries of a kind not before experienced. Imports of silver table ware, bronze plated furniture, fine pottery, ivory, jewellery, glass, and especially wine, were gladly accepted in exchange for iron, cattle, gold, silver, hides and clever hunting dogs. There was a brisk trade in slaves for no neighbours of a profiteering native kingdom were exempt from slave raiding. At first, most of this trading was concentrated in the south-east but before the arrival of the next wave of Roman invaders, Celts at trading posts on the Trent, the Severn and the Humber were welcoming imports from the Roman Empire. Examples of some of these goods were uncovered at Cawood in the early 1930s. Dr. Philip Corder, at that time on the staff of Bootham School, York, had carried out excavations at the Brick and Tile works at Cawood. A small amount of red-glazed Samian ware was discovered there. The best Roman table ware was made of this pottery which came from the Greek island of Samos. Fragments of amphorae were also unearthed at the Tile Works. These came from tall two-handled vessels that had been specially made to carry much prized wine to Britain from Gaul.

In AD 43 the Emperor Claudius, seeking to have a triumph in Rome, ordered his legions to invade Britain. They overran most of England and Wales but it was not until AD 70 that they crossed the Humber into Yorkshire. The Brigantes had earlier entered into a truce with the Romans which encouraged the invaders to believe that there was no need to penetrate the wild and seemingly profitless lands beyond the Humber. To help seal this treaty, Queen Cartimandua handed the Welsh leader, Caractacus, over to the Romans when he fled to the Brigantes for sanctuary. Her husband, Venutius, and many other tribesmen, disagreed with her actions and civil war broke out. The Romans found it necessary to move the IXth. Legion from Lincoln to York to subdue the hostile northern tribes and in AD 74 the Brigantes were routed. Prisoners were treated as slaves and forced to work in the lead mines in places such as Swaledale and Greenhow and the iron ore deposits in the Bradford and Sheffield areas. The invaders very quickly began to exploit the timber and mineral resources found in Yorkshire. For example, jet was mined at Whitby during the Roman occupation. One surface find at Drax, near Selby, was of a small curved section of an armlet of spiral pattern. Made from jet, it must have once been a much treasured ornament.

The conquest of the north did not bring lasting peace. The warlike Picts from the north were never subdued and there were more sporadic uprisings amongst the tribes in the wilder parts of Brigantia, The Romans answered this by building a network of roads to speed the movement of the legions, messengers and goods vehicles. Those built across Yorkshire mainly followed the uplands which, unlike the Selby area, had little in the way of forests to clear or marshes to drain. One of the main routes went from Lincoln, along the Chalk Wolds to the Humber west of the present Humber Bridge. A ford or a ferry was used to reach Brough, which had become the capital centre of the Parisi. The road then traversed the Yorkshire Wolds, crossed the Derwent valley and the Vale of York to reach the important river crossing around which York developed. The principal road up the Vale of York linked settlements such as Doncaster, Tadcaster, Aldborough and Catterick to York. The area that became Selby lay within the framework of these Roman roads. Evidence gradually unearthed during the last hundred and fifty years has revealed that the invaders did not keep to those straight Roman roads but spread across the areas between, even as far as Selby.

The construction of these roads and of Hadrian's Wall in AD122 to hold back any warring factions from the north made life more peaceful for both Roman and native Britons. Civil settlements developed at places such as York and Aldborough. There was a merging of Roman and Celtic cultures, especially around Holderness and the Wolds where the Parisi had settled; eventually nearly all the Vale of York had become Romano-British. A building which was definitely identified as Roman was discovered in Drax. The existence of Roman material in that parish had been officially recognised in 1956 by a symbol on an Ordnance Survey Map of Roman Britain. This followed the notification of the finding of Romano-British potsherds in Drax parish by the late Miss A.W. Richardson, who had been the headmistress of Camblesforth Primary School and Hon. Secretary of the Local History Study Section of the Yorkshire Archaeological Society. The fragments became visible beneath crops of potatoes in a field on the Scurff Hall Farm estate, owned at that time by Mr. T.B. Thompson. The artefacts were gathered together after the crops of potatoes had been lifted. More than half of the hundred or so pieces collected from the field were identified by Dr. Kenneth Steer of Edinburgh, as being from coarse vessels of the type produced in Yorkshire kilns during the third to fourth century AD. From 1961 to 1964 a planned survey and excavation was carried out in the area known locally as "The Stannels", a derivation, it is believed of the name, Stone Hills. The field had been so named because of the large quantity of stone found there which was not indigenous to this part of Yorkshire. It was at this time that the archaeologists unearthed the remains of a Romano-British building dating from the same period as the sherds. It had been erected during a time when trade was good, Yorkshire kilns were set up and many farms flourished. The farmers who had become wealthy had built bigger and better working establishments known as 'villas' on their estates. Many had wall plaster, hypocaust heating and even mosaic floors in their homes. The building at Drax had had five rooms, a verandah made formerly of timber then later of stone, plus a timber-lined storage pit. On the Ordnance Survey Historical Map and Guide of Roman Britain, published in 1991, this Romano-British 'farmhouse' is not classed as a villa but as an *'other substantial building'*. Artefacts found at the excavations included burnished Romano-British pottery, sherds of plain and decorated Samian ware and iron articles such as a sickle and nails.

Sherds of Roman pottery were also discovered during excavations on the site of a moated manor house that once stood on a ridge of sand, on the north bank of the River Aire, in East Haddlesey. In 1992, field-walking exercises carried out on a small headland further up the river, again resulted in the finding of sherds of Roman pottery. This work and other surveys were carried out by people connected with the Royal Commission for Historical Monuments of England, the West Yorkshire Archaeology Service and English Heritage. These archaeological activities followed the discovery of the outline of a Roman Fort on photographs, taken in July 1991, by staff from the RCHME, York Office. Crop marks revealed the presence of a previously unnoted fort north of Roall Manor Farm, Kellington. The fort, now a scheduled site, National Monument No.30128, is sited on a small sandstone outcrop above the old course of the River Aire with its main gate immediately above the steep bank. The river had once cut a deep, narrow loop, which later became the boundary between the parishes of Kellington and West Haddlesey. Roall means 'rough land in the bend' whilst the abandoned oxbow came to be known as the 'Old Hee'. It has been suggested that the fort at Roall may be dated to the Flavian or Hadrianic period; also that it was purposely built facing the water to either guard a crossing or hold the river as a route way. No evidence has been found of a Roman road in the vicinity of the garrison which suggests that it was supplied via the river. This factor adds to the importance of this rare example of a Roman fort in this country.

Querns that had most probably been in use by Roman soldiers were found at Cawood, Hirst Courtney and Balne. A beehive shaped quern used for grinding wheat was uncovered by Mr. Arthur Pearse when he was working on the land at West End Farm Balne and had been given to Miss Richardson. Wheat was an important part of the diet of a Roman soldier. It was given to them as grain which they ground for themselves when needed, using the querns. Rough but hard stones were necessary to avoid grit mixing with the flour. At first these stones had been imported from the lava deposits in the Rhineland but later, hard British stones, mostly of millstone grit came into popular use.

The Romans in Britain interfered little in religious matters. Paganism had been widespread in the country but by the second century people were converting to Christianity. By the end of the fourth century many of the wealthy villa owners had become Christians and there were bishops in the country. Both cremation and inhumation were carried out according to the prevailing fashion of the day. Evidence of some of these Roman burials was found within the area around Selby. A large receptacle used by the Romans for internments was dug up in a field near to the little Norman church at Birkin. The solid-looking millstone grit coffin, complete with its lid, now stands on view near the north door of the church. In 1949 another massive stone coffin was brought to light during quarrying operations at Pollington, near Snaith. Made of gritstone it weighed 1527kgs. (30cwt.) and was thought to date from the fourth to fifth century. Its position lying east to west, was indicative of a Christian burial. The bones inside belonged to a woman of around 50 years of age whose eggshell thin skull was so well preserved that it was possible to ascertain that one of her teeth had been extracted during her lifetime. Almost one hundred years previously, a burial without a coffin had been unearthed in the Priory Garth at Snaith. The find, made by Aaron Fish, was recorded by Charles Best Robinson, the assistant curate at Snaith at that time. The skeleton was that of an unusually large man who, it was believed, may have been a Roman soldier at the time of the Occupation. Roman roofing tiles were found placed, not unlike the ridge of a roof, over the grave, which had caused the soil to lie lightly upon the body. A number of coins were found close to the head of the deceased which, it is said, would most probably have been placed there in the belief that the soldier would then have had the passage money for his soul to travel across the muddy waters of the River Styx.

A report written by Miss Richardson described the finding of Roman coins in Selby. It was the first intimation that some kind of activity had taken place in the actual area of the town after the Roman invasion. Mr. George Ross, recorded in Kelly's Directory of 1936 as being a Nurseryman and Seedsman of 14, Market Place, maintained that in the early 1880s, enterprising young schoolboys searching along the banks of the River Ouse, at low tide, had found numerous Roman coins. The Ross family were living at the same Market Place address in 1887. Miss Richardson's report also stated that a few years later more Roman coins had been unearthed some ten miles downstream from Selby, near to Baxter Hall, in the parish of Drax. A definite identification of two Roman coins found in the vicinity of Selby was made in 1989. The first was discovered using a metal detector in a field behind Whitley Bridge school. It was identified at the Yorkshire Museum as being a bronze coin from the reign of Tetricus II (AD 270-3). The second was unearthed in the British Oil and Cake Mills' allotments, which are situated between the north bank of the River Ouse and Recreation Road, Barlby. Mr. Ian Neale, a teacher of Latin at Selby High School, helped to identify the find. It was a commemorative issue of the period AD 330-346. On the obverse side of the bronze coin was a helmeted head of ROMA facing left and wearing the imperial mantle with the inscription, VRBS ROMA (City of Rome). The picture of a she-wolf standing facing left and suckling Romulus and Remus, was on the reverse. The letters PLG inscribed below the figures signified that it was minted at Lyon.

More data concerning the possible presence of Romans in the town was provided during the 1990s when various archaeological experts carried out some digs in Selby. 'Sample Excavations' carried out by MAP Archaeological Consultancy Limited of Malton, produced a smattering of Roman pottery south of Selby Dam in land at the rear of Finkle Street and Gowthorpe. The scratched condition of the material suggested that the area had been open cultivated land during the Roman period. In 1993 the York Archaeological Trust sank 14 boreholes between Gowthorpe and Selby Dam and four holes on the north of the Dam. They found no evidence of human habitation on the north side below the bricks, tiles and mortar. The only pottery found dated from the 19th. century which, it was suggested, had been used as material to help create a flood bank. At the lowest level of the 13th. hole, situated on the south side of the Dam, field workers found a fragment of Roman grey ware believed to date from the second to third century. A watching brief carried out for Selby District Council by Alison Clarke, MA, AIFA., an Archaeology Consultant, concentrated on Finkle Street and Micklegate. Amongst the numerous sherds found there five were recorded as Roman. Two were classed as Samian ware, the others as calcite-gritted ware from the first to second century.

Further concrete evidence of the presence of the Romans in Selby was found in 1998 by the York Archaeological Trust. Previous to this, David Brinklow of the Trust, had pondered on the belief put forward by W.W.Morrell in his *History of Selby* that the traces of a building discovered in 1854 during excavations for drainage work in Micklegate had been part of a castle. Brinklow had stated that the description of *"solid compact masonry and the concrete so perfect that the workmen found it impossible to lift the stones at the joints, as is usual, but had to break up the entire mass as if it had been rock,"* was highly reminiscent of Roman material. This thought was reinforced, when in 1998 the Trust carried out an Archaeological Watching Brief on excavations taking place on the corner of Ousegate and New Street, Selby, prior to the building of a block of flats there. Ditches that were without question of Roman date were revealed. A substantial 2.05 metres wide by 0.77 metres deep ditch was found in an area now situated at the back of the new flats. On a SW-NE line, it was dated to the Roman period by the presence of six sherds of second to third century pottery. The large dimensions and profile of the ditch suggested to the archaeologists that its role had been more for defensive purposes rather than as a boundary or drainage ditch. It was reported that the narrow slot cut in its base was very reminiscent of the 'ankle breakers' employed in Roman military defence ditches. There were signs also that suggested the ditch had been regularly cleaned out and maintained before it became redundant. As the ditch ran at a right angle to the River Ouse there was speculation that it may have continued to the south bank of the river, thus forming a defensive barrier on the eastern approaches to any settlement that may have been near the Ouse at that location. A single sherd of Roman pottery was found in a slightly narrower ditch which formed a right angled return to, or joining, with the first ditch. Excavations that took place at the eastern end of Ousegate in 2003 also uncovered evidence of Roman activity in Selby. The trench containing the sherds believed to be from the Iron Age also yielded up a piece of Roman pottery. Another sherd was found in the next trench and a small amount of abraded Roman bricks in other trenches. Together, these finds from the last few years, make it increasingly clear that there was some kind of Roman presence in Selby during the Romano-British period.

Ancient Burials

The latest dated pottery found at the Romano-British site in Drax were pieces of mortarium made between AD 370-400. This suggested that the area had been abandoned no later than AD 400. Any Roman presence in Selby would have been diminished around that time because successful attacks being made on the Continent by their enemies caused the withdrawal of legions from Britain. The Roman garrison at York was recalled by Stillicho, the regent of Emperor Honorius, as Roman control over Western Europe began to collapse. The country had been strongly defended by the Romans. They had repulsed continuous attacks being carried out along its coastline and up its estuaries by the Picts from the north of the Rivers Forth and Clyde; the Scots from Ireland and the Angles, Saxons and Jutes from Northern Germany and southern parts of Denmark. Saxon pirates had been a menace to the Romans since the third century with their continual looting and killing along the Channel and the North Sea coasts. The fortifications at Selby may have been there as a defence against such intruders. By AD 410, Yorkshire, like the rest of Britain, was left to defend itself against the fierce raiders, many of whom had given up piracy and came instead to take the land as their own. Little is known after AD 410 concerning how many Romans stayed in Britain or what persons were in authority. By the sixth century most of the Western Empire had fallen into the hands of the barbarians but the complete defeat of Britain took a long time to happen. The Kingdom of Elmet, which lay between the rivers Wharfe and Calder, stayed under British rule long after the Romans had left. Some invaders who crossed from the Continent settled in the south whilst others entered the Humber and sailed along its rivers and made their homes on land between this estuary and the Firth of Forth. The territory was split into two kingdoms, Bernicia and Deira. There was much strife between the Anglo-Saxon leaders. Edwin of Deira took over the rule of Bernicia and in AD 616 he wrested the Kingdom of Elmet from British control to become King of all the region then known as Northumbria. This included the land that was later called Yorkshire.

The Anglo-Saxons were pagans who worshipped many gods. However, the spread of Christianity had gained momentum after the arrival of St. Augustine in AD 597 and Edwin was baptised in York in AD 627. Much of the fighting that followed that century for control of the various kingdoms was between pagan and Christian tribes. In AD 633 the pagan king Penda of Mercia who had joined forces with Cadwalla of Wales, faced and killed Edwin at the Battle of Hatfield Chase, near Doncaster. In AD 642, Edwin's successor, Oswald, was slain by Penda but in AD 655 Penda, and many other kings, met their fate at the Battle of Winwaed. The exact location of this battlefield is unknown. Some historians believe it was in the vicinity of Leeds, others are in favour of Thorp Audlin, near the River Went, north of Doncaster. The victorious leader at that conflict was Oswy, a Christian like his brother Oswald. Oswy continued to support the spreading of Christianity. He converted the Mercians and many other pagan tribes to the faith. Wooden churches, preaching crosses and then monasteries and convents appeared throughout the Yorkshire area. A timber built chapel was erected near to the remains of the Romano-British farmstead in Drax in the mid tenth century and is believed to have been of Saxon or Danish origin. A charter dated AD 959, stated that there was *"a chapel at Ealdedrege (Drax) at the meeting of the Aire and Ouse."* It is believed by many local historians that a little wooden church was erected in Selby during Anglo-Saxon times and evidence of its existence may be hidden under the car park on Church Hill.

Verification that there had been an Anglo-Saxon presence in Selby was found in the trenches dug by archaeologists working for MAP at the rear of Finkle Street in the 1990s. Observations made by the team led them to state that it was possible that one or two of the dykes in that area, anciently known as Kirk Dyke and Back Dyke had been in use during the Anglian period. Definite proof that there was a burial ground in Selby during Anglo-Saxon times was uncovered in 1857. In that year men making a drain on Church Hill had come across some internments eight feet down. Each coffin had been made from the trunk of an oak tree which had been split open and then hollowed out. The receptacles had been shaped with an axe and had lids that fitted on snugly with no evidence of any fastenings. About 14 coffins were uncovered but it was reported that not all were raised because of difficulties caused by the shape of the drain. It was said that of those recovered, one went into private hands and another was presented to the Yorkshire Museum. The skeleton of a female in a good state of preservation was found in one of the oak coffins. She had a necklace around her neck made up of seven large beads that graduated in size. In her notes, Miss Richardson stated that this most important archaeological find was, it is believed, given to a child who subsequently dropped it onto a kitchen floor where it was trodden underfoot. These beads were destroyed but a solitary Anglian type bead from the same site and of the same description was safely deposited in the York Museum. It is biconical in shape and made of clay that has been baked hard. It also still retains traces of the red colouring matter which once filled the series of finely incised lines with which it is circumscribed. In 1876 when excavations were taking place for a beer cellar under the Crown Inn, 10 Church Hill, more ancient burials came to light. The public house, now known as *No 23* was then run by Moses Lomas who had also been a builder and monumental mason. Between 15 to 20 oak coffins were uncovered in an area 915cms. by 610cms. (30x20 feet). The coffins which had all been laid in an east to west direction were in various states of decay. Most were saturated and dripping with moisture making them too rotten to be moved. The warp, stones and pieces of wood found in the coffins when opened showed that the containers had been subjected to the tidal actions of the River Ouse. The best preserved ones were lifted out of their resting places. One of the coffins, just over two metres long, contained the skeleton of a male whose teeth were considerably worn. Also in the coffin were three long thin hazel sticks laid from the bony fingers of the right hand down towards the left foot. Hazel plants were used by our pagan ancestors in the same way Christians use the olive branch, as a symbol of peace. A smaller coffin held the skeleton of a child. It was half the size of the other containers and had been ingeniously wrought from boards of wood neatly fastened together with wooden pegs. It was in a state of great decay but a hazel stick was still in evidence laid in the same position as in the larger receptacle. In the vicinity of at least three of the longer tree coffins were thick oaken headposts about a metre in length, which must have originally marked the place of the burials. The fate of some of the coffins disinterred from the ancient cemetery on Church Hill is unknown but others are safely stored in the deep recesses of the museum at York. The combination of all these things suggest that the area of Selby near to the River Ouse, which the Romans had used as a defensive point, was later occupied by settlers belonging to an Anglo-Saxon community.

The Formation of Yorkshire

Christianity continued to spread through the various kingdoms but there were still outbreaks of strife between the different leaders. This was a source of weakness capitalised upon by the next wave of invaders to raid the shores of Britain. These were the Vikings from Scandinavia, who, at first, like the Saxon pirates before them, restricted their looting and pillaging to the coastal settlements. Their first recorded raid was on the island of Lindesfarne in AD 793. From AD 835 onwards the Vikings carried out continuous raids from Wessex to Northumbria, destroying and plundering everything in their path, especially the monasteries and churches of the Christian communities. In AD 866 a Viking army led by Ivar the Boneless entered Deira. York was besieged then burnt down. Eventually the invaders gained rule over Northumbria and Mercia whilst the south of England remained in the hands of the Saxons. The areas settled by the Danes were governed by Danelaw which prevailed over Saxon laws and customs. It was recorded in The Anglo-Saxon Chronicles, which had been compiled during the reign of Alfred the Great (AD 871-99) that *"Halfdan shared out the land of Northumbria and they were engaged in ploughing"*. The Saxon invaders had slaughtered the Britons, driven them out, or, used them as slaves, but the Vikings, once the conquest was over, settled down alongside the natives. The Anglo-Saxons had chosen the forested lowlands near to the rivers. They farmed the land and grew crops of wheat, rye and barley. They also kept pigs, sheep and goats and used oxen to pull the plough. The Norse-Vikings occupied the upland country above the forests and reared sheep in single farms as they had done in Norway. The Danes settled on the plains and in the valleys where they grew crops and raised animals. Both groups of invaders brought skilled craftsmen with them; examples of whose work may be seen in museums around the country.

There was still much conflict between the kingdoms. Northumbria was ruled over by a succession of leaders and, for a time, the northern province found itself being ruled by Athelstan who, in AD 926, was acknowledged as king of all the English. Northumbria had tried to regain its freedom in AD 947 under the leadership of their appointed king, Eric Bloodaxe, but the struggle for autonomy was lost seven years later at the Battle of Stainmore. The kingdom, including the area that became Yorkshire was once again part of England and Danelaw ceased to exist. The formation of Yorkshire as a county appears to have happened during the late 10th. or early 11th. century. It was the only northern county to have been created before the Norman conquest of England, which started in 1066. Named after Jorvic (York), capital of the North, its boundaries stayed roughly as they were then until the major local government changes of 1974. The new county was split into thrithings, the Viking word for a third part, with York as an independent area. By the time of the Domesday Survey carried out in 1086 the Ridings had been divided into administrative sub-divisions, known as wapentakes. Each of these was responsible for levying their own taxes, raising fighting men and maintaining law and order. The wapentakes replaced the Anglo-Saxon 'Hundreds' which had also been units of local government. The East Riding remained divided into eighteen hundreds for a long period before gradually being converted into six wapentakes. The settlement that became known as Selby was in the Wapentake of Barcheston or Barkston Ash. Many place names in and around Selby have been derived from Anglo-Saxon and Viking words. 'Hirst' the Saxon word for wood or grove is found today in the names of two villages not far from Selby. Formerly known as East and West Hirst, they now carry the names, Hirst Courtney and Temple Hirst. Hambleton is derived from Hammil, a Saxon leader, and 'ton' the Saxon for settlement whilst Hemingbrough is made from Earl Heming, a Viking leader and 'brough', their word for a fortified place. The name Selby has been described as coming from 'Sele' the Saxon word for 'fortunate' and 'by' the Viking for town. The modern translation for Selby is 'a settlement in a willow copse'. 'Thorpe' the Viking word for an outlying farm or hamlet is seen in Thorpe Willoughby and also in the town of Selby. Its main thoroughfare retains the name Gowthorpe whilst the Norse word 'gate' for 'street' is found in Ousegate, Millgate, Micklegate and Bondgate.

During periods of peace many industries developed in the towns. Workers in bronze, leather and wood set up their premises in wooden buildings. Trade with other countries flourished as more trade routes were opened. Then, in 1013, fresh bands of Danish invaders entered the mouth of the Humber and proceeded to devastate the lands of Lindsey and Northumbria. The fyrds, which were bodies of local countrymen obliged to rally to the call to arms, did not fare well against the plunderers. Indeed the Anglo-Saxon Chronicle records that the gathered forces followed their leaders' example by fleeing from the scene of battle.

Danes and English fought for the lands and the crown of England. The overall ruler changed many times. From 1016-35, Cnut, king of Denmark, ruled over a generally peaceful land. It was during this period that Selby had its name recorded in a charter dated 1030 which listed some of the lands and possessions belonging to the Archbishop of York. It included many of the villages that surround Selby.

Two parts of Cawood and all of Wistow and all upper Selby, and two oxgangs in Flaxley, and half of Barlow, and all Brayton except half a plough; and all Burn and all Burton except half a ploughland and all Gateforth and all the two Thorpes and all the two Hirsts and all the two Haddleseys and five oxgangs in

the third Haddlesey and half of Birkin   all Hillam, all Fryston, all Milford, all
Lumby, all Brotherton, all Fairburn except two and a half ploughlands....

The finding of a flax seed capsule in one of the boreholes between Gowthorpe and Selby Dam by the York Archaeological Trust during the 1990s demonstrates that flax was grown in that area and was possibly the origin of the place name 'FlaxIey'; 'lay' being the Saxon word for a 'clearing in the wood'.

Stamford Bridge

Cnut was succeeded by two of his sons whose early deaths left an empty throne. Their father had taken Emma, the daughter of Richard I of Normandy, as his second wife. Emma had previously been married to the West Saxon, Aethelred (the Unready) and it was the son of their union, Edward, who in 1042 succeeded to the crown of England. When Edward died in 1066, he left no heirs, which led to a desperate struggle amongst the claimants to the throne of England. It is said that Edward had designated William, Duke of Normandy as his heir but the crown had not been his to give. William had become Duke in 1035. He had inherited a court full of intrigue and treachery, but had successfully survived rebellions amongst his retainers and attacks from various foreign powers. William claimed a long connection between Normandy and Anglo-Saxon England through Emma whose father, the Norman duke Richard I, was William's ancestor.

Another claimant was Harold, son of the Earl Godwin of Wessex. Godwin had been a man of tremendous wealth and power, accumulated when he had served as Cnut's right hand man. Harold succeeded to the earldom of Wessex, two of his brothers gained East Anglia and Middlesex whilst the fourth, Tostig, friend and brother-in-law to Edward the Confessor had been made Earl of Northumberland. It is reported that when Harold was a guest at the Court of William he had promised to support the Duke when he laid claim to the throne of England. The third contestant for the crown was Harald Hardrada, King of Norway, whose wife could trace her ancestry back to Cnut.

The struggle to possess the crown began the moment Edward took his last breath. Harold immediately seized the throne and was crowned King of England. William wasted no time in ordering a fleet to be constructed. In the meantime Tostig, who had become unpopular in Northumbria because of his aggressive and brutal ways, was driven out by the inhabitants and went into exile in Normandy. One of the manors under his control had been Hemingbrough. It was not long before Tostig began to plunder along the south coast of England before moving unhindered up the Channel and into the Humber where he continued to ravage the countryside until stopped by two of Harold's earls, Edwin and Morcar. Undeterred, Tostig joined Harald Hardrada on the Tyne where that king had brought a great Viking fleet ready to aid him in his attempt to win the English throne. Meanwhile Harold waited near the Isle of Wight for William of Normandy to appear with his fleet. When weather conditions made it clear that no ships were going to make it across the Channel and with winter approaching, Harold went back to London. The same anti-cyclone that had held William back caused a northerly airstream down the North Sea which Hardrada took advantage of to bring his long ships down the east coast of England. Tostig and the Norwegian king laid waste to Cleveland then sacked and plundered Scarborough. In September 1066 their impressive invasion fleet entered the Humber and sailed up the Ouse to anchor at Riccall. If the vessels did number around 300 as it was stated in the Anglo-Saxon Chronicles, it is estimated that Hardrada may have had at least 10,000 fighting men at his command. The invaders marched on York but found their way barred by an English army led by the two Earls, Morcar and Edwin. Morcar had previously supported the Northumbrian rebellion against Tostig and had succeeded him as their leader. The English fought valiantly but were beaten back into the marshes at Gate Fulford. At least a thousand of the best troops in the north were killed that day. York surrendered a few days later but was left intact. The army took hostages from the city and were promised more from the Shire. Supplies were also carried back to the anchorage at Riccall. Selby is not mentioned in the recordings of these battles but it is feasible that the settlement, along with others near the banks of the Ouse, were sacked for supplies to feed such a mighty army. It is also possible that the inhabitants of these places may have already abandoned their homes at the sight of the huge fleet of Viking ships passing along the Ouse.

Harold, maybe aided by the use of beacons and speedy messengers, had quickly learnt of the landing by the Norwegians and had hastened up the still existing Roman roads towards York. With him were his house ceorls, tall, fierce fighting foot soldiers who had chosen to follow him. They were accompanied by levies of local men gathered on the way north. Unaware of this, Hardrada set out on a foraging quest in the direction of Stamford Bridge, the place where he expected to be given more hostages. He left his son Olaf and most of his men with the ships at Riccall. The weather was warm and so Hardrada allowed his raiding party to leave their body armour at the camp. It was, therefore, an ill-prepared army that came face to face with the vigilant Harold and his fighting force on the 25th. September, 1066. Mounted messengers raced to Riccall for reinforcements but these arrived at the battle too exhausted to be a forceful fighting machine. Harald Hardrada, Tostig and an Irish king were all killed in a most savage and conclusive confrontation that can be considered as one of the most decisive battles in English history. The Anglo-Saxon Chronicles recorded:

"The Norwegians who survived took flight and the English attacked them fiercely as they pursued them until some got to the ships. Some were drowned and some burned and some destroyed in various ways so that few survived and the English remained in command of the field."

Olaf, the son of Hardrada, survived the onslaught and was allowed to leave the country. It is reported that there were only enough survivors remaining to man about 20 of the ships that had been anchored at Riccall.

Around 1832 a quantity of bones and old iron were turned up in a field near the place known as Riccall Landing. Fifty years later ten human skulls were disinterred in the West Fields, Old Landing, in Riccall. One day, in December 1956, Mr. Outhwaite of Dam End Farm, Riccall, had gone out to make a clamp of mangel-wurzels. The field he went to work in adjoined the River Ouse, close to Riccall Landing. As he was digging the clamp he cut into a number of human skeletons at a depth of about 30 cms. below the surface. That same year, the York historian and archaeologist, Peter Wenham, assisted by some of his students at St John's College, York, and others from Nunthorpe Grammar School, supervised the excavations of the skeletons. In 1957 he was helped in his work by Mr. J. Bailey, Headmaster of Riccall County School and his senior pupils. At least 39 skeletons were discovered and were identified as being 28 men, 2 women, 5 children and 4 unknown. All lay with their feet to the east and heads to the west, bodies fully extended with arms either down by their sides or across the pelvis. They had all clearly been buried at the same time and were closely positioned side by side. No artefacts were found with them. Further skeletal remains were also unearthed in several places by the staff at the Ouse Catchment Board Depot at nearby Counting House Hill when they had been engaged in digging holes for gateposts. Several more skeletons were uncovered in 1976 during trenching in what is now known as the Environmental Agency Depot at Riccall Landing. In 1985 men employed by Yorkshire Water on Selby's new flood bank at Riccall unearthed further skeletons. The York Archaeological Trust recovered 23 skeletons there. The density of the burials and the area over which the total remains were found suggested to the scientists that there may have been approximately 500 burials all carried out at the same time. The only catastrophe that could be thought of that had wiped out so many people in that area in a single incident was the battle at Stamford Bridge. No artefacts were found to help date the skeletons so the mystery of the burial ground remained a closed secret until the beginning of the 21st century. In 2001, the BBC contacted the York Archaeological Trust in pursuit of suitable topics for a new series entitled, "Blood of the Vikings". The Riccall skeletons were chosen for further study. An examination of the bones revealed that some showed signs of mutilation consistent with wounds caused by swords and spears. Paul Budd of Durham University undertook to do an oxygen isotope analysis of samples of teeth from six different individuals. The analysis revealed that none of these people had been born in the British Isles. They apparently originated from a geographical area that included Norway and other places around the Baltic Sea. Women and children would have made up part of the Viking company that sailed up the Ouse to Riccall, for it is recorded that Hardrada had one of his wives and several of his children with him. Also, if local inhabitants had been left to intern the bodies for Harold and his victorious army it is believable that they would have quickly stripped them of any useful or valuable articles before they buried the dead. Could these skeletons, therefore, have been, as the York Archaeological Trust suggest, a rare archaeological phenomenon, part of a battle cemetery from the Viking Age; the result of the routing of Hardrada and his army? Further work is being carried out by the Trust to try to answer these questions.

After the battle that took place on the 25th. September, 1066, it is believed that Harold and his men took the opportunity to have a celebration in York. Harold would have had to call upon the land fyrd in the Vale of York to assist him in his struggle to keep the throne of England. The levy would have consisted of farmers, ploughmen, craftsmen etc. who would all have had to leave their tasks to join the fighting force. It is probable that some came from the hamlets and villages in the Selby area and as Harold rejoiced in York they would have made their way home, glad to be amongst the survivors, completely unaware that whatever liberty they enjoyed was about to be severely curtailed. It is recorded that on the 28th. September, at 9 o'clock in the morning, William of Normandy landed at Pevensey. An event that was to change many lives including those of the community inhabiting a small site at Selby.

CHAPTER 2

THE FOUNDING OF SELBY ABBEY

The Norman Conquest

On the 1st October, 1066, Harold received the news that the Norman duke, William, had landed on the south coast of England and was ravaging the countryside which Harold had once ruled. He quickly prepared to leave York but was only able to raise a small complement of men because of the terrible losses suffered by the English during the battles at Gate Fulford and Stamford Bridge. The king had to rely on what remained of the staunch warriors in his bodyguard and available mercenaries until he could augment his troops with men levied in the southern counties. The earls, Edwin and Morcar, were ordered to gather what men they could before they followed Harold. After a series of forced marches, only broken by a short break in London, Harold arrived within nine miles of Hastings. It was the evening of the 13th. October. William had had a motte and bailey castle hastily erected in Hastings. The Normans reconnoitred the countryside whilst still continuing to cause havoc amongst the inhabitants there. On the morning of the 14th October, William led his army out of the town to face Harold and his men massed along a ridge at Sandlake. A great number of Norman lives were lost in the ensuing conflict but, despite the magnificent defence put up by the Anglo-Danish house earls and thanes, Harold and his two brothers were killed and the battle lost. The earls, Edwin and Morcar, appeared in the southern counties after the battle at Hastings had drawn to a close. In November, they with other notabilities elected Edgar Aetheling, a prince of royal blood, as the next king though no coronation took place through lack of support. William suffered little opposition from any other quarter and in Westminster Abbey on Christmas Day 1066, he was crowned King of England.

Over the next twenty years there was a drastic redistribution of wealth in England as the Norman king rewarded his warriors and magnates with lands and revenue wrested from the Anglo-Saxon aristocracy. Count Mortain, the half-brother of William, who had taken part in the Battle of Hastings, became the largest landholder in England after the king. In the district around Selby he held Hemingbrough, Hensall, South and North Duffield, Cliffe, Osgodby and Stillingfleet. Ilbert de Lacy was in the second rank of the Norman Lords who gained rewards through their military skills. He was awarded many acres around Selby, including parts of Brayton and Thorpe Willoughby.

William's reign did not begin peacefully for many Englishmen would not accept Norman rule. Riots and insurrections were frequent occurrences, especially in Yorkshire and the North. One supporter of these revolts, Merleswein, held land near to Selby. His name occurs in many documents dateable to the reigns of King Edward the Confessor and William the First. One manuscript known as the York Gospels or Anglo-Saxon Gospels, contains a list of men acting as festermen. In England the duties of such persons included acting as sureties in legal transactions within the Danelaw, guaranteeing the validity of a seller's title to the land he was selling, and ensuring the appearance of a wrongdoer at court. The name of Merleswein was second on the list which also included Ulf, owner of the manor of Birkin; Wegga or Wiga, who held Carlton-in-Snaith and Womersley; Barat, who had Burton Hall, Brayton and Thorpe; also Alfcetel, who possessed the manor of Hambleton. Merleswein, an exceedingly wealthy official, held manors in many places including an enclosed and fortified dwelling place at Drax, an official residence in Lincoln, and another within the fortress at York. As sheriff of Lindsey and a legal representative of the monarch, Merleswein was the person Harold left in charge of the north when he had ventured out on his fateful journey to Hastings. In the unlikely event that more Nordic invaders should sail up the Humber, the sheriff was to defend the river route to York with the depleted local militia. This probably included men from the river-side settlement of Selby who were, by custom, duty bound to defend their own and their neighbours' families, dwellings, crops and cattle; to be ready also, to leave their work at the first signs of danger.

After news of the death of Harold, Merleswein accompanied Edgar Aetheling and members of his family to Scotland under the protection of King Malcolm. They remained with the king until 1068 when the company returned to Yorkshire to join the earls, Edwin and Morcar, and many other rebels in a concerted revolt against the Normans. The feelings of the inhabitants of York and the surrounding district were roused to fever pitch; many forsook their homes to live in tents whilst taking part in military exercises. Despite this the uprising achieved nothing. William quickly made his way north, successfully quelled the insurgents, then left William Malet as sheriff with 500 knights to guard his newly erected fortifications in York. A second rising began at Durham where William had appointed Robert de Cominis to replace Gospatric as the Norman Earl of Northumberland. In January 1069, the new earl and his army were massacred within the city by the Northumbrians. Again, Edgar returned from his refuge in Scotland. Accompanied by Merleswein and a great number of exiles he joined Gospatric and his followers in an advance on York. William, sent for in post haste by the governor there, came and fell upon the besiegers from the north, killing, capturing or driving them into headlong flight. He then sacked the city and erected yet another wooden fortress.

The indomitable Northumbrians tried a third time to defeat their Norman overlords. In September 1069, Viking marauders who had taken advantage of the chaos caused by the rebellions and had been exploring along the north-east coast, entered the Humber. A force of some 240 ships led by the brother of King Svein of Denmark, and with crews made up of Norsemen, Danes, refugees and discontents, sailed into the Ouse to be met by Edgar and his supporters. They were joined by men from all over the north. The local population was not hostile to the invaders. It is credible that some of the inhabitants of Selby and others taking refuge in the forests helped to swell the army of rebels on the banks of the Ouse. York was stormed and destroyed by this motley horde of assailants who killed around 3000 Frenchmen in the battle. The victorious Danes and Norsemen retreated back to the river after ransacking the city. William, in a tremendous rage, marched from the south determined to have his revenge on every man, woman and child in the north. His temper was not improved when having to divert his troops to cross the Aire he found the bridge at Pontefract was broken and the river was in flood. A frustrated William was held up for three weeks by the high waters even though, as tradition has it, his men, looking for a safe crossing, followed the course of the river up into the Pennine Hills and down as far as Snaith. Once across the Aire, William and his men, with unparalleled ferocity, ravaged the whole of the north country as far as the Tees. In this 'Harrying of the North' as it came to be known, lands along the North Sea coast came in for especially savage treatment to discourage further invasions by the Scandinavians. The Danish fleet finally left the Humber and after forays with the outlaw thane Hereward, the marauders returned home in 1070, having gained much in the way of bounties but little in political achievement. Merleswein, after helping to lead the northern uprisings disappears from historical records.

After the quelling of rebellions in the Midlands and the North, more manors were distributed amongst the Norman leaders. Society was run on a feudal system which was based on the holding of a unit of land in return for a stated service. This was usually of a military nature with homage owed to the overlord. Knights were an essential part of William's power. They held vast portions of land which they let to tenants who, in return, had to show fealty not only to these overlords but also to the king. It was documented that:

> Hambleton-Earnwine has it from Ilbert de Lacy; Birkin-Gamall has it under Ilbert; Ryther-Hugh (a Norman) has it. Hugh sublet it to Chatel and his brothers (English tenants).

The family of Ralph Pagnel extended their lands after the unrest through further grants from Ilbert de Lacy, and advantageous marriages. Ralph became tenant-in-chief of almost all the lands and manors, including Drax, previously held by Merleswein. It was estimated that by 1087 only eight per cent of the land was still in the hands of Anglo-Saxon thanes. One Saxon who held a royal grant of land was Barat, whose name appeared on the list of festermen. He was a rare example of an Englishman who retained the land he had held during the reign of King Edward. This property included Burton Hall, Brayton, Thorpe, Roall, Eggborough, Kellington and probably, Beal.

The majority of inhabitants in England were not affected by the changes for the local government system of counties, hundreds, sheriffs and courts was retained as was the collecting of taxes known as Danegeld. The compilation of the Domesday Book arose from the growing complaints concerning titles to lands etc., and the king's desire to know how much land was available for geld. Thorpe (Willoughby), a manor that included Burton Hall and Brayton, was described in the survey as *"a berewick with three and a half carucates for geld."* In general, William wished to know the state of the lands and the customs of his new kingdom. The history of many English villages begins with an entry in the Domesday Book of 1086. The survey supplied ample evidence of the widespread devastation caused by William following the uprisings in the northern counties.

> "Barlby- Merleswein had one carucate for geld. Land to half plough. Ralph Pagnel has it and it is waste. Howden- all the outliers are waste; Lund-waste; land belonging to Breighton-waste; Camblesforth, one carucate taxable, land for half a plough - waste."

The Founding of Selby Abbey

The spread of Christianity developed during the Norman period. The churches flourished in contact with Europe. The Pope gave full support to William whose followers eventually came to venerate the English saints. Churches became the centre of life in the villages. Baptisms, marriages and burials took place there. Mass and feast days were celebrated and village affairs discussed within their walls. Monasteries and nunneries grew in number; the latter becoming havens for the unfortunate womenfolk of dispossessed landowners. Many bishops were monks but some began to live like great barons as they amassed property from their Christian estate owners. The Archbishop of York possessed vast tracts of land. One entry in Domesday, in connection with some of these holdings, mentions the name of Selby. It recorded that the archbishop had 96 carucates of land in Sherburn. Some of it was divided between the archbishop's knights, a thane, two clerks and the Abbot of Selby.

The abbot referred to in the share out of land was Benedict, the first monk to be ordained as an Abbot of Selby (AD1069-1097). He had been a member of the great Benedictine monastery at Auxerre, a hundred miles south-east of Paris until, according to tradition, he had had several visions in which he was directed to travel to Selby to build a monastery there. The figure that had appeared to Benedict was that of his patron saint, Germain or Germanus, (AD378-448). Germain had been born in Auxerre where he had grown up to become a brilliant, eloquent and very knowledgeable advocate, well versed in civil and military matters. He had a zest for life and all its pleasures. This was, it is said, until the Bishop of Auxerre, wishing to use the advocate's talents for God's work, had him seized and forcibly tonsured. Tonsuring involved the clipping of a person's hair to show that he had made solemn promises to devote his life to God. It is said that a great change came over Germain; he distributed his wealth amongst the poor and followed an abstemious life-style bereft of any bodily comforts whilst striving to do the Lord's work.

In AD418 he was consecrated Bishop of Auxerre. At the request of the pope Germain travelled to Britain in AD429 and again in 447.This was to assist the Christians to put down outbreaks of heresy instigated by the followers of Pelagius, a British monk (c360-c420) who denied the Catholic doctrine of original sin. The essence of the Pelagians' beliefs was freedom of the human will which, they preached, was capable of doing good without the help of divine grace. This was condemned by religious leaders as heresy. Besides these religious activities Germain used his military skills to organise bands of the local militia in their frequent skirmishes with invading barbarians such as the Picts and Scots. One encounter had become known as the Hallelujah Victory, for the hills had echoed with the joyous cries of this exultation coming from the throats of Germain and his followers as the defeated enemy took to their heels. Germain was known in Roman-Britain by the Celtic name - Garmon and, yeoman-farmer, William Storr, noted this name amongst the field-titles of his lands in Wistow in 1711. The name is perpetuated today in a field in Wistow-Lordship known as Garmon Carr which might have been the place where the rural faithful gathered to pay due homage to Saint Germain. This holy man died in Italy in July AD448, and his body was carried to Auxerre where his tomb soon became a shrine.

The life and deeds of this pious saint were recorded in AD449, by a monk at Auxerre named Constantine. Tales of the tasks the saint had undertaken would have been retold through the ages. Around six hundred years later, Benedict, the founder of Selby

Abbey, may have heard these stories whilst a monk at Auxerre. They could have kindled his interest in, and his love of, Saint Germain. A study of well-authenticated documentary evidence on the works of the saint held in the archives could have aroused in Benedict a desire to emulate Germain in some way; a wish that resulted in the visions. Alternatively, Benedict may have been one of a number of itinerant monks searching for a suitable place to settle in England.

An important manuscript written by a monk in Selby in AD1174 detailed the early history of Selby Abbey. The *Historia Selebiensis Monastrii,* now in the French Bibliotheque Nationale, was translated into English in 1984 by I.S.Neale. Entitled *A History of Selby Abbey Monastery to AD1174*, the semi-legendary historical narrative described how Benedict was refused permission to leave Auxerre and was bitterly reproached by the other monks for wishing to abandon their religious house. Benedict did not reveal the contents of his visions, or how he intended to travel to Selby, but secretly stole away in the night taking with him an ancient relic from the altar - a finger of Saint Germain. Arriving in England the young monk mistakenly went to Salisbury. There the exhausted and bewildered traveller was befriended and cared for by a benevolent businessman, Edward of Salisbury. During a troubled sleep Benedict was again visited by Germain who, it is recorded, urged him to continue on his journey. Helped by a guide, the monk reached King's Lynn where he boarded a ship that eventually took him up the River Ouse to Selby. As soon as Benedict was ashore he raised the sign of the cross in honour of the Lord; then, under an oak of extraordinary size, he built a small hut of branches and leaves. The year was AD1069 and the land he was on belonged to King William. Benedict soon became loved and venerated by those around him for there was at that time a dearth of monks. Except for the monastic community at Durham, no new religious houses had been formed in the North since the devastation of the monasteries by the Vikings around AD867.

The time when Benedict began to gather followers around him was during the period when many in the north had not acknowledged defeat by the Normans. Many families, especially Danes, had fled to Scotland; one group were the ancestors of a well known Selby family called Staniland. It was reported that even after 1070, when the country north of the Humber was in Norman hands, the Viscount Governor of York still would not venture outside the city walls, even as far as Selby. In 1069 the sheriff of York, Hugh, son of Baldric, escorted by a company of soldiers, was one of those who, when sailing up the Ouse, saw the monk's cross in its prominent position above the river bank and went to investigate. Hugh promised Benedict his protection and assistance in setting up a religious centre at Selby. After taking leave of the monk the nobles in Hugh's entourage assigned carpenters to build an oratory of wood in honour of the blessed Germain on a site on Church Hill where for many centuries to follow, the town chapel stood. The sheriff continued to help Benedict in every way possible. He arranged an audience with William who received the monk favourably and gave him permission to build a monastery at Selby. When Benedict had first landed at Selby it is believed that there was a settlement there divided into Great Selby and Little Selby. Great Selby was situated on the Ouse, a waterway which was used as a regular route to the north from the Midlands. This involved sailing down the Trent from Torksey and then up the Ouse to York. William gave Benedict one carucate of land in Great Selby, plus parts of Flaxley Wood, Rawcliffe, Brayton and a fishery at Whitgift. Benedict was only given small portions in Great Selby and the other places listed because they were part of the socage of Snaith. This manor and lands were not surveyed in the Domesday Book because they were then in William's hands and reserved for the support of his table. Socage referred to a feudal tenure of land, involving payment of rent or other non-military service to a superior. The ancient socage of Snaith included twenty-five settlements grouped along both banks of the Aire. It extended from Adlingfleet westward to Birkin on the left bank and to Whitley some distance beyond the right bank of the river. In the twelfth century the course of the River Don formed the boundary of the parish on the south-east separating it from Lincolnshire.

Benedict and his growing band of brothers constructed other buildings of wood next to the chapel. King William then commanded that the monk be ordained as Abbot of Selby Abbey by Thomas Senior, Archbishop of York. After a year had passed Benedict's followers were given the tonsure. They lived in their house according to the rules of St. Benedict which included the following solemn promises - to live as poor people; to obey the abbot in all matters; not to marry. The new Abbot then energetically set to work to acquire as many profits and property as he could for his monastery through service and purchase. He acquired two charters from the king confirming the abbey's possessions and rights. William endowed the convent in this manner as a thanks offering to God for, among many reasons, granting him a victory over the independent northern people.

Grants, Gifts and Spiritual Possessions

Selby Abbey, like other monasteries, soon attracted benefactors who gave the monks rich endowments in the hope of much spiritual gain for themselves. The grants and gifts bestowed on the monastery during its existence are too numerous to record in full here but many of the places concerned have been presented on a map. They included not only lands around Selby but extended into South Yorkshire, adjoining counties, Leicestershire and Northamptonshire. Benedict was wise, he cultivated friends who endowed his monastery with land and possessions. Domesday states that Benedict received Stanford (on Avon) in Northamptonshire and Misterton in Leicestershire from Guy de Raimbeaucourt ; Crowle, a hundred in Lincolnshire was presented to the abbey by Geoffrey de la Guerche. Many acres of land around Selby became part of the monastery's estate. Thomas, the Archbishop of York gave the monks of St. Germain land in Monk Fryston, Hillam and Little Selby. This was later confirmed by his successor, Thomas the Second, who added two bovates in Thorp; the donor cited as Clamarhoth, ancestor of the family of Stiveton of Steeton Hall. When Nigel the provost, ancestor of the family of Huddleston, became a monk of Selby during the reign of Hugh, the successor to Benedict, he granted two and a half carucates of land in Hillam plus part of his tithe in Huddleston to the abbey. In return, the Archbishop of York gave Gilbert, son of Nigel, two carucates of land in Wetwang. The abbey also gained Haddlesey, and fifteen acres that adjoined Gateforth, plus Hambleton, which Ilbert de Lacy gave to them.

There were different types of gifts and various reasons for them being bestowed on the monastery. Awards granted by John de Lascelles to the monks of Selby included one bovate of land in Brayton given on the day of the burial of his brother, Robert, and one carucate promised there on the day of his own death. He gave the monks other plots of land for the provision of lights nightly in the cloisters, and so that the monks might yearly make an anniversary for the soul of Robert, as for a departed brother of the monastery. Alexander de Ruhale quitclaimed- gave up- to the monks for lights in their church the rent of four shillings which they were in the custom of paying him for *"two bovates in Thorpe by Selby and two bovates in Burton by Brayton"*. A grant by Emma de Lascelles, with the consent of her son Adam (father - Peter de Birkin), of her mill in Sitlington was for the purchase of mass wine. It is interesting to note that Peter, son of Assolf, an Englishman of considerable estate in the West Riding, had obtained for wife, a lady who was clearly of Norman blood. The monks gained control of two landmarks in Selby that had been formed during the end of the last Ice Age:

> William de Gateford, son and heir of Nicholas de Burstal quitclaimed his right in the wood called Hoga de Hamelton (now Hambleton Hough) that the said Abbot of Selby might enclose the same.

> Robert Basset of Brayton quitclaimed all Brayton Bergh, (Barff) with the ground.

> Simon the cow-herd gave all his right in Brayton Bergh.

The description of parts of the lands given by John de Lascelles in Brayton included examples of boundary markers:

> Langelei and land with its vestures by the hedge of Ralph the knight, (Ralph de Stiveton), and by oak-trees signed with the cross by both John and the monks for land-marks on that side towards Brayton unto Tranamor.

When Richard, Abbot of Selby, granted tithes in the wood of 'Birne or Berlay' to Robert, prior of Drax, he used the River Aire as one boundary and an oak they called 'Fair-haia' as another border marker. "For", it was quoted, *"Adam de Bellaqua gave this oak-tree as a boundary, binding himself and his successors never to cut it down or uproot it"*. The exact limits of many of the lands exchanged or gifted caused divers legal wrangles and disputes. Henry de Campeaux and his son Robert were accused of taking property from the monks by going beyond the boundaries of their manors in Fryston and Hillam. A charter, notifying the monks that Henry de Lacy had, with the consent of Robert the son, restored the land to the abbey, indicated that the transgressions had been of long standing. The impression was that Henry had been cursed by bell, book and candle because of the length of time the monks had spent making numerous demands for the return of their estates. He had died before the matter was settled and his soul had been excommunicated. The agreement drawn up in the Charter was that on return of the land the soul of Henry de Campeaux was to be absolved in perpetuity and the soul of Robert should be included in the communion of alms and prayers--remembered for some benefaction.

The convent of St. Germain gradually appropriated many churches and chapels. Gerard, Archbishop of York (AD1101-1108) became involved in a dispute between Henry I (1100-1135) and the Archbishop of Canterbury concerning the importance of the See of Canterbury. The result of this was that Gerard received a gift of six churches including the one at Snaith. The Archbishop then granted that church to Selby Abbey. The tithes from the ancient parish of Snaith, which at that time extended from Hensall on the west to Adlingfleet on the east, were for many centuries amongst the most valuable possessions of the convent. The church at Snaith was often at the centre of a controversy as to the rights the abbey at Selby had over its running. In May 1310 Archbishop

Greenfield decided on *"the appropriation of the parish churches of Snaith and Aethelingflete to the abbot and convent of Selby."* It was also decreed for the better holding of services there that the monks provide the church with two resident chaplains, one of whom was to be known as the prior. It was stipulated that the two brothers were not to exact tithes of turf or windmills from the parishioners beyond what they were used to paying. They were granted four wax candles for the High Altar and one for each altar on feast days in return for wax-scot (tax), as was the custom.

Other religious places also came under the auspices of the abbey during its existence. "Church of Crowle gifted to St. Germain's, Selby, by Geoffrey de la Guerche, confirmed by Henry I." In 1257 Sir Richard de Berlay, knight, quitclaimed the park of Staynor Hall which then served as a grange where the monks stored provisions. A chapel was erected outside its moated enclosure in the year 1286. Three years later, Ralf and Cecil his wife, and their heirs were given a plot in Selby in return for annually covering the costs for lights in the chapel at Staynor. Records also show that the monks paid a man sixpence a year for cleansing the passages around the small building. There had been a church and a priest at Brayton before the Domesday Survey. During the reign of John (1199-1216) rights to a third part of the church at Brayton were given by Ralph de Ruhale to Selby Abbey. In 1263 a contest developed between Thomas, Abbot of Selby and Henry de Vernoil concerning the latter's advowson of Brayton Church. At a meeting of the Justices Vernoil gave up his rights in return for one hundred marks and one hundred solidates of land; these included messuages and gardens in Pollington and Balne. It was recorded that in 1220 the church had been giving one third of its tithes from corn, hay, wool and lamb to the prebend of Wistow who had then volunteered instead to accept an annual sum of fourteen pounds. By 1348 any tithes, whether in kind or money, plus rents and profits gained by Brayton Church belonged to the monastery at Selby. It was at this time that, thanks to the efforts of Archbishop William Melton of York, a portion was allotted to Brayton for the maintenance of a secular vicar. It was ordered that the monks should have a fit and proper mansion erected in a place known as Parson's-Intak, lying on the north-side of the church for use of the vicar. It was to stand in two acres of land with a further 23 acres, locally named Courtnay's land and some common pasture put at the disposal of the vicar. He was also to receive one pound pension per annum, which former rectors had had from the prebendary of Wistow. Other items give an insight into some of the ways that the priests derived an income- tithes were collected of foals, pigs, calves, geese, swans, pigeons, line and hemp, milk, honey, and bees; also of wool paid in fleeces or money.

In 1292 the Abbot was granted a licence for a chantry in Hambleton.

"The Abbot of Selby to John de Craucumbe, Commissary to the Archbishop of York, that he appoint a priest to the chapel of Hamelton built in honour of the Blessed Virgin Mary because of the difficulty for those living in Hamelton, Gateford and Lund to attend services in the parish church of Brayton. The Chaplain is to be supported by the Abbot of Selby."

John de Brotherton was the first chaplain there and the payment of ten marks for him and a clerk were ordered to be paid out of the profits of the church at Brayton.

In 1304 Henry de Lacy, Earl of Lincoln, gave licence to the abbot to rebuild the chapel of St. Magdalene at Whitgift so that inhabitants of Ousefleet, Whitgift, Eastoft, Reedness and Swinefleet and tenants of eleven bovates of land in Fockerby and thirteen bovates in Haldenby (all in the parish of Snaith) could hear divine service and partake of sacraments. Twenty eight years later John de Lacy was given a licence to found a chantry at Gateforth; for the following two hundred years the priest there was appointed by the Abbot of Selby. Recorded accounts belonging to the abbey for the years 1416-17 reveal that there were also chapels under their jurisdiction at Hook, Carlton, Rawcliffe and Turnbridge. The last mentioned lying midway between Snaith and Rawcliffe on the old course of the Don.

Another little chapel that came under the authority of the Abbey was situated near to Gowthorpe in Selby. It was dedicated to a fifth century saint of ancient Gaul, St. Genevieve. When at the early age of seven, Genevieve or Genovefa, committed her life to God she was specially blessed by Germain himself. The young girl grew up to have considerable powers of leadership in all that was good; Germain held her in great esteem and gave her his support when she faced her many ill-wishers. There is a reference to the chapel of St. Genevieve in the Selby Coucher Book in a charter dating from the eleventh or twelfth century. In it Adam, son of Richard Marshall stated:

> I have by this charter given, granted and confirmed...the toft and croft which belonged to Hugh Blundus (maybe Bland) in Gowthorpe opposite the chapel of St. Genevieve, four acres of land...

This chapel may have been situated on or near the triangular area that is bounded on its north by the main street of Gowthorpe, and on its other sides by Armoury Road and Brook Street. This religious building is also mentioned in the Account Rolls of the monastery for the year 1434-35. The place of worship was in need of refurbishment for it is recorded that two hundred laths were purchased to use as beams for the chapel. Eight cart-loads of mud were also delivered and four men paid to mix it and use it as plaster for the said beams. Planks and nails were bought to make benches for the place of worship and to provide a door to the adjoining garden.

There is a strong belief that there was a place of worship in the vicinity of Church Hill long before the founding of the abbey but not enough evidence has been uncovered to prove its existence. There is, however, sufficient data to show that there was a minor church in that area during the life of the monastery in Selby. This will be referred to in detail in Chapter Three.

The Abbots and Officials of Selby Abbey

The *Historia* described the site of the religious house where Benedict and his brothers worshipped as being in the proximity of three royal rivers, the Ouse, Derwent and Aire, lying in an area dotted with lakes, ponds and waterways, all of which teemed with every kind of freshwater fish. The slightly raised ground was enclosed on all sides by forests in which there were numerous timbers of outstanding quality. There was also close at hand a large quantity of stone perfect for carving and suitable for every building purpose. The only drawback to this seemingly idyllic situation was the presence of wandering bands of Saxons who lived deep in the forests only venturing out when they needed to plunder for provisions or when an opportunity arose for them to make a strike against the hated invaders. The monk-author of the *Historia* identified the leader of one gang of outlaws as Swain, son of Sigga, believed to have been a disinherited Englishman. The little church and its offices soon attracted the unwelcome attention of the band but, it is recorded, when one of the outlaws assaulted its door the power of Germain caused his hand to stay firmly stuck there until, with the help of the monks, he confessed his sins and vowed never to wrong them again.

Benedict was Abbot of Selby Abbey from approximately 1069 to 1097. Besides acquiring much in the way of property and funds for the abbey it was recorded, by some historians, that in 1076 Benedict procured from Pope Alexander II the authority to use the ring, mitre, pastoral staff, dalmatic coat, gloves and sandals and to bless church ornaments, such as altar cloths, and to give first tonsures. It was later stated by other writers that the grant had been wrongly ascribed to Alexander II for he had died in April, 1073. The privileges, it is believed, were bestowed by Pope Alexander IV in May, 1256. At whatever time Selby Abbey acquired these honours it appears that they were not fully appreciated by the monks there. On the 11th April, 1308, a formal letter from Archbishop Greenfield was delivered to the monastery. The abbot was informed that the Archbishop of York had inspected the Apostolic Letters and, with the consent of the dean and chapter, had granted that the abbot might take advantage of the aforesaid indulgences which, up-to-date, the head of the convent had omitted to use. These honours were confirmed that year on the Abbot of Selby and the Abbot of St. Mary's in York, making them the only mitred abbots in England, north of the Trent.

Benedict did not begin the building of the monastery and its church in stone nor did he manage to stay true to all his vows. The final rift between the leader and the monks came after an incident involving the stealing, by two monks, of a large amount of silver from the treasury - money intended for the use of the monastery. Benedict let his anger at this atrocity colour his judgement. He pursued and caught the culprits then ordered them to be castrated- a punishment that far outweighed the crime. The abbot's actions were condemned by the king and caused dissatisfaction amongst his brethren. Unable to regain their respect Benedict eventually resigned his charge.

Benedict was succeeded by Hugh, a former prior of the monastery. He was described as a god-fearing, charitable and energetic man. Hugh came from Durham where Benedictine monks had started to build a cathedral. A master builder, the new abbot began the construction of a monastery using stone as well as wood. According to the *Historia*, Hugh laboured alongside his men wearing the traditional workman's smock and carrying to the site, on his shoulders, stone, lime and other materials needed for the buildings. Every Saturday he received a workman's wage which he gave to the poor thereby fulfilling the instruction *"Give to the poor from your own just labours."* It was around the year 1100 that the monks, dressed in their black habits, some with hooded cloaks, others with cowls, and with boots or sandals on their feet, left the wooden church to dwell in the stone convent. It was written that:

> The monastery should, if possible, be so arranged that all necessary things, such as water, mill, garden and various crafts are situated within the enclosure, so that the monks are not compelled to wander outside, for that is not at all expedient for their souls.

Inside the walls of Selby Abbey the Benedictine monks' day was long and hard for the Saint's rules, which had been introduced into Britain near the end of the sixth century, were very strict. Their waking hours were taken up by three tasks; worship, which included eight daily services; writing, which involved painstakingly copying and translating of religious works; and labouring, in the fields and gardens to provide food.

The abbey belonged to the diocese of York. Its head was the abbot who was chosen by the monks and ordained by the Archbishop of York. The archbishop had episcopal rights of visitation over the monastery whilst, at the same time, the abbot was expected to regularly attend convocations - an assembly of clergy - at York. The lord abbot had his own dwelling which has been described as being near the south-west corner of the church overlooking a court, 200 square feet in area. The abbot had supreme control over all aspects of the life of the monastery but to help matters run smoothly he needed to delegate. Hugh had been Benedict's prior. He had helped to supervise the religious life of the abbey. Priors were often placed in charge of cells set up away from the convent. Brother John Selby, a novice in 1416, had by 1436 been elevated to the position of prior at Snaith. Abbot Richard (1195-1214) had also been a prior at Selby.

The bursars dominated the handling of the finances of the house. So important was the position that two monks were always appointed to carry out the task. Sometimes two-thirds of the normal income went through the bursars' hands. They recorded multiple financial transactions carried out in the running of the monastery. These account rolls were compiled with special care from around 1338 when superiors of Benedictine houses were instructed to present annually an account of the year's financial business at a specially summoned chapter.

The study of surviving accounts have helped to build up a picture of life not just within the abbey confines but in the local area and nationally during medieval times. Other monks had special responsibilities in specific areas. Many of the brothers may not have chosen to take on these onerous tasks but few at Selby could expect to avoid being appointed to at least one of the numerous offices in the abbey. On the positive side, the officers were exempt from duties such as keeping silent, reading and writing in the cloisters; they also had the opportunity to travel and to develop their own particular talents. One position was that of sacristan. He cared for the holy vessels. The valuables and vestments in his trust were stored in the sacristy which was also his responsibility. It is still to be found today situated on the south side of the eastern arm of the church. This official had to keep the vestments clean and repaired. He had to provide candles, lamps, incense and wine for masses. It is interesting to note that the sacristan paid a clerk five shillings to maintain the abbey clock. The history of the modern clock is not easy to trace but it is recorded that by the eleventh century monasteries in Europe were using weight-clocks. These, it is believed, were probably only used to strike a bell at certain intervals as a call to prayers and had no dial to show the time. In the accounts of Selby Abbey it is stated that Anthony Swerdsliper was paid twopence for making a leather baldric for one of the bells at the monastery. An unusual duty for the sacristan was described in 1404 when it was noted that he was given four bushels of wheat by the granger for baking into 'pain demaine', white bread of the finest quality, for the convent in Lent. Some of his expenses were met by the rents he received from farms in places such as Selby, Burton, Brayton and Byram. This did not always cover the costs. At the beginning of the fifteenth century the sacristan had to provide 4000 hosts for masses and the parishioners' holy communion; also gloves for the bell-ringers and white linen cloth for making priestly garments called albs. These reached to the feet and enveloped the wearer. He also had to cover the expense of having mats and footrests made for the stalls of brethren in the choir and to have the organ repaired using sheepskin and glue.

The almoner had his offices next to the great gateway which faced north and was situated at the head of what is now known as James Street. This official, with the help of the kitchener and other abbey servants, looked after the poor. In 1404 the granger gave him 21 quarters of beans and peas to distribute amongst the needy. Other food given for charitable distribution at Advent and other festivals included six quarters of rye, a whole pig and two quarters, plus a bullock. One act of kindness included the buying of ten rods of russet cloth for clothing three poor persons. The almoner had mantles made for them, purchased shoes and paid to have the three shaved. He bought them wax tapers at the feast of Candlemas and gave them 3000 turves (peat) to keep them warm. Gifts of money and clothes were given to various poor strangers and debts written off. A sum of 4s. 5½d. was given to the former wife of Robert Tombarum in Hillam, described as a poor old woman. John Hudson of Thorpe Willoughby had his debt of 12d. pardoned for he was a poor blind man. John de Duffield, shoemaker, had a debt of 2s.6d written off because *"he has nothing"*. Beggars were not turned away. In 1399 is recorded *" To a certain young man, son of one of the esquires of the lord earl of Arundel, a beggar-20d"*. A knight called Adam who had become a beggar, brought a charter from the king as evidence of his condition. He was given 6s. 8d.

Every Maundy Thursday the almoner was responsible for gathering the needy together in the cloisters of the Abbey for the giving of alms, which one year included 1,200 red herrings. In 1404 money amounting to 30 shillings was apportioned for the poor. In 1969 Queen Elizabeth II carried on the tradition when she distributed Maundy Money in the Abbey Church at Selby - the first time such a service had been held in a parish church. The almoner, like many other officials derived some income from the rents collected from farms and houses. In the early fifteen century he was receiving rent from some tenements in New Lane, Selby. Out of this income he paid the wages of a servant in the almonry and the bearer of the mortuary roll. This roll was carried from monastery to monastery to secure for the soul of a dead monk the prayers of members of other religious houses.

In the early days of the monastery the monks themselves had no wealth. A bequest left to the abbey during the thirteenth century was given for the feeding of the poor, the care of the infirm and for pittances for the monks - all were equal in the eyes of the benefactor. Pittances were, at first, given in the form of small gifts of food and drink on special occasions. This gradually changed to small allowances given annually to the monks by a Pittancer. In 1362 Abbot Gilfrid de Gaddesby received 20 shillings and the monks 13s. 6d. The average number of monks in the monastery from 1412 to 1517 was twenty six. Like the monks before them their clothing was provided by the chamberlain. He too relied on farm rents for some of his income but it was sometimes boosted by the profits from the sale of crops. *"Received from sale of rushes, reeds and hay growing in Selby Dam-46s"*. At the opening of the fifteenth century the almoner annually transferred 20s. rent money to the chamberlain to pay for the clothing of Brother John Acastre, the accountant. During the early years of the monastery the chamberlain provided cloth or finished garments for the community but at sometime between 1415 and 1431 this changed; the pittance paid out to the monks began to include an allowance for clothing. In 1441 Abbot John Ousthorp was awarded 66s. 8d. for pittance and clothing. Monks such as Thomas Crull received 40 shillings. Officials also began to receive fees for the positions they held or for saying masses at endowed chantries.

The Lord Abbot had his own chamberlain to see to his needs. In 1398 John de Selby was granted a salary of 13s.4d. to do this work. During that year he purchased for the use of the abbot nine ells of black cloth (one to be made into a cowl), three ells of cloth burnet, 16 ells of blanket cloth, eight ells of stamyn cloth plus one ounce of silk for stitching the clothes. John Shether, skinner, was paid to mend the abbot's furs and to line other apparel with fur against the approaching winter. At the same time John de Brighton was paid 42s. for boots and other things useful in the cold. The chamberlain paid out ten shillings for enough cloth to make himself, his clerk and his page in the kitchen William de Duffield, gowns with hoods. Other expenses he had to find the funds for included ten lambs' skins for the livery of the abbot's squire and two ells of cloth of ray for the livery of the workman, Richard Smyth, working at the Abbot's pond. The page attending his chaplain had to be fitted out with a lined tunic and given a gown and six pairs of shoes. Some articles purchased for the abbot's dwelling place, during the period of a year, were listed as linen cloth for his chamber, ells of canvas for his tablecloths and for use in his kitchen, 20 stones of paris candles, 16 dozen goblets, eight candlesticks, four bowls, half-a-dozen decorated pewter pots and copper vessels that were sometimes repaired. Two andirons were also purchased for the abbot's hall to supplement the ones already there.

Thomas de Howeden became a monk in 1375. During his presence in Selby Abbey he was kitchener twice and in 1401 took over the minor role of an Infirmarer. He was given a small amount from the rents paid by farms in places such as Balne, Osgodby in Lindsey and Menthorpe. His largest contribution however came from the sale of turves (peat) and wood even though he had to pay for its transport to the abbey. In one transaction he paid for turves to be loaded onto a boat at Rawcliffe, the shipowner reimbursed for bringing it to Selby, and paid the wages of eighteen women for carrying the fuel from the boat into the turfhouse. The infirmary was not just for those who were sick, old retired monks also found refuge there. Aged or infirm people who were awarded a corrody were often cared for by the infirmarer. A corrody was a pension awarded to certain people for their services to the Abbey or in return for gifts. In 1292 Roger de Selby, marshal, was granted a corrody for life. He received a bowl of broth daily, and a loaf of bread, if there was anything eaten which required bread, and an allowance of ale. Every two days he was given a loaf of bread for his servant and every year he received a robe. All this was a reward for his faithful service to the convent. Alice Spicer became a corrodian; she was given five shillings annually for clothes and turves for fuel. In return, on her death, her messuage in Selby was to revert to the abbey. John Tuch and his wife, Margaret, bought a pension of ten marks for the term of their lives for the princely sum of £80. Peter Talbot and his wife, Beatrice, paid a lesser sum of £26.13s.4d. for the office of porter and a corrody belonging to same, sold to them for the duration of their lives. It was common practice for the Crown to demand corroderies for its servants. In 1291 King Edward ordered that because John de Brayton was too old to continue his work as Clerk in Chancery he should receive support in his old age at Selby Abbey. John was informed that he was to spend his retirement in the shelter of the monastery with a corrody of one free servant, twelve shillings sterling, plus necessaries and shoes; all to be received by him annually on the feast of St. Martin.

When the monastery was in its infancy all the brothers went into the infirmary at one time or another for blood-letting - a practice that was believed to be therapeutic. It gave each monk the chance to have a break from the strict regime of the abbey; an opportunity to relax and taste richer foods! One bill for the infirmary listed beef, lamb and cheese amongst its items, goods not usually found included in a monk's diet. Another charge paid out by the Infirmarer was the sum of ten shillings due to Robert Barbour for doing the tonsures. Other tasks carried out by this talented man were those of surgery and dentistry. It is believed that the infirmarer, Thomas de Howeden came from the place from which he took his name. Records show that during 1397/98 his mother was supplied with wheat and barley by the proctor of the Abbot of Selby at Whitgift and Reedness - eight kilometres south-east of Howden. In the Pittancer's accounts for 1403/04 two thirds of the surnames listed were of places within 50kms. of Selby. Later records showed that eventually the monks did not necessarily come from the area depicted in their name. Later still some began to use their family titles. The last abbot in the town, Robert Selby (1526-1540) was referred to in some documents as Robert Rogers.

"Let all guests be received as Christ would be," was an instruction given by St. Benedict. The Guest-House Keeper was in charge of this duty. Guests expected to be treated in a manner befitting their status, and as the abbey received many distinguished visitors suitable accommodation had to be provided. The main guest house at Selby had a Hall with a long table for dining in it. The comforts for upper class life by the fifteenth century included rushes on the floors, candles, curtains, covers woven with red roses and decorated walls. The house also contained a superior apartment known as the High Chamber. This had an inner and an outer room and boasted a feather bed with luxurious covers. There were stables and granaries within the precincts of the monastery for the guests' horses and south of these there were lodgings reserved for the less important visitor. Fodder to feed the horses belonging to the lord abbot and his visitors was brought in from the farms at Wistow, Monk Fryston and Rawcliffe. The full cost of hospitality at the abbey must have been burdensome. Some of the expenses incurred one year included the cost of purchasing seven stone of paris candles from a candle-maker in Riccall, towels, blankets, goblets, plus plates, dishes and saucers made of pewter. These plates etc. were bought in London at the cost of three pence farthing per pound weight; twelve of each were ordered, the weight of which came to 49 pounds. When William de Skipwith, John de Amyas and Robert Mauleverer stayed at the guest house whilst the abbot was absent the following expenses were incurred. Eight gallons of wine were purchased for 6s.8d and meat and fish for 3s.4d. Ten shillings was spent on more horse-bread for the animals in the guests' stable plus nine pence for some candles to light the same. Meanwhile a man working in the quarry at Monk Fryston was earning 5d a day. Hidden expenses were caused by gratuities. When Thomas, Duke of Clarence, (second son of Henry IV) visited the convent, accounts show that the Keeper gave money to the servant who announced the duke's arrival; and during his stay 20s. was spent on members of his household in the form of small gifts and tips of money.

Three officials, the kitchener, granger and extern cellarer were together responsible for victualling the monastery. The kitchener was in charge of the kitchen, the cook and other servants. He also helped the extern cellarer keep up the number of stock. This varied from year to year. During 1416-17 over 400 cattle, pigs and sheep were bought. From 1475 to 1476 there was no record of any animals being purchased. The cellarer acquired livestock to supply the community's need for meat. At first, except for the sick, monks practised self-denial in the matter of eating meat from four-footed animals, but by the end of the twelfth century this prohibition was being increasingly ignored. In 1336 there was an official acceptance of the relaxation of the Rule when Black Monks were permitted, reluctantly, to eat meat four days a week, on a regular basis. Exceptions were at Advent and the nine weeks between Septuagesima and Easter. In the fifteenth century attempts were made by representatives of the Benedictine Order to reintroduce the stricter rules on meat-eating, amongst other things, but this was opposed by the monks' spokesmen. The granger was responsible for the bakery and the brewery, both situated near to the abbot's lodgings. He drew on a large area for his supplies because of the great demand for grain. Bread and ale were staple items in a medieval diet. In his book on the economy of Bolton Priory, I. Kershaw suggested that the average consumption per day by one individual in a monastery was two and a half pounds of bread plus one gallon of ale. Accounts for Selby Abbey 1413-14 showed that 283½ quarters of grain were baked into bread and 714 quarters of malt used for ale. The malt used that year produced 42,840 gallons of ale which, on the figures given, implies that the community in the monastery, consisted of 117 persons. This is similar to the number present in 1416-17 when there were 35 monks, 50-60 servants, 10 corroderies and an unknown number of guests.

The Keeper of the Refectory was a minor official whose responsibility it was to look after the monks' dining hall. He purchased the necessary articles to equip the place properly. His income from the farm rents averaged around 27s. a year so the Keeper was not asked to be responsible for the upkeep of the fabric of the place. During 1421-1422 Brother John Grayngham spent ten shillings of his income on the following items. He purchased four yards of linen cloth for the cupboard in the refectory and an equal amount for napkins. A further nine yards were bought for long towels for use in the lavatorium where the monks washed their hands before meals. The monks had to be as fastidious before they had the use of any books or manuscripts. *"Wash lest touch of dirty fingers on my spotless pages linger,"* was another rule laid down by St. Benedict. The Keeper of the Refectory paid sixteen pence out of his ten shillings annually to a laundress to keep the linen clean, and William Pyper the same amount for making two reed mats for the benches in the dining hall. Thomas Goldsmith gained fourpence for repairing a maplewood cup and Adam Smith an equal sum for mending the handle of a vessel used for ale. Twopence was given to Henry Cleric for making some candles and the clerk of the Refectory received sixpence as a Christmas present.

To help the officials who were responsible for the abbot's well-being they had recourse to the bursars' income. In 1398 Henry Droury was cook to Abbot John de Shireburn. He received a wage and at intervals was reimbursed by the bursars for victuals purchased by him for the lord abbot and his visitors. These included flavourings used to enhance or disguise the taste of the food such as spices, green ginger, saffron, mustard, sanders (from sandalwood) and cummin. Many of these plus figs, raisins and wine were brought from Hull. Others like almonds (bought in dozens) came from York. One payment was made to two men and a fisherman for bringing a boar, some swans, rabbits and capons from Crowle for the abbot's consumption. The bursars also covered the cost of 55 capons at four pence each. The steward at Crowle sent the head of the abbey an offering of a deer. Half a barrel of sturgeon and six barrels of salted eels were also amongst the foodstuffs purchased for the use of the abbot. These were bought from William Spenser, whilst a further quarter of a barrel of sturgeon and one barrel of salted eels were obtained from William Hamerton. A barrel, fully packed, held 32 gallons of sturgeon or 30, and sometimes 42, gallons of eels.

Gifts of Food and Entertainment

Being a mitred abbot the father of the convent had gifts from many people of standing and influence. These were usually of food except in one case in 1399 when Abbot John de Shireburn received a gift of two hunting dogs from Lady Roos; William, Lord Roos of Hamelake had an important seat at Helmsley. Other gifts received that year included twelve partridges brought by a servant of William Barker near the festival of St.

Hilary, (13th. January); William of Tadcaster was an alnager, the king's cloth inspector, in the West Riding of Yorkshire in 1395 and 1399. A month later the abbot received a porpoise from Sir Stephen Scrope who had a favourite residence at Faxfleet near Goole. It is interesting to note that porpoises have been sighted several times during the last few years in the River Ouse, especially around Cawood. The older residents of the village believe that they are following the migration of salmon up the river. Further gifts included two herons delivered by the servant of William Ketring, esquire of John of Gaunt, Duke of Lancaster. This young nobleman had been granted the manor of Kirby, near Ouseburn, Yorkshire and it is believed he may also have held the manor of Osgodby where the Abbey had an estate. Many gifts of food were sent at Christmas. The prior of Drax sent the abbot on this festival day a present of apples, pears and cheese.

The head of the monastery also dispatched gifts of food. The Archbishop of York received a bounteous present of six pheasants, six swans and twelve rabbits, sent by water to his residence at Cawood. Also, by the order of the lord abbot, a boar was given to Brian de Stapleton, Knight, of Carlton, near Snaith. This knight served Henry V in France and died in Normandy in 1418. A number of gifts were sent to Gokewell Priory during the time that William Pygot (1407-1429) was abbot. In 1416 the kitchener accounted for two salted fish sent to the prioress there, by order of the lord abbot. The bursars' lists of 1431-32 records Lady Joan Pygot, former head of the small Cistercian priory, as the recipient of a pension from Selby Abbey. In 1440 Gokewell Priory which was situated in Lincolnshire housed eight nuns and had a revenue of £10 per annum.

Gifts were annually presented to a special visitor to the monastery- *"and to the boy-bishop of York yearly 6s.8d.".* The festival of the Holy Innocents, which fell on the 28th. December, was celebrated by the election of a boy-bishop from amongst the cathedral choristers. The boy-bishop, chosen by his peers, toured his diocese and was entertained and given gifts by various members of the nobility and ecclesiastical institutions along the way. Entertainments at Selby and elsewhere would have included tumblers, dancers, fruit sellers, harp players, organists and minstrels. Many of the minstrels told stories and performed conjuring tricks besides playing music. The nobility often provided the entertainers. Minstrels belonging to the Duke of Lancaster, Sir Henry 'Hotspur' Percy and Sir Philip Darcy all came to Selby to amuse the abbot and his guests. Sometimes the King's Royal Acting Company, usually six in number, beguiled an audience. They received 6s.8d. for their performances at Selby. Many of these diversions took place on festival days. On one Christmas Day four boys from York performed before the abbot whilst on St. John the Baptist's Day, clerks from Selby acted out a miracle play. The Abbot of Selby often went to the manor house at Rawcliffe for recreation. He also went to Snaith and to Wheel Hall. The latter, situated by the River Ouse, near Riccall, was the residence of the Bishops of Durham. After the monastery had acquired Stainer Grange it became a place where both the abbot and his community went for short periods of rest and recuperation from the normal monastic regime. Hunting was another popular form of entertainment enjoyed by the nobility, abbots and the monks. Forest laws were set by the king. In the year 1200, King John awarded the Bishop of Durham a charter confirming to him and his church and successors the manor of Sedbergh and villages of Crayke and Cliffe, with woods free from forest laws and with power to clear and enclose the ground at their pleasure. The Abbot of Selby was also favoured with a Charter allowing him to hunt in a Royal Forest that extended from Cow Lane in Selby, to Wistow Lordship. An area of this Abbot's Chase covered parts of Selby, Wistow and Cawood commons including an extensive forest of oaks near Wistow known as Moss Carr Hagg Wood. Many royal personages came to hunt in the forests around Selby. When King John visited Cawood he hunted for fox and deer in what is today known as Bishop Wood. The accounts for 1416-17 showed that the kind of victuals taken by Brother Thomas Bolton when organising hunts in the North Wood included a whole lamb or quarter of mutton. Brother Thomas was the abbot's chaplain and it was possible that his duties included the providing of entertainment for lay visitors enjoying the abbot's hospitality. The lord abbot also employed an usher whose tasks included the care of hunting dogs. Many of the monks kept such animals within the precincts of the abbey. The wildness of these curs can be judged by the fact that in 1417 the kitchener had to write off ten sheep which had been savagely and totally torn apart by dogs belonging to Brother Thomas Bolton and others in the abbey.

The Lords of Byram Hall were the King's principal bowkeepers and attended the Abbot of Selby at the Chase. The Basset family also attended some of the hunts. Margery, daughter and heiress of Miles de Basset of North Moreton in Berkshire and of East and Middle Haddlesey, near Selby, was married to Sir Nicholas de Stapleton. He was a Justice of the King's Bench who in 1280 was granted a house and five bovates of land in West Haddlesey. Roger Dodsworth, the seventeenth century antiquarian, described Basset Park as being in the area of Brayton and noted that the Bassets were bow-bearers (in the chase) of the Abbots of Selby. It was also recorded that if the head of the family came and blew his hunting horn at the great gateway of the abbey on Christmas Eve, he and his retinue were entitled to the hospitality of the Benedictine monastery throughout the twelve days of Christmas.

CHAPTER 3

THE GROWTH OF SELBY

The 'Little Chapel in the Town'

The existence of the monastery in Selby affected the lives of the inhabitants of the town and surrounding villages from its founding to its dissolution in 1539. It was the nucleus for the expansion of Selby over almost five centuries. Before the advent of the abbey there had been a small rural settlement around Church Hill and near to the banks of the Ouse frequented by fishermen. Much of the land in the area was still mainly marshy and thickly forested hiding in its depths many outlaws. A hundred years or so after the arrival of Benedict, Selby had grown into a substantial Yorkshire town through the influence of the monks and its position as an inland port. Steps were being taken in the struggle to reclaim land from the marshes and to deforest some wooded areas.

When Abbot Hugh and the Benedictine monks left their wooden structure for the confines of the new abbey, the people of Selby acquired the little chapel on Church Hill for their own worship. There are several references in historical books and documents to a "little church" at Selby. It was recorded in the year 1200 that a young lady, Cecilia by name, daughter of Nicholas, physician of Selby, gave her toft, "near the little church" to one Thomas Bustard, who appears to have been her nephew. Later, King John (1199-1216) gave the toft to John, the chaplain serving the parochial chapel of Selby. In another charter it is stated, the chaplain, perhaps when close to death, gave the toft, with all its buildings and appurtenances lying near to the "little church", to the Abbot and Convent of Selby. He stipulated that in return they were to annually set aside six denarii with which to provide a pittance for the monks.

In 1275, Walter Gifford, Archbishop of York, who kept himself fully informed of the activities of the religious houses in his diocese, sent one of his officials to visit the "little church" or, as it was known, the chapel of St. Germanus. The chaplain there explained to the archbishop's representative that the rite of baptism had formerly been administered in the chapel until it became customary (on whose authority he did not know) for children to be christened in the monastery. Today many infants are received into the Christian faith in Selby Abbey Parish Church at a totally plain and simply hewn stone font. It is believed it is the one at which babies born in the town, as far back as the twelfth century, received their baptism. It is not known at which point it was removed from the minor church but it stands today under a beautifully carved fifteenth century oaken canopy- the only remaining example of medieval woodwork in the Abbey Church. In 1275 the chaplain had presented the official from the archbishop with an "inventory of the temporal possessions of the ancient parochial chapel". It showed that it had no communion vessels, save two phials of tin or pewter, because, at that time the sacrament was only administered at the monastery. The chaplain declared that neither the church nor the altar within were dedicated and that the dead were interred in the burial ground of the abbey.

Grants and charters were often affirmed or changed by incoming kings or religious heads. Those concerning the chapel at Selby sometimes changed the rites and customs carried out there. When in 1310 Archbishop Greenfield gave Snaith to the abbey at Selby he also confirmed to them the "little chapel in the town". The later charter of 1349 testified that the Abbot of Selby appointed Sir William de Helperthorne, chaplain, to be their proctor:

> *to receive and demand in their name all offerings, lesser tithes and fees, coming into the chapel at Selby from the feast of St. Valentine 1349 to the end of the year completed in full, following the next one.*

One or two exceptions were referred to, including the offerings made at the four principal festivals, namely Easter, Christmas and both festivals of St. Germanus. These were to be given to the sacristan of the monastery who was then to pay Sir William, forty pence at Eastertide. Out of the tithes, offerings and fees collected he was to pay the kitchener of the said abbey, twelve silver marks in equal portions on the feast of Pentecost and of St Martin in winter. It was written down that Sir William was to occupy the rooms next to the chapel and was to maintain them at his own expense. His duties included officiating as a priest at the chapel in all divine offices and providing sufficient quantities of communion bread, wine, candles and incense for the parishioners. John of Haddlesey and John of Spalding acted as sureties for Sir William. They ensured that the payments of money and the fulfilling of his duties were carried out faithfully by the chaplain. Any lapses in their watchfulness carried a severe penalty for the guarantors; it involved the distrainment of all their, or their heirs' goods, land and property!

In 1352 the little religious house was again put under scrutiny, this time by Geoffrey de Gaddesby, the Abbot of Selby (1341-68). In a letter he stated his intention to pay an official visit to the parochial church to see for himself whether or not all its affairs were in good order. Authority over the minor chapel changed hands many times during its existence. State records for 1370 clearly show Edward III (1327-77) had advowson of the parochial church that year. As lay rector he had asked John, Abbot of Selby, to permit him to present a worthy person to the chapel of Selby, for the living at that time was vacant.

The account rolls of the abbey for the years 1416-17 reveal many changes in the running of the chapel. John Bulkyn was parish chaplain at that time. He was given a salary that year of £4.13s.4d plus 13s.4d for collecting the Lenten tithes. From the profits of the minor church, which partly came from small offerings and burials, the abbey received £7.12s.5d, along with any donations in a money-box dedicated to St. Zita. This patron saint of servants was believed to be from Lucca in Italy. Some of the expenses incurred that year by the chapel included such purchases as: one stone of paris candles for lighting at dawn on festival days in winter, nine pounds of wax for making candles, and 480 wafers together with wine and incense for mass. The chaplain had also to pay Henry Clerc to prepare tapers and wax-candles for a wheel-shaped chandelier for the building. John Bulkyn was more fortunate than Sir William de Helperthorne as he was not responsible for the upkeep of the chapel or the dwelling house. These were all in the hands of the convent. The repairs done that year were recorded in the accounts and show how the monastery not only purchased its materials from a wide area around Selby but also provided work for the people in its vicinity. Peter Geve was employed to make a wall between the chapel and the dwelling house and to repair the foundations of other walls there. The materials bought included two wagon-loads of stone from Monk Fryston, two wagon-loads of lime from Sherburn, six quarters of sand and 1680 bricks. The monks paid for the stones and lime to be carted to the monastery. The house was also in need of repair and for this work many lengths of oak timber and boards of wainscot were purchased and two men paid to saw them. Vast numbers of nails were bought -1680 brad-nails, 900 medium spike-nails and 720 stowering nails. Seven wagon-loads of mud were brought for daubing the said house at a cost of eight pence. John Orwell, a carpenter, was hired by agreement to do the repairs and also paid to make and strengthen a porch over the door. A lock and key were purchased from John Nesse for this door. Forty thraves of thatch, each thrave usually containing from 12 to 14 sheaves, were needed for the roof, and a man was paid fourpence to collect some withies for the same purpose. Patrick the thatcher and his mate were then paid nine shillings, by agreement, to thatch the roof of the house.

This small parochial chapel of St. Germanus was still functioning thirteen years before the dissolution of the monasteries. Its authority had also been extended for it is recorded in Cardinal Wolsey's Register, dated 26th January 1525-26, that a licence was issued to the curate of the little chapel permitting him to officiate over the marriages of John Rathby and Margaret Gretcham and of Thomas Slater and Joan Goodyere. It was already the custom for a bride to have a dowry for it is recorded in the late twelfth century William de Aton:

> *gave to Hugh da Langthwaite in marriage with Alice, his daughter, four marks and four pence of rent in Barlby and various liberties.*

Archaeological Digs

In 1275 the chaplain at the minor church had informed the Archbishop's representative that the dead were interred in the burial grounds of the abbey. In 1996, workmen laying pipes in the shadow of Selby Abbey Church for the Yorkshire Water Authority, unearthed a skeleton. An archaeological dig was then undertaken in the area of Church Avenue, Abbey Place and Market Place and more bones were uncovered. Most of the complete skeletons found were all aligned east to west and came from burials immediately to the north of the existing burial ground adjoining Selby Abbey. Joy Langston, who did a study of the bones reported that there were twelve complete skeletons recovered, ten adults, one juvenile and one infant, whilst other bones were left in situ. The deepest interred and the shallowest were subjected to radio carbon dating which established that they had not come from the Cholera Burial Ground. It was also concluded they belonged to two working people who had died at a young age. The deepest burial was dated between 1450-1520, the other between 1560-1630. Both were found to have been suffering from extensive osteo-arthritis, tooth loss and a poor diet. From a study of all the bones discovered it was concluded there was no evidence to show that anyone had survived beyond their mid-forties. Roughly a third had not reached the age of eighteen. Their average height was given as 173.8cms for the males and 157.5cms for the females. There was evidence of degenerative changes in their spines whilst four of the skeletons showed definite signs of a medical condition that signified they had endured a gruelling life style from a very early age.

It was put forward in the reports on the skeletons that it appeared the burials had not been in a favoured part of the graveyard. Items in the account rolls of the monastery for 1413-14 confirm that there was a separate burial area for the people of the town of Selby. One task accounted for in the Rolls was the construction of a stone wall and arch between the cemetery of the town and the monks' burial ground. The monks relied on the local people for materials and labour. John de Bakhous provided most of the 620 alder stakes needed for the foundations of the walls and the rest came from Stainer (Staynor) Park. Cart-loads of clay, lime and sand were transported by road to the abbey and only four loads of sand were carried by boat from York. The monks also had to pay for the carrying of these materials either from the banks of the Ouse or the abbey's gates to the monks' cemetery.

The last of the materials needed for the construction of the walls and the arch was stone, of which there was a plentiful supply near to the town. The main quarries used by the brothers were at Monk Fryston and Huddleston. Account notes refer to quarries at Fryston, Hillam and Wrekiln. Morrell states that there is a deed in the archives of the Vavasour family that relates how these generous benefactors gave a 'Quarrey' pit to the monks at Selby. In 1291 the convent also obtained a charter from the Prior of Marton, in the Forest of Galtres, granting them leave to remove stone from three acres of a quarry in Thevesdale, near Tadcaster. This area was sandwiched between a quarry used by the Abbot of Thornton Abbey and one used by the Prior of Drax. Stone for York Minster and Howden Church also came from this valuable property. In 1371 Abbot Shirburn (1368-1407) bought a thirty year lease of a quarry in Huddleston and ten years later was involved in the opening of one at Monk Fryston. Huddleston Quarry has been described as lying roughly a mile due west of Sherburn-in-Elmet, just south of Huddleston Hall. It is believed it was worked until Victorian times but all that is left now is a yawning cavity on the flank of a hill.

An official known as the Keeper of the Fabric was responsible for the maintenance of the buildings but his income was so small that large alterations or repairs were subsidised by the bursars. Most of the stone and lime the Keeper ordered for the cemetery walls came from Monk Fryston. This limestone was very popular for the stones split easily to make 'flagges' for paving. Before the stone was prepared for the walls at the monastery, the Keeper of the Fabric paid two labourers to dig out the roots of hazel trees in the monks' cemetery. This took two and a half days after which another two men were employed to fix 131 sharpened stakes into the ground for the foundations of the wall between the cemeteries. The masons in charge of the building hired a further five workers to help fix the stakes because of the shortness of time. A William Pyper was paid for carting 28 loads of clay needed for the top of the stakes. Robert Bouland and his son then earned 12s. 6d. carrying the stone from the abbey to the cemetery at ten pence a day. Two masons, employed by the bursars, took ten weeks to prepare the stones for use, then, after the following Easter, with the help of two labourers they raised a wall with an arch and gate to separate the two grounds. The Keeper had then to find the funds to buy materials such as Spanish iron, lead and nails and pay for Adam Smith to make bars and hooks from them for fixing and fastening the gate. The last payment the official made was 3s. 4d. a gift to the masons on the orders of the lord abbot.

During the digs that took place in the 1990s the archaeologists uncovered the foundations of a substantial wall, made of limestone blocks, in the area of Church Avenue and Abbey Place. Others working for the York Archaeological Trust discovered a partly demolished limestone wall in the vicinity of The Crescent which, they suggested, may have been the remnants of an Abbey precinct boundary. It is possible that the first was part of the cemetery wall and the second a segment of another wall built during the year 1414. The accounts show the Keeper of the Fabric and the Bursars paid for the services of masons constructing a stone gate at the northern side of the monastery, the stone wall, gate and arch between the cemeteries, and another wall on the eastern side of the abbey. When the digs took place a team, working for MAP, found several wooden stakes in situ at the rear of Gowthorpe, all dating from around the thirteenth to fourteenth centuries. Records written by the monks during that period contain many references to the use of stakes:

> *For the services of one man felling alder trees in order to make stakes from them - 6d.*
> *For the services of men helping the masons to dig and prepare the soil to fix the stakes in that place...*
> *For the service of two men sharpening and fixing 497 stakes in the foundation of the wall - 8s.*

In 1413 the bursars paid ninepence for each cart-load of stone brought from Monk Fryston to the abbey during summer-time and, by agreement, tenpence in autumn. There were 319 cart-loads of stone delivered that summer and eight more as autumn began. At that time a cart, with untired wheels cost 10s. 8d. but the Granger at the monastery, who bought such a vehicle, paid a further 43s.9d. to make it roadworthy. For this money a smith fitted the wheels with metal tires and nails; pitch was bought and smeared on the naves of the wheels; two axles were fitted using 18 clouts (plates of iron fitted to prevent wear), and plenty of grease was applied to them and the wheels. Traces and halters were included in the price and a horse hide for repairing the harness of the cart. The expense of keeping such a vehicle makes it believable that the monks owned most of the carts and hired local people as drivers. A further payment made by the Granger at the time he bought the cart was for 64 horse-shoes to be fitted onto his cart horses. He also paid for 112 shoes to be removed and then refitted to other animals. The size of this stable might indicate the possibility of the existence of a transport service owned and run by the brothers of Selby Abbey.

Waterways

Many buildings in York were partly made of magnesium limestone blocks brought from quarries in the Tadcaster area. In 1385 the Dean and Chapter of York took a lease out on Huddleston Quarry and continued to use its stones for their building work until the sixteenth century. The Gatehouse is all that remains of Cawood Castle, which was the principal palace of the Archbishops of York. It was built using the creamy-white stone from the quarry. Until well into the fifteenth century the material was taken to Cawood by road and then some of it was transferred to boats on the Ouse. Records show that a new quay was constructed at the riverside settlement during 1421-22. Cawood seems to have developed into a small river port which began to prosper well before the rise of Selby. It is certainly mentioned in a charter of 963, by King Edgar (959-975), concerning an estate at Sherburn. In a memorandum dated 975, Oswald, Archbishop of York (971-972), stated he held half of Cawood, the other portion still belonging to the Sherburn estate. There are indications in historical records that the Archbishops of York created Cawood as a port. They note wharves in the settlement owned by the Archbishops. The ferry, whose tolls were a valued source of revenue was held by them. It is believed that an artificial waterway, Bishopdyke, which still exists today, was once navigable from Sherburn to the River Ouse at Cawood, ten kilometres away, and was, at some time, used to transport stone from Huddleston Quarry. In 1504 it was recorded that:

Richard ffarechild sledded stone from a basin in Cawood to a boat.

Bishopdyke, was possibly in use during the Roman era when boats, mostly laden with grain, anchored there awaiting the tides. The water in Bishopdyke comes from a lake at Barkston, which is fed by a copious spring known as 'Scarthingwell' and several other minor springs and streams.

Waterways were also developed by the monks of Selby Abbey to assist in the carriage of goods and people. The most important of these dykes came to be known as Selby Dam. On modern maps it begins its journey as Fox Dyke, a small tributary that is crossed, north west of Hambleton, by an aqueduct carrying the waters of Bishopdyke. Somewhere along its route, roughly in the area of Rest Park farm, Fox Dyke becomes known as Selby Dam, a name it carries for the rest of its journey until its outfall into the River Ouse at Selby. In medieval times the western terminus of Selby Dam was named as Paradise Landing. This was in the vicinity of Hambleton, where many streams and drains fed into the small river. Later records name the wharf as 'Godsalf Lendyng' at Hambleton. The waterway, known along some of its stretches as the 'Pool of Selby', was very important for transporting goods to and from places along its course from Hambleton to the Abbey or Selby.

The rights to the passage along its waters often caused disputes. In 1321 there was a suit between the Archbishop of York and the Abbot of Selby concerning a length of Selby Dam. It ran from the park of the archbishop to the manor of Thorpe, and was edged by the primate's land on one bank and the monks' land at Hambleton and Thorpe on the other. The right of passage must have been successfully claimed by the abbey for there are many requests recorded in the Selby and Diocesan Registers regarding the granting of licences to servants of the Archbishop. These usually concerned the carrying of timber from his woods along the Pool to the Ouse. In 1349 the Abbot of Selby, Geoffrey de Gaddesby, gave Henry de Stockbridge and John le Berker permission to transport along the Dam timber bought in the woods belonging to the Archbishop at Scalm. They were allowed, from the middle of Lent to the next feast of St Michael, to carry it in their boat to Selby and given leave to sell it there. It was stipulated that the transporting of these goods had to be carried out in broad daylight and not at night under penalty of the revoking of the permission. Henry and John were held responsible for any men they employed in the moving of the wood. The monks also allowed local people to transport their goods along the Dam. In 1357 workers who had bought the underwood of the Easthagg of Hambleton were granted right of way to Paradise Landing in that village and along the Pool into Selby. Many of the people who were allowed to use the waterway also benefited from the monks' sound knowledge of agriculture. When Thomas Daniel and John Aughton were sold the herbage in Aughton Hagg Coppice at Hambleton, save for the oak, apple and maple there, they were shown how to fell the wood properly and how to make it ready for the ships to carry it to Selby. The men were granted use of a garden at Ousegate End where the monks demonstrated how to stack the timber correctly. Thomas and John were ordered to carry their cargo along Kirkdyke by day for no small boats were allowed to navigate along its waters at night save merchants from the Elmet region.

Kirk Dyke, or Back Dyke, was a water course, which, on a modern town map, would cross Finkle Street, Church Lane and New Street before it went along the back of Ousegate to enter the river somewhere near to the present Haddlesey to Selby canal. The York Archaeological Trust in their survey of Selby concluded Selby Dam was a natural stream that had its outfall near Ousegate and had been in use during medieval times. The work done by MAP Archaeological Consultancy Ltd covering an area at the rear of Gowthorpe, Finkle Street and Micklegate confirmed the alignment of Kirk Dyke and uncovered evidence to show that it was also in existence during the twelfth century, if not earlier. Their conclusions were that the dyke had been modified during medieval times and then lapsed into disuse by the sixteenth century. It was then replaced by a narrower ditch in the seventeenth century; backfilled about a hundred years later and finally superseded by a brick culvert on the same alignment. During their excavations the archaeologists found evidence of other ditches, especially in the region of Gowthorpe. Two dykes, dating from the twelfth century, were aligned north to south and carried signs of having been timber revetted - probably necessary due to changing water levels and the silty nature of the soil which was easily eroded. Another ditch was found which ran up the western side of Micklegate towards the Ouse and parallel to the modern north-western edge of Micklegate. It appeared to be as old as the other trenches and was probably there to channel excess water towards the river. Another suggestion is that, like many others in and around Selby, it had been dug out as a boundary marker.

> *80 rods of ditch around Warde Shawe with as many rods of hedge made on the same...2d. a rod.*

A survey dated 1543 states that Warde Shawe was a wood covering four acres about one mile from Pontefract.

The brothers were usually diligent in any work concerning waterways. Commissioners regularly met in York to inquire into the state of river embankments, dykes, gutters and sewers. In 1413 a meeting was held at Crowle to discuss the state of Mere Dyke, and to apportion responsibility for its repairs. This ditch seems to have been an important sewer beginning in the Hatfield area and running through Eastoft and Crowle to the River Trent in the County of Lincolnshire. One of the persons present in 1413 was Thomas Egmanton, steward of Rawcliffe and Stallingborough. He, and two other representatives of Selby Abbey, received an attendance fee from the monks. The extern cellarer also provided five gallons of red wine for the meeting.

The monastery employed many labourers to maintain their ditches and sewers both in Selby and on its other properties. At one time two men were paid for removing roots, earth and dust from the banks of a ditch near to the turf-house and brewhouse in the abbey precincts. Four men in Hambleton were paid fourpence a day to clean out the great ditch:

> *at that place from the western end of the township to a point on the causeway known as le Fox.*

It took the labourers four days to complete the work. The services of ten men were needed for one day to repair defects in portions of a new sewer within the soke of Crowle. They were paid a total of 3s.4d.

The numerous drains and sewers were very important in an area that still contained many acres of swamps and marshes and was subject to much flooding from the rivers that flowed through the lowlands. Some of these ditches doubled as moats to help protect manors and farmsteads when threatened by local or national disputes. There were still stretches of forest land that hid all types of outlaws and vagabonds. By the thirteenth century Cawood Castle had been enlarged and was protected by moats on three sides, with the River Ouse as a natural defence on the fourth. A manor known as Kenbury is believed to have once existed on a small rectangular moated site on the south-eastern side of the village of Cawood, between Broad Lane and Wistowgate. Holme House in Camblesforth, a manor house at East Haddlesey, Scurff Hall Farm near Drax, all had moats around them. The manor house at Thorpe Willoughby and that at Staynor, both owned by the monks for a time, were used as retreats and they too were moated residences. It appears that Selby Abbey also had its moat. In a survey of 1543 concerned with the valuation of timber it was stated that some trees were,

nere the scite of the late monastery there, without the mote within the compass or precincte of which mote all le scite or scytuacion of the saide late monastery is sytuate and sett.

The rivers Ouse, Aire, Trent and the Humber were major waterways necessary to the trade of both townspeople and monks. The account rolls refer to staithes, used for loading and unloading cargoes, at Amcotes on the Trent, Whitgift and Reedness on the Ouse. In her lectures on Selby Miss Richardson noted that around the turn of the thirteenth century there was a cleared space of ground near the outfall of Selby Dam that was known as Cnar-landing. The use of this word adds support to the belief that the Vikings came to Selby for 'Cnar' was most likely derived from the Scandinavian 'Knarr', meaning a ship of all work. The Norwegian Vikings had the best vessels of all the European people during the eighth to the twelfth centuries. This particular ship, the Knarr, could carry 20-30 men, with their women and children, domestic animals and food; or it could be used for cargo. Cnar-landing was given by the Abbot and convent of Selby to a Robert of London but was later returned to them by his son, Martin. The land was identified with his son's name for some two hundred years. In 1432 Robert Skipwith, the bursar at the monastery, recorded that he had paid out twelve pence to the labourers working on the repairs of the banks in Martin Croft and 'knerlendyned'. The landing stage was most probably near to the area that is known today as Abbot's Staithe. In 1404 the cost of renovating the wharf and the crane there came to over thirteen pounds. The landing stage is believed to have been situated down The Quay, a short passage off Micklegate that leads to the Ouse. Adjacent are some substantial remains of medieval stonework that over the centuries have been used as warehouses or garages but whose time of construction is still in doubt.

In the late fifteenth century the water transport used by the abbey consisted of a large barge, a small ship and two 'Cathes'. The last most probably resembled flat, punt-like vessels; a granger's small expenses included sixpence spent on a cord for hauling a cathe. In 1413 Robert Bird received a wage of 26s.8d. as master of the Abbey's ship. When alterations needed to be done to the manor house at Rawcliffe the materials were shipped there in the Abbot's barge. In order to build a new chamber and a chapel at the recreation place, seven wagon-loads of timber, which had been lopped and shaped into posts in the West Hagg of Hambleton, were taken to the banks of the Ouse then loaded onto the abbot's ship to be transported up the Aire to Rawcliffe. Two boat-loads of plaster were shipped along winding waterways from Crowle to the manor-house. It is interesting to note that during the work involved in erecting the new buildings the extern cellarer accounted for drink "by courtesy" but pay was by the day, "without food". The monks were not given to wasting good materials. A stable was also needed at Rawcliffe and this was built with the timber, thatch and stone taken from a disused one at Thorpe Willoughby.

Fuel was another commodity that was often moved by water. It is written in the accounts that chaldrons, (25½cwts) of sea-coal were bought from ships bringing the fuel from Northumbria. The most popular source of heat was turves. Robert Bird, using the largest abbey vessel, and with the help of a crew of three, was paid for bringing a ship load of turves from Rawcliffe to Selby. When 28 boat loads were delivered it was written down that the porters were given the customary payment of 12 full nets of turves to each boat load. These turves of peat were to be used as fuel in the abbot's chamber and other monastic buildings but, as it has been shown, they were often given as part of a pension, corrody or exchange of gifts. For example, a couple in Rawcliffe were given a toft there and two parts of an acre of moorland, with permission to dig 20,000 turves on it. They were granted permission to sell these turves or burn them in their own home. In addition they were also given free pasturing of animals, free herbage, corn from the monks' place at Rawcliffe, white or russet cloth for their tunics; all in exchange for what must have been some highly prized land and tenements in the same village. Payments were often made to women for carrying the turves from the ships to the abbey turf-house. It appears to have been situated south of the abbey gatehouse in an area where James Street lies today. In 1398 two men were paid to cut down willow wood in Skaholm marsh. It was then carried by water to the turf house where it was made into fences to separate it from the brewhouse. The latter was known to be near the Great Tithe Barn which was in evidence down James Street until late in the twentieth century. Another fuel used for heating houses and offices was wood. Many people in the area were employed in gathering this material. In one instance local men were sent to cut down 31 poor oaks in Thorpe Willoughby Park and the North Wood to be used as fuel in the offices. They received both money and food in payment. Two men were paid to lop and split the fuel from the oaks. It took them 37 days, at fourpence a day, but with no food provided. Pieces of firewood were also made from the underwood in various places. This went by cart to the abbey. Bundles of sticks, known as faggots, were made in the North Wood then taken to the banks of the Dam at Thorpe Willoughby thence by water to Selby. The bundles brought to the abbey sometimes numbered over two thousand.

The ferry-boat was often pressed into service to bring faggots or hay from Rosscarrs. This ferry which was mainly used for carrying persons, livestock and goods across the Ouse between Barlby and Selby was given to the abbey by Hugh Ward of Thorpe, son of Robert de Thorpe. He also gave the monks the profits from the landing tolls and barge tolls on traffic going to, from, or passing his property along the Ouse. As well as these tolls Hugh gave the monastery a group of houses and cottages anciently known by the name of Selby Waterhouses. They were situated on some elevated land in the bend of the river, across from Selby. The monks had two pastures for animals, one was in a park area to the south of the abbey; the ferry was needed to reach the other one which lay on the Barlby side of the river, "near the hamlet of Selby Waterhouses". The accounts show that one year the kitchener paid John Croxdale to scour out one hundred rods of ditch around the pastures "across the Ouse". He also paid John an additional sixpence to clean out a horse pond there; a pool of water which may have given rise to the present name of Pond Street in Barlby. In 1441 the chamberlain included in his expenses the purchase of a ferry-boat from Brother Thomas Crull, bursar of the monastery that year. The vessel cost him 66s.8d. The chamberlain then paid out a further 11s.4d. for repairs, alterations and labour. These involved the sawing of timber into planks, the shaping of timber into posts, the sawing of one sapling into ledges for the boat and the purchase of the appropriate nails to use with the timber. Trenails used for the ledges were cylindrical pins of hard wood used mainly for fastening together woods that were going to be exposed to the action of water. The chamberlain and the pittancer were both responsible for the Keeper of the Ferry. They supplied him with clothes money, presents of food and looked to the state of his office; they, for instance, made sure he had enough paris candles to light the premises. They had also to look after the welfare of other ferry keepers:

> *One shoulder of ox delivered to the keepers of the ferry at Carlton in the customary fashion.*

At other times the gifts consisted of a carcase of a sheep or a salted fish.

When the ferry-boat purchased by the chamberlain had been declared fit for use, 7½d. was paid out for some ale which was given to the men who dragged the vessel from the dam to the waters of the Ouse. There was no clear passage from the tributary to the river because the waters of Selby Dam had been harnessed to provide power to run the water-mills belonging to the monks.

The Mills of Selby Abbey

Millgate in Selby takes its name from the four mills built in that area by the monks. They were powered by water or by wind but the monks also record the use of a horse-mill.

> *1405 Fixed rent of 26s.8d. from the farm of Peter Milner for the horse-mill leased to him in the town of Selby yearly.*

Most of the mills were still in use in the nineteenth century when steam power replaced that of wind and water. It was during that century they either fell into disuse or were demolished. The old Hippodrome Picture Palace (1917-1955) pulled down in 1978, is believed to have been built on the site of the last one. This mill had stood close to the north side of Mill Bridge from around the eleventh or twelfth century until at least 1886. When the monks built the first mills they dammed Selby Dam near to its junction with the Ouse to provide the drive for the water-wheels. The surrounding district was flat, little of it being 20 feet above sea-level, so to raise the mill dam to obtain a head of water for their wheels large areas of the land were flooded, including that owned by Robert Wilgheby. This caused disputes between him and the abbey until, in return for the gift of the then enclosed park of Thorpe, Robert gave leave for the brothers to flood his property when the need arose. The estate given to him consisted of a mansion, dovecote and buildings on two acres of land surrounded by a moat. The manor was retitled Thorpe Willoughby to distinguish it from the numerous other Saxon Thorpes or villages. However, it did not stay in the hands of the Willoughby family long for during the reign of Edward I (1272-1307) Robert's son returned it to the abbey. The old manor house, Thorpe Hall, was rebuilt in 1830 and it was recorded that as late as 1867 it was still encircled by water.

The mills in Selby were known as the Soke Mills. The Soke, a Danelaw term, gave the lord of the manor, in this instance the Abbot of Selby Abbey, jurisdiction over his tenants; it gave him the right to hold court and bound all within his manor to grind their grain at his mills. This was not accepted gracefully by the people of Selby and disputes arose throughout the working life of the mills. The tenants had to pay a percentage of grain, known as a multure, to the millers for grinding their corn. In 1470 the millers at Selby were fined two shillings for taking too great a multure of the tenants' corn. The inhabitants continued to display dissatisfaction regarding this act which resulted in the Soke Court threatening the millers with a further fine of twenty shillings if they transgressed so again. More complaints from the townspeople brought forth this ruling in 1503:

> That the millers grind for the Selby tenants of my Lord Abbot before any outside folk.

This edict was repeated and confirmed more than once during the reign of Henry VIII (1509 - 47):

Keeping the mills in good working order provided plenty of work for local people. In 1404 twenty men were employed in renovating the mills in the town. John Wright, carpenter, was paid for searching in the woods to find suitable timber for repairs. He also renewed one inner wheel for the upper mill in Selby and made mill-spindles, cogs and other necessities during five weeks in winter. John Bond, carpenter, helped with this work, as did Richard Fox, apprentice of John Wright. With the help of John de Binglay they then renovated the trough that carried water down to Selby Dam. This trough ran from the mills to near the stone bridge over the mainstream. Robert de Bouland was paid for two days' work transporting clay for the men. A further twelve men were then employed for a day stopping up the holes in the long trough. This would have been a form of 'puddling', a term used later during the great canal era meaning to make something water-tight. Puddle was a mixture of clay and water used as a rough cement for lining embankments etc. The men also broke up four cartloads of stone in Monk Fryston quarry and brought it to the mills. John del Wod, mason, helped by Peter Geve, took a week to lay the split flagstones as a pavement under the bridge. Unlike the other workers the mason and helper were supplied by the granger with bread and ale from the stores in addition to their wages. An unusual item included in the expenses for the renovation of the mills was that of 6s.2d. for a net for 'catching fish there'! The millstones used at the mills came from Monk Fryston quarry. In the monks' accounts for 1320 it was stipulated that the towns of Fryston and Hillam were to carry the millstones for the watermills at Selby from the cross-roads of Leeds to Fryston. They were also to carry the timber and other materials needed to make or repair the windmill and the watermill in their towns as often as required. In 1320 there were 23 unfree tenants in Hillam and 17 in Fryston.

How much grain was milled was dependent on the weather. In the summer of 1404 one quarter of grain was paid as multure at Knottingley, instead of the usual twenty, because of the lack of water in the Dam to turn the wheels. The monks made little profit on grinding cereals during 1413-14 for the same reason. In autumn and winter heavy rainfalls from its large catchment area frequently extended the Millpond as far as the carrs shown on modern maps. Whole areas suffered losses from the overflowing of the Ouse and other rivers that ran through the abbey lands. Selby Abbey received relief from taxation for their estates adversely affected by such floods, especially those near the Humber. In 1346 when the monks were seeking permission to appropriate Brayton church, to help with funds, they described how two hundred pounds had been spent in drainage work which had all been swept away by floods before it had been finished. Many crops were destroyed in this manner.

Ten acres of meadow grass purchased in Wistow meadows and tithe. When mowed and spread out it was all flooded and carried off by suddenly rising flood-water.

No tithe hay at Carlton this year - flooded and destroyed by flood-waters.

220 thraves of grass and rushes coming from produce of the Selby Dam this year, 3d. a thrave - not more because of flooding.

The town and parts of the monastery were often inundated with flood water. Sometime in the twelfth century the water entered the cloisters and other buildings but the worst conditions were around the town chapel with its wattle and daub walls. When the banks of the Ouse were breached at another time the water flooded the monks' dormitory (near the end of the South Transept) and some of their premises situated where James Street lies today. The area around Millgate was often under water, an occurrence that was repeated over many centuries and was blamed on the presence of the water-wheels. The residents of Millgate and Dam Bank suffered much from attacks of ague, a feverish and shivering condition, they said, brought on by the wheels. In 1805 an Act of Parliament was passed which ordered the abolition of all the ancient machines at corn mills. Following this edict the old water wheels at Selby were demolished but it is not recorded whether or not the health of the residents down Millgate was improved.

In the fourteenth century some flooding of the land was blamed on innovations introduced by Abbot Gaddesby (1341-68) described by Morrell as being one of the earliest English engineers. Legal proceedings were brought against him and the anger of some people erupted into vandalism. Using abbey funds he reclaimed a tract of land, owned by the monastery, useless for agriculture because of constant flooding. The quagmire, near to Rawcliffe and known as Inclismore consisted of 600 acres of moorland. It is reported that to help drain the land there Geoffrey de Gaddesby caused a strong sluice of wood to be made upon the River Trent at head of the Maredike sewer which ran through Eastoft and Crowle. The wood was of a sufficient height and breadth for the defence of the tides coming from the sea, and likewise, from the fresh waters descending to the sluice to enter the river. This appeared to have been a good example of reclaiming land for the local field workers but, in 1350 it was presented at court that by damming and divertng the water at Maredike the abbot had caused 3000 acres of land belonging to Edward de Langley, lord of Hatfield, to be flooded, resulting in a thousand pounds' worth of damage. The abbot must have defended his case well for the sluice remained in place during his term of office and it was not until after his demise that some 200 tenants from Hatfield and Thorne finally gave vent to their feelings concerning the sluice. They converged upon the banks of the Trent and destroyed the monk's work so that for some time the tides ebbed and flowed without restriction. Abbot de Shirburn (1368-1407) replaced the broken wooden construction with one made from stone. Some difficulties arose with the new sluices for it was said they were too high and too broad. At a meeting of Commissioners at Crowle the jurors there recommended that the Abbot add two 4 feet by 6 feet high wooden sluices as flood-gates to strengthen the stone works. They also instructed the monks to build a bridge over the sluice to enable carts and carriages to pass that way. It was also decreed that, if the sluice stood against the tides for a year, the Abbot of Selby and the free-holders in the villages affected by the drainage should henceforth be responsible for keeping the sluices in good repair. They should also provide enough labourers to regularly scour and cleanse Maredike as far as the bridge of Ludington. This care must have lapsed after the monks departed for by the reign of Charles I (1625-1649) the drains were all silted up and much of the land lay beneath at least three feet of water. It was said that grain laden boats were able to pass regularly over the water-logged Haxey Carr from the River Idle to the banks of the Trent. Charles I sold the manor of Thorne and Hatfield to Sir Cornelius Vermuyden. This man deserved the grateful thanks of the local people for the vast improvements he made to the land with his draining and embanking of the marshes and fens but, like Abbot Gaddesby, his efforts were much maligned. In a pamphlet entitled *The State of that part of Yorkshire adjoining the Level of Hatfield Chase, 1701*, Vermuyden was described as:

> *a monster of a man, whose natural qualities no one English epithet can answer.*

The main grievance put forward, apart from the dislike of change, was that drainage disturbed the balance of the varied and rich resources found on the margins of the marshes which had sustained a large population for decades. Vermuyden also found that draining one area can cause problems elsewhere. The Dutch engineer employed Flemish workers to dig canals in his endeavours to drain Hatfield Chase. Local people complained that instead of it being carried away the water was flooding neighbouring land. Fierce rioting broke out during which Flemish workers were assaulted and some killed. Their work was destroyed as embankments were levelled. The problem arose because, by mistake, the drainage system had caused the River Don to drain into the Aire and not the Ouse. Vermuyden corrected this error by spending £20,000 on a new canal from Snaith to Goole – a high price to pay in both lives and money. Steam driven engines eventually helped to control the waters more adequately but as those who were present in the Selby district in 1947 or the year 2000 can bear witness, the flooding of some areas continues to this day.

Thorne, within the manor of Hatfield was one place that benefited from the drainage. Many of the poor labourers found employment digging the abundant turf on the common in the summer, whilst the wives and children made it ready for sale. When the harvest was over, the turves of peat, which made up the principal fuel for the peasants, was taken in small boats down the newly made canals and drains to the river Don through Thorne Sluice. The turves were then put on board other vessels which carried them to the markets at places such as York, Leeds, Lincoln, Hull and Selby where they found a ready market.

The abbey leased out mills in the proximity of Hatfield Chase and elsewhere. Many of them had been given in grants to the monastery.

Helington-South...Emma de Lascels gave a mill here for one messuage, which her son Adam confirmed by hanging a knife on the altar, only reserving the right of having the corn ground for his own house use; and Adam de Preston, and Maud, his wife confirmed the same in 1287.

Profits came from mills in such places as Brayton, Thorpe Willoughby, Monk Fryston, Rawcliffe, Hook, Crowle, Sitlington, and others as far away as Stanford-on-Avon. In one instance the keeper of the fabric received 40s. from the mills at Thorpe Willoughby, but in return he had to pay out 14s.1d. on renovations there. Sometimes the abbey lost revenue from the mills when the premises were untenanted or sold. In 1446 the mill at Sitlington, in the parish of Thornhill, near Wakefield, returned no rent for it had no miller and was in a ruinous state. One of the mills that was sold by the monks in 1405 and then removed, had been situated at Upper Langley, Brayton. Maud, the widow of Ralph de Hanburg had given all her land in Langley, with two shillings and eightpence annual rent to the monks of Selby. Langley is no more but the site of the windmill was described as having been near the south-west corner of the former brickworks on the Camblesforth Road. It has been put forward that the modern Longman's Hill may be a corruption of the sixteenth century name Langleymilne Hill, for records show a windmill in that area in 1579. It must have been a good situation to have a windmill for one is shown there on a 6" OS Map dated 1851. A collection of photographs taken by William Rawlings, a local man, includes a picture of a post mill there dated around 1880. The monks also lost any multure they may have been receiving from the people of Drax when William, the eldest son of Ralph Paynel, gave the mill at Drax 'with all its Soke' to the Priory there. This religious house had been founded by him somewhere between 1130 and 1139. To ensure that the tenants and other villagers in the area did not rob the Priory of its tax by grinding their own grain, their rotary querns or hand mills used in preconquest days, were deliberately damaged to render them useless. This was a practice likely to have been carried out in other places where there were Soke Mills.

The Provision of Food and Employment

The Abbey needed large supplies of food-stuffs, especially grain, to support its community. The chief crops grown were wheat, oats, barley and rye. The monks depended on a handful of farms, their tithes and the market for most of these products. The custom in Norman times was to have a lord's manor worked by villeins. These were looked upon as unfree tenants who worked on the lord's estate in return for their own holding. Where they gave their free labour was known as demesne land. To help the monks supervise their scattered possessions and be responsible for the cultivation of the demesne lands, serjeants, similar to salaried estate agents, were appointed. Many of them collected and stored the tithes due to the monastery-

And for 22 quarters of barley from the serjeant of Carlton,

And for 126 quarters of dredge from the tithe-barn of Hook.

Near the end of the fourteenth century the monks began to lease out their demesne land to the tenants. Places where this practice was carried out included Crowle, Rawcliffe, Holme-upon Spalding-Moor, Gunby, Thorpe Willoughby and Acaster Selby. The rent collected from these leases was referred to as 'farm'.

And for £14.14.0 from the farm of the demesne of Rawcliffe yearly.
and £10 from the farm of the demesnes of Thorpe Willoughby yearly.

There were many tenants in the North who chose to farm their holdings on the manor and pay a rent in money and not in kind.

Fixed rent of £25.6.0 from the old farm of Hillam with the rent of the tenement lately leased as a penny farm.

Many tenants in Monk Fryston and Hambleton also opted to work on 'penny' farms as they came to be called. They suffered much hardship in times of droughts and floods but they told the monks they would have it no other way. Crops were also raised in monastic granges at Stainer, Rawcliffe and Holme House, near the village of Holme-upon-Spalding-Moor. An important source of grain for Selby Abbey came from the tithes of appropriated churches. The collected cereals were stored in tithe barns at Reedness, Hook, Goole, Garthorp, Balne, Stainer, Adlingfleet, Crowle, Snaith and numerous other places. The bulk of this tithe corn came to Selby by barge along the Humber, Trent, Aire and Ouse. It was unloaded at the Great Staithe, also one in Ousegate near to where the canal now has its outfall, or at the Barlby ferry landing. The Great Barn in Selby, used to store the collected tithes was situated next to the malthouse. It was connected to the Gatehouse by a path laid with Monk Fryston 'flagges', roughly on the line of James Street. The barn had walls three feet thick and was 313 feet long and 29 feet wide. It stretched from New Lane to the other side of James Street. The barn was divided into sections to separate the different grains, root vegetables, stock fish and beer. The building began to be neglected following the Dissolution of the monasteries; its final destruction began in 1842 when a great gap was made through the middle of the barn to make way for a thoroughfare. The eastern part disappeared in 1892 when it was destroyed and replaced by Selby Cattle Mart. It is not clear when the western remains were taken apart but during its decline it was occupied by a brewery, a garage and a clubhouse. Mr. W.H. Whisker, whose family ran a long established wholesale and retail fruit and vegetable business in town, came to Selby before the First World War. The initial family home was in Harper Street and their first shop was at 67, Brook Street. A warehouse down Beech Grove and part of the Tithe Barn were used for storage. The Whisker family had a shop on Gowthorpe from as far back as 1932. They continued to use the premises down Beech Grove for storage until, sadly, early in 2004, the family ceased trading. All that remains of the magnificent barn where their grandfather stored his goods is a commemorative plaque and a few remaining stones which, in 1984,were incorporated into the Abbey Vaults public house.

Wheat was one of the main crops used by both monks and people in and around Selby. The bursars accounted for the tithes collected, for money from the sale of some of it and for cereals bought elsewhere.

10 quarters of wheat purchased from William Brown from Gowdall with transport of the same from the Carlton crossing to the abbey.

And for the service of John Adcock in transporting 120 quarters of wheat by water from Garthorpe to Selby on 3 occasions for the use of the granger.

The grangers were responsible for the distribution of the grains. Wheat was delivered to the baker to provide bread for the abbey household and the corroderies. The kitchener was given a share to make pastry and the lord abbot's cook for use in his recipes. The finest bread, pain demaine, was made for the lord abbot and his guests. An allowance was made for the wheat used in making of bread for the poor and portions of it given as gifts to the servants of the baker and the brewer. Crops were grown in Monk Fryston and Eastoft besides the areas already listed as having tithe barns. In 1405 the granger received 412 quarters of wheat. Four baskets of this grain, which was equivalent to 11 quarters, were paid as rent from tenants holding four bovates of land in Hillam. It was recorded that no more was given because all of the remaining bovates in that area were leased as penny farms making money payments to the bursars. The granger stated the officials had accounted for almost £17 in lieu of 67 quarters of grain leased at the penny farms; thus, the rent of corn in grain and money was just as it had been for the last 80 years. The rest of the wheat came from the serjeants of the various places already noted. Sometimes part of the tithes had to be used for repairs or maintenance.

…with the tithe of the corn-sheaves of Swinefleet between Reading Gate and the quay, in addition to £9.9.1 deducted for the new barn, gates and wharf there.

Quantities of rye and maslin were also received from places such as Carlton and Reedness. In 1404 gifts of rye were given to two brewers, the carter at the brewery, a clerk in the church, two workmen in the pool, the forester of the North Wood, the one in the Haggs and the one of Hambleton. These were annual gifts but the same year Henry Milner also received a portion for assisting with the making of malt for 30 weeks whilst Thomas Rosell, brewer, was indisposed. It was also noted that the granger gave the brewer, his two grooms and his carter, a quarter of wheat each because of the poor quality of their allowance of rye. The supply of oats came mostly from the same districts as the wheat. The largest amount itemised was 110 quarters of oats brought in twelve wagons from Carlton to Selby. The bursars purchased quantities of this crop as fodder for livestock. They paid for some to be transported from Wistow to feed the horses belonging to the abbot and his visitors. Oats from the store were fed to the cart-horses and to animals belonging to the extern cellarer and the kitchener. Hay and straw was also purchased for the stables. When there was no tithe hay from Carlton because of the floods, 25 cart loads were purchased at Hemingbrough plus 60 thraves of straw for bedding. Meadows at Rosscars and five and a half acres at Haysted, Wistow Ings, were set aside to supply the hay for the mill-horses. Local men were employed to do the mowing, and the making and stacking of the hay in those places. They were paid by the abbey's stableman and groom. The workmen taking the cartloads of hay to the abbey also received victuals paid for by the stableman.

Barley, and a mixture of barley and oats known as dredge, also came from the same districts as the other grains. Men from Thorne were paid to use their ship to transport these cereals from Eastoft to Selby. As it has been stated ale and bread were important parts of a medieval diet. The local population used rye and wheat for their bread whilst everyone needed barley for their ale. During one year a total of 752 quarters of barley were delivered to the brewer for making ale for the monks and the corroderies. The staff in the brewery consisted of a brewer, carter, groom and page. They were provided with liveries similar to those worn by the lord abbot's servants. Other minor employees included a man who kept the office supplied with turves, others who brought the barley from the manors to Selby and many who helped with the process of making ale. The malting method may have been carried out in the traditional way in which steeped grain, after it had been drained, was spread in thick heaps on the floor to initiate germination. After 24 hours the grain was spread more thinly to help moderate the temperature.

Two men paid 10s. without food for spreading barley, dredge and oats before malting for 15 days.

One man paid for winnowing 772 quarters of malt

To winnow was to allow air to be blown through the grain in order to remove the chaff. The granger also employed workers to make sieves out of cloth and to sew sacks out of sack-cloth for him. A cooper was sometimes needed to make great hoops to put around the vat in which the wort was left to ferment in the brewing process. Repairs were always having to be made in the malt-room for a deal of malt was lost to mice, rats and weevils. In 1432 Mr. John Rattener was paid 12 pence for:

his diligence in catching rats at Thorpe by order of the lord abbot about the feast of St. Lawrence.

Other losses occurred through careless work and the purchase of poor quality grain. The latter was fed to the animals. Evidence that the inhabitants of Selby made their own ale was found in the chamberlain's rolls. In 1404 he accounted for the reroofing of two malt-kiln houses in the gardens of tofts in Micklegate. One held by William Belnays, the other by Robert Eleson. Almost 40 years later another malt-kiln within the garden of a house in Micklegate in the tenure of Lawrence Wylson was completely renovated. It had stone foundations and a mud floor; sand and mud were used to daub its walls whilst 200 wall-tiles from Cawood adorned the inside. Wine was also enjoyed by the abbot and his guests. It was purchased from various places including a tavern situated near the Abbey gates. When Ralph, the son of Robert de Thorpe was granted a tenement in Hambleton it was stated he was also given some land 'between the vineyard and the millpool'. Figs and raisins were bought in for the convent's use but whether sufficient grapes were grown locally for eating or wine-producing purposes is not verified.

Beans and peas were other crops grown on the manors. Garthorpe, Reedness, Hook and Stainer were the main suppliers. Some of these legumes were delivered to the lord abbot's stables as fodder for his horses and large amounts were fed to the pigs in the kitchener's working place. Beans and peas were also used in pottage, a kind of soup or stew, sometimes eaten by the monks, especially during Lent. A quantity of oats was given to the kitchener for him to make into flour for thickening the pottage. The almoner was allocated a supply of these vegetables to sell to the townsfolk. Through the centuries meatless pottage has often been the only meal poor people could afford to eat. Other vegetables such as cabbages and leeks were bought in from local people whilst gardeners were engaged to dig over the soil in the monks' plots so that herbs could be planted or sown there.

One small crop grown was mustard. The accounts showed that the monks bought seeds at Adlingfleet. When the grinding stones used to crush them were in need of repair, a man travelled from York to fulfill that task. The brothers travelled further afield to purchase other condiments used to flavour or preserve their food. Pepper was purchased from John Bouche, a spicer in York, but in one instance a large amount of it was brought back from London by one of the monks. Sometime in the thirteenth century Richard de Castellain, with the consent of Emma his wife and Ralph his son, gave a salt-works upon the Humber to the abbey. It was 'three perches broad and sixty in length'. Much of the salt used by the monks in the fourteenth and fifteenth century was bought from mariners or merchants; there were no records to be found of the condiment obtained from the monks' salt-works. Honey was used as a sweetener and for medicinal purposes. In one transaction the monks bought 20 gallons of honey gathered together from various sources.

The growing of crops to feed the monastery and the local inhabitants provided plenty of employment in the district as did the rearing of livestock. Rabbit or coney meat was a popular delicacy. It was not part of a staple diet but was eaten at banquets and feasts by all but the minor manorial tenants. In 1417 Brian de Stapleton, Knight, was given six adult rabbits, known as coneys, as a present. This animal's skin, especially the fur, was highly prized for garment linings. The warrens where the rabbits were reared were usually surrounded by a ditch and a fence or hedge as barriers against other animals and poachers. Hunting dogs were kept at the warrens belonging to the abbey. Two of the rabbit rearing places were at Thorpe Willoughby and Crowle. There was also a reference to one at Acaster Selby. Supplies of oats were sent to these warrens. They were not only used to help fatten up the rabbits and coneys but were given to the partridges and pheasants being kept there and to the hunting dogs. Swans, capons, ducks, geese and even herons were raised in many of the manors that produced the grain for the monastery. They were sent to Selby as gifts, tithes or purchases. Thirty three herons came from issue at a place named Schaghgarth and twenty swans and cygnets from those kept at Crowle. Fifty-five capons at fourpence each were also acquired; all were for the abbot and his guests.

Swans were also to be found on Selby Dam and the ditches in and around the abbey precincts. These lovely birds were only for the table of the lord abbot and his visitors or given as gifts to such notables as the archdeacon of Richmond and William Gascoigne, Chief Justice of the King's Bench. The arms of Selby Abbey and now of the town of Selby are sable, three swans argent. The shield is so illustrated on a processional roll of the lords to the parliament in 1512 in which the Abbot of Selby occurs eighth in order of the peers. It is recorded that there was another coat for the abbey having a mitre with a crosier passing through it to show it represented a mitred abbot but the consensus is that the former is the real shield. A legend has been passed down the years that Benedict saw three swans alight on the River Ouse at Selby which strengthened his belief that he had found the place depicted in his dreams. The unknown author of the *Historia* does not recall such an event even though he describes many visions in detail. The number three was frequently chosen by religious groups to represent the Trinity. Fountains Abbey used three horseshoes, Bridlington priory had three Bs whilst the

Abbey of Whitby had three coiled snakes. The presence of numerous swans on the waters around Selby made them a logical choice for the shield of Selby Abbey.

Another magnificent bird to be seen in Selby at that time was the peacock. These birds which were fed on oats and chaff were considered not to be very palatable. The Romans had thought the flesh was only suitable for rissoles whilst the Anglo-Saxons condemned the bird as being too difficult to digest. However, the rich in medieval times agreed with the Romans that the peacock was outstanding as a celebratory bird for feasts and festivals; that is, when served up in the full splendour of its skin and feathers. John Sharrow, Abbot of Selby from 1466 to 1486 attended, what is believed to be, the greatest feast in history. It took place on the 15th January 1466, in Cawood Castle and was to celebrate the induction of George Neville, Chancellor of the Exchequer, as Archbishop of York. The meal of seven courses included amongst the bird flesh eaten 400 swans and 104 peacocks. Pigeoncotes and dovecotes were a feature of many manors although the right to keep the latter was given to only a privileged few. Pigeons and doves were valued for their meat, eggs and their dung which was used as a fertiliser. The lord abbot of Selby had a dovecote situated over the Chapter House. He also had a pigeon cote which one year produced 207 birds for him to add to the 200 he received from Stainer and 80 from Thorpe Willoughby. Cocks and hens were given to the kitchener in the form of tithes and rents from many places. At Christmas 1320, the 23 villeins in Hillam had to take 69 cocks and hens to the Kitchener in Selby in payment of tithes. In 1417 hens were valued at twopence and cocks at one and a halfpence. Eggs were also part of some rents or tithes and that same year Reedness sent 1440 out of the 2,760 eggs received as tithes.

Milk was not drunk to the same extent as ale. There was a dairy at Stainer from which in one year 173 gallons of milk and seven and a half stones of cheese were delivered to the abbey. The milk was carried in earthenware jars. Supplies must have also come from other places for the same year it was recorded that the granger used 20 stones of cheese in the food he provided for the workers in his office. Livestock available to the monks for consumption were deer, bulls, cows, bullocks, heifers, sheep, lambs, oxen, boars, pigs and piglets. Lambs and piglets were given to the abbey as part of the tithes from the people of Selby. The majority of these animals came from the same area as the crops but there were some exceptions. John Barlay, the convent's cook in 1417, travelled to York by water to buy ox-feet. Bullocks were purchased in Pontefract and Doncaster whilst sheep were brought from as far afield as Stallingborough.

> *And for the expenses of John Wotton and William Pinne (poulterer in the Kitchener's office) going to Stallingborough to drive 80 sheep taken from stock to Selby, with the ferry-toll at Burton on Stather.*

This ferry crossed the River Trent from Garthorpe in Lincolnshire. The sheep brought to Selby may have grazed on land given to the monks for that specific purpose. Galfrid de Castellain had given a meadow there and confirmed a pasture for one hundred sheep; Richard de Bellaqua of Stallingborough also confirmed this gift and added another pasture for one hundred and forty sheep. The number of sheep purchased one year was 383, all for consumption by the abbot, convent and visitors. Women found employment shearing sheep for the abbey. In one instance eight of them were paid 20d. each and given food for washing and shearing 120 sheep. Sheep and lamb-skins were sold, as was the wool received in parochial tithes. When Robert West, farmer at

Whitgift, gave 26 stones of wool as tax it was, in turn, sold to Robert Courtney for a sum of four pounds. The hides from oxen, cows, bullocks and heifers, calf skins, animal intestines and fat were all sold for profit. In 1399 Agnes Bernard was paid 6s.8d for preparing the intestines. The tallow from slaughtered stock was used for lights or sold to a chandler in Riccall. In the excavations that took place during the 1990s at the rear of Gowthorpe, Finkle Street and Micklegate enough animal bones were uncovered to fill two standard size packing crates. The majority of the finds all dated from the twelfth to the sixteenth century and were mainly from cattle, sheep, pigs and horses. One of the medieval dykes produced bones of cattle, oxen, sheep, goats, pigs and dogs. Fragments of cat and one fallow deer were also unearthed. The remains of the cattle and oxen were chiefly horn cores which suggested to the archaeologists that primary butchery had been done in that vicinity.

This vast production of food provided much agricultural work for the people in the large estates controlled by the monks. The ditches and drains that criss-crossed the area and the rivers that flowed down to the Humber provided both sustenance and employment. When affordable, fish was included in the diet of many during the Middle Ages; religious observances played a major role in its consumption, especially by the monks. The cost of salmon ranged from 13d. to 3s.4d. The salary received annually by a groom in the lord's stable was 10s. and a carpenter earned an average of 6d. a day. Sturgeon and porpoise were only on the menus of people of high rank. Salmon, whale, grampus and seal were also sometimes found in the royal rivers, Ouse, Derwent and Aire. From as far back as the reign of Edward the Confessor (1042-66) they all ranked as royal food and were reserved for the support of the king's table. In one instance, Henry I did grant away the royal right to take porpoises but there was a proviso added in his Charter Rolls which stipulated:

Except the tongue which I reserve for myself.

Salt sturgeon and 'jowles of fresh sturgeon' were included in the great feast held at Cawood Castle in the fifteenth century. Miss A.W. Richardson noted that as late as 1829 a sturgeon, stated to weigh 176 pounds and measuring 7 feet 3 inches in length, was taken out of the Ouse near Selby. It was purchased by the Museum of the Leeds Philosophical Society.

The fish eaten in large numbers was the herring. Over 38,000 red and 1,440 white herrings were purchased for the abbey at York during one financial year. Of these fish 1,200 were distributed to the poor on Maundy Thursday. To preserve quantities of this kind of food for those who lived away from water, or to build up reserves for the winter some of it was dried or salted. The monks had salted fish brought from Scarborough and dried fish from York and Hull. Many of the dried fish were described in the accounts as ling, lobs or keeling. The top price for a dried fish, species not recorded, was 3d. whilst the price of a salted one varied from 7d. to as high as 1s.4d. The fishmongers were subject to the vagaries of the weather as much as the crop growers for it was reported in the accounts that on one occasion the fishermen's stalls near the Humber had been carried out to sea.

The freshwater fish eaten in Selby were listed as tench, pike, pickerel, roach, perch and eels. During one year 4 pike, 18 pickerels, 406 eels and 3,600 roach and perch were caught in Selby Dam. A kitchener paid two shillings for a tranmel to catch fish in the Dam. The tranmel was a three layered long narrow net set vertically with floats and sinkers. It was so designed that a pocket formed when fish attempted to swim through, thus trapping them inside. Most of the 104 salmon consumed at the abbey came from the Selby Fishery near Rosscarrs, about 2.5kms. down the Ouse from the monastery. Others were bought at Turnham Hall and Airmyn. It is believed that in recent times salmon have again been migrating up the Ouse. Pike, roach, perch, eels and numerous other types of freshwater fish are still to be found in many of the waters around Selby but the people attempting to catch them are not hunter-gatherers, they do it as a sport. It is very rare that any of the fish are eaten.

There were many rules governing fishing in medieval times. Special licences were needed to fish in a manor. Fishing at night was forbidden and there were penalties for this and for placing a fish-hook in forbidden waters. Selby fishermen often found themselves in court. Several were given fines for 'taking salmon and salmon peel against the rule' whilst fishing in the Ouse below Selby. Even the millers in Selby were charged if caught fishing in the mill-ponds without permission. Fisheries and fishponds were owned by religious houses and the middle ranks of society. They were formed to supply their owners with fresh fish, much more nutritious than dried or salted ones. At its foundation Selby Abbey was given a fishery at Whitgift which it held until the time of Abbot Thomas Whalley(1255-62).

> To John de Folevill and his heirs and assigns for homage and service - our fishery at Whitgift which is called Grishars. Which we had as a gift of King William the Conquerer of England; paying annually one pound of cinnamon.

Fisheries which took the form of a weir or a base in a river on which nets or baskets could be secured were under the control of the manor in which they lay. In 1305 it was agreed, before the sheriff at Selby, that the abbot and convent of that town could have three weirs on the bank of the Ouse by Selby for catching fish without:

> any damage to the King or hurt to others.

At one of the meetings held at Selby to settle local matters, merchants and sailors using the Ouse between Selby and York and others from Drax, Airmyn, Hemingbrough, Cliffe and Barlby were present to hear the abbot confirm that the weirs owned by the monks would not interfere with any shipping. Following this promise another licence for a further weir across the Ouse was granted in 1319. The Abbots of Selby were not the only landowners to be summoned to court with regard to the safe passage of cargo ships. Much of the Abbey's goods came from Crowle and beyond or came through York. Communications with the Selby area were difficult at that time because of the vast stretches of waste and marsh land to the west of Crowle so the most convenient way to travel was along the Trent and Ouse. In 1362 the Archbishop of York was summoned to explain to the Commissioners the existence of weirs on the Wharfe and Ouse. It is believed that from time immemorial there had been fisheries by the wharf in Cawood for the taking of salmon and other fish which, it was argued, still left sufficient passage for ships. In 1394 the Archbishop was again summoned in regard to certain fisheries on the Ouse which had been enlarged and submerged, resulting in the sinking of two ships coming from the Trent to York. The ships had been laden with cloth; a loss valued at £60. In August 1484, following complaints from many merchants concerning the fish-garths and weirs that were interfering with their shipping on its way to Kingston-upon-Hull, members of the York City Council assembled in their chamber upon Ouse Bridge to discuss the problem. They came to the decision that the sheriff and two chamberlains were to:

take certain rowers and pass through the waters of Ouse unto Yalflet and search all fishgarths standing in the river.

A week later a list of the fisheries together with the names of the landowners and the men who 'farmed' them was given to the Mayor of the City. The Prior of Drax was one of the 'lords'; he was found to have three weirs. His tenants were John Collinson who farmed two spaces and William and Andrew Grice who each farmed three spaces. Weirs varied in length from 12 to 20 spaces. These 'spaces' were most probably the distances left between vertical poles to which the nets or traps were attached. The weirs had numerous spaces also known as 'rowmes' set strongly across the whole width of the water with piles, stones and hedges. Many years after this inspection the Council ordered that the erection of weirs on the River Ouse was, in the future, to be by licence only.

The monks accounted for some repairs done to the fishery they had near Rosscarrs. Eight oak saplings were felled for new poles. They were stripped and cut to a point before being carted in three trips from Spark Hagg, three kms. north-west of Selby, to the fishery. John Copyn with the help of two other men spent three days pulling up and taking out the old timbers of the office fishery. Three other men worked for four days replacing the piles to make a new fishery. All the men received twopence a day but it was recorded that only the men removing the old wood received bread and ale from the monastery's store. Robert Bird, master of the abbey's ship, was paid 12d., by agreement, for bringing the fishery's boat by water from Donemouth at Adlingfleet, where the old south course of the Don joined the Trent. The abbey had a fishery at Crowle which in one year supplied the brothers with five great eels and 810 small ones. Many pike, pikerels, roach and perch were included but only one tench. Fishing nets called dikenets or kiddle nets were purchased at this fishery. Kiddle was another word used to describe a weir, dam or barrier in a river having an opening in it fitted with nets for catching fish.

Fish ponds, some with complex breeding tanks were kept by many of those in the middle ranks of society to provide the large quantities of fish consumed in their extensive households. Some fish-ponds were situated in towns. The word 'vivary' was used by the monks of Selby to describe some of the waters in and around their manors. Selby mill-pond was sometimes referred to by this name. The word survives today in 'Vivars Way', a modern access road from Canal Road and in the name 'The Vivars' which for a long time has been the name given to a seven acre piece of land in the same area. It was given this title because that was where, it was believed, the monks had their fish pond. Recent work done by MAP has thrown some doubt on this theory. The Enclosure Map of 1808 depicts the Vivars as open land with no sign of development. The first edition of an O.S. map in 1851 puts the area in question as being south-east of the railway but later publications have it further eastward. The Archaeological Watching Brief undertaken by MAP in 1994 concerning the Vivars found that the only medieval features there were a silted pond and ridge and furrow, of pre-enclosure date, which avoided the water site. The excavations and environmental evidence put forward supported the belief that the pond had gradually silted up during its lifetime with little interference from man. The distinct lack of fish bones in the lower silts also did not support the use of the feature as a fish-pond. The evidence suggested that the Abbey fish-pond was not located within the south-west corner of the Vivar site as recorded by C.C.Hodge in *The Architectural History of Selby Abbey* 1863. Fish-ponds in Selby are referred to in many ancient documents but their precise locations are difficult to place because of the loss of medieval names. It is documented that sometime between 1115 and 1128, Henry I confirmed to the abbot and convent of Selby the gift of a fish-pond endowed to them by his father:

> *However long and broad it is from boundary to boundary.*

He also warned that anyone fishing in it would incur forfeiture in the King's Court. The vivary or stew was said to lie near Dayridding, described as being not far from the boundary of Brayton. Around thirty years later, a vivary was mentioned in a deed in which Henry de Lacy confirmed the gift of a piece of land previously given by John de Lasceles:

> *and the land, both woodland and otherwise, lying next the boundaries of Selebye and between the monks' vivary and the midst of the marsh called Tranamor, and on the western side to the clear water (or stream) on the near side of Todhill, which separates two moors, and thence across to the vivary by an oak-tree which is set as a boundary on the near side of the wood.*

John de Lasceles also gave up any rights he might have had in the monks' vivary.

Markets, Fairs and Tolls

The monks and the people of Selby relied on the markets and fairs to provide some of their needs. They also gave employment to local folk and helped the monks sell off any surplus goods. Selby became a popular market centre supported by the many visitors to the abbey, the frequent ferry service and the town's growth as an inland port for the busy traffic between the Humber and York.

Before the advent of good roads and transport services most of the trading was carried out at markets and fairs. Many pre-dated the Norman Conquest but after this event they were granted an existence by charter. Over 3,300 of these were given during the 13th. century with an additional 1,560 in the fourteenth century. It was another way for the Crown to obtain revenue from local land-owners and for them, in turn, to exact tolls from the tradesmen. A charter was more a right to collect revenues than it was to hold a market or fair. William I granted the monks at Selby complete exemption from paying any of the tolls at all English fairs and markets. Fairs were often centred around one particular item; horses, wool, hides or cloth for example. It was a holiday time for the locals for there was plenty of food and drink available and jugglers, acrobats, musicians and other entertainers were all ready to amuse whilst taking their share of the profits. By 1258 it had become an offence to hold fairs on the Sabbath day but the tradition continued for many years. The annual medieval fairs at Selby took place at the Feast of St. Peter, (two days) and at the Feast of St. Michael for three days. Markets were held on a particular day in the week. The main venue for a market in the early days was in the churchyard on a Sunday so people who had to travel far could worship then trade on the same day. Archbishop Melton on a visitation to Selby Abbey in 1324 forbade any further use of the cemetery for markets. The populous therefore moved their buying and selling operations to an open space in front of the great abbey gates which would have included the area now occupied by Barclays and Lloyds banks and the Londesborough Arms Hotel. Part of Selby market is still held adjacent to these premises. By 1324, the market at Selby was being held on a Monday; a custom continued to this day. Archbishop Thoresby issued a similar order concerning markets at Whitgift in 1367. He forbade the use of the church porch and yard for markets and prohibited eating and drinking there. Nearly two centuries later the church wardens at Riccall ordered that the custom of peddlers selling their wares in the porch of the church on feast days had to stop. The place of sale was moved from the church grounds to the market cross.

As Lord of the Manor the abbot of Selby Abbey was accustomed to take stallage, standage and other charges for the buying and selling of goods brought into the market. The monks paid a toll-keeper 15s. per annum to collect their dues which were many and varied. It is believed that in the early days cattle and horses were tethered near the church walls, but by the fourteenth century the traders had to pay stallage for their animals on market day as well as at other times. The owners then had to pay a toll on any animals they had for sale. The toll-keeper was also allowed to collect 4d. for each creature that strayed from its grazing ground. There seemed to have been a tax to pay on everything sold at the market. The toll paid on cow and horse hides and wool-skins in 1343 included a halfpenny on each hide from the vendor and purchaser alike; there was an extra charge of one penny for every bundle of ten sold. Merchants paid to have items such as corn, salt and coal verified as being the correct weight. It cost the bakers and the ale-sellers a small amount for officials to check they were selling the right sizes of bread and measures of ale. Mercers, drapers, cobblers and fustian makers all paid a fee, as did those selling iron or iron goods. Some of the stalls were situated in front of the Abbey gates. These stalls cost around 1s.4d to rent and they were not always occupied. In 1417 it was reported that a stall at the Abbey gates had had no tenant for a year and three other stalls had been in the Abbot's hands for the same reason. Itinerant merchants like drapers, doublet-makers and bow-makers who brought their own booths did not escape the tolls for they had to pay for a site.

Many traders from both Selby and further afield did not accept the payment of these tolls gracefully. Some of them ignored the rulings and the fines that followed these actions. Roger Whatman of Burn and John Barker of Gowthorpe were amongst 21 people listed by the tollkeeper, at one time, as having paid their fines whilst William Hudson of Wistow and Robert Pedelyn, barker of Selby, were included in the roll of 27 offenders who had paid neither tolls nor penalties. The wives of some of these objectors were also noted down as toll-evaders and, as the toll-keeper reported, there were many others of the town of Selby whose names at that time he could not bring to mind. William de Aston did not pay any tolls or other duties demanded by the monks. Therefore, Abbot John de Wystowe (1293-1300) aided by two of his brothers impounded twelve oxen used by the culprit for ploughing his land in Barlby. William did not accept this punishment for, one night with the help of his friends, he stole into the Abbot's pound and recovered his animals!

Another objector, Walter, son of Ralph of Selby, left the town and found a place to live where there were no charters or taxes. This was on the island of 'Rawenserod' or Ravenser, which, according to tradition, had been cast up by the sea during the reign of Henry III (1216-1272) and was said to have been "distant from Grimsby by the space of one tide". Fishermen found the island an ideal place to dry their nets until in 1250 a ship was wrecked on its shores. An enterprising young man made a hut from the wreckage of the vessel and settled down to eke out a living supplying passing ships with food and drink. This must have proved to be quite a profitable business for by the time Walter arrived there were four dwellings on the island. The Selebian joined the others in the brisk trade being carried out on Ravenser. They did not just settle for any ship that happened to pass their shores. The men regularly went out in their small boats to meet ships in the Humber that were heavily laden with merchandise and persuaded them to call at their island. Actions were then taken to delay the ships whilst pressure was put on the traders to unload there and not to journey on to Grimsby, as was their custom. Walter and his partners warned them that the Burgesses of Grimsby would make such deductions on their wares that, for example, herrings worth 40s. would only fetch half that price. As a result of this and other dire tales almost all the vessels stayed and unloaded at Ravenser. Business thrived until in 1290 the Mayor and Burgesses of Grimsby laid a complaint against the islanders and an Inquisition was held the following September. At this the Mayor complained that since Edward's coronation in 1272 the actions of Walter and his fellow conspirators had resulted in a depletion of trade in Grimsby; it had caused so much poverty amongst the tenants in the town that most of them could not pay their rents and had been forced to leave the area. The islanders argued that the ships stayed away from Grimsby because the Burgesses were always making wrongful deductions and were so slow to pay the crews that the ships missed the tides. The Mayor insisted that these accusations had been investigated and any errors rectified. The outcome of the Inquisition was not clear but Ravenser must have continued to flourish for it eventually became an important port with its own Member of Parliament. However, the threat to Grimsby's future as a prosperous trading and fishing town gradually disappeared in a way not dissimilar to the manner in which it had unexpectedly arisen. The sea slowly began to claim back its own so that by around the year 1360 Ravenser no longer existed.

The island had enabled Walter to make a good living free from the tolls and customs laid down by the abbots of Selby. Those trading in his home town were not so fortunate. In 1343 ships docking at the wharves paid a minimum of twopence a ship which increased in relation to the number of vessels. The additional tax due on the freight carried was fourpence for each ship. Selby's position on the lower reaches of the Ouse worked in its favour for the navigation above the port to Cawood, York and Linton was not easy for medieval ships. By the thirteenth century it was amongst the principal ports such as York and Hull which had to pay tollage to the King. During the fourteenth century Edward III gave York merchants permission to send their woollen hides, on which export duty had to be paid, in "little ships" to Selby because of the state of the River Ouse above the port.

Trades and Crafts

As the little inland port of Selby grew in importance there was more work for the local inhabitants. The monks also employed the townsfolk to do duties other than that of producing food. There were three main groups of hired labour in the abbey defined by the amount of payment annually received from the monks. The servant in the Guest House and the tailor in the abbey were each paid 13s.4d. The groom in the tailor's shop and the abbot's laundress each received ten shillings whilst the lowest paid which included the page in the kitchen and the repairer of vestments were given 6s.8d. These servants of the monks had employment all the year round but those who worked on the land to support themselves and their families faced hard times during the winter months. They were mainly self-supporting and when they could not work outside they occupied their time making useful articles for their homes. The men made wooden platters and spoons and rough tools for cultivation such as scythes and rakes; the women folk prepared food and made clothes and household items. Reeds and willows were woven into baskets for catching fish and flails were made using holly or thorn.

Thomas Turnour earned a living by making objects out of wood. He received 18d. in one sale for supplying the monks with 80 wooden dishes, plates and shallow bowls known as saucers. Other talented village people made pottery and bronze wares that were sold at the markets and fairs. It is believed by some researchers that there were pottery kilns either in Selby or, more probably, at Thorpe Willoughby that produced Humber Ware. This ware was mainly jugs and pitchers made for the kitchen, cellar or the poorer folk's homes. It was seldom seen on the high table or in a manor house. The early pots were plain with a greenish brown glaze but by the fourteenth century more decorative ones were being produced. An example of a Humber jug in York Museum is coloured in grey and red with a matt green-brown glaze on its upper half. It has a fine seal on it depicting ears of corn and leaves. The archaeological digs that took place in the 1990s turned up numerous sherds, several dating from the eleventh to the sixteenth centuries. Of the 759 pottery pieces discovered in an area covering Church Avenue, Abbey Place and Market Place, 108 of them were medieval. Numerous sherds from the 13th. to 17th. centuries were found close to the Griffin Hotel in Micklegate whilst others dating back to the 12th. century were recovered near to Wren Lane. There was a preponderance of Humber Ware amongst the sherds found in both places.

A sixteenth century potter's kiln that made this type of ware was discovered in 1963 by archaeologists at West Cowick. The search for the kiln began when some children took pieces of pottery to Miss Richardson, who contacted some interested parties. They in turn brought in the archaeologists. A magnetic survey of the area soon revealed the location of the kiln in the garden of Mrs. E.P.Cooper, Top House Farm, West Cowick. It was ten feet in diameter and had seven flues through which heat for firing pots passed into the kiln; the maximum number of flues seen previously in that type of kiln had been five.

It has not been proven that there were kilns in the town of Selby but there is no doubt that leather work and tanning were major industries in the locality during the time of the monks. Seven of the traders named for objecting to paying the market tolls in 1343 were listed as barkers--tanners. A number of years later it was noted that John Barneslay, barker, received the hides of 14 oxen, 49 cows, 15 bullocks and one heifer from the monks of Selby. He also bought 16 calf-skins, 67 lamb-skins and 156 wool-fells; in addition, by agreement, he was given a gift of one ox-hide and one cow-hide.

An example of medieval leather work was found by Donald and Joyce Eyre in the area of Church Hill in 1974. They had been given permission to carry out excavations prior to the building of homes for the elderly which now stand on Gant Walk. The two amateur archaeologists discovered, amongst other things, a small child's shoe. It was in almost perfect condition even to the presence of tiny stitches on the soles.

The many finds unearthed in the 1990s helped the researchers to draw the conclusion that three branches of leather work were carried out in Selby in medieval times; they were currying, cobbling and shoe-making. Excavations in the town not only revealed signs of primary butchery having taken place, they also uncovered large quantities of the waste product from the leather tanning process. This consisted of a predominance of sheep and goat leg bones amongst the material found in a trench behind Gowthorpe. The waste product from the leather tanning process was also evident on various other sites in Selby.

The survey carried out for Selby District Council revealed substantial evidence of leatherwork in Micklegate. A large collection of well-preserved leather articles was recovered amongst which were several shoes in the styles popular from the thirteenth to the fifteenth century. There were also samples of three types of waste leather. The first consisted of shavings from the paring down of thick hides; the second was made up of unusable parts such as bellyskin, udders and hide edges. The third consisted of the bits left after the cutting out of shapes. Other leather goods found amongst the waste in Micklegate included an archer's brace, a suspension strap and a cut down knife sheath. The last had a panel decorated with two three-leaved clovers or shamrocks, each with a roundel separated by a double parallel vertical line made by an impressed tool. Cobbling waste was found in the area now cut through by Finkle Street. Three items had been cut to salvage reusable leather before being discarded. Shoes found there carried signs of having been heavily worn and frequently repaired. One of the shoes had a pointed toe stuffed with moss. This piece of footwear also had the upper part of the shoe slashed vertically from the throat towards the toe. It has been put forward that this may have been done to ease a shoe too tight across the instep rather than as a fashion statement. Tim Padley made a study of the articles of shoe leather found in Selby in 1995/96. Most of them dated from between the late twelfth century and the fourteenth century and were mainly from Micklegate. Twenty seven shoes or shoe parts came from that vicinity; two shoes were found in Finkle Street and three more in the Market Place. All but one of the 57 off-cuts and fragments discovered originated in Micklegate. The most common shoe component recovered was the sole. Triangular shaped pieces with stitching on them were identified as heel stiffeners placed at the back of the upper on the inside of the shoe to strengthen the heel and used with the flesh side towards the foot. Medieval shoes were described by Tim Padley as having uppers of wraparound construction which led to gaps when the shoes were assembled. These were filled with insets to the uppers which were attached by binding stitches to make the uppers function correctly. Upper fragments found showed that the shoes had rounded toes whilst strips of leather were believed to have been from fastenings for the shoes or from bags. It was concluded that the collection of leather from Micklegate probably came from cobbling. Off-cuts could be used for making or repairing shoes but damaged and discarded shoe parts would not have been found where no repairs had been carried out.

The only evidence unearthed of the weaving of cloth having taken place in Selby was a stone loom-weight found at the base of a trench dug in Micklegate. However, there is a mention in the account rolls of a fulling-mill in the town. A fulling-mill was where the bare and thready material produced on a loom was shrunk and pounded to matt the fibres closer together. To do this the cloth was soaked in a solution of fuller's earth powder. The current from a fast flowing stream was then harnessed to turn a wooden beam, with hammers on it, placed across the water. The hammers, or fulling stocks, pounded the cloth as they fell on it. A procedure which, pre twelfth century, had been carried out by the stamping of people's feet. In the early part of the fourteenth century the monks granted Adam the Folour (Fuller) of Selby and his wife, Margaret, a messuage and one mill with appurtenances in the town. In 1404 a fulling-mill in Selby, for which the pittancer received 10s. annually, was moved to an unspecified place. By this period Selby had four clothiers and was still producing cloth at the time of the demise of the monastery in 1539. Ancient documents also reveal that the growing of flax and hemp with some form of linen cloth making were carried on in a small way during the monks' rule.

1413. And for 8 ells of cloth of lake(linen) purchased for one tablecloth, 2 long towels and 2 short towels.

Flax plants, most probably grown in the area of modern Flaxley Road, were harvested when 19 – 120 cm. high and then bundles of the stalks were stacked together and left for about two weeks to dry. Hemp, which grew to a height of at least 300 cm. was processed in the same way as flax but, being coarser, needed harsher treatment. In 1519 the people of Selby were forbidden by the court to dry hemp in their homes, in the dam or in the landings going to the dam. Bundles of flax and hemp needed to be submerged in pools or gently flowing water to rot the woody matter away from the fibres within the stalks. This 'retting' took about a fortnight. It polluted the water and gave off a very unpleasant smell, which is maybe why in 1533 the Court of Selby ruled that "No man rett neither hemp nor line". The only other method left was to lay the bundles on the grass and water them or rely on the dew to ret them. Line was the name given to the longest fibres of flax which were used to make the finest yarn. Some industrious inhabitants must have managed all the processes needed to make the threads for, in 1324, when Archbishop Melton forbade the use of the cemetery for a market, he also declared that it was no longer permissible for women to bleach their linen cloths in that place.

Streets and Houses

Most of the dwellings in Selby were rented or leased from the monks.

And for 6s. yearly from the rent of the tenement in New Lane formerly in the possession of John Marshall of Brayton.

Much of the property and land in Selby was held by the abbey from the king and so a royal charter was needed to confirm any grants of tenements and estates to individual people. The lands were held for life at a fixed rate paid to the abbey. On the death of the tenant the land reverted to the abbey. Some of the properties confirmed by royal charters in the early fourteenth century included – a toft with a forge built upon it and other appurtenances for Peter le Feure and his son Roger; a messuage and a shop with appurtenances for John, son of Robert le Shepherd; two shops and appurtenances for Martin the Tailor and, six acres of land for John of Airmyn, sailor.

The building and repairing of the many properties in the town provided plenty of work for the skilled worker and the labourer. One of the conclusions drawn from the twentieth century excavations was that where today there is a shopping complex and a car-park behind Gowthorpe, during the thirteenth to the fifteenth century it was open land. At that period it was broken up into backyards for the houses fronting onto Gowthorpe. In these gardens were found a number of small pits and depressions; there were also stakeholds with several wooden stakes in situ. One other feature was the remains of three hoops of wood not unlike barrel hoops inside of which were the remains of a circular wooden top or base of a barrel which were suggestive of a barrel well. There were many references to hedges, fences and outbuildings in the account rolls. Reginald Wright and his companion earned two shillings for working for three days repairing the fence of a tenement in Gowthorpe formerly in the tenure of Geofrey Dynelabe. William Butler and his co-worker cut down underwood by the Dam to make a hedge round a garden in Micklegate. In 1434 three cartloads of thorns were felled in the North Wood and used make a hedge around a house in Cow Lane. Rents were lost for various reasons:

> *16d. allowed for depreciation of the holdings in Cowick which Henry de Horden holds.*

> *And 16s. for loss of the rent of one messuage in Ousegate in the lord's hand this year for lack of tenant.*

> *And 6d lost from the rent of Robert de Boland this year because he refuses to pay.*

> *One barn in Micklegate - rent lost because it is filled with thatch for the office's use.*

> *One house in Wren Lane, rent lost, it is filled with sand, lime and tiles.*

Many buildings had thatched roofs. Reeds and rushes from Selby Dam and other ditches were used for this purpose. In one instance grass and rushes mowed down along the Dam, were bound into 220 thraves and sold for ¾d. a thrave. Walter Coke of Thorpe Willoughby was paid to carry the said rushes by water from the main waterway to the houses of the various buyers in Selby. He took his craft along Kirk-dyke to reach some of the dwellings. Sixteen thraves of thatch were used for the roofs of four cottages situated near the water-mills. A woman assisted the male worker in this thatching and ridging. Women were often employed in 'drawing the thatch'. This entailed sorting out the long reeds, straws etc. from the short, pulling them out and laying them straight for the thatcher. Oak saplings were purchased for making into beams for the cottages. Oaken boards were used to make a louvre for the Poor House but its whereabouts in the town was not recorded. Payments had to be made to the abbey for any oak branches taken down in the woods for timber. Most of the buildings had walls made of wattle and daub. The builders daubed mud onto upright posts known as stowers on which twigs and branches or laths had been fixed or interlaced. A house in New Lane had its walls plastered with mud brought from Bondgate; a portion of it was used for daubing various defects in the walls of houses in Ousegate, which Richard Beawe held by contract. Numerous materials were brought into Selby from the surrounding area. One delivery consisted of 1,500 tiles from the tile-kiln at Cawood which were transported to the Ouse and then brought by water to Selby in the monastery's barge. Tiles were also carried from Long Drax and with those from Cawood were used for various purposes. One thousand were used for paving a number of houses whilst some from Long Drax were needed to renew a chimney. A drain was made between this chimney and a chamber attached to it using eight stones of lead purchased from John Plummer and melted by William Plummer.

This William is also recorded as having melted and reworked office lead into one vessel weighing 32 stones for cooking meat in the monastery's kitchen. The original lead would have been transported from Boroughbridge, via the Ure and Ouse. Boroughbridge was a new town that had developed following an increase in population and trade during the twelfth and thirteenth centuries. For hundreds of years lead and other goods from West and North Yorkshire were shipped at Boroughbridge for York and Hull. Pipe Rolls (1179-1183) contain many references to lead being sent from the new town to York and Selby for the transhipment of most of it to London or abroad.

Another material used in building was clay. Two cart-loads of clay were used in repairing the walls of a shop "at the corner near the cross in the market place". Robert Slater repaired the chamber of the shop with his own tiles but the Keeper of the Fabric paid out three pence for a ladder to enable Robert to enter the chamber! Henry Joyner used a varied amount of materials to build a house on Gowthorpe including stone from Monk Fryston and lime and slates from Sherburn. In addition he bought staples, crooks and iron bars for strengthening the doors and windows of the dwelling which, besides having a kitchen, had a kiln-house, brew-house and a lean-to in its garden. Stone flags and cobbles were used for paving. The archaeologists uncovered a finely cobbled area, possibly from the thirteenth century, at the south end of Micklegate.

Medieval Selby

The account rolls gave plenty of information regarding the kinds of employment open to the local people during the existence of the monastery. They also helped to build up a picture of Selby as it may have been at that time. No suburbs had developed outside the town because of the fear of flooding and the danger of attack by groups of Anglo-Saxons still averse to the rule of the Normans. At night the entrances to the town proper, which were most likely situated at Millgate Bridge, Brayton Lane end of Gowthorpe and Ousegate, (near the Nelson Inn), were barricaded and guarded. The main part of Selby grew around Church Hill where the little chapel was situated. A track from there led down to the ferry and to Ousegate which, because of its proximity to the Ouse, was an important part of the town. An archaeological dig undertaken by Y.A.T at the east end of Ousegate in 2003 revealed some evidence of medieval activity in that area. Pieces of twelfth century pottery, a medieval pit and some ditches were excavated in three trenches. The full nature and extent of the ditches could not be ascertained because of the restricted nature of the explorations. The team, however, saw that most of the ditches formed right angles to Ousegate, so may well have served as some kind of land divisions for the properties fronting onto the street. Long narrow properties end-on to a street were well known in many medieval towns. The water-logged state of the coffins found interred on Church Hill demonstrated how high the river water reached at various times. The close proximity of the dwellings on Ousegate to the river's banks caused many problems for the inhabitants.

> *"Manor Court 1483*
> *Great default in Ousegate, the ground goes away and may in process of time, without it be mended is like to mischief all the streets of Ousegate and all the houses that edge the water. Wherefore we desire that my Lord and his brethren lay their heads together, that there may be found a remedy therefore before it be worse."*

People who lived along the banks of the Ouse sometimes benefited from the actions of the river. When Nicholas de Selby was mayor of York (1287-8) he was present at an Inquisition at which it was confirmed that citizens who had dwellings near the 'Use' could freely enlarge their property or yards on either side of the water, on land recovered from the river. This was an ancient custom but it is not clear whether Nicholas, who was most probably educated at Selby Abbey, included the inhabitants of Selby in this ruling.

A track going west from Church Hill was recorded as Wren Lane. It led into Micklegate which became the main industrial and trading part of the town with its access to the monks' staithes. It is recorded in the Coucher Books that Walter Hall of Selby gave his daughter, Margaret, one messuage in Selby which lay in Ousegate next to a toft once belonging to William Tibby, on one side, and the *"main street of Micklegate towards the Ouse on the other"*. The cemeteries were referred to as being in Church Lane. This lane which ran south-west from Church Hill may have led from the little chapel to the townsfolk's burial ground and the abbey church. It may also have provided access from the monks' quarters to their tipping ground. Evidence of medieval rubbish pits was found during the archaeological digs carried out in 1998. They were uncovered on a piece of land known as Irwin's Yard which lies in a right angle formed by Wren Lane and Church Lane. Its proximity to the abbey suggests the rubbish pits may have been used by the monks. The dig provided evidence of activity there as far back as the eleventh century. The earliest discoveries pointed to the use of the ground for rubbish and cess-pits; a typical 'back-yard' in medieval times. The people had no designated places for tipping, no organised collections of rubbish and no water supplies, so everything was disposed of in their own back yards. Further finds in Irwin's Yard such as clay floors, large hearths and charcoal, pointed to some kind of light industry being carried on there at a later date. The size of the hearths suggested metal work, which needed a source of great heat. Evidence found of the construction of a large stone building in the yard dating from the fifteenth or sixteenth century makes it believable that the industry thrived.

Gowthorpe was the main entrance into the town for people and goods coming from the direction of Monk Fryston, Hambleton and Thorpe Willoughby. Also at the western end of Gowthorpe where Armoury Road lies today, possibly close to the chapel of St. Genevieve, was a trackway leading towards Brayton. The officials at the monastery always listed the market place, with its stalls near the abbey gates, as being in the eastern part of Gowthorpe. The only way south from this end of Gowthorpe seems to have been New Lane. This trackway was most probably formed after the monks had built their perimeter walls around the abbey for it appears to have followed the walls or ditches that led to the posterngate from where travellers could make their way west to Brayton or east towards Staynor. This trackway had a hermitage at the end of it. Hermits were common figures in late medieval times but the site at Selby seems to have been vacant for long periods for it was let out when possible to tenants for fourpence rent. In the account rolls that have been available there has been no reference to Finkle Street which today connects Gowthorpe with Micklegate. The northern end of this short thoroughfare has often been referred to as "King's Street", a name that does appear in ancient documents concerning the Court Leet of 1519.

All fennces buttnyg on the kynge's strett be mayd be Saynt George Day.

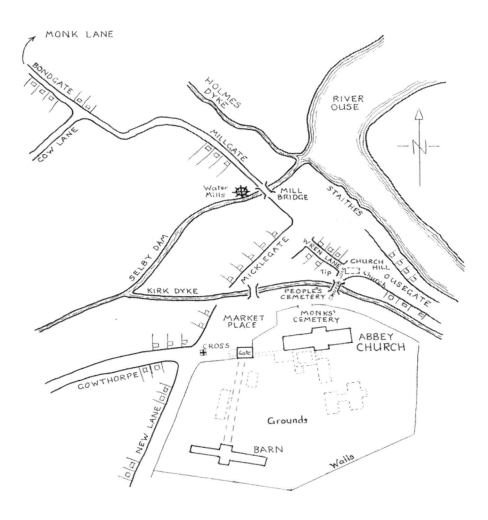

Figure 3. Medieval Selby

It was the custom at that time that the king gave his protection to certain roads, often referred to as "The King's Highway". In 1519 The Court Leet may have been referring to all streets that were under the king's jurisdiction - hence the ruling. It is also possible that during the presence of the monastery the market place spread further north than it does today with open access into Micklegate.

There is much evidence to show that at the far end of Micklegate, almost opposite to Wren Lane and leading north-west was a track that later became known as Mill-gate. This road crossed Selby Dam by way of Millbridge and led to the water-mills of the town. Beyond the mills the road followed the old course of the River Ouse to Over, or Minor Selby. This small manor, whose boundaries are not defined, was mentioned in records dated as early as 1030. The route through this area became known as Bondgate, a place where the tenants were bondsmen obliged to serve the abbot as part of their tenure (the conditions under which their land was held). Bondgate, now part of the B1223 to Cawood, led to Monk Lane. It was described by W. Wheater in his "History of Sherburn and Cawood,"1882 , as being:

> *This once wretched quagmire, now scarcely a passable road leads from the end of Bondgate, the peasants' gate, therefore outside the town of Selby into Wistow Lordship and has, I imagine, been the road used by the monks to get to their estate at the Haystede, where their mill horses are kept. It follows the old course of the Ouse and was, most likely, the shore of an extensive swamp.*

Another path used by both monks and townsfolk led westward from Millgate. It was known as Cow-Lane and led to Flaxley, the common, and the woods. This area forming Over Selby where the houses were mostly occupied by farmers and their labourers, formed the boundary of the town. It and Bondgate were also safe-guarded especially at night. Today, an area to the north and east of Bondgate and Millgate is known as The Holmes. At the time of the monastery it belonged to the lordship of Barlby. One hundred acres in area its boundary was traceable by the course of a ditch which separated it from Selby, on the one side, and from Wistow on the other. It was known as 'Bardleby cum Holme'. In 1883 the Local Government Board transferred the Holmes, for parochial and rating purposes, from the East Riding to Selby in the West Riding.

Courts, Laws and Punishments

When the monks were granted gifts of land by the Kings of England they were also given full right to sac, soc, toll, team and infangenetheof. 'Sac, soc and toll' gave the abbots the right to exact tolls on their estates and to have their tenants' corn ground at their mills. 'Team' gave the lord of the manor the right to punish offenders in his fee. 'Infangenetheof' empowered the abbot to judge and hang thieves taken in his manor. The holding of these manorial courts was an old custom built upon by the Norman rulers. The villagers were answerable to the lord of the manor for their failings but during the reign of Henry II (1154-1189) it became the practice for twelve men in each Hundred to meet before the sheriff to represent all those in their area accused of a crime. Many local people were called to plead for the innocence of a person from their neighbourhood. When a fight between John from Thorpe Willoughby and William Belle from Gateforth ended with the death of William, John was imprisoned in Nottingham.

On the 10th. February 1293, twelve men chosen from the villages of Wistow, Read, Drax and Brayton stood before the court at York to plead before the sheriff and four coroners for the life of John of Thorpe. They argued that he was not guilty of the man's death by 'malice and hatred' but had killed William in self-defence; using a staff had been the only way of preventing his own death at the hands of William. John was reprieved. If he had been found guilty he could have been outlawed, fined or hanged.

Bursars' accounts 1399 Allowances: And 20s.8d. from the holdings in Acaster Selby which John de Glasedale, a thief (who was hanged), held in the lord's hand.

John de Glasedale may have met his fate on Gallows Hill Road which is shown on the 1804 Enclosure Map of Brayton. It was a private road branching off in a north-easterly direction from Thorpe Willoughby Church Road, now known as Brackenhill Lane. Today it is a track marking the boundary of a field whose northerly edge borders on the Selby-Leeds railway.

During medieval times courts were held at several places in and around Selby including Monk Fryston, Hillam and Hambleton. All fines were accounted for and the income from them sent to the abbot. When a man from the Selby area was fined 6s.8d. for grievously harming another man, half of the payment went to the abbot and the rest was given to the church. In 1399 the abbot received 50s. from the court of Crowle but nothing from the courts held at Queniborough, Stallingborough, Thorpe Willoughby, Brayton and Acaster Selby; there had been no fines or amercements at those places during that year. A separate court was also held at Over Selby:

The court of the lord abbot of Selby for his tenants in bondage in Over Selby, held in the office of the granger of the abbey of Selby. 7 June 1399.

The tenants were expected to be present at these meetings. The abbot derived an income of 10s.8d. made up of fines for non-attendance at this court and a fee paid for a grant to a holding. Selby Waterhouses, a hamlet on the Barlby side of the Ouse, given to the monks by Hugh Ward of Thorpe, also held its own court. At one hearing in 1326, Robert and his wife Alice, brought a case against Hugh Scute and wife Agnes, concerning a payment for trespass. Alice appeared but not Hugh so the court dispossessed him of one ox which was handed over on the sureties of John de Selby and Walter Dunning to produce the husband at the next court.

The abbot or his representatives held court in Selby in chambers above the abbey gates. Many people came up before this court for causing an affray.

1472 Ryc' Emson maid afray of John Broun and drue blod on hym.

John Kyng maid afray upon the goldsmith of Selby.

When John Byrd and Remenghyngton were involved in a brawl during which both drew blood they had to pay a fine of 12d.each. Vagabonds were a constant problem to the eleven men sworn to uphold the law for the lord and his tenants at the Court Leets or manorial courts. At one meeting they declared upon oath, that Patryk, dwelling in Middlethorpe, was a vagabond who had no craft and was known as a pursuer of other men's wives. Many of the men listed as vagabonds were described as having no craft. The jury's verdict on all these men was;

> *We order all vagabonds mentioned to be of good rule in time to come. If found guilty again to leave town by Michaelmas next and if they return to be fined 40s.*

A difficult enough amount of money for even a working man to have found at that time! The jury also objected to those who disturbed the peace at night. A servant of Henry Couper was accused of rioting late at night with three friends. John Coke, fisherman, was charged with allowing men to "play at the tables" for money in his house at night. It was said Robert Courtenay received unruly persons at night and was suspected of doing misdeeds with them. The opinion of the jury concerning Roger of the Marchalsye, servant to William Broun, was:

> *He is a suspect person and we desire to have him out of town.*

Women accused of various crimes were also under threat of having to leave town. One servant described as being, 'ill-disposed of her hands.' was ordered to 'void' the town by St. George's Day or face a fine of 20s. An 'evil-disposed' wife who, it was said, cut corn at harvest time and took other food, especially eggs, from the fields, was threatened with imprisonment if she did not leave the town immediately. The saddest cases forbidden the town were the lepers. Leprosy had become prevalent from around 1000-1250 AD but quite rare after the fifteenth century. Ryc' Derreke was a leper who was forbidden to mix with his fellow men in Selby and threatened with a charge of 40s. if he did not leave the town. In a further ruling concerning this poor man it was ordered that he be taken into Selby Woods and anyone offering him shelter was liable to a fine. It became common for large towns and even some villages to have a leper house. These were wretched places due to the lack of funds. It does not appear that there was one in Selby but, in the records of grants, it was stated that in 1154 the monks of Pontefract were given thirty acres of land in that town. Some years later the son of the benefactor gave them an extra 'five acres there, lying between house of lepers and Carleton'.

Cases of slander were brought before the Court to be settled. In 1505 Robert Calthorne of Selby was charged with speaking ill of Jane, wife of William Roper. To make amends Robert offered Jane a jewelled belt and some beads belonging to his wife, with the one condition that she would not wear them in Selby during his lifetime. The Ropers advised the Court that the offer was acceptable to them as 'trew kyrsyn folk.'

Parents were responsible for the actions of their children! If a child was found breaking hedges or fences the father was fined fourpence. Further such behaviour and the penalty went up to 3s.4d. Dogs were also a subject of contention. A man was only allowed to keep one dog in his house. In 1477 William Bacon was accused of unlawfully keeping two such animals. He was ordered to keep one and 'put away the other in pain of 20s'. An order in 1519 enlarged on the previous law concerning dogs. No man, it said, was to keep hounds, greyhounds or spaniels which could be used in the hunting of the lord's game. It was illegal for any man to hunt or hawk on the lord's estates without a licence. The muzzling of dogs, a subject still under discussion today, was obviously a problem in the sixteenth century. At the Court of Selby in 1533, Robert Strynger, John Petty and Robert Doule were ordered to muzzle their dogs. This may have been because they were ferocious animals, sheep worriers or, because the three men were butchers; the court had made it a rule:

That all bochers kepe wele theire blode in bolles, and mussell theire dogges.

During the last centuries of the abbots of Selby Abbey being Lord of the Manor it became the custom to hold a Great Inquest in April and October to pass judgement on the guilty, introduce new rules and enforce old ones. They were presided over by the constables and a jury of eleven men. The abbot and monks still owned the town but they too were answerable to this court.

In the first, we fynd a great defawt in the crosse in the merkythe place, that it is in pounte to fall, and lyke to doy gret hurt bot it be mendid

They also declared that Mill-bridge and Cockret-bridge were in need of attention. All, they declared, belonged to the Lord Abbot and were to be repaired by the following Easter. John Sharrowe was abbot from 1466 to 1486 and during his time the officials made many rulings concerning the state of the cross but it was still "like to fall"at the end of his term of office. The cross was a focal point in the town. Many transactions were carried out there and news relayed to the inhabitants. The few broken steps of an ancient cross that were replaced by a new cross in 1775 may well have been the remains of the one that was so neglected in the fifteenth century. The court had the right to admonish the monks but it also defended them. Robertus Michall, barker of Cow Lane, despite a ruling forbidding such actions, repeatedly cut down oaks in the North Wood. The court fined him for this and took away his axe until he had fully repented of his actions to the abbot. John Shepherd and Colling the shoemaker, were fined for felling holly and oakwood in the same place.

The records helped to give an insight into how the townsfolk were governed by the rulings and decisions made at the court meetings. In many ways they were there to help and protect some of the more vulnerable people. It was brought to the notice of one court that the butchers of Selby were selling meat to the poor that was under weight. The lord and stewards were ordered to have a weekly search made of the butchers' shops to make sure they sold a "reasonable pennyworth". It was also a rule that if any butcher kept until after Thursday meat from an animal that had been slain the previous Saturday he was to forfeit the meat and pay a fine to the lord. The lord and stewards also examined the fish sold in Selby; they checked the weighing machines, the money paid at the coast for the fish, then fixed the prices. One seller was fined for selling herrings at four for a penny "against orders of the town". One of the worst offenders was Richard Dishford who kept fish in his shop for fourteen days. They stank so much he was ordered to throw them into the Ouse and threatened with a large fine if he transgressed so again. Ale was the staple drink of the people. There were alehouses in the villages and wayside taverns on the roads. Many townsfolk brewed their own ale so ale-tasters were appointed to check its quality and the selling prices. In 1472 a brewer was allowed to sell ale in his house at twopence for a gallon. The weakest ale was drunk by children and the very poor. Brewers were ordered not to deny a needy man or woman a pennyworth or halfpenny worth of ale. The wife of Nycolson was fined two shillings for selling ale at not less than twopence a gallon and Ric' Marshall's wife fourpence for not letting poor folk buy her ale. At the Great Inquest of October, 1533, Robert Pewe and Thomas Shyppyn were appointed ale-tasters for Gowthorpe and Robert Doule and John Dobb, officials for Micklegate - the two main areas of Selby. From 1266-67 it was the custom for the court in every locality to lay down the Assize, that was the price, size and quality of bread. Officers appointed to oversee the selling of bread in Selby around 1483 must have been neglecting their duties, for the court that year ordered them to make a weekly check:

> *for pur pepell yt lyffhis of the penny complens tham grettly yt the sys is nct kepid. (for poor people that lives off the penny complain greatly that the assize is not kept.)*

Pigs were the most common domesticated animals kept in the town of Selby. There were many regulations read out at the courts concerning the keeping of swine. All pigs, except sows with piglets, had to be ringed. Acorns were a favourite food but no-one was allowed to freely gather them in the woods. John Wright of Faxfleet had to pay a penalty of ten shillings for repeatedly ignoring this edict. It was not permissible for anyone, especially woodkeepers, to take their pigs into the woods or the church-yard without an authorised person. A payment known as 'pannage' had to be made to the owner of a woodland for the right of pasturing pigs there. No pannage was collected from the penny farms at Monk Fryston, Hillam and Hambleton one year "on account of the poverty of the tenants there". Herpam of New Lane was the appointed pig herdsman in 1519. Each day, with the help of a chosen few, he rounded up the pigs in Selby and took them to the woods to feed. When the pigs were returned they had to be confined to their sties for the night. Any man who did not let his animals go with the herd, except those confined in their own grounds, was fined fourpence. Rules were laid down concerning the pig-sties in the town. John Mitteley came up before a jury presided over by Thomas Elles, esquire, deputy to Sir Thomas Darcy, knt., charged with not keeping an efficient pig-sty. He was ordered to make proper drains and gutters and to wall up and make sound the whole west side of his pigsty towards the tenement of his neighbour so that:

> *no fylth, nor corropion, or dunge, come or discend into the grounde of John Goldall except that it be seeping.*

Thomas was advised on how to make suitable grates under his sty. He was also told to keep the dung within his own grounds or in the passage where it would not annoy his neighbour. Other animals were grazed on the common but the owners were warned not to put any unfit ones, such as "skabbed horses" to pasture there. Trespassers were not welcome:

> *That Symond Rae de Braton take of his cattle off our commen of Selby be Saynte Elene day.*

Symond was also fined 12d. for eating on the common, a practice forbidden by law.

The Court Leet encouraged people to maintain their property and the thoroughfares in the manner taught by the monks. Fences were ordered to be made and maintained between neighbours and around the common; gutters to be cleaned out to stop water flooding the pavements. At one April meeting the officials commanded all water-sewers and ditches were to be diked and scoured by Whitsuntide. It was also ordered that:

No man scaste no caryon in the newe layn,ne in no nother commen waye wher the Kynge's pepill passes.

Also, carrion was not to be thrown into the Dam nor "dung or muck" into the channels or upon the causey - a raised road over marshy ground.

The officials at these meetings, the forerunners of magistrates and parish councils controlled the markets and set the prices:

No man by no corn to the bell be gon aboght the town.

Yt every baxster maike goode brede and holesom for man's body, and sell acordyng as they by the corn.

They were especially against forestalling, a practice that was still causing great concern as late as the nineteenth century. William Broun met women at the town end with their geese which he bought from them and sold as his own at the market. Hobson and Heryson, two men from Gowdall, purchased salmon from the fishermen before they reached Selby market. These forestallers were ordered to leave town and threatened with a fine of 6s.8d. if they were found guilty again.

At the Great Inquest held in October 1533, not many years before the monks were no longer rulers in Selby, the officials meted out the punishments, laid down many rules for the inhabitants to live by, and then made it clear what they thought were the most important occupations in the town at that time. They exhorted the cordwainers to sew well their shoes and entreated them not to buy or use horseskins; the tanners or barkers, to tan or bark well their leather; the glovers to: *sewe wele theire glovys.*

1. Iron Age Burial Site

2. Selby Abbey showing the Cresent and New Street

3. Temple Manor

4. Tomb of Sir Hugh Pickworth, Selby Abbey

5. Selby Cross

6. Half-timbered houses on Gowthorpe

CHAPTER 4

ABBOTS AND KINGS

The Upkeep of the Abbey

The abbey was a dominant feature in the town of Selby for over four hundred years. The abbots, as lords of the manor, ruled over the lives of the people on their estates. The townsfolk practised the monks' religion for there were no other faiths for them to follow. As the centuries passed the fabric of the abbey church and its adjoining buildings was constantly in need of repair or being updated to incorporate the latest styles in architecture. There was nothing in the Benedictine Rules that forbade corporate wealth or magnificent buildings as long as the monks led a simple life. Repairs and alterations were dependent on the state of the abbey's finances. To run an establishment the size of Selby Abbey the man at the helm needed to be a businessman as well as a devout Christian. The raising of funds involved an ability to acquire gifts of land and property, to raise loans, to sell annual pensions and corroderies and to have the experience to manage all the assets of the abbey wisely.

In 1307 Abbot William de Aslaghby (1300-1313) successfully petitioned Pope Clement V *for the physical possession of the church of Adlingfleet in the diocese of York and a portion in perpetuity for the vicar who will serve in the church.* The abbot explained that the monks needed extra funds to do some very costly repairs which included the abbey church that was, *wasted by great age and the monastery, owing to the ravages of time, is so diminished in its revenue and greatly weighed down by so many debts that their own resources are not sufficient for making repairs of this sort.* William added that their funds were not even large enough to cover other necessary expenses such as maintaining their accustomed hospitality or other pressing needs. On the authority of the pope, William Pickering, Archdeacon of Nottingham, papal delegate, together with the Lord Bishop of Coventry and Lichfield, informed the abbot that his wishes had been granted. The parish church of Adlingfleet, south-east of Goole, was given to the abbey, with all rights and appurtenances. The gift was intended to help with the repairs, increase worship at the church and cover the expenses of a vicar. It was stated that if the rector retired or died the brothers of Selby Abbey could freely and legally enter and take possession of Adlingfleet church without the assent of any other authority. The part of the grant reserved to support the vicar and cover his episcopal and other dues was similar to that given to the vicar at Brayton. Land was provided for him in Adlingfleet with common pasture and the right (turbary) to dig enough turves for his own use only, in addition the vicar was to have a sheepfold, next to the one owned by the abbey, 60 feet long by 25 feet wide. He was to receive the priest's tithes and lenten tithes in goods and livestock from the tenants, mortuary payments for the dead and also marriage fees. Robert Thorp, vicar at Adlingfleet at that time, accepted the agreement on behalf of himself and his successors.

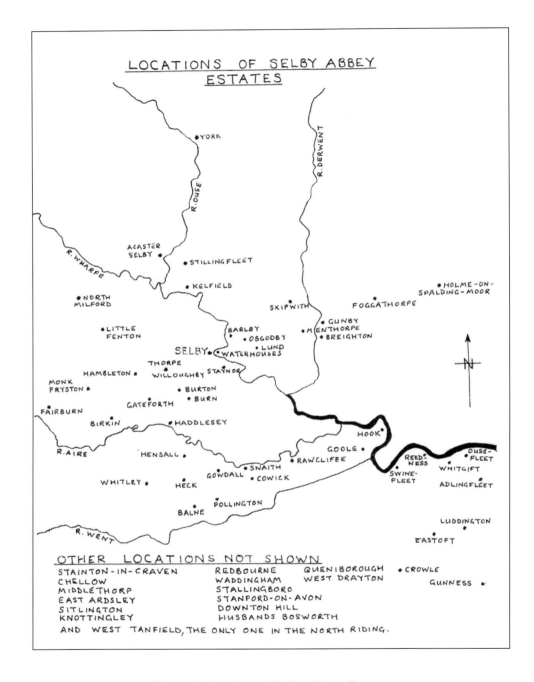

Figure 4. Location of Selby Abbey Estates

Not all the abbots of Selby possessed the skills required in maintaining a flourishing abbey. Along with outside influences, this sometimes resulted in the accumulation of large debts. The size of the debt did not always reflect on the efficiency of the abbot in office but on past events. In 1322 the abbey had built up a large debt through the rebuilding of the choir. Begun around 1280, it is said only the lower sacristy was ready for use at the beginning of the fourteenth century. Further work was seriously curtailed by the hostilities that broke out between England and Scotland. Ready money was not always available for small transactions such as buying grain or paying for minor repairs. Some officers raised extra funds from the sale of wood, turves and excess produce. This was not the case in 1404 when the granger's expenditure exceeded his income by over £107. This monk, Peter de Roclif gave details of why this had happened. He explained that recently corn and malt had not been sold but kept for the office, and boards and timber from oaks delivered to them for fuel were not sold on, as was the custom. He had also not received the full amount due to him in rents. The profits and tithes of Selby from the northern side of the town had been smaller because of the lower price of grain or sometimes, the lack of water for the mill in summer. Brother Peter had raised money by buying corn, barley, dredge and oats, which he had then sold on through his servants; the funds raised were used for improvements within the monastery and elsewhere. Extra expenses incurred by him in 1404 included the purchase of hay for the horses of the extern cellarer which, by custom, had normally been paid for by the bursars. These officers had also left the granger to pay for the servants' livery; another custom ignored! No help had been forthcoming from the bursars for repairs that had obviously been neglected by their predecessors but which Brother Peter carried out despite lack of funds. He undertook extensive repairs on houses, mills, and other property outside the walls of the monastery. Renovations were also carried out on the malt-kiln house, horse-mill, turf-house roof and the stables, all of which were threatened with ruin. It was Brother Peter who tackled the costly repairs to the wharf and crane on the banks of the Ouse.

The work involved in the building and repairing of the monastery buildings was undertaken by craftsmen from around Selby. The nave and north transept were worked upon by masons who had helped to build Durham Cathedral. When the north aisle of the abbey was being rebuilt, Robert Cooper, a mason, was brought to Selby to give advice on the making of the stonework. Masons were held in high esteem, as is clear from the following:

> *1288: To Thomas de Thornet the Mason, for his work and service, 20s. a year from our Treasury also one robe as is issued to our armour bearers, And if the said Thomas shall be unable to work at any time through infirmity he shall receive his full corrody and one robe and 10s. per annum.*
> *Thomas is not to depart from our service without special licence.*

Glaziers and plumbers were in great demand. When the west gable of the monastery needed new glass, a glazier glazed three lights using 49 square feet of glass, costing ninepence a foot. Adam Smith made bars out of Spanish iron for the windows. These were smeared with pitch and the glass secured using 2000 brad (flattish) nails. A plumber then melted 191 stones (in weight) of lead from lead ash using two quarters of charcoal. Most of the charcoal was made in Hambleton woods. Plumbers were kept very busy. One was paid to solder the gutters of the cloister then to search for and solder any

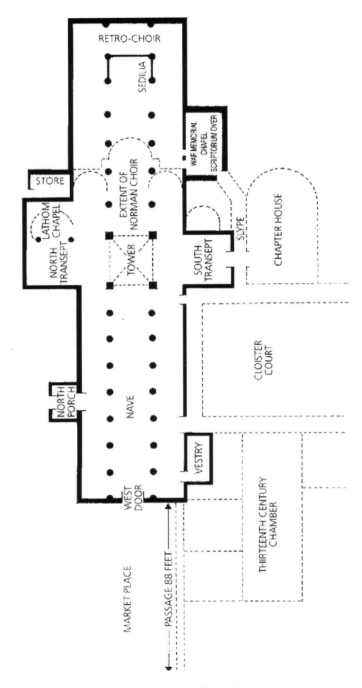

Figure 5. Plan of Selby Abbey

defects found on the roof of the choir and the gutters around it. He was also employed to take down the old lead roof of the vestry on the north side, repair and solder it before replacing it. The Keeper of the Fabric was responsible for buying the tools and other small items needed for many of these tasks. He purchased ladders, ropes, chains, chisels, axes and other tools. Adam Smith was paid an annual sum of 3s.4d. to keep some of these implements sharp and in good condition. The Keeper paid for odd pieces of wainscot out of which masons' moulds were made using tackets, (later known as tacks) for joining the pieces together.

William de Suthwell, a master mason, and three other masons were involved in the dismantling and rebuilding of the cloister in 1398-99. Numerous other craftsmen and labourers were also employed in this task which cost the bursars almost £69. Stone was quarried at Monk Fryston, then carted to the abbey. Labourers helped the masons dismantle the old cloisters and then prepared the ground for the craftsmen. Alder trees were felled and stakes made from the wood. Men were paid to carry boards of wainscot from the wharf to the abbey; this was then sawn into pieces for use in the cloister's roof. A master carpenter was paid four shillings a week to work on the roof whilst John Brennard, carpenter, received 40 pence a week to carve bosses for the joints of the ceiling of the cloister. The nine carpenters working on the building did not receive food with their pay except for those who, at the beginning, had to go into the woods to search for suitable trees. All of them, however, received an allowance for gloves. New lead sheets were cast from the old roof and none of the surplus went to waste. John Hare, plumber, used it to roof eight corners of the higher lantern of the great kitchen; this important room also sported a weather-cock. Ropes had to be found for hauling the lead sheets onto the roof. Other items purchased during the building of the new cloisters were lime, sand, wax and resin for repairing the stones, Spanish iron, and barrels for making tubs for the masons. Tools and nails for preparing a bowl for casting the lead sheets were bought, and one lock with a key for the door of the lead-house, *"to keep safe the lead"*.

At times like this, when money was available the monastery was a hive of activity as buildings near to ruin were repaired, whilst others were rebuilt in the latest architectural styles. Abbot Hugh's successors soon altered the simple cross design he had shaped for the church. Whilst the abbey enjoyed a very large revenue Hugh's solid pillars were replaced with the simple Transitional style of delicate shafts encircling the central column. Between 1280 and 1340 as the community grew, a new Gothic building was developed around Hugh's choir, which had only been built to accommodate a small number of monks. Stained glass was put into windows that had previously been filled with trellis work until the abbey abounded with samples of the art. One stained glass window fitted into the church during the fourteenth century, depicted the Washington family's coat of arms. The shield was described in 1585 as being *"argent, two bars and in chief three mullets pierced, gules"*. It is one of a minority of examples of the Washington arms that show the mullets holed. These star-shaped mullets or rowels represent the spiked revolving discs at the end of the spurs that were worn by knights in medieval times. The belief held by many people, that the present day American Stars and Stripes flag, was derived from the Washington family arms as depicted in the window in Selby Abbey Church, has never been satisfactorily proven. Ancestors of the Washington family came from the village of Washton, near Richmond. It was in the seventeenth century that one of their descendants, settled in Virginia and became a tobacco planter. The presence of the arms in Selby Abbey suggests a benefaction. A Nicholas

Wessington was mentioned in the 1397 account rolls of Selby Abbey. Along with other servants of the abbey he had been left a legacy by William, son of John de Escryk, priest of Selby. This included food and an annual salary which was quoted by the bursars as being 26s.8d. Nearly twenty years later John Wessington became prior of Durham (1416-1446). He contributed to the fabric of Hemingbrough Church; it is only five miles from Selby so the prior would have had some contact with the abbey and may have made a donation to its upkeep. There is also a connection with the Tempest family; Eleanor, daughter of William de Wessington, (died 1399), was married to Sir William Tempest. At some time both their coats of arms were on display in the Abbey.

The Early Abbots

During the time the monks were lords of the manor of Selby the abbey was ruled by 33 abbots. Over the same period, from 1069 to 1539 20 kings were to occupy the English throne. The first of the 33 abbots was Benedict (1069-1097) who set up the small religious community in the area of Church Hill and whose story has been told. Under the second abbot, Hugh (1097-1123) the monks moved from Church Hill to the area where the Abbey Church stands today. Hugh was the son of Ilbert de Lacy. Following the Norman Conquest Ilbert was awarded lands in Lancashire, Nottinghamshire, Lincolnshire, and 166 lordships in Yorkshire. Out of these possessions he gave the manor of Hambleton to Selby Abbey. His son, Hugh, laid down the foundations of the Abbey in stone on slightly elevated ground in otherwise flat landscape, but even there the water table stood only three feet below the surface. The last Ice Age had left a layer of wet, impervious clay about one foot below the water table. Today layers of clay still cover much of the Selby area making for drainage problems which over the years has led to frequent flooding, the cause of so much havoc and distress. During the twelfth century wet clay and the speed with which the Norman tower of the abbey church was built later caused sinking problems. The cracked and distorted arches that can be seen today in the nave of the church were the result of this early subsidence. The raising of other parts of the monastery was spread over a longer length of time so the weight of it was slowly applied to the clay. The water was gradually squeezed out giving the clay time to dry out and become hard and firm. Hugh had begun the building of Selby Abbey in stone and by the time of his departure the town had one of the most impressive and majestic churches in the north. Over the centuries much of Hugh's work has disappeared. For example, an aisled chancel built by Hugh was destroyed two centuries later to make way for the decorated choir and in 1690 the twelfth century south transept was ruined by the fall of the central tower.

C.C.Hodge, in his *"Architectural History of Selby Abbey,"* 1893, stated it was clear that Hugh had built the whole of the eastern arm and had, at some time, enclosed the cloister from the then open ground on the north in order to stop unauthorised persons entering the building. Hodge also gave a brief description of part of the lay-out of the church and adjoining buildings. He stated that the western range abutted against the church which, in the fifteenth century, consisted of a timbered structure on a stone basement, thirty three inches thick and buttressed. Connected to it was a dormitory with cellarage beneath it, the abbot's chambers and a long passage, with chambers adjoining, which led to the abbey gate, some 88 feet to the west of the western end of the church. The buildings were initially half-timbered with wooden tracery in the windows and frescos painted on the interior walls. There were two newel stairs connecting the dormitory with the church and with the cloister. One was a day stairway by which the monks reached their sleeping cubicles from the cloister for their siestas. The second enabled the brothers to gain access to the church at matins without having to venture outside. Hodge believed that the stairs at Selby did not lead directly into the church but into a passage between the undercroft of the dormitory and the south aisle of the nave. The built- up doorway can still be seen in the aisle wall of the abbey church.

The First Crusades

William the Conqueror had given Benedict one carucate of land at Selby on which to build an abbey. The Conqueror died in September 1087, ten years before Hugh became abbot of Selby Abbey. The ancestral lands of Normandy were left to the eldest of William's nine children, Robert II (Robert Curthose), and England to his second son, William Rufus, who as William II ruled from 1087 to 1100. He was a strong king and was successful in finally bringing the rebellious northern counties under Norman control. His elder brother caused William continuous trouble in disputes over who was the rightful heir to the English throne. William Rufus gained some respite from this problem when, in 1096, Robert joined the First Crusade to the Holy Land.

After the fall of the Roman Empire, lands had been broken up and Palestine ruled by Arabs and then Turks. During the presence of the Romans, buildings had been erected at holy places and pilgrims had begun to travel from many countries to worship at them. The Arabs respected other religions and left the Christian travellers in peace. The Mohammedans were more fanatical; they attacked and drove out the pilgrims as they attempted to cross Turkish owned territories in Asia and Africa. The passions of the Christians at home were greatly roused by the pitiful tales brought back by surviving pilgrims. In 1095, at the Council of Clermont, the Pope appealed for help to fight the Turks. Bishops, barons and knights from numerous lands swore to avenge the cause of Jesus Christ. They agreed to wear a cross on their breast and shoulders as a pledge to their engagement. During the long struggles with the Turks, one tenth of the benefices received by the Pope from the churches were given as a tax to the Crusaders. This would have included contributions from Selby Abbey and the churches under its jurisdiction. It is reported that thousands joined the cause to regain access to the Holy Land. However, the first Crusade was a disaster; great numbers of pilgrims perished on the way from hunger, privation or disease, whilst many were killed on reaching Palestine. A second Crusade had some success. By 1099, after a dreadful carnage, Antioch and then Jerusalem were taken and the standard of the Cross raised. It is believed that Robert, Duke of Normandy, was one of the leaders of this expedition.

After the capture of Jerusalem, lodgings were assigned to the crusaders in a building close to Solomon's Temple from which the Knights Templar took their name. The Knights Templar was a religious military Order constituted around 1118 by nine French knights. They joined together to wage perpetual war against such people as the Turks in order that Christians everywhere could travel in safety. They took vows of poverty, celibacy and obedience, similar to those taken by the monks at Selby Abbey, but they led a military life. The Templars also received gifts of land, money and privileges in the same manner as the community at Selby as the following report shows:

1287: lnquisition made at York before the Sheriff by two knights and ten others who say on oath that it is not to the damage or annoyance of the king or others neighbouring that Roger, son of Roger Forester of Hathelesye (Haddlesey) and his wife convey to Roger de Turbeulye, Master, and Brethren of the Knights Templar in England of one messuage and two bovates of land with appurtenances in Warley, in parish of Halifax.

The Templars eventually held over 70 properties in Yorkshire, of which the most important was at Temple Hirst, a village six miles south of Selby. The abbey was involved with this Order throughout its existence and at its demise.

Henry I

Hugh was still Abbot of Selby when William Rufus died in August, 1100. The king was succeeded by his younger brother Henry, who was to rule England for 35 years. During his reign he, like William Rufus, faced opposition from Robert II, Duke of Normandy. Supported by powerful magnates the war of succession lasted until 1106 when Henry finally conquered Normandy and captured his brother. Robert was Henry's prisoner for the remaining 28 years of his life but Henry had to fight very hard, and at great expense, to hold on to the Duchy of Normandy.

It has been said by several historians that Henry I was born in Selby but this claim, and the actual date of his birth remain controversial. Orderic Vitalis (1075-c1142) author of *Ecclesiastical History* noted it was around Easter 1068 when William sent to Normandy to request his wife, Matilda to join him in England. Also in London on the 11th. May, that same year, Aldred, Archbishop of York, anointed Matilda as the King's consort. This event was noted in the Annals of Winchester followed by these words, *"and not many days later she brought her son, Henry, into the light of* day". Orderic, who counted the years as beginning and ending at Easter, recorded that after Matilda had been crowned, and before the year came to an end, she gave birth to a son called Henry whom she made heir of all her land in England.

There has been no mention found of the actual birthplace of Henry I in any documents predating William Camden's *'Brittania"*. When describing Selby Abbey in his nationwide survey of the counties, published in 1586, Camden wrote: *"The year after the foundation (AD. 1070) King William repairing hither with his beloved queen to settle the endowment, she is said to have been delivered here of her youngest son, afterwards Henry I"*. Later scholars enlarged upon this statement, many stating that Matilda was on her way to join her husband in the north when she had to seek help with the birth of her baby in Selby. As late as the eighteenth century a room in the remains of the abbey buildings, next to the abbey gateway, was being displayed to visitors as the place where Henry was said to have been born. Inscriptions and arms pictured in the chamber in question showed it had been part of the buildings added to the house at the gateway, in the early sixteenth century, by Abbot Robert Deeping, from Croyland Abbey!

Many researchers see the story of Henry's birth at Selby as a legend that came into being after the dissolution of the monasteries. They believe the Selby monk, writer of the *Historia Selebiensis Monasterii* would have been aware, when he wrote his manuscript in 1174, that William's son Henry had reigned as King of England for 35 years but significantly, nowhere in his narrative does he make any reference to his possible birth at Selby. This event surely would have been worthy of note.

Also, neither Henry nor his father, William, ever hailed Selby as his birthplace in any of their charters concerning the monks or the town. One of the mandates issued between 1100 and 1108 by Henry with regards to the monks, intimates that at some time the brothers may have been casting their eyes over other estates gifted to them, and had made it known to those in higher authority that a move to a more salubrious place than Selby would be welcome. Henry emphatically blocked this move but did not claim it was because Selby was his birthplace.

> *Henry, King of England, to Archbishop Gerard, Osbert the sheriff and all his French and English barons in Yorkshire. Know that I will and command that the abbey of Saint Germanus of Selby remain with immunity in the place where it was founded by my father and mother, nor should it be removed from that place to another but should remain there with all the customary dues and privileges which it possessed on favourable terms in the time of my father, mother and brother, and whatever my father wanted for the benefit of the same church for God and for my soul, I want and grant.*

Whether Henry I was born in Selby or not has yet to be proven either way. What is known to be true is that the monks stayed in Selby and, during his 26 years as Abbot, Hugh laid the foundations of a beautiful monastery and greatly increased the wealth of the convent. He looked after the religious needs of his brethren, the people in the town and those in the surrounding areas. In 1123, at a meeting in the chapter house of the abbey, eminent dignitaries, including the Bishop of Durham, Bishop of the Orkneys, Abbot of York, the Prior of Pontefract and many others, reluctantly gave Hugh permission to resign his office. It is said that after visiting many holy places he returned home and retired to a farm, south of Bishop Wood. It was then known as 'Scablu', but later changed to 'Scalm'.

New Abbots and Royal Usurpers

Herbertus (1123-1127), the next abbot came from the abbey of St Albans. His election was approved by Henry I. A good, devout person, steadfast in his prayers and religious duties he lacked the skills of administration and leadership needed for his position. Without a strong person at its helm the once thriving monastery quickly began to deteriorate. Fields were left uncultivated, buildings began to collapse for want of repair, barns were empty and cattle died for want of herbage. A timely visit to York by the pope's legate saved the monastery from ruin. Herbertus consulted this official about his difficulties and was advised, quite simply, to retire back to his favourite abode, the abbey of St. Albans.

His successor Durannus (1127-1137) had a completely different character. He came from St. Mary's of York and was described as a man of considerable ability, shrewd but generous, and endowed with a great variety of skills. Durannus was also a handsome and attractive person who had, as the writer of the Historia put it, "a *vile familiarity with women of ill-repute*". This caused him to be the subject of gossip throughout the shire bringing disgrace to the ordained. Finally, when after many reproofs by his brothers, he still did not conform to his vows, Durannus was compelled to resign. He retired to Cluny where, many years later, he became prior of a Cluniac monastery. It was not recorded whether he had become a reformed person!

Henry I died during the time Durannus was abbot of Selby. He had lost his wife, Matilda II, the sister of Edgar of Scotland, in 1118 and his only legitimate son in

1120. Seven years after this he had made the barons swear to recognise his only legitimate daughter, Matilda, as his heir. King Henry I died in 1135, supposedly, it is said, from a 'surfeit of lampreys'. Prior to his sudden demise the king had been involved in violent quarrels with his daughter and her husband, Geoffrey of Anjou. This discord re-opened the old divisions between the Anglo-Norman baronage and allowed one of these barons to seize the crown from the designated heirs. The opportunist was Stephen, younger son of Stephen, Count of Blois and Adela, daughter of William the Conqueror. Not only had Stephen been made a wealthy magnate by his uncle, Henry I, he had also been present when the barons had sworn the oath to support Matilda in her claim to the throne. Nevertheless, Stephen was popular, his wife came from English royal blood and he was present in the country and not always abroad as Matilda tended to be. Also in his favour was the uneasiness felt by the English at the thought of having a woman on the throne. The Norman knights nursed a hatred of Geoffrey of Anjou which had been further fuelled by the savage behaviour of his troops in Normandy. Empress Matilda, however, did have strong support from Scotland and Wales. As the barons took sides, years of civil war followed Henry's stern but peaceful rule. There was an orgy of destruction as conflict followed conflict.

David, King of Scotland, uncle to Empress Matilda, took her side against Stephen. He launched attacks on Northern England in the years 1136 to 1138. When he advanced to enter Yorkshire, forces from the county moved to Thirsk and from there to Northallerton. They were led by Archbishop Thurstan of York and Walter Espec, Lord of Helmsley and Wark, supported by many barons. Ilbert de Lacy, one of their leaders was the grandson of the Norman knight, Ilbert, who fought with the Conqueror. William had introduced Knight service whereby certain landholders had to provide a number of knights, fully equipped and ready for battle. In this respect the monks at Selby Abbey were obliged to give the service of one such knight to the de Lacy family. It is probable that Selby was represented in the fight against the Scots. The 'holy war' against the Scots culminated in a battle near Northallerton on the 22nd. August, 1138. The archbishop and his English army marched with banners of St. Peter of York, St. John of Beverley and St. Wilfrid of Ripon flying from a mast surmounted by a pyx (religious container) and carried on a cart, thus earning the conflict that followed the title of 'The Battle of the Standard'. It was a hard fought contest but David was defeated and fled the field. He continued to attack Northumberland but Yorkshire was spared further hostilities. It is interesting to note, *"for acqittance of forfeitures which he had committed against the church of St. Germaine"*, Ilbert's brother, Henri, subsequently confirmed to the monks of Selby Abbey the manor of Hambleton and released them of Knight service.

Many people in the north of England had joined Archbishop Thurstan in his battles against King David because they were perturbed by the actions of certain 'native Scots' who used the campaigns as an opportunity to collect slaves. This practise had ceased in England sometime in the twelfth century although ancient documents reveal that 'natives' or serfs, were still being given as gifts, especially to the church:

Grant by John de Lasceles to monks of Selby of Archel his native, with his land which extends from his house in Selby, with two bovates in Brayton.

A serf or native, was the property of his lord and was bound to do whatever work his master ordered him to do. Sir Adam de Neufmarche (or Newmarket) whose family held lands at Womersley and Askern gave his serf, Peter, son of Hugo de

Moseley, to the Templars residing at what is now known as Temple Hirst. He was given to them, along with all his goods, chattels and his offspring, on condition that Peter and his descendants should be free. This meant that neither Peter nor his family could be handed over to another master but they were still obliged to work as 'free' labourers on the Templars' estates. Under the feudal system Peter, like every other man, had to acknowledge a superior lord. In return for this 'freedom' Peter paid a penny per annum to provide a light for the altar in the Templars' preceptory at Hirst.

Following the removal of Durannus as abbot, the abbey at Selby was without a leader for two years whilst the many applicants from inside the monastery vied with each other for the position. The monks had a licence from the crown to elect their own abbot but in this instance the matter could not be settled; they therefore appealed to Archbishop Thurstan for help. Taking his advice they united to elect Walter, head of the nearby Pontefract priory. Walter (1139-1143) was a man of mature years, deeply religious and esteemed for his spiritual duties. Unlike Herbertus, secular affairs were not neglected but put into the capable hands of one of his brethren. This monk was known as William the Great who was described in an earlier document as a bursar. Although Walter devoted himself with zeal to spiritual matters he did not entirely divorce himself from other affairs of the abbey and its estates. He did his best to see that the house did not incur unwanted expenses such as loans or run the risk of losing any of its assets. The loss of this able abbot through illness after only four years in office must have dealt a devastating blow to the abbey and the community around it. The well-being of the monks and the prosperity of the abbey directly affected the lives of the ordinary people.

They Built Castles

Walter was succeeded by Helias Paganellus (1143-1153). Helias had followed the military career of a knight until he took monastic vows and entered the Benedictine Order at York's Holy Trinity Priory, refounded by his father. This devout, learned man was elected as Prior by his fellow monks and soon after, on Walter's death, was called to become Abbot of Selby. His military skills must have been especially useful during the turmoil caused by Stephen and Matilda as they fought for the crown of England. Barons erected strongholds on their estates in defiance of their king. The Saxon chronicler stated;

> In this king's time all was dissension, and evil, and rapine. Against him soon rose the rich men. They had sworn oaths but no truth maintained. They built castles which they held out against him. They cruelly oppressed the wretched men of the land with castle work. They filled the castles with devils and evil men. They seized those whom they supposed to have any goods, and threw them into prison for their gold and silver, and inflicted on them considerable tortures. Some they hanged up by the feet, some by the thumbs or by the beard, and hung coats of mail on their feet. They put them into dungeons with adders and snakes. They burned all the towns. Thou mightest go a day's journey and not find a man sitting in a town nor an acre of land tilled.

Selby did not escape this turmoil. It suffered greatly during the early years of Helias's time as abbot when Henri de Lacy built a castle in the town. Though no evidence of where it was actually sited has been uncovered it is believed that it was erected on slightly elevated land flanked by Selby Dam, Kirk Dyke and Micklegate. Part of this area was examined by MAP in the 1990s. It was found to contain signs of occupation and several dykes that had undergone many changes dating as far back as the twelfth century. Selby castle most probably would have been of the motte and bailey type. That is, a wooden defensive tower built on a mound, or motte, which had been formed from the earth dug out from an encircling ditch. A palisade of stakes would have then formed one or more surrounding lines of defence. The peasants of the neighbourhood were possibly, under duress, forced to help build this castle. They were caught up in the hostilities that broke out when Count William d'Aumale, an enemy of Henri de Lacy's, learnt of the fortifications being erected in Selby. William, accompanied by his fighting men and many mercenaries invaded the town intent on collecting plenty of booty. The anonymous writer of the *Historia* recorded that William tried to enter Selby many times but was thwarted by the steadfastness of the defenders, until he found a secret entry through the monastery buildings. By this time, however, the townsfolk had gathered their belongings together and fled to the church and churchyard for safety. Angered by so many empty houses the troops caused much havoc and destruction and then gathered in battle array to attack the castle. A whole day was spent in fruitless efforts to breach the castle's defences. Furious at their failure to do so they gave vent to their anger by torching the town. The Selby monk recorded, *"The fire found fuel from every quarter and once alight did not abate until it had begun to reduce the fabric of almost all the town to one blazing inferno"*. The *Historia* also related how in the midst of the flames, even though houses were packed closely up to it on every side, the chapel remained unscathed. William did eventually gain possession of Selby castle and dwelt there for a considerable time, plundering and terrorising the whole neighbourhood.

Helias Paganellus ruled wisely over the abbey for nine years whilst hostilities continued to break out all over the country. He put his future as abbot in jeopardy, however, when he vehemently opposed the election to the primacy of Henry Murdac, Archbishop of York. The embittered archbishop ignored the virtuous conduct of Helias and in 1152, by cunning and underhand behaviour, obliged the abbot to resign. He had posed as Helias's friend and confidante and had eventually extracted an oath from the unsuspecting abbot that he would always trust and obey the archbishop's counsel. Therefore, when Henry advised him to resign his office on the grounds he was inadequate for the position he held, Helias could not oppose the archbishop and regretfully laid down his pastoral office. The monks elected a fellow brother, William, to take his place, but again the archbishop wielded his power. He chose Germanus, a monk from St. Albans as Helias's successor. The monks refused to accept this ruling for over a year demanding that Helias be allowed to return or be permitted to resign through the proper channels. It was only when Henry threatened them with excommunication that the protests stopped and Germanus was accepted. Three months later Henry Murdac died; Helias restored to office for, as it was said, he had been removed unlawfully and contrary to canonical procedure. Meanwhile Germanus had ridden back to St. Albans where he sought the help of the Pope through his legate, Theobald, Archbishop of Canterbury. Germanus was reinstated as Abbot of Selby for Archbishop Osbert and the majority of the clergy who had supported Helias turned away from him and went over to the other side. Fully confused, Helias returned to York to spend the rest of his life there in peace.

Temple Hirst Preceptory

It was during this unrest in the abbey that one of the first of the Knights Templar preceptories, in Yorkshire, was founded near Selby. The manors were so named because the Order of the Temple of Solomon lived by rule, or precept. The preceptories served as refuges for the few knights who, from time to time, were out of the combative activities of the Crusades. Like the monks, they guided and controlled the large number of farm-workers, both free and servile, who worked on their estates. They also kept the people on whom they relied for tangible support aware of their presence and their cause. The preceptory established near Selby was at West Hirst, later Temple Hirst, in the ancient parish of Birkin. Ralph de Hastings of Fenwick near Doncaster, as well as of Suffolk, gave the Templars the manor in 1152. The hamlet of East Hirst, which stretched from the boundaries of Carlton up to the "ploughland of West Hirst", was given to the Templars by John de Courtney and his wife, Emma, who had inherited the land. This village eventually became known as Hirst Courtney. The Courtneys held property in Brayton. Documents show that when Walter Hall of Selby was granting land to his daughter, he gave her seven acres lying in Langley, Brayton, described as being next to the land of Robert Curtenay. The Templars were given lands in Burn and East and West Haddlesey; part of the latter included *'a croft in which is a corn mill, opposite to the gate of Hirst'*. There was much interchange between Selby Abbey and the Knights Templar in both secular and religious matters. In one instance tenements in Potterlawe, near Eggborough, were gifted to Selby Abbey by the Templars in exchange for the tithes of Willoughton, in Lincolnshire.

The End of Stephen's Reign

King Stephen and Empress Matilda were still in conflict over the throne of England whilst Henry, Matilda's eldest son was helping his father in France. Following many successful campaigns in Normandy by Geoffrey of Anjou and Henry, the Duchy of Normandy came under their control. When Geoffrey died in 1151, Henry ruled over both Anjou and Normandy. When, at nineteen, he married Eleanor of Aquitaine and governed her land, he became the richest prince in France. He then turned his attention to England where he set out to gain the crown for his mother, the Empress Matilda. Stephen could not control the barons and many in the civil services and the church had turned against him. In December 1153, after many confrontations, Henry was reluctantly accepted by Stephen as the heir to the throne. It was agreed that the king would rule during his lifetime but they would strive together to get rid of the mercenary soldiers and the unlicensed castles built during the unrests. Actions by the French then made it imperative for Henry to return to Normandy. This left Stephen free to continue his own policy of destroying only those fortifications built by the barons who had been in arms against him.

There appears to be no record of what happened to the castle at Selby but Stephen came in person to the town on his way to lay siege to a fortification at Drax. Robert de Gaunt was the second husband of Alice Pagnel. They had chosen to support Matilda during the conflicts. One of Robert's knights, Sir Philip de Colville of Lincolnshire, was holding the castle at Drax for the Pagnel family. He refused the orders sent to him to dismantle or destroy the fortress. He also stood firm against delivering up the castle to be burnt hoping that the faithful support and strength of his comrades and the copious supply of food and weapons he had at hand would win him the day. Stephen assembled his army from the nearest provinces and led his men from Selby through Brayton and Barlow to reach Drax. The king and his entourage must have been received favourably in Selby for it is definitely known that three charters were signed by Stephen at that time, all to the benefit of Selby Abbey. The abbot took advantage of Stephen's presence in the area to get royal confirmation of the gifts bestowed on the monastery by William the Conqueror and later monarchs. One of the documents was witnessed and signed on the field where the king was laying siege to Drax castle. It was acknowledged by such powerful magnates as Hugh de Puiset, Prince Bishop of the Palatinate of Durham; Robert de Chesney, Bishop of Lincoln and Richard de Lucy, Royal Justiciar, a loyal servant to King Stephen throughout his reign. A mandate to the sheriff and ministers of Yorkshire, was also signed by the king. It directed that the abbot and the monks of Selby should have the same liberties and customs as they enjoyed in the time of King Henry, his uncle.

Mercenaries in Selby

The castle at Drax was destroyed in the summer of 1154. In October of the same year, King Stephen died; he was buried in the Abbey of Faversham in Kent. Henry, the eldest son of Geoffrey Plantagenet of Anjou and Empress Matilda ascended the throne. Henry II (1154 - 1189) spent the first years of his reign in territorial expansion. He became unpopular amongst his people when he was accused of having corrupt judges and of oppressing the Church. His reign was also marred by the behaviour of his rebellious sons. Henry did, however, collect together a team of able administrators to help him rule over his vast domain. They introduced many remarkable legal reforms and their doings contributed towards the centralization of government and the development of the judicial system. Germanus was abbot of Selby during the first seven years of Henry's reign. He was described as an excellent and decent man who possessed every virtue that became a monk. His time as abbot seems to have passed peacefully until it was cut short by a severe illness from which he died in 1160.

Gilbert de Vere was a member of the Lincolnshire branch of the Vere or Veer family. After taking holy orders he entered the monastery at Selby and was elected abbot in 1160. It is probably in consequence of this that his father, Guy de Vere, gave the abbey the advowson of Bottesford, Leicester.

In 1174, during Gilbert's time in office, the townspeople of Selby invoked the wrath of Henry II by allowing Flemish mercenaries to enter the town and plunder their homes. The events which brought Flemish soldiers to Yorkshire began the year before. With Henry II at the height of his power, good administration had produced the monies he needed to pay for strong fortifications and a well-organised field army. Then a family quarrel broke out resulting in a great rebellion that spread through England and abroad. The discord began when Count Humbot III of Maurienne and Savoy agreed to the marriage of his heiress, Alice, to Henry's youngest son, John. He also promised to give a dowry in the Alps and Rousillon but asked that his future son-in-law be similarly endowed. Henry decided to give John three castles in Anjou. This was when the seeds of discontent already sown amongst his family increased. Since 1170 his eldest son had been referred to by many as, Henry the Young King. For reasons that are not clear he had been crowned king that year by the Archbishop of York; an act which became part of the sequence that led to the murder of Thomas Becket, Archbishop of Canterbury. The young Henry, even though he was the titular king of England, Duke of Normandy and Count of Anjou, did not possess one single castle. He strongly objected to his father's gift to John and demanded to have the effective government of his inheritance. When this was forcefully denied him by the king, Henry fled to France. His mother, Eleanor of Aquitaine, sent his brothers, Richard and Geoffrey to join him there; the queen was unable to follow for she was captured and put in prison.

Louis VII took Henry, his son-in-law, under his protection and rallied his followers to the young man's cause. King Henry's rebellious son made extravagant promises of riches and estates to the French barons, especially to Philip, Count of Flanders. His promises to the pope and the church of sweeping reforms, was the signal for a general insurrection. All the hidden grievances brought about by over twenty years of strong, firm government came to the surface; resentful subjects joined together to rebel against their rulers. There were several uprisings in Gascony, Normandy and Anjou, followed by a revolt in Brittany. At home English Earls including those of Chester, Norfolk and Leicester, all took up arms against the king. The North was attacked by William, the Lion King of Scots and his brother, David. By Christmas, however, the uprisings abroad had been subdued whilst Richard de Lucy dealt successfully with the English rebels. In September the Earls of Leicester and Norfolk, together with Flemish mercenaries, had invaded Suffolk, but by October they were defeated.

Pockets of resistance remained, especially in the North. In 1174 the Bishop of Durham invited Flemish mercenaries to assist in the revolt against the king. Before they arrived the sheriff of Yorkshire, Robert of Estouteville, aided by supporters of Henry II, captured the Scottish king whilst he was besieging Alnwick. Within weeks of this, the Bishop's nephew, Count de Bar sur Seine, landed at Hartlepool with 40 knights and 500 Flemings. The battle already being lost with the capture of the Lion King, the bishop gave the soldiers 40 days' pay and leave to return home. Whilst Count Hugh and his knights were employed to safeguard the castle at Northallerton, many foreign soldiers stayed to roam the countryside. It was at this time that Henry II accused the townspeople of Selby of allowing Flemish mercenaries to enter the town and rob them of their goods and chattels. The town was fined 100 shillings for letting this happen. It is recorded that a William de Selby was accused of not stopping the rebel soldiers when he saw them enter the town, and for this he had to pay a further fine.

Gilbert, the Abbot of Selby, is believed to have died ten years after this event, which left the monks without a leader. The abbey, as was usual in such circumstances, was placed in the hands of the king. Henry II appointed Hugh Murdac his chaplain, who was from the same family as Archbishop Murdac, to hold the office until an abbot was chosen. This process was not hurried for whilst the abbey had no leader its revenue went to the Crown. Out of the income accrued by 1185 around £216 was allowed for food and clothing for the monks. The amount that went to the king at the end of those two years was described as being £169 in new money and £278 in old money (marks).

Richard I

Roger de London was promoted from prior to Abbot of Selby in 1189; the same year Richard I was crowned King of England. Richard (1189-1199) had been entrusted with Aquitaine after his father, Henry II had pardoned him for his part in the revolts of

1173-4. His father had also helped him in a confrontation with his elder brother, Henry the Young King. It was in 1183 during one of these conflicts that the heir to the throne lost his life. Henry II's concern in providing for his youngest son, John, apparently at Richard's expense, made Richard, like his brother before him, flee abroad for support. This came from Philip of France who, at Henry's death in 1189, helped to ensure Richard's succession to almost the whole of the Angevin/Plantagenet Empire. This consisted of England, Normandy, Aquitaine, Anjou, Maine and Touraine.

The Knights Templar and other crusaders were still striving to gain the free movement of religious groups across Palestine. Despite appeals from many quarters Henry II had refused to take part. When in 1187 Jerusalem was captured by Saladin, Sultan of Egypt, Henry still did not join a Crusade but he did levy a heavy tax on those of his subjects who had not 'taken up the cross'. When Richard became king, he, and the King of France, led a great body of followers in a Third Crusade. Richard the Lionheart, as he came to be known, performed many deeds of valour but the Turks also had a wise and brave leader in Saladin. The Crusade finally came to an end when, at negotiations that took place in 1192, Saladin promised to let the Christian pilgrims travel and worship in peace. Evidence of how much the people of Selby were involved in the Crusades has not been found. However, the number of benefactions confirmed by Richard to the abbey suggest the King's protégé, Roger de London, had won his goodwill. This may have been through the amount of revenue that went out of the monks' hands and into the Royal Exchequer, or the number of vassals sent from the Selby area, by the abbot, to join the Crusades. One of the leaders was Richard Tempest. It is recorded that he took up the pilgrimage to Palestine in 1192 but where he met his death is unknown. The cross-legged effigy of a knight, together with one of his wife in the north aisle of Selby Abbey Church was believed by some to have been erected to his memory. Further research has established that they represent Sir Hugh Pickworth and his wife. Hugh was one of many knights involved in the hostilities with Scotland during the reign of Edward II in the fourteenth century.

Another great warrior was Sir Robert Turnham, who led many valiant fighters on the Third Crusade. He was lord of the manor of Cliffe, inherited through his wife, Joan, daughter of William Fossard, the feudal lord of Doncaster. Sir Robert shared with King Richard all the military glory gained by England in the East. Together with Richard de Camville, he was given command of the island of Cyprus. Sir Robert became Admiral of the Fleet, whilst his son, who was with him in Palestine, was the king's armour bearer. In recognition of his services, Richard I gave his faithful servant around 480 acres, of what was chiefly alluvial land, that lay along the banks of the Ouse between Barlby and Osgodby. Sir Robert had Turnham Hall built on this land. It was a timber structure covered with tiles and surrounded by a moat. Many illustrious families owned Turnham Hall; some were involved in political intrigues whilst others were smitten with the crusading fever and died in its cause. One of these was Sir John Ros who died in August 1393 at Paphos, on the Isle of Cyprus, whilst on a crusade to Jerusalem. It was rare, because of many difficulties, for the bodies of dead Crusaders to be returned to England; sometimes just the hearts were brought back. The wife of Sir John Ros survived him by barely a year; in her will, dated July 1394 she stipulated she wished to be interred near her late husband in the choir of Rievaulx. This illustrated that he was one of the few whose remains were brought home. Turnham Hall underwent many alterations and rebuilding. It was rebuilt between 1795 and 1800 by William Burton of Kingston-upon-Hull. The Hall had been inherited by his wife, whose father, Mr.

Keighley, had bought Turnham Hall in 1769 for the sum of £12,000. A native of Cawood, her father had become master of the grammar school at Cliffe when aged eighteen. Shrewdness, familiarity with the law, good business sense when dealing with the sale of corn and other goods, had all helped to make Mr. Keighley an influential figure with the means to purchase Turnham Hall when it came on the market. In 1918 the grandson of William Burton, sold the Turnham Hall Estate to Olympia Oil and Cake Mills. Ten years later the Selby firm, now known as BOCM Pauls Ltd., also bought the manor house. In January 1929 they conveyed Turnham Hall and its grounds to Mr.C.E.Wetherell, whose family have been running a drapery business in Selby since 1898. Just before the turn of the century the Wetherell family sold the Hall to another private owner. Today the rambling red-brick buildings of the Hall are a landmark for walkers and cyclists on the Selby to Howden section of the Trans Pennine Trail. They stand at the junction where cyclists leave the banks of the Ouse to follow Field Lane into Cliffe.

Richard I of England spent most of his reign abroad but he still lent his support to Selby Abbey when it was needed. During the 1190s, Geoffrey Plantagenet, an illegitimate son of Henry II held the see of York. In 1194 a dispute arose between him and the chapter of York concerning the appointment of a dean. When Geoffrey did not receive their support for his choice the archbishop excommunicated the Cathedral dignitaries. King Richard was in Germany at that time so the Abbot of Selby and the superior of the houses of St. Mary, York, joined the ill-treated clergy in a long, arduous journey to find their sovereign. King Richard, angered at their treatment at the hands of Geoffrey, gave the complainants permission to travel on to Rome to put their case before a papal court. In putting forward their case the travellers described how Geoffrey Plantagenet continuously neglected his spiritual duties putting all his efforts into hunting, hawking, military affairs, and taking an active part in the political events of Richard's reign. Geoffrey was suspended from the office of archbishop. There was no rest for the Abbot of Selby when he returned for the Pope's legate, Hubert, Archbishop of Canterbury, had arrived at York to enforce discipline and order. During his stay Hubert held a large assembly in the minster attended by most of the northern ecclesiastics. Roger de London, Abbot of Selby, played an active part in those proceedings as he had done in the appeals to the king and the pope. This, coupled with the stresses and discomforts of twelfth century travel may have caused the onset, during the meetings, of an illness from which he quickly died.

King John in the North

Another prior of the monastery was promoted to abbot. Richard (1195-1214) appears to have been the only abbot of Selby to have been installed in his office by the Archbishop of Canterbury. During the reign of this monk as abbot Richard I died whilst fighting to regain some frontier castles in France and John, the youngest son of Henry II became ruler of the whole of the Angevin Empire. John had often rebelled against his absent crusader-king brother but Richard had forgiven him and eventually designated John as his heir. As Earl of Montaigne, John had spent much time in the neighbourhood of Selby. It is known that he passed the Christmas of 1192 with the Bishop of Howden. It is quite possible that then and at other times he had also enjoyed the companionship and the hospitality of the Abbot of Selby.

Soon after John became king his tactless methods quickly lost him Normandy and much of his inheritance abroad. John, therefore, spent more of his time in England than had his predecessors and travelled on many occasions to the north of England. Richard the Abbot of Selby was in office during most of the days of John's troubled reign. He lost no time in having the monastery's position verified by the king. In the year 1200 the monks at Selby gave John 100 marks of silver and one palfrey for the confirmation of his charters. A palfrey was a docile horse suitable for ordinary riding especially by a lady. In the bursar's accounts for 1398 a similar mount was described in the following manner

And to the servant of Edward de Clynton, who brought to the lord abbot one letter for one ambling horse - 18d

On the 26th February, 1204, a full confirmation of the possessions of the abbey was received from the king. Morrell in his *"History of Selby"* states the writs were tested at York, 1st March and at Nottingham 5th. March 1204, and quoted the contents as follows:

The king confirms his possessions in wood and plain, in meadows and pastures, in waters and marshes, in ways and footways, and in all places, as well within the town as without free and quit of tax, danegeld sheriff's aid, frankpledge, and with all these liberties which belong to the said abbey. And the king commands that the monks and their men have our safe conduct and are quiet and free of passage, pontage, tollage and stallage, through all cities and burghs, and they may sell freely and quietly whatsoever they have, and buy what is necessary for their sustentation, free in all things in the liberty of the city of London. The abbot and monks were to be free in all the king's ports, and in case of shipwreck their men were to have their goods in peace, provided that one escaped from the wreck. Claims against them were only to be heard in presence of the king or one of his chief justices. The abbot and monks were to have warren in their manor of Stamford, which was in the king's forest, and in the manor of Crowle with its appurtenances, and nobody was to hunt in their warrens except under a penalty of ten pounds, and they were to have the right to capture all kinds of fish in all waters, except the royal fisheries.

The inhabitants of the monastery at Selby were kept aware of, and often took part in, national events; these often involved the townsfolk. In 1206 a quarrel broke out between King John and Pope Innocent III concerning the latter's choice of Stephen Langton as Archbishop of Canterbury. The king was so frustrated by this and the process of election that he refused to let Langton enter England. The differences lasted until 1213 when the king rescinded his decision and made peace with the Church. Selby did not stand aloof from these events for during the disputes Abbot Richard's name appeared second on a list of principal churchmen in the country who sent an appeal to the pope. The Abbot of St. Mary's of York, the only other mitred abbot in the North of England, headed the list. In 1208 Richard was recorded as being asked to pay 40 marks and two palfreys to the exchequer in order that *"the king may remit his ill will towards him"*.

The town of Selby continued to grow in importance during the reign of King John. This was mainly because of its position on the lower reaches of the Ouse. Its port, which may have centred round the mouth of Selby Dam was accessible to many of the large vessels that could not navigate any further upstream in order to reach York. Selby therefore became a centre for imports and exports, a place where cargoes could be transferred from small river boats to large sea-going vessels. In 1204 it was listed amongst the sea-ports where all merchants were obliged to pay a duty of one fifteenth. The value of Selby's trade from July 1203 to November 1204 was assessed as just over £263. Lincoln with £9,849, Hull £5,170 and York £2,631 far exceeded Selby but the little inland port surpassed contemporary ports such as Whitby with its £3, Norwich £104 or Ipswich with £113.

Unlike his predecessors, Abbot Richard was promoted to higher office. In 1214 he left Selby to become Abbot of Ramsey, one of the wealthiest monasteries in England. At the dissolution its revenue was more than twice that of Selby; only seven in the country had higher incomes. The story of the succession of some abbots after 1214 is complicated and not very well documented. There were many instances of severe disagreements and mismanagement. Geoffrey (1214) was nominated by the king but never installed. Alexander (1214-1221) saw the sealing of the Magna Carta and the death of John. The king had made plans to regain Normandy but his political and diplomatic manoeuvres ended in failure. His expensively bought allies were defeated abroad whilst at home the barons rebelled against his rule and forced John to seal the Magna Carta at Runnymede in June 1215. The charter was a fundamental statement of English liberties which, it is said, the king never intended to honour.

Unsettled Times for Kings and Abbots

However, before John could implement or disgrace the Magna Carta he died from a combination of dysentery, fatigue and over-indulgence in food and drink. His eldest son, only nine years of age, became Henry III. He inherited a country torn by civil war but his advisors dealt wisely with the military, financial and political problems left by his father. Alexander, Abbot of Selby, made a payment to Henry to ensure the abbey's continued exemption from the paying of Danegeld. When the abbot died through old age another Richard was elected but he was quickly replaced by Richard de Kellesay (1222-1244) under whose leadership the disputes and misgovernment of the abbey increased. He did, however, fill an important post as one of the king's justices itinerant for the County of York. It was the first instance recorded of legal services which, in succeeding reigns, continued to be carried out by members of the monastery of Selby. Richard was succeeded by Hugh de Brayton (1244-1254) who founded a seminary for boys which began a long tradition of learning in the abbey. Free tuition in grammar and music became available for those boys who wished to learn.

1413-1414 Accounts: One William Kay paid 13s.4d. for instructing the monks and boys in the almonry in grammar.

After his marriage to Eleanor of Provence in 1236, Henry took full control in the governing of his realm. It was not long before the people were being heavily taxed to cover the cost of his extravagances. At the same time, substantial contributions were also being levied by the Pope for the services of the holy church. Agents of the crown and the church were sent all over England with orders to use whatever methods were needed to gather in riches for their masters. The monks at Selby were forced to pay large sums of money to the king; many of the abbey's possessions and most lucrative revenues were lost to the tax-collectors. The people of Selby and district would also have suffered deprivations as their rents and tithes were increased to meet the needs of the abbey. Hugh de Brayton died in office in 1254 at a time when the fortunes of the monks were at their lowest. The king ordered all that was left of the abbey to be rendered up to his treasury. It is recorded that the men of Selby paid a fine of ten pounds to the king to ensure they would still enjoy the same liberties and customs they had had under the last abbot, and not have a tax levied on them by the monks whilst there was no head appointed at the abbey.

The new abbot was Thomas de Whalley whose first term of office as abbot was from 1255 to 1262. This was when the resentment of the barons towards the king grew into rebellion. Some of their anger had been caused by their exclusion from the governing council and the lavish way in which Henry III treated his relations, who included the queen's foreign kinsfolk then resident in England. They felt that the king continually ignored their advice and they wished to regain their power in the country. Simon de Montfort, Earl of Leicester, became the leader of the more extreme reformers; with the support of powerful allies in Wales, he challenged the Crown. Llewelyn, Prince of Wales, who had driven the English out of his country in 1256, was a strong supporter. Using the disarray in England to his advantage he gained numerous victories whilst in alliance with Simon de Montfort. The people of Selby were drawn into these civil wars. On the first of August, 1260, the Abbots of Whitby, Croyland and Selby were ordered by the king to send contingents to Chester to help the monarch in his fight against Llewelyn. The conflicts lost momentum after the Battle of Evesham (August, 1265) when the royalists led by Henry's son, Prince Edward, defeated and slaughtered Montfort's supporters. The barons had commanded great sympathy in the country and Simon de Montfort, who died a hero's death at Evesham, was worshipped as a saint by the common people for a long time.

Three years before this event Thomas Whalley gave up his position as Abbot of Selby. David de Cawood was elected in his place and held the office until 1269. Memoranda from this period show the different ways in which the abbots as lords of the manor controlled the lives of the ordinary people of Selby:

> *Memorandum that the said Adam and his household were given in a charter by the Abbot and Convent freedom for ever; Charter February 1269.*
> *Adam to Pay to altar of Saint Mary in the monastery of Abbey-one penny each year on the Feast of the Nativity.*
> .

Adam was the son of Adam, the forester of Hambleton who held three acres of land around the village. Another charter authorised by David, Abbot of Selby declared:

> *I give and demise to Eve, former wife of Adam de Barkston, and her daughters Isabella and Hawise, one messuage and bovate of land with all its appurtenances, in the town of Hausey, (Haddlesey) which is a gift to the aforesaid women until we provide maritagium for Isabella and Hawise, and for Eve, a service by which she can get food and clothing, iii solidos (three shillings) being paid to us and our church half yearly so that aforesaid Eve, Isabella and Hawise can neither sell the land nor alienate it, nor marry without our permission.*

'Maritagium' was a duty which was to be carried out by the owner of a serf. It behoved him to provide marriage for the daughters of his vassals, for they could not marry without the consent of their masters. The charter also declared that if the women broke any of the rules put down, the property would revert to the monastery.

A Wayward Abbot

Thomas de Whalley returned as Abbot of Selby in 1269. From his second term of office there was plenty of documentary evidence to show how unsuitable he was for the position and how he was a bad influence on the brothers. Thomas was described as being a haughty and quarrelsome man with a malicious nature; he revelled in disturbing the peace and tranquillity of the monastery setting brother against brother. In 1275 Archbishop Giffard visited Selby Abbey and its dependent cell at Snaith. He found much to condemn. The abbot and several of his fellow monks were accused of misconduct with married women in Selby. Matters did not improve but were even worse when Archbishop Wickwane made a visitation in 1279. In his report he declared that Thomas de Whalley did not observe the Benedictine Rule, did not sing mass, rarely heard matins out of bed, seldom attended chapter and never stirred himself to preach or teach. He never advised anyone or visited the sick. Thomas slept away from the dormitory and rarely ate in the refectory. He flaunted the concessions that had been made to the monks concerning the eating of meat. He ate it openly before the laymen in his manors and elsewhere outside the abbey. The abbot even dined on meat on forbidden days. It is said he despised and neglected the statutes of the abbey at Selby. Lands, manors, tithes, corroderies and pensions were sold or transferred at will, without consent of, or discussion with, anyone else in authority. The money realised by these deeds was spent according to the abbot's whims. An even worse charge brought against the head of the monastery was that he was having illicit liaisons with a lady of 'Whenby' and a girl named Bodeman. The latter lived at the monastery gates and had already borne him off-spring. Thomas was also accused of laying hands on at least three of his brothers to the extent of "drawing blood". One was Thomas de Snayth, clerk, who had been sent to Snaith to recover "certain tithes" there. The result of the Archbishop's visitation came in 1280 when Thomas de Whalley was excommunicated.

New King, New Abbot

Thomas had still been in office when Henry III died. There had been little peace in the country for a long time after the Battle of Evesham but eventually affairs did settle down. In 1270 Edward, the heir to the throne left the country to go on a Crusade. The capture of Jerusalem, against all odds, in 1099, had sparked off an enduring enthusiasm for crusading throughout much of Europe. The Crusades fostered courage and chivalrous deeds; the defending of the weak against the strong. Crusaders, such as Edward I and his supporters kept Jerusalem free until the fall of Acre in 1291. Crusading against non-Christians, however, remained an ideal until as late as the sixteenth century. It was whilst Edward was away "defending the weak" that his father died. The heir to the throne stayed abroad for another two years to settle affairs in Aquitaine but returned to England in 1274. He had had much sympathy for Simon de Montfort and his ideals which he was to draw upon during his time as king.

William de Aslakeby (1280-93), former prior of Selby, replaced the disgraced Thomas as abbot. He was the antithesis of his predecessor. William had a strong character and used his boundful energy to rule wisely over the abbey. Through his efforts its revenue increased and plenty of new work on the monastery buildings and elsewhere was undertaken. In 1257 Sir Richard de Birlay, knight, had given the house and park at Stainer to the monks and the house had become one of the granges supplying provisions to the abbey. In 1286 Abbot William Aslakeby had a chapel built there. It was during his office that Edward I confirmed to the monastery the churches of Selby and Brayton and another valuable addition, the manor of Thorpe.

The prosperity of the abbey and its peaceful atmosphere encouraged learning. Many good scholars were produced in William's time whose successes took them far beyond the confines of the abbey. The education they received within its walls enabled them to move to the City of York where many attained municipal and parliamentary honours. Nicholas de Selby was sheriff at York in 1279 and 1283. Nicholas later held the prestigious position of Mayor of that city for three successive years. In 1295 he became the first member of parliament ever elected for York and thus attended the parliament of 23 Edward I, held at Westminster. William de Hamelton had been a monk at Selby Abbey before becoming the Dean of York and Vice-Chancellor in 1302. Three years later he had become the Lord Chancellor of England.

It is likely that the following important figures also gained their early grounding at the abbey. Adam de Osgodby was Clerk in Chancery during the reigns of both Edward I and his son, Edward II. In 1307 he was Master of the Rolls and was twice in charge of the Great Seal. In 1389, Richard II conferred on the chief citizen of York, William de Selby, the title of Lord Mayor of York. As this status was not granted to London until later, William, therefore, became the first Lord Mayor in England. Morrell records that the family "de Selby" seems to have sprung from a William de Selby who, in 1200, was the abbot's forester. It was a sufficiently honourable and lucrative position to enable the possessor to have his children educated at the abbey and at York.

When Edward I became king he went on a further crusade to the Holy Land. Since the time the pope had first asked for funds to help in these ventures, Selby Abbey had had to pay its contribution. In 1292 a tax return, known as the "taxation of Pope Nicholas IV" was made for each monastery. It was to aid the estimation of a grant from the pope of one tenth of the possessions of the Church to Edward I, to help defray the cost of his expedition abroad. The income of Selby Abbey that year was £832.11s.1d. The churches at Adlingfleet and Snaith had each contributed £153.6s.8d. to the total; the little chapel at Selby, £13.6s.8d. It is interesting to note that when the crusades began to diminish in number the revenue collected from the churches initially went to the Papal exchequer until Henry VIII usurped the Pope and it then was kept by the Crown. During the early eighteenth century it became known as Queen Anne's Bounty when she generously used the tax, around £17,000 annually, to augment poor livings.

William de Aslakeby died a few months after the tax returns of 1292 and was succeeded by John de Wystowe who served the abbey for two terms. His first years as abbot seemed to have passed peacefully. John was believed to have been a distinguished ecclesiastic. It is known he acted as referee in a disputed case before the papal court and, in 1295, was appointed by the English court to be the collector of the tenth from the clergy. He retired in 1300 and William de Aslaghby became the new abbot.

Edward I was constantly at war during William's term as Abbot of Selby. The king put great efforts into attempting to rule the whole of Britain. He won Wales and tried to solve the long-running problem with Scotland by conquest. However, when Philip IV of France took Aquitaine, Edward found himself fighting the French, the Scots and many Welsh rebels. His subjects were heavily taxed because huge sums of money were needed to pay for the conflicts with the Scots and the castles being built in Wales. Edward spent much time in Yorkshire from where he tried to deal with the resistance of the Scots. In 1299, the year he married his second wife, Margaret of France, Edward again travelled north to face his enemies. He entreated his new bride to join him there. His queen journeyed north in easy stages, as he had commanded, but in 1300 the progress of the heavily pregnant queen was brought to a halt. Whilst travelling near Brotherton she went into labour and was forced to remain in that place. Margaret gave birth to a prince, afterwards known as Thomas de Brotherton, Duke of Norfolk. During the following years the queen often resided at Cawood where Edward visited her in the winter months. The Archbishop of York often held prayers within the castle walls for the safety and success of his monarch in his forays against the Scots. He ordered the same to be held in all the churches of his diocese including Selby Abbey and its religious houses. Many of the Selby 'volunteers' called to take up arms would have been amongst the armed men and soldiers that gathered at Cawood ready to follow their king to the Borders and beyond.

Selby Abbots Summoned to Parliament

Using York as his base, Edward moved his law courts and his Parliament to the city. Local matters were also still considered and settled.

> *Inquisition 2 March 1301, before the sheriff of York by twelve men including representatives from Burn, Gateforth, Brayton, Lund, Hambleton:*
> *Petitioned not to loss of King if he gave leave to William de Hamelton, dean of Church of the Blessed Peter of York and John Merkyngfield, clerk, to grant a messuage, a mill, four tofts and three bovates of land in Brayton, which they had purchased, to parson of Brayton, John de Nassington, for support of a chaplain to celebrate daily divine service in Church of Brayton. Granted-23 February 1302.*

Between 1302 and 1307 William de Aslaghby, Abbot of Selby, was summoned to attend four Parliaments in York. Attending these assemblies provided some of the few occasions when the Abbots of Selby and a few of their brothers were allowed to leave the confines of the abbey. Selby Abbey was one of five independent Benedictine monasteries in the province of York but in comparison with the other institutions, its size and revenue placed it in the second rank of such houses. Despite this, the Abbot of Selby had the distinction of being one of only twenty-four Black Monk superiors who were regularly summoned to attend Parliament;

> *To messenger of lord king, who brought to the lord abbot a writ of summons to parliament about the festival of St. Giles, 1st. September....2s.*

It is reported that when William de Aslaghby attended Parliament he used every opportunity to further the interests of the abbey. Other abbots were not as vigilant. When Gilfred de Gaddesby was summoned to Parliament he often sent a proctor to act in his place. During the abbacy of John de Shireburn there were 38 Parliaments. Details of 27 of them held in the Public Records Office reveal that the abbot only attended two Parliaments, one in 1382 and the other in 1383. John delegated different people to represent him at the meetings:

> *And to Alexander de Stayndrop, who went as proctor of the lord abbot to parliament at London about the festival of St. Matthew (21st. September) by command of the lord abbot...6s.8d.*

Alexander acted as the abbot's attorney in the Court of Common Pleas. John de Shireburn appointed many clerks, amongst others, to act as his proctors. In 1385 three people travelled to London on his behalf~ John de Waltham, archdeacon of Richmond, Thomas Stanelay, canon of Lichfield, and Thomas de Haxey, clerk. The records also listed many of the excuses put forward for non attendance at the Parliaments:

> *1371....hindered by the concerns and difficulties of reforming the condition of the abbey.*
> *1379 ...poverty of the abbey and ill-health of the abbot.*
> *1407....abbot broken by old age and continual sufferer of ill-health.*

When John Cave was Abbot of Selby (1429-1436) he had twenty shillings sent to the clerk of the Parliament *"for his diligence in excusing the lord abbot for not coming to the same"*.

More Visitations

William Greenfield, the Archbishop of York from 1304 to 1315, was the distinguished prelate and statesman who settled the long dispute concerning the rights of Selby Abbey over the church of Snaith. He was diligent in his visitations to the monasteries and quick to punish wrongdoers. In 1306 Selby Abbey was put under scrutiny. The archbishop found matters were seriously amiss there and meted out several punishments. One monk, Henry de Belton, "for his enormities" was put into the hands of the Abbot of St. Mary's, York. It was ordered that he be escorted to the far-off cell of Rumburgh, Suffolk, and that Selby Abbey pay an annual fee to them of four marks. The monk, however, remained at St. Mary's until the archbishop finally directed the abbot to send him with a safe convoy to St. Bees. Another wayward monk was dispatched, for the same fee, to Whitby.

In 1307 Edward I died on the Solway marshes at Burgh-by-Sands, Cumbria, as he was leading his army on yet another campaign against the Scots. Edward had married twice and it was the last born son of his first wife, Eleanor of Castille, who became Edward II. He had been the first to bear the title of Prince of Wales but he was an unworthy successor to his father; weak and intemperate, Edward II proved to be neither a good soldier nor a good statesman. The new king and William de Aslaghby, Abbot of Selby, were both involved in the intrigues that resulted in the dissolving of the Order of the Knights Templar.

The Downfall of the Knights Templar

The Order had used its preceptory at Temple Hirst and those at other venues as repositories for the safe-keeping of their wealth and treasures. They also filed vital documents away in them; some contained important details of the actions of others, including kings and nobles. Those they had helped but who could not later settle their debts were beholden to them. This, along with the wealth they had amassed may have contributed to the feelings of fear, hatred and envy that grew around the Templars, and which, eventually, caused their downfall. There were other contributory factors. By the fourteenth century the Templars no longer had any positions to hold in the Holy Land and, by that time, the age of the feudal knight was coming to an end. Many knights who had been given land for their fighting prowess and support of their lord or king began to take more interest in maintaining the estates they had acquired. They concentrated on increasing their assets through the marriages of their children rather than by the sword. The duties of a knight were also becoming an irksome burden to many. For example, four knights in every shire had to attend the meetings of the shire courts and list all the complaints of injury brought by individuals against the sheriff and other officers.

The wiping out of the Templars began abroad. Their existence, the acquisition of extensive properties, and their riches were questioned. Philip 1V of France, motivated by greed and an urgent need of a fresh source of revenue, eventually coerced the Pope into dissolving the military order. It was decreed that the Templars' property and wealth should be transferred to the Knights of St. John of Jerusalem. However, when Edward II married Philip's daughter, Isabella of Boulogne, her dowry was made up of spoils from the Knights Templar. The King of France had plundered, tortured and murdered the crusaders in order to gain their riches. The Pope had not intervened so it was not long before Edward II overcame his previous reluctance and ordered the arrest of all the Templars under his rule. He confiscated the lands they held in England, Scotland and Ireland.

There were 28 known Templars in Yorkshire, two of whom, a preceptor and a chaplain, were normally resident at Temple Hirst. A royal writ was issued in 1308 commanding the Sheriff of Yorkshire to hand over to Sir Miles Stapleton, Lord of Haddlesey, the manors of Temple Hirst, Kellington and Potterlawe. In 1310 the Knights Templar were summoned to York to appear before a large assembly of ecclesiastical dignitaries; these included the Abbot of Selby and the prior at Drax. Out of the 28 Templars summoned, 23 were accused of blasphemy and other crimes. The malicious accusations brought against them included the charge that, at a feast in the Grand Preceptory at Temple Hirst, they had, allegedly, worshipped a calf, a man's head and a black cat. In other words, they were accused of dabbling in devil worship. On the 14th. August, 1312, William Greenfield, Archbishop of York, issued a decree from his palace at Cawood, dissolving the Order of the Knights Templar. It stated that all the knights were to be removed from the preceptories. Some Templars recognising the hopelessness of their position pleaded guilty and threw themselves on the mercy of their enemies. They obtained absolution and a corrody and were directed to be sent to neighbouring monasteries, such as Selby Abbey. William de Graftonsen, preceptor of Ribstan was ordered to Selby, but was then quickly given leave to travel for a month on business in the dioceses of York, Lincoln and London. It is recorded that in 1331 he was absolved from his vows and allowed to turn to secular pursuits. Other Templars courageously denied the fabricated charges brought against them and many faced torture. One English

Templar, Brother Humbert Blanke, Grand Preceptor of Auvergne, was tortured and half-starved for five years. He was finally loaded with double chains and left until, mercifully, death put an end to his suffering.

Sir Miles de Stapleton gave an account to the Barons of the King's Exchequer concerning the revenues arising from estates of 223 acres owned by the Templars at Temple Hirst. Fourteenth century documents listing the goods and chattels found on the estates are housed in the Public Records Office. The lists include descriptions of crops, stocks and other possessions and are similar to those found at Selby Abbey and its manors. Everything was sold, including two ancient boats and three old fishing nets found on the banks of the Aire, and a pigeon-cote, of the 'moveable variety'. The pigeon-cote resembled a little house on a post and was sold for ten pence. To give an idea of the great difference which exists between the value of money six hundred and seventy years ago and its value today: a horse and foal, three large sows and twenty-two piglets, nine capons and twenty-four fowl were sold for four pounds and twelve shillings. Included in the inventory of articles found in the chapel was a silver chalice. This showed that the Templars had had their celebrations with the accompaniment of wealth, for only richly endowed churches had silver or gold chalices; the poorer ones used glass. Some payments were made from the proceeds of the sales. The heirs of John de Courtenay and the monks at Selby Abbey were compensated for their loss of revenue. On behalf of the king, a corrody, valued at twopence a day, was continued to be paid to William Constable, keeper of the Templars' manor at Potterlawe. A shepherd was given twopence a day for five months and provided with enough money to purchase salt and medicines for the animals left in his care.

The Preceptory had a special feature, peculiar to Templar buildings, a narrow gateway through which only one mounted horseman could pass at a time. The king gained most of the property, but the church at St. Edmunds, Kellington, was one of the few assets transferred to the Knights Hospitallers. The manor at Temple Hirst was eventually granted to the Countess of Pembroke for life. After her death Edward III gave it to Sir John D'Arcy. In the late fifteenth century his descendant, Lord Thomas Darcy transformed the preceptory into a fortified brick house. In the nineteenth century the preceptory and other buildings formed part of a farmhouse known as Temple Manor Farm. Today Temple Manor houses a private specialist nursing home for the elderly. Over the years extensive alterations, both good and bad, have been carried out but some historic features still remain. A number of turrets were erected by Thomas Darcy; evidence of two of these can still be seen today. One was reduced to a buttress but the other stands out as an octagonal stair tower. The oldest remains are to be found in the moulded arch around a south door. This arch was built in the thirteenth century as part of the preceptory.

Conflict with the Scots

Edward I had died whilst fighting the Scots and his son was expected to carry on the hostilities. However, as soon as Edward II was proclaimed king he acted contrary to his father's wishes. His private affairs superseded everything. He abandoned the Scottish wars and got rid of the wise counsellors who had guided his father. Edward II earned the hatred of many earls through his lavishness and his use of favourites at court. The barons finally took up arms against their king until one royal favourite, Piers Gaveston, was eventually captured and executed. The Scottish wars were resumed but

Edward II had lost much support, especially from the Earl of Lancaster. Robert Bruce, King of the Scots (1306-29) took advantage of Edward's lapses to regain land and castles in Scotland. He then crossed the border into England. The Scots devastated the countryside; they looted and burned such places as Hexham, Corbridge and Durham. In 1314 Edward II, ignoring parliament's advice, professed himself ready to travel north to fight for Stirling Castle, a strategically important fortress.

When Edward II entered Yorkshire he stayed for some time in the area around Selby. The royal party stayed in Haddlesey on several occasions and also visited Cowick and Sandhall, which lay on the east bank of the Ouse. Most of the travelling was done by water. Itemised accounts list;

> *Passage of Use water,*
> *Passage of Bugwith water --(Derwent)*
> *Passage of Karleton --(Aire)*
> *Carrying goods from Selby to York by water.. 12d*

The king had travelled in his own royal barge from Boston to Lincoln. When he and his retinue crossed the Humber they were carried in a fleet of eleven barges belonging to Galfrid de Selby and several of his friends. They were engaged for two days and paid thirteen shillings. It is reported that the King and Queen visited Beverley on the 29th. May 1314, Holme (upon Spalding Moor) on the 30th, and Selby Abbey on the 1st June. They then moved to Riccall where they were ferried across the Ouse by Ralph, the ferryman of Cawood, but not before they had purchased *"Herba for the horses at Selby"*. It must have been a splendid sight for the townsfolk of Selby to witness the arrival of Edward II and Queen Isabella at the abbey. Edward had his reasons for coming to the town for he was engaged in raising contributions towards the war. The Abbot of Selby loaned the king 240 marks; this was twice the amount given by Rievaulx but equal to the loans from Fountains Abbey and St. Mary's of York.

The religious leaders would also have had orders to muster men ready to go to war, for every military effort seemed to have been made to ensure the success of the king's expedition against the Scots. Edward summoned all the barons who owed him military service to meet him at Berwick upon Tweed. Men from the Selby and Sherburn area were part of the large army that set out for the border in 1314. It also included some highly skilled archers from Wales and the Marches. Edward's army of around 20,000 men met the Scots, led by Robert Bruce, near Bannockburn. Where the English crossed the burn and where the battle was actually fought has not been fully determined. What is clear is that, despite the presence of those highly skilled archers, the English led by their weak king, Edward II, suffered a major defeat at the hands of the Scots at the Battle of Bannockburn. This left the northern counties open to attack. The victorious Scots swept through the land as far as York wasting all before them. All the surviving religious houses were ordered to collect their vassals and to put their houses in a state of defence. Poor harvests brought about by torrential rains in 1315 and 1316 added to the misery of the people. Parliament forbade the use of corn for brewing; famine and disease were rife. The invaders took all they wanted, meeting little resistance from a defeated and starving population.

A New Abbot at Selby

During these troubled times the monastery at Selby acquired a new abbot. It is not clear what happened to William de Aslaghby but in January 1313, Simon de Scardeburgh, a monk at Selby, was appointed. The abbey was without a leader for some time; as per custom, some of its revenue went to the king. Edward was hard pressed for money. It is recorded that the brothers received notice from him that, of the £80 due to the Crown, £40 had been granted as part payment, along with other amounts from similarly vacant houses, to foreign money-lenders. The monks were, therefore, commanded to pay it, without delay, to the merchants. It was not long after this that Simon, as Abbot of Selby, contributed the 240 marks to the king. This abbot took an active part in political events that also affected the people of Selby. Simon attended six Parliaments in the space of seven years and, on five occasions during one of these years, he was asked to send his service against the Scots. The large loans of money, the supply of fighting men and equipment, poor harvests and the state of the country at large, combined to seriously deplete the revenues of the abbey. The erection of new buildings and the repair of old ones came to a halt.

One of the local men who went to war was Sir Hugh de Pickworth, whose effigy is in Selby Abbey Church. In 1314 and 1316 he attended the Parliaments held at York and Lincoln as one of the knights of the shire for Yorkshire. A 'census' known as 'Nomina Villarum' listed Sir Hugh as joint Lord of East (or Kirk) Ella and of West Ella. There are many references to this knight in historical documents. Records reveal that he had already been involved in the wars, for State papers show that in September 1310, letters of protection were ordered for him as he was about to set out for Scotland. The knight later complained that during his absence on the king's service a band of men entered his manor at 'Holme by Seleby', assaulted his men and took away two of his oxen. Two years later he was one of five men appointed to stop the passage of ships along the rivers Ouse, Derwent and Humber, between York and Kingston-upon-Hull. The men were instructed to accomplish this by either, drawing the boats and ships ashore or, by sinking them. It is not improbable that the inhabitants or workers in places such as Ousegate would have been drawn into this exercise. In June of that year Hugh de Pickworth was again summoned for military service and ordered to meet the king at Stamford Bridge. In August an order appointing Hugh de Pickworth and others to choose foot soldiers to go on a Scottish expedition was countermanded. During the years 1334 and 1335, Sir Hugh appears to have no longer been required for military service and was appointed to enforce the statute for the preservation of salmon in the rivers Ouse, Aire and Wharfe. The knight attended many 'inquests' and his name appears on various land agreements for the area.

In 1338, Edward III granted Sir Hugh de Pickworth and his wife, Margery, (daughter of Sir John de 'Usflet') a lease on one of his houses in Selby, held by the Abbot. They most probably died there and were accorded burial within the Abbey Church, around the middle of the fourteenth century.

When Parliament met at York in 1318, every city and town was ordered to contribute men for the war against the Scots under penalty of forfeiture of life and limb. This must have been effective for a muster at Newcastle in 1319 was well attended. The English then laid siege to Berwick which had fallen to the enemy. During the siege Robert Bruce managed to send a raiding party into Yorkshire to capture Queen Isabella who, he had been informed, was in York. However, on the way, the Scots sacked

Boroughbridge which alerted York to their presence and the Queen was saved. The Scots carried on with their plundering, burning Pontefract before heading into the area now known as North Yorkshire. Archbishop Melton, leading a motley army of priests, monks, farmers and townsmen, made an effort to repel the invaders. On the 20th September, the two sides met at Myton-on-Swale. With the help of a northerly wind the Scots had set alight great bales of hay which helped to conceal their position. They swiftly bore down on the confused English and the Archbishop's men were scattered far and wide. Hundreds were slaughtered whilst others drowned in the Swale. Nicholas de Fleming, the Mayor of York was killed; the Archbishop had a narrow escape and, it is said, the Abbot of Selby made his escape from the carnage with the help of a swift horse. The conflict became known as the "White Battle" because of the number of ecclesiastics there. It is believed that over 300 of them perished in the Battle of Myton-on-Swale. Edward gave up the siege of Berwick and for a time there was a temporary truce between the English and Scottish kings.

Civil War

Simon de Scardeburgh did not live to enjoy this peaceful interlude; he died in 1321. John de Wistowe, who had been Abbot of Selby from 1293 to 1300, took up the mantle again. Like his predecessor, John became involved in the events occurring in the north of England. Edward II, though inadequate as a military leader had, for a period, shown himself capable of governing the country. However, he again became susceptible to the flatteries of his favourites. Hugh Despenser and his son were leading figures at court and by 1321, Hugh Despenser junior, was clearly the king's special favourite. Feelings of hatred against the Despensers by the barons grew until they broke out into a renewal of civil war. Thomas of Lancaster, cousin to the king, led the revolt to force Edward to dismiss his favourites. Thomas was the richest and the most influential earl in England at that time. He had headed the government during 1315-17, when the king had been deemed unfit to rule. When the revolts began the Abbot of Selby was ordered:

> to raise as many men-at-arms and foot soldiers as he can to march against the rebels or adherents of the earl of Lancaster, and muster at Coventry.

What part these 'recruits' took in the conflicts is not clear. Edward sent the Earls of Kent and Surrey to pursue Lancaster and lay siege to Pontefract Castle. It is said that Lancaster had wanted to make a stand at Pontefract but was pressed to withdraw further north where many hoped they would receive assistance from the Scots, with whom an alliance had been made.

The Lancastrians reached the south bank of the River Ure, at Boroughbridge, on the 16th March 1322, to find the King's men, led by the Earl of Carlisle, gathered at the northern end of the wooden bridge. Thomas Lancaster and his men were defeated and prisoners were taken to York. Edward ordered Lancaster to be brought to Pontefract where he was sentenced, as a rebel, to be hung, drawn and quartered. In the end Thomas Lancaster was beheaded in sight of his own castle. His body was taken by the monks and buried in their priory church. Other earls and knights were hanged at York, Canterbury and London. The Earl of Lancaster had had a great number of sympathisers. This probably included the monks of Selby Abbey and many people in the locality, for Thomas's wife, Alicia de Lacy, owned extensive estates around Selby. The town also enjoyed a friendly relationship with Pontefract through their respective religious houses.

More Conflicts

Following the death of Lancaster, hostilities broke out afresh between England and Scotland. The Scots swarmed over the border, ravaging and burning villages as far south as Preston. They made their way into the heart of Yorkshire. Again the abbot at Selby was ordered to raise men-at-war, foot soldiers and provisions. The king, on a journey from London to York, passed the night of 6th. December 1322 at Selby. The invasion by the Scots had thrown people into panic. Many of them, including the heads of many religious houses, were tempted to make their own peace with the enemy. How this affected the Selby area is not recorded but in 1323, a Walter de Selby was listed as a prisoner in the Tower and a constable was specially engaged by indenture to keep him in safe custody. When John de Wystowe was summoned to attend Parliament in 1324 and 1325, the abbot pleaded illness and sent two proctors in his place. It is not stated whether this was to keep him safe from the Scots or his king!

Edward II had narrowly escaped capture in battles near Byland and Rievaulx. He was surrounded by nobles and barons still smarting from their defeat at Bannockburn, the death of Thomas of Lancaster, and their treatment by the Scots who continued to burn and plunder their property with apparent impunity. The weather also seemed to have conspired with the enemy to wreck their crops, flood their lands and help spread disease amongst both humans and animals. To help maintain their manors, the monks at Selby began to follow the trend away from growing crops to the more profitable occupation of keeping sheep. Everyone needed an end to the war which was ruining the country and dishonouring the earls, barons and knights. The Earl of Carlisle - hero of Boroughbridge, defected and arranged with Bruce for a committee of Scots and English lords to conclude a peace. A thirteen year truce was agreed upon for there could be no lasting peace as long as Edward II refused to recognise Robert Bruce as King of the Scots.

There were no more skirmishes with the Scots during the rest of Edward's reign but his ineptitude in dealing with French affairs led to hostilities breaking out abroad. His wife, Isabella of Boulogne, was sent to discuss peace with her brother, Charles IV. The queen took her son, the future Edward III, and her lover, Roger Mortimer with her. When established in France she declared she would not return to her husband. In September 1326, Isabella accompanied by Mortimer and a small force, sailed for England intent on annihilating the Despensers and removing the king from power. Edward found very few supporters and was easily captured. When Parliament agreed that he should be deposed the king abdicated in favour of his son. Edward was imprisoned in Berkeley Castle, Gloucestershire. On the 21st. September it was announced that he had died. The belief held by most people is that he was gruesomely murdered but a few believe that Edward escaped and ended his days as a hermit.

After the Battle of Boroughbridge, Edward's favourites had ruled the court and their avarice and cruelty had led to a reign of terror. There were countless arrests and executions. This all came to an end in 1326 when they were captured during the uprisings. The Despensers were put to death and all their estates confiscated. Around four years before his death, Hugh Despenser junior, became the owner of Turnham Hall, near Cliffe. This was the estate later owned by the Wetherells of Selby. Hugh had been given the Hall in payment for a loan given to a member of the Mauley family during their ownership. The family was unable to reclaim the property after the death of Hugh and Turnham Hall was granted by the Crown to John de Ros, seneschal, (steward) of the royal household.

Apart from dealing with the national events that affected the abbey at Selby, John de Wystowe also had to sort out the problems they had caused within its environs. Soon after his installation as abbot, John sent Archbishop Melton an account of the state of the monastery as he had found it in 1321. The abbey had a debt of £551. Some of the reasons for this were a very poor harvest and low revenues to the abbey which included rents that were depreciating by more than 100 marks a year. The abbey was also burdened with the payments of several pensions and fees amounting to nearly £45 a year. There were fifteen corroderies who received food and drink daily; eight also received food for their servants whilst eleven were given a yearly allowance for clothes. Archbishop Melton paid a visitation to Selby in July 1324 and agreed that the abbey was heavily in debt and burdened with pensions. He exhorted the abbot and all the officials to use moderation in their dealings. For example, the monks were instructed to return to wearing the simple habits used by the first Benedictines and not to introduce any "novelties" to them. They were also to stop selling their discarded clothes when receiving new ones and to give them to the poor. The archbishop observed that the infirmary had been built in an improper and low situation so that the sick brethren were subject to, and in danger from, the stench and the polluted atmosphere surrounding them. It was ordered that as soon as funds permitted, another infirmary had to be built. Matters did improve for during the peaceful years of the truce John de Wystowe began the re-building of the choir which was stipulated to begin, "as soon as the monks of Selby had money enough".

Edward III

When Edward III was crowned King of England in 1327 the truce with Scotland had some years to run. There had been several minor breaches of the peace with neither side happy with the situation. Battles for the Scottish crown and lands continued. The abbey at Selby, and the people of the area were called upon from time to time to participate. In 1332, Edward Balliol led a group of dispossessed Scottish landowners in a successful battle against a larger force at Dupplin Moor, near Perth. The group were known as the 'Disinherited' because they had lost their lands to Robert Bruce. Edward III had aided and abetted the 'Disinherited' in their journey from their gathering place near the Humber to Scotland. Balliol was crowned King of Scotland but further upset his countrymen by vowing his allegiance to Edward and granting the king extensive territories in the Scottish lowlands. Edward deemed it necessary at this time to call out levies in four shires to help defend the Border. He also moved Parliament to York where it remained for five years and to which the Abbot of Selby was summoned. The king had many of his grandfather's attributes. At the Parliaments in York he sought for a mandate for a Scottish war but was disgruntled at the result of one attempt. The Archbishops of Canterbury and York had not been able to come to an agreement concerning the bearing of their crosiers (hooked staffs) which resulted in the Archbishop of Canterbury, and all his clergy, not attending in York. The Bishops of Lincoln and Carlisle, the Abbots of York and Selby, and the Archbishop of York were present but no official business was carried out because of the absentees. Another meeting had to be arranged at considerable cost to all those concerned. Edward III showed his frustration in the wording of the next summons to Parliament.

> *strictly enjoining all persons to attend, and on no pretence whatever any longer*
> *to delay or hinder the king's mighty affairs by their non-appearance.*

However, developments in Scotland, including the banishment of Balliol, made Edward disregard the views of others and prepare for war. He besieged Berwick and in 1333, at the Battle of Halidon Hill, defeated the Scottish force sent to relieve the town. The monks at Selby were again ordered to commit themselves in the hostilities against the Scots. The following order was contained in a writ sent to the Abbots of Selby, Fountains, Jervaulx, Meaux, Whitby and the prior at Bridlington:

> *25th. April, 7 Edward 111, 1333-4*
> *....to send immediately to Durham, one strong cart well bound with iron, and*
> *prepared with other necessaries, together with five sufficient horses to convey*
> *some tents and other baggage of the king then proceeding against the Scots.*

John de Wystowe died in 1335. John de Heslyngton (1335-41), a monk at the abbey, was appointed the new abbot. As he began his term the political wrangling, battles and truces between the English and the Scots were still in progress. Edward III also faced problems in France. The support given by that country to the enemies of England, especially to Scotland, was a major cause of the increasing hostilities between the French and the English.

Unruly Monks

John de Heslyngton also had to face the wrath of the Archbishop of York who had made a recent visitation to the monastery. In December 1335, the new abbot received a damning report from Archbishop Melton, concerning the behaviour of six of his brethren. Adam de la Breuer was accused of having forbidden relationships with Alice, daughter of Roger the Smith of Selby, and also with her sister! Adam was described as a drunken, lecherous and rowdy person who delighted in causing friction amongst his brothers. It had been declared, to the scandal of the order, that he had often been found gossiping indecorously with women in the cloister, the church and elsewhere, particularly with Alice and her sister. Adam must have been one of the monks who had added 'novelties' to the design of his habit. In his case they were secret little pockets in which he hid goods stolen from the monastery. Many of these illegal possessions found their way into the houses of the women whom he had been accused of visiting. Adam paid scant attention to his religious duties and was often charged with leaving the choir before the end of a service. The final accusation brought against him was that he had abused every monk who had told the truth concerning his activities. Adam was given a year to repent of his sins. He spent this time imprisoned in a building remote from his fellow-men with no access to any females. Every Wednesday and Friday he was taken to the chapter and given a whipping by everyone present at the meetings. On those days he received bread, soup and light ale as sustenance; on other days he was given the same as his brothers but without any delicacies.

Thomas de Hirst was similar in character to Adam. He was accused of sending alms and monastery property, to at least seven women in Selby. It was his attitude towards women in general that first aroused the suspicions of his fellow monks to his activities. John de Whitgift, Robert de Flexburgh and Nicholas de Houghton had all been convicted of having relationships with certain women of the town. They disregarded this and continued in their lecherous behaviour including the sending of alms and stolen goods to various houses in Selby. It is interesting to note that another malefactor, Roger de Pontefracto, sent his purloined articles to the house of a Maye de Pontefracto. Thomas, John and Robert were forbidden to go outside the cloister for a year. They were to have no contact with women without a special licence from the abbot, and then only openly in the presence of two monks. These offenders were also fed on bread, soup and light ale on a Wednesday and Friday and suffered whippings at the hands of all those present at the chapters. It is not clear what punishments were meted out to the other two miscreants who were alike in that they each had only transgressed with one female for which they had already been convicted.

The year after the report, Archbishop Melton issued further orders to the abbot. These followed the general pattern for a visitation. For example, the abbey was in debt so pensions were not to be granted without the consent of the archbishop; yearly accounts were to be kept and scrutinised by the abbot; women were not to bleach clothes in the churchyard; monks were not to sell their habits and were to pay proper attention to the sick. There appears to have been no more visitations to Selby recorded in the Registers but a list of questions put to the abbot in 1343 are stored in the Records Office. The questions are too numerous and complicated to be quoted here but it is worthy of note that the abbot was asked whether, after the notice of the visitation, or the rumour of it, had reached the ears of the brethren, a silence had been imposed concerning certain matters!

In 1335, the archbishop had noted serious defects in the church roof. He also remarked upon an evil odour rising from the latrine in the infirmary which, he said, must have been highly offensive to persons sitting in the cloister. These may have been rectified for, at some time during his six years of office, John de Heslyngton had funds to continue work on the choir- an enduring monument left by the monks.

Conflicts at Home and Abroad

However, like many leaders before him, the abbot had to cease the work and prepare for war with the Scots. Edward III had been using all his resources to enforce his claim to the crown of France. He feared that without troops in the North the Scots would take the opportunity to cross the border. To counteract this, the king issued a proclamation, on the 6th.March 1339, ordering the abbots and priors of the larger houses in the north, and other great landowners, to use every means at their disposal to prevent any invasion by the Scots. The Abbot of Selby was reminded of his duty to use all his resources to ensure the safety of his house. He was to spare neither trouble nor expense to prevent the devastating effect of a Scottish occupation of Selby and its neighbours. This did not materialise for a while for the Scots were not in a position to take advantage of an open border. Their allies in France were busy defending themselves against the English forces. King PhilipVI had stated that any treaty with England had to include King David of Scotland and all the Scots. David, son of Robert the Bruce, had been sent to France for safety in 1334 when he was disinherited by Balliol. This French/Scots alliance was one of the causes of what became known as the Hundred Years' War.

Gilfred de Gatesby (Geoffrey de Gaddesby) appointed Abbot of Selby in 1341 kept the position for twenty-seven years. It was he who used his engineering skills to drain the land near Hatfield thereby upsetting the local inhabitants. He was in control at Selby when Edward III, won one of the main successes of the Hundred Years' War. In August 1346, at the Battle of Crecy, the king employed tactics painfully learnt in England's clashes with the Scots. He used his archers, supported by dismounted men-at-arms, to win a resounding victory. Calais, Edward's next objective, was ideal as a port of embarkation. It gave access to the raiders in the Channel and provided excellent wharves for bringing in English goods. During the French campaigns supplies for the armies were drawn from Hull which was situated on the edge of a region where, except in times of famine, there was always a corn surplus. A good harvest yielded enough crops to feed 20,000 troops for a year. Selby's position on the Ouse made it an important inland port through which to channel vital goods. In 1346 when corn, bacon and other provisions were requisitioned from Derbyshire, Nottinghamshire and Yorkshire, they were transported to Hull via Tadcaster, Doncaster, Wansford, Beverley, York and Selby. From Hull the goods went to Portsmouth for embarkation. With the help of these supplies Edward III laid siege to Calais and the English army prepared to spend the winter in the fields outside the town.

The Scots were again causing trouble. David II, son of Robert Bruce, had sought sanctuary in France but in 1341 had returned to his homeland. He gained great support through his acceptance of the alliance between France and Scotland and forced Balliol to retire to England. In 1346 David led a Scottish army across the border. The invaders attacked Liddel Strength, a small castle situated high above the south bank of the River Liddel which, at that point, forms the border between England and Scotland. A garrison of 200 men-at -arms, led by Sir Walter Selby, held the castle for four days before it was taken and destroyed by David. Sir Walter and both his sons were executed. Today Liddel Strength, 18km. north of Carlisle, is described on O.S. maps as "motte and baileys". After taking Liddell the Scots spread into the area around Durham. Wisely, when Edward had left for the wars in France he had not raised levies from counties north of the Trent. Besides entreating the religious houses to be prepared for attack, he had placed Lords Percy and Neville, with the Archbishop of York, in charge of the border defences. On the 17th. October 1346, at Neville's Cross near Durham, 12,000 Scots were intercepted by an army led by northern lords and outraged churchmen. The intruders unable to stay on the defensive against the English archers attacked, but were defeated. The greatest triumph was the capture of David II of Scotland. In 1347, Lord John Darcy, owner of Temple Hirst manor, near Selby, took David and other prisoners from the conflict to the Tower of London. The Scottish king remained there in reasonable comfort for eleven years. Abbot Gaddesby must have been summoned to supply men and arms in the battle against the Scots but the names of those called upon from the common people are not known. One of the lords present at Neville's Cross was William de Ros. He was a descendant of John de Ros, late Admiral of the North Fleet, who had been granted the estates of Turnham Hall after the death of the Despensers. William de Ros and Lord John Darcy had also been present at the Battle of Crecy.

The longbow had first been used by Welshmen in the employ of Edward I, but was not used effectively until the Battle of Boroughbridge. When the campaigns in France began the archers were at the forefront of the battles, fighting shoulder to shoulder with dismounted men-at-arms. Fighting men were now receiving payment. Mounted archers, who could swiftly dismount and use their Welsh longbows were paid sixpence a day whilst foot soldiers received twopence a day. A ploughman, meanwhile, earned roughly 12s. a year. The longbow was not easy to use and an archer needed continual practice to become proficient. A good longbowman was able to shoot ten to twelve arrows a minute compared with two from a crossbowman. To achieve this standard, shooting at the butts, especially on a Sunday, was encouraged by proclamation and Statute. Boys were expected to begin practising this skill from the age of seven. The custom must have lapsed from time to time. For example, at Inquests held in Selby in 1483 and 1519 it was announced:

> *Our butts in the Out-wood be made by the township of Selby by next Whitsuntide or fine - vjs. Viijd (6s.8d)*

The Black Death and its Aftermath

Edward III did not enter Calais until August 1347. The king evacuated most of its inhabitants and replaced them with English colonists whose descendants held the port for over two hundred years. The outbreak of a mysterious illness which later became known as the Black Death halted the military expeditions in France. England's failure to capitalise on the victory at Neville's Cross has also been ascribed to its outbreak. The disease first appeared in this country in the county of Dorset in 1348 and within a year it had reached the Highlands of Scotland. It killed off one third to a half of the population of England, wiping out whole villages in its path. More than two-thirds of parish priests in the West and East Ridings died of the Black Death.

Their number decreased so quickly that the clergy had to admit as rectors, a number of young men known as 'shavelings'. Their shaven heads indicated their chosen occupation was that of a clerk.

For hundreds of years it has been believed it was the bubonic plague that swept through Europe in 1348/1349 and killed a quarter of its population. Recent research in the United States has thrown some doubt on this. The symptoms of the Black Death included high fevers, swollen lymph glands, coughing, vomiting of blood, accompanied by fetid breath, foul body odour and bruising of the skin. Many of these symptoms do appear in bubonic plague but the researchers found they were also characteristic of many other diseases. The evidence against it being bubonic plague included records of priest replacements kept by the English bishops between 1349 and 1350. They show that the death and infection rates amongst the clergy from the Black Death were far higher than those usually associated with modern cases of bubonic plague. Also the bubonic plague was carried by fleas on infected black rats and its mode of transmission to humans was slow compared with the Black Death which swept swiftly through the land going directly from person to person. It spread like wild fire along major routes and rivers defying natural barriers that would have halted the transmission of a rat-borne sickness. There were no reports of the bodies of dead rats filling the streets or of a mass death of these rodents as was evident in modern epidemics of bubonic plague. The research indicates that the Black Death may not have been bubonic nor pneumonic but a type of fever, originating in Africa and connected to animals. It was possibly like the modern named "Ebola" a kind of fever which still occurs periodically in Africa, the Indian sub-continent, South America and the Far East. This answer is not acceptable to everyone and researchers are now trying to find an answer through DNA tests on the remains of Black Death victims.

Selby and the neighbouring villages all suffered during the spread of the Black Death. An Inquisition post mortem at Hemingbrough in 1349 revealed how the land, such as that around Turnham Hall, near Cliffe, had depreciated in value. Its pastures had gone down in price for they had been trampled by wandering cattle. The herdsman were lying in the churchyard at Hemingbrough whilst the neglected cattle were breaking down the hedges and destroying the meadows. It was also reported that all the 'bondigers' and carters of the abbey in Selby were dead so that goods such as turves and hay had to be carried by water. This was much more expensive to do. The granger at the abbey justified the extra costs in the accounts for 1348/49 in the following manner;

> *For unloading of two ships of turves at Selby purely because of the plague...*
> *Two shillings for the unloading at Selby of hay carried by water because of the plague in the preceding summer.*
> *Twenty eight shillings for the transport of 16 oaks by special delivery, only because all the transporting was done after Michaelmas because of the plague in the preceding summer.*
> *Twelve shillings for 33 ells of hair cloth because of the plague.*
> *Two shillings for various workers on occasions in the brewhouse because of the illness of various servants from time to time.*
> *Five shillings and sixpence for jars and cups for wine and beer for Christmas. This also specifically because of the plague.*
> *Two shillings to William Bond of Hambleton for the transport of millstones from Hambleton to Selby because the bond men of Selby have died and their land is in the possession of the feudal lord*

The feudal lord in this case would have been the Abbot of Selby but this was not so when John Pouger (or Poucher), and his wife Margaret died during the summer of 1349, presumably from the Black Death. Margaret was one of two daughters and co-heiress of John Paynel, Lord of Drax. In October 1349, it was Thomas, son of Hugh de Pickworth, who was appointed to take into the king's hands the lands which had belonged to John Pouger and deliver them to the Chancellor to whom custody of heir had been granted.

The great depopulation of the country by the Black Death was followed by a social revolution that changed the whole course of English history. The decrease in the value of land was followed by a sudden increase in the value of a labourer. By the end of the fifteenth century the trend towards sheep-rearing had increased because fewer hands were needed and the profits were greater. Large flocks of sheep, each tended by only a shepherd and his dog, filled the hundreds of acres once occupied by villain tenants and their dwellings. The workers seeing the scarcity of servants demanded higher wages. The king and council ordered the masters not to pay more; servants, free of bond and under 60 were to continue to serve their lords for the same wages as before the plague. Villeins, under pain of imprisonment, were also expected to stay in their manors. It was considered a serious offence not to do so because of the loss of revenue to the manor. For many years after the Black Death landowners complained of villeins absconding to the trading towns. During a case in a Bradford court in March 1360, a landowner in Craven referred to villeins from the manor who had fled as far afield as Pontefract, York and Selby. The tenants and villeins rose up against the feudal system. Stewards were unable to enforce the accustomed services, work was often left undone and there were organised strikes. After the Black Death it took 50 years of strikes and hardships before the freedom of the English serfs was secured. The terrible scourge that had taken so many lives served one good purpose; those workers, who so wished, were able to become rent-paying tenants - still poor but free.

It is not known how many monks at Selby Abbey succumbed to the Black Death but after the initial catastrophic loss, which affected all religious houses, the number of brothers did recover. The monks, however, at Selby and elsewhere, discovered that many of their demenses could no longer be run effectively using servile labour. In 1355, to help deal with this problem a survey was carried out at the manor of Crowle, including work done by certain tenants. Shortly afterwards 85 acres of arable and pasture lands were leased out for fifteen years.

It was decided in the Chapter House, in September of that same year, before Abbot Gaddesby, that John Peterburgh and John Burgeays, of Selby, were to lease the eastern part of the monks' grange within the manor of Thorpe. The charter drawn up clearly showed how much land was theirs to use and the help given to the two prospective landowners. The lease included the demise of the eastern part of the monks' grange which was divided from the rest by a wall and the southern part of a stable with a granary attached. There was a dovecote and 'doghouse' with all the herbage and fruits of the gardens situated within that part of the manor of Thorpe. Outside the site the men were allocated two byres, a foalhouse and also many meadows and pastures within the monks' demesne lands. The two Johns were given leave to take wood, except for young oaks, fruit trees, maples and brushwood, on condition they made reasonable provision for the growing of maturing plants to replace those taken. They were given permission to dig out turves and disturb the soil if it was for the improvement of hedges, ditches and sewers. The lessees were also allowed to provide fodder for their cattle in winter and have a piggery in the woods, but were to be careful not to waste any wood. They had the use of one boat on Selby Dam in which they could carry goods as far as the Millbridge in Selby. They were to be responsible for the men working on the boat who were only to use the waterway during daylight hours. No-one was permitted, however, to fish in the Dam or the ditches.

The lease was for a term of fifteen years with the lessees paying an annual rent of thirteen marks of silver plus any pigeons bred above the normal allowed each year. The two Johns were warned that if the rent should fall into arrears beyond fifteen days or the lessees died, then all the lands would revert to the abbey *"until satisfaction is made"*. The charter also stated that if their cattle were at any time seized by the servants of the king or by any one else on account of the monks' debts, then the cattle would be released without delay and at the abbey's expense. Both men were offered a robe each year and, from time to time, a barrel of brine. To help them to begin working their land the monks gave the two men five quarters of corn, a number of quarters of barley, ten quarters of oats, two cows, two wagons, one plough with all its equipment and eight haywains. All of these articles had to be replaced at the end of their lease. They had also to return the land and property as they had found it except where damage had been caused by accident of fire, wind or any other great calamity. John de Baruneby and Robert le Fischer of Selby offered themselves as *"bail and pledges of the said John and John"*.

The problems faced by Geoffrey de Gaddesby during his time as abbot included a fire, which caused damage to the Dorter, Chapter House and Treasury, and the troubles caused by a runaway monk. The offender, Brother John de Hemmynburgh, had in his time at Selby represented the abbot in Parliament and later become prior of the abbey. A year before the last event, he had been instrumental in the release of a brother monk. A memorandum, allowing Henry de Salley to leave Selby Abbey in order to join a mendicant order, was signed on the 24th. January 1350, in the presence of several monks, including John de Hemmynburgh. At a later date, due to circumstances not fully known, John also left the monastery, but without the necessary licence. Geoffrey, like other abbots before him, sought help from the crown and its officers in securing the return of the fugitive. With the assistance of the Sheriff of York and several landowners, all in possession of Royal Commissions to do so, the runaway monk was soon seized and returned to the abbey. He did not settle for records show he was in London in 1372, then in Rome and Avignon, seeking guidance from the Pope on matters that concerned *"his soul's health"*. An undated entry in an abbey register suggests his confessions there so alarmed the monks that a proctor was appointed to protect their interests.

A seal believed to have belonged to one of the abbots of Selby in the fourteenth century is now part of Selby's mayoral chain of office. It was discovered in the late nineteenth century in ground somewhere between the abbey church and the toll bridge. In November 1898, the vicar of Selby, A.G.Tweedie, sent an impression of the seal to the British Museum. The experts there declared it an interesting example of the use made of ancient gems in the Middle Ages, for the red stone in the centre of the seal was of late Roman work. The engraving on the stone represents two boxers, one of whom is wearing a low-brimmed hat. To their left is a herm, a palm branch for the victor, and a water jar. A 'herm' is a square stone column with a carved head of Hermes on top and was often used by the ancient Greeks as a boundary marker outside a house. The seal, found in Selby, is oval in shape, the stone being encased in medieval silver. Around the edge of the stone, in medieval characters, are the words, *"SECRETUM FERO LUCE"(I carry [this seal] hidden from the light"*. This was to show it was the monk's private, or secret seal, as apart from the official one as used by the abbot.

A fee had to be paid when an agreement was properly sealed. When, in 1398, a deed was drawn up by the monks concerning the selling of a pension to John Tuch and his wife, a payment of 3s.4d. in addition to the same previously given by John, was paid to the lord prior. This was the fee due for the common seal with which the deed was authenticated. In medieval times the engravings on many seals reflected the names of the owners. In the 1180s, Alan Wastehose, granted Peter, son of Godfrey de Roxtun, one bovate of land in South Duffield, for the yearly rent of one pound of cumin. In order that, as many grantors stated, *"my gift, grant and confirmation of this may remain ratified and valid"*, he placed his seal on the manuscript. Alan legalized his gift with one of white wax on a brown silk tag. This bore the impression of a boot (or hose) with a decorated top. A circular white seal used by William Esveillechien (Watchdog), when confirming the grant, showed a hound running. These seals were most probably made of $\frac{2}{3}$ beeswax and $\frac{1}{3}$ turpentine. By the time of the Dissolution of the Monasteries, shellac, coloured either red or black, was beginning to be used as the chief component, then gradually, as signatures began to be used more generally, except by corporations, seals became unimportant.

Subsidies and Taxes

The victories at Neville's Cross and Crecy swung the fortunes of war in the King's favour. Tournaments to celebrate the victories asserted Edward III's claim to be at the head of European chivalry. Between the years of 1360 and 1371 his subjects experienced the longest respite from direct taxation for more than a century. The profits of war and wool subsidies allowed Edward to embark on a prodigious building programme, including the rebuilding of Windsor Castle. The wool subsidy was a customs duty imposed on wool exported from England to the Continent. Edward 1 had imposed the first regular duty in 1275 at the rate of 6s.8d. a sack. In times of war with the French the subsidy quickly rose to as high as 40s. and above.

There were strict rules regarding the quality and width of cloth. From the time of Edward I ulnagers had been employed to impose these rules. At first two had worked together to examine all cloths exposed for sale in their area. They confiscated all wares, whether home-made or of foreign manufacture that were not in accordance with the legal dimensions. Selby had a few cloth-makers and not all of them followed the regulations. In 1274 men from Selby, Whitby and Hedon were accused of manufacturing material that did not conform to the Assize of Cloth - rules which stated the size and quality of cloth required before sale. The accused men in this case would have forfeited their wares to the king. Almost a hundred years later, when Parliament had gained control over indirect taxation, the right was granted for a subsidy to be collected on English woollen cloth put up for sale. A tax was not paid on any cloth made for own use but now, the cloth-makers marketing their goods not only had to pay the ulnager a fee for measuring any material intended for sale, but they also paid a subsidy. Only then would their wares be sealed by the ulnager or his deputies. The officials had dies made of copper or lead to use as seals. It was not unknown for counterfeit ones to be in use in Yorkshire and elsewhere.

By this period an ulnager was appointed for each designated area where he usually kept the position all his working life. The ulnager of the king in the West Riding, for the years 1395-96, was Wiliam Barker of Tadcaster. His name appears in the abbey account rolls 1398/99 under 'Pensions and Fees". He was receiving 20s. a year from the monks; in his will dated 1403 he left 6s.8d. towards the fabric of the abbey. His accounts, as ulnager, listed the payments of subsidies and ulnage and the forfeiture of saleable cloths not sealed. The towns recorded included Pontefract, Leeds, Wetherby, Wakefield, Doncaster, Barnsley, Ripon, Skipton and Selby. Four cloth-makers listed for Selby were John Escrik, John Marschall, Robert Graynham and Thomas Danyell. The number of cloths for sale was 22½ for which 7s.6d. was paid in subsidies and 11¼d. paid to the ulnager. Leeds had the same number of cloth-makers listed, but one of them alone produced 52 cloths. Their total came to 120 cloths for which they paid 40s. in subsidies. The cloth-makers of Selby were still trying to flaunt the laws. It was recorded by William Skipwith, the ulnager for the County of York in 1396, that he seized and sold, as was allowed, several pieces of cloth exposed for sale before they had been sealed or any subsidy paid. Eight offenders were named; one of them was a William Wath of Selby who had been trying to sell six ells of blue cloth, unsealed, and valued at 6s.8d.

The cloth-making industry became well-established where the population was gathered around a castle or abbey. It was the main occupation for some, whilst others did it as an extra source of income. Many, even parish priests, made cloth in their spare time for their own use. Cloth-making did not become a major industry in Selby as it did in other West Riding towns. The ulnagers' records show that between 1469 and 1478, whilst Leeds produced an average of 335 saleable cloths, Selby still only sold 22½. During the first four years of this period Thomas Boteler, or Botler, and Anthony Kydall were amongst the chief producers of cloth in Selby. From 1473 the name of John Crosse featured quite often in the ulnager's accounts.

Edward III died in 1377 and was succeeded by his young grandson, Richard II. Most of this king's reign was to be dominated by his uncle, John of Gaunt, fourth son of Edward III. The king's inability to command his magnates caused him much trouble. The increasing costs of the Hundred Years War led Parliament in 1377 to grant the levying of a tax of one groat (four old pence) on every lay person over fourteen. In Selby 586 persons paid the tax which indicates the town may have had a population of under 1000. York had near 7000 taxpayers and Kingston~upon-Hull, 1,557. This was the first poll tax suffered by the people since 1222 when money was levied to help the Kingdom of Jerusalem. The earlier tax had been graduated according to a person's wealth, a practice followed in 1378 when a second tax was imposed. Under this the Duke of Lancaster paid £6.13s.4d.

Examples of the different grades paid, taken from the *"Rolls of Collectors in the West Riding"* for the Wapentake of Barkston, reveal that there were six merchants in Selby, including a Robertus Potteman, who each paid a tax of 3s.4d. - a level indicating that they were moderately prosperous people. Two innkeepers paid two shillings whilst another two were taxed at thirteen pence. Roger Barker, a tanner, Ricardos Milner, a carpenter, and Willelmus de Grayne, a lister (dyer), were amongst 32 inhabitants who paid sixpence. In Cawood, 37 inhabitants paid fourpence in tax whilst there were seven innkeepers who paid sixpence and one person, John de Cawood, who was taxed the large sum of 6s.8d. John was described as a 'franklin', a landowner who was free but not of noble birth. The majority of people described as franklins paid a lesser amount of 3s.4d. The larger tax was levied on Thomas Dawtre, Esq. of Brayton; 18 other people in that place paid fourpence. Thomas de Gayteford, an attorney of Gateforth, who received 20s. a year for his services to Selby Abbey, was also taxed 6s.8d. Figures for 1379 showed that Doncaster, a wealthy and populous town, paid 233s.6d., whilst Sheffield yielded 131s.2d., Selby 126s. and Leeds 60s.4d. The details collected with the taxes also revealed the variety of crafts and trades carried out at that time. Amongst the 198 families in Selby there were six carpenters, one couper, three barkers or curriers, one shoemaker, five weavers, five dyers, one blanket maker, seven tailors, one dauber or plasterer, one slater, one fletcher, three butchers, five blacksmiths and one draper.

The graduated tax did not yield the expected large revenue, so in 1380 a poll-tax of three groats on all lay men and women over fifteen was instituted. The poll-tax was similar to a census in that it necessitated inquiries into the personal affairs of the king's subjects. This, and the harsh, uncaring methods used by the collectors, were deeply resented; evasion, on a large scale, took place. This practice may account for the drop from 586 taxpayers noted in Selby in 1377 to the 460 recorded there two years later. Many people appealed for no more taxes except for the fifteenths accepted by their fathers and those before them. The fifteenth, paid by lay people, was a tax levied on moveable property. The duty, of which the clergy paid a tenth, had been at a fixed rate since 1334 but was becoming more and more unrealistic. The ulnager, William Barker, who was at some time employed by the abbey, was a collector of the fifteenths and tenths in 1398.

The more vociferous amongst the taxpayers openly rebelled. The poor state of the land, and the ineptitude of the government during Richard's minority, together with the new Poll-tax, caused a 'Peasants' Revolt' in both rural and urban areas. Numerous social and economic grievances, including the treatment of labourers after the Black Death outbreaks, all found expression in fierce revolts in the south. The main one was led by Wat Tyler who was killed during a confrontation with the king during the rebels' actions in London. There were outbreaks in other counties including three isolated ones in York, Scarborough and Beverley. Labourers from the area around Selby may have taken their grievances to York. The revolts were quickly put down and the main instigators punished. Even so, it made the government then, and for many years to come, more cautious about inflicting taxes on the populace. The continuing shortage of labour meant that the fifteenth century was to be a more auspicious time for the poor. The wealthy were subjected to a tax in the seventeenth century but almost three hundred years were to elapse before the next universal poll-tax.

Political Intrigues

Richard II continued to experience conflicts with his nobles. The people tired of his weaknesses objected to his extravagances and his over indulgence of favourites. In 1387 a group of lords and earls, who became known as the Lords Appellant; accused the king's friends of treason. A battle took place at Radcot Bridge, Oxfordshire, at which the accused were defeated. Those who failed to escape were executed thus depriving the king of many of his supporters. One of the Lords Appellant, who now gathered round the king, was Henry Bolingbroke, son of John of Gaunt. Born at Bolingbroke castle, he was heir to the richest lands in England, for his father, by marriage, had inherited the entire Lancaster estates. In 1371 Henry had been created Earl of Derby and twenty years later was given the title, Duke of Hereford. He was another knight of chivalry who went on crusades to the Holy Land. King Richard used tactics similar to those previously employed by the Lords Appellant to remove some of the strong opponents of his rule. They included Henry Bolingbroke who was finally sent into exile. Whilst he was absent from the country John of Gaunt, who had managed to keep the peace between the opposing factions, died, and the king seized the Duchy of Lancaster. Henry returned to England with just a few hundred men determined to claim back his inheritance. He also put himself forward as a champion of the rule of law, against a tyrant king. Richard had left on another peacemaking visit to Ireland when, early in July 1399, Henry landed at Ravenspur, on the lower Humber. Ravenspur, like Ravenser, where Walter of Selby had moved to avoid the taxes, was another place that had risen up from the sea only to disappear into its depths many years later. After Henry left Ravenspur, he was joined by the Earl of Northumberland and other nobles. Supporters continued to flock to his standard until his small army had increased to a force of 60,000 men.

John de Shireburn had been Abbot of Selby Abbey for thirty years when the struggles for the crown took place. His age and ill-health were put forward as his reasons for not attending Parliament but he could not afford to be too much out of touch with the political changes taking place during the closing years of the fourteenth century. Whether he wished to or not John became involved in the national events of that period.

The account rolls for the years 1398/99 record the sum of £6.13s.4d. being paid to Sir Richard de Redemane, knight. Sir Richard, who held the title, Master of the Horse, had brought a writ under the privy seal of the king. In it the abbot was commanded to send horses for the use of his sovereign. The knight was given money to buy some horses. He was also presented with one colt complete with saddle-cloth and bridle and ten shillings in gifts for the servants accompanying the king's representative. Sir Richard, of Harewood in Yorkshire and Levens Castle in Westmoreland, was one of the richest Yorkshire Parliamentary representatives. He had received many valuable grants from Richard II.

It is presumed that the horses were for the king's second expedition to Ireland. A little time after this the gift of a horse was given by the monks to Robert de Waterton whose family were devoted to Henry Bolingbroke. Their name was taken from the manor of Waterton in the Hundred of Crowle. Robert was an esquire of Henry Bolingbroke and one of the earliest to give his support after Henry landed in the north. He was later in receipt of a large annual pension from Selby Abbey. The accounts for 1398/99 show that 6s.8d. was paid to Master Thomas Wright of Rothwell, for bringing to the lord abbot a letter from Henry, Duke of Lancaster, asking for the loan of some money. A Thomas Wright had been a servant of John of Gaunt and had received a grant of a house in Cowick, near Snaith, for his services to his master. Another messenger to the abbey was given two shillings. He was John Moslay, cook to the lord bishop of Durham who, on the second of August, brought news of the Duke of Lancaster to the abbot.

Henry Bolingbroke was, by that time, in the southwest of England. King Richard left Ireland on the 27th. July, and lost two armies in battle within two weeks. Eventually he surrendered to the insurgents at Conway, in Wales.

Writs for a Parliament to meet at Westminster on the last day of September were sent in Richard's name, from Chester on the 19th. August 1399. The bursars at Selby noted that they paid two shillings to a messenger of the lord king who had brought the abbot a writ of summons to a Parliament to be held on the 30th. September. They also recorded 6s.8d. paid to Alexander de Stayndrop who left the abbey on the 21st to act as proctor of the abbot at the Parliament in London. Alexander, may have joined the party of the Archbishop of York who was on the same mission to London. The archbishop was attended by three employees from Selby Abbey. The three men paid 20s. to carry out this duty were, Robert Broune, who was described in the next abbot's accounts as the lord's butler, John Bewe, a page at the abbey, and John Bernard, whose occupation was not stated. By this time King Richard was Bolingbroke's prisoner. His act of abdication was read out on the 29th. September to an assembly of knights and representatives of both secular and religious bodies. The writs of summons to a Parliament sent to the abbot of Selby and others, were regarded as nullified by the king's abdication on the previous day. The persons present in London on the 30th. attended a short assembly and were then summoned to attend the first Parliament of Henry IV to be held on the 6th. October. Alexander de Stayndrop, as proctor for the Abbot of Selby attended both meetings. Richard was imprisoned in Pontefract Castle where, it is said by many, he was murdered in February 1400, after a failed rescue attempt.

Although Selby was a small town situated in the north of England, far away from the King's Court, it is clear the members of the Benedictine Order within the abbey and the inhabitants of Selby itself were aware of, and often became involved in, national affairs of great importance. This was also the case when it came to lesser affairs of the nobility and Parliament. For example, there was the bill of Parliament put forward by Thomas Haxey. Thomas was amongst the people who, after the Black Death, leased land from the monks. It seems from the records available that twenty years or more had elapsed after the first leasing out of land. The monks must have managed up until then by using servile labour and day workers. By the end of the fourteenth century, however, lands at Hillam, Monk Fryston and Hambleton had been farmed out. This left the Selby demesne with property in Thorpe Willoughby and Wistow which was worked by day labourers. Estates in other counties were also farmed out. Property owned by the monks in Stanford-on-Avon, was leased to an association of 14 men for 21 years. This included the manor house with its arable land, pastures and meadows, and, for additional rent, the services of servile tenants. The lessees were obliged to carry on certain customs, such as the holding of courts and the provision of hospitality expected by abbots and others on their travels. Thomas Haxey was one of a group of three men who leased a manor in that area.

Thomas was also a clerk who acted as proctor for Abbot Shireburn at several meetings of Parliament. He made his first appearance as proctor in 1386 but it was his attendance there in the late 1390s that almost led to his execution. Thomas was clerk of the Court of Common Pleas and for this duty he often received considerable 'rewards' from the king. Despite this he became instrumental in bringing forward a bill which included a complaint concerning the extravagances of the royal household and the numerous bishops and ladies who attached themselves to the court. Because Thomas represented a northern abbot it is possible he was encouraged in his act by the many disgruntled prelates in that region who had not gained access to the court; or he was perhaps swayed by the general hostility felt by many clerics to the king's association with the French. Whatever the reason, Richard was not disposed to tolerate such criticisms from his subjects. After taking advice the king forced the commons, who had sponsored the bill, to apologise and admit that their bill was against his *"regality, royal estate and liberty."* Thomas Haxey, however, did not escape so lightly for he was adjudged a traitor and threatened with death. The lords, when questioned by Richard, had informed him that it was treason to induce the commons, or anyone else, to try to interfere with the running of the royal household. Thomas was only saved from execution by the timely intervention, and pleas, of the clergy. He did eventually receive a pardon. This must have been before 1404, for in the October of that year Thomas was again, in his role as proctor for the Abbot of Selby, present at a meeting of Parliament.

John de Shireburn was abbot at Selby for almost forty years and, during those years he received many gifts from his influential friends. However he had to wait through most of his time as abbot for a present bequeathed to him by Henry de Snayth. Henry had been Prebend of York, Lincoln, Beverley and Howden. He was a native of Snaith and had been educated as a youth at Selby Abbey. Amongst his gifts to the monks, willed to them in February 1380, Henry left 100 marks towards the rebuilding of the abbey and 40 marks for the improvement, or repair of a house at Snaith, used as a priest's resting place. He bequeathed to the abbot his complete set of satin vestments lavishly embroidered with golden suns, but, he stipulated, the abbot was to wait until the Lord Bishop of Lincoln, an executor of the will, had no further need of them! John de Buckingham, Lord Bishop of Lincoln, died in 1398. Eighteen years after the will had been written, John de Shireburn at last received his gift. He was abbot until 1407 so may have had the opportunity to wear Henry de Snayth's gorgeous vestments for at least a few Festivals before he, too, no longer needed them.

Higher Education

In the fourteenth century Pope Benedict XII encouraged the religious houses to provide more facilities for higher studies. Each monastery with the necessary resources was to maintain a master to teach the monks grammar and to assist the ablest students to go to university. Selby Abbey managed to send several carefully chosen members of the community to Oxford and Cambridge. Though all of them may not have returned with degrees many, as it has been recorded, reached high positions in the town and elsewhere.

Items in the account rolls for 1459-60 show that the Bailiff at Stanford-on-Avon was paying an annual pension of £10 to a monk at Oxford. He also sent the student a further £1.15s.0d. to cover his travelling expenses and other needs for the Long Vacation in autumn. Twenty years later it was noted that four pounds had been sent to aid the scholars at Cambridge.

Two monks who gained degrees returned to the town to become abbots at Selby Abbey. One was John Ousthorp who graduated as a Bachelor of Theology at Oxford and became abbot in 1437. The other was William Pygot who succeeded John de Shireburn as abbot in 1407. Pygot was chosen to go to Oxford University in accordance with the Benedictine Statute that stipulated each house was to send one student, out of every 20 members of its community, to Oxford or Cambridge. There were many references to William Pygot in the rolls of 1398/99. He was given £6.13s.4d. to cover expenses incurred at his admission to the degree of Bachelor of Canon Law. The ceremony of inception to this higher degree, whose rules stipulated five years study, was an expensive one. In the same period it was noted that the abbot commanded a gift of 20 shillings be given to Brother John de Cawood, Dominican of York, at his inception in theology; this also involved an elaborate and costly ceremony. William received a yearly pension of £10 which, on one occasion, was taken to him by John Palfreyman, a regular traveller for the abbey. On his travels to Oxford, John rested at the manor leased out by the monks at Stanford-on-Avon. In one instance, William Pygot, using eight horses, was accompanied by John de Birne and others from Selby to Stanford. William then continued on to Oxford. John Palfreyman was later paid expenses to bring the horses back to Selby. John de Birne was given funds to go on monastery business from Stanford to London. This included speaking to Master Ralph de Selby, a Doctor of Canon and Civil Law who was Baron of the Exchequer and Archdeacon of Buckingham. He was also a creditor of the abbey who, it is recorded later in the accounts, was paid £13.6s.8d. in part payment of 200 marks borrowed from him in preceding years.

Horses were an important part of travel in the medieval period and featured often in the rolls. Expenses of 28 shillings were noted for William Pygot and others going to Oxford with four horses in September 1399; plus a bill for medical attention needed by sick horses on the return journey. An amount of sixpence was later paid to William Farrier for shoeing horses hired by Pygot at Oxford to bring him back to Selby. John de Birne left the abbey with six horses and travelled with others to collect rents at Queniborough and Stanford. They then took the horses to Oxford where they met with William Pygot and accompanied him to Northampton. Before leaving the town John had given the scholar a gift of 3s.4d. to buy a pair of boots. The general chapter of the Benedictine Order in England was held in Northampton every three years under the statute of Benedict XII. John de Shireburn, the Abbot of Selby, must have once again, used his age and feebleness to be excused attending the chapter and appointed William as his proctor.

CHAPTER 5

THE DISSOLUTION OF THE MONASTERIES

The Battles for the Crown

Three Henrys ruled England during the time William Pygot was Abbot of Selby. The first, Henry IV, who had been outspoken about the extravagances of his predecessor, Richard II, soon received complaints regarding the increasing expenditure of his royal household and the misappropriation of taxes. He also earned the enmity of the Percy family who had been instrumental in putting him on the throne. They rebelled against a king who had not paid the huge sums due to them or allowed them to keep the ransoms taken for prisoners. Henry 'Hotspur' Percy lost his life in 1403 during an insurrection against Henry's rule. When his father, Henry Percy, Earl of Northumberland, was killed five years later at the Battle of Bramham Moor, near Tadcaster, the rebellion was brought to a close.

Richard Scrope, Archbishop of York, had also joined the rebellion against Henry's rule. He was critical of his taxation of the clergy and harboured fears that this might be followed by clerical disendowment. The Percys failed to support the archbishop in his actions against the king which forced Scrope to disband his army and surrender himself to the king's supporters. It is not clear whether the Abbot of Selby or men levied from the region were part of the archbishop's forces. Richard Scrope was executed at York, the only pre-Reformation bishop to meet such a fate. His body was interred at the east end of York Minster where it was shortly joined by that of his brother, Stephen who had died at Turnham Hall, near Cliffe, and whose body had rested overnight at Selby Abbey.

The state of the king's finances improved after the cessation of the revolts but Henry's health gradually deteriorated ending in his death in 1413. His son, Henry V succeeded him. He was a young man of 25 years, full of confidence in his own abilities and determined to restore order and peace to his realm. He also aimed to justify his right to the throne of France where there was much civil unrest. The importance of ships for both trade and war was recognised. Attempts were already in progress to protect merchant ships by the formation of a kind of coastguard force. Some of these ships were stationed off the east coast ready to protect trading vessels and to levy the duties owed for the services they rendered. Henry V created his own navy consisting of 38 vessels but found they were not sufficient for his campaigns against the French. He therefore commandeered any vessel that could be found of 20 tons or over, and hired others from Holland. Men were press-ganged into his navy to crew the ships.

Shipbuilding was a growing industry in and around Selby. Local ships appropriated by Henry V in 1415 included the following: *The Clement of Rocliffe, Master Mariner, John Hunt; Nicholas of Fysshelak- John Butler; Catherine of Selby- Robert Colly; and Mary of York,* whose master was *Robert Gryce.*

Henry sailed to France with 1,500 vessels carrying 2,000 men-at-arms, 6,000 archers with supporting units, stores and arms. Harfleur was captured but not before the king had lost half his men to illness during a lengthy siege. Henry then began a long hard march across Normandy towards Calais. After several skirmishes with the enemy he was intercepted by a large French force near the village of Agincourt. In the ensuing battle the overconfident French suffered great losses at the hands of English long bow archers supported by dismounted men-at-arms. A contingent of men from the Selby area was commanded by Sir Brian Stapleton of Carlton. He was counted amongst the friends of the abbey for the kitchener recorded that not long after Agincourt, the abbot sent the knight a gift of a boar and two swans. Another man from the Selby region, who had probably been educated at the abbey, was Sir Robert Babthorpe of Hemingbrough. He was Controller of Henry's Household and executor of the King's will. Robert drew up a roll containing the names of every Englishman present at the Battle of Agincourt. This resounding victory on the field gained Henry the unstinting support of Parliament and the respect of the French forces. In 1417 the king led another army into France and in the following three years ruthlessly reclaimed the whole of Normandy. Sir Brian Stapleton died during this campaign, after the taking of Caen. Henry had plans for more expeditions in the conquest of his kingdom but in 1422 he died of dysentery.

His son, Henry VI was only nine months old when he became King of England and France. The country was governed well until 1437 when Henry declared he was of age and took over the ruling of his lands. His reign proved a disastrous one for his subjects. Lacking the energy and purpose of his father, he seemed ready to accept peace at any price. The English suffered humiliating defeats in the wars abroad and without a strong leader by 1453 had lost both Normandy and Aquitaine. The king who had stayed at home during these conflicts suffered a breakdown and from that time on participated only rarely in the government of his realm.

With this weak ruler on the throne noble families contended for position and power. It had been shown that the crown could be held not only by right of descent but also through conquest. This led to the Wars of the Roses, between supporters of the House of York and those of the House of Lancaster. The first fierce conflicts between the two houses ended when the victorious Yorkists usurped Henry VI and put Edward IV on the throne. His father, Richard of York, had been a contender for the crown but had lost his life at the Battle of Wakefield in 1460.

Selby does not feature in any details concerning these wars although its inhabitants may have been part of the levies gathered by both sides and it may also have given shelter to fugitives from the battles. The nearest fighting to the town took place at Ferrybridge. Edward, advancing north to meet the Lancastrians, had made his headquarters at Pontefract. The only crossings on the Aire for a considerable distance were at Castleford and Ferrybridge. A ferry at the latter had been superseded in the fourteenth century by a wooden bridge which, by the number of repairs recorded and the tolls collected, was in constant use by medieval traffic going to and from York. In 1461 a struggle for the possession of this vital crossing developed into a major engagement whose outcome could have destroyed the Yorkists' plans. Edward dispatched a small force to hold the bridge over the Aire but his men found it had been destroyed by their enemies. The Yorkists set about making a temporary narrow crossing but were taken by surprise by Lord Clifford's cavalry who killed them all and secured the bridge for the Lancastrians. This disaster for Edward most probably took place in the early hours of the 28th. March. Determined to win back control of the crossing, he sent troops to

Castleford where they traversed the river then came back down the north bank and attacked Clifford and his troop. A fierce battle took place in which both sides lost many men. The Yorkists won the day; Clifford and his cavalry fled towards the Lancastrian lines. That same night Edward moved his troops safely over the Aire at Castleford and Ferrybridge. They then made their way by various routes towards Sherburn-in-Elmet and the main Lancastrian army. Lord Clifford and his men who had hit the Yorkists hard were cut down later that day before they could reach their main force. On the 29th March, 1461, the bloodiest engagement of the Wars of the Roses took place. Edward IV gained the throne after a fiercely fought contest that became known as the Battle of Towton. The Lancastrians had sorely missed having a king of the calibre of Edward to lead them in their conflicts.

Among those supporters still loyal to HenryVI was Thomas Roos, grandson of the Earl of Warwick. He was three years old when his father died and as a special favour Henry VI had made it permissible for Thomas to have the livery of his lands when he was only eighteen. Those estates included the manor of Turnham Hall, near Selby, where so many men of note seemed to have resided, but when Lord Roos took up arms in his support of the House of Lancaster these lands were forfeited.

King Henry, supported by his Queen, Margaret and the Prince of Wales, had been in York when news reached them of the devastating defeat at Towton. They fled north towards Berwick accompanied by the Duke of Somerset, Lord Roos and several others who had managed to make their escape from the battlefield before the Yorkist cavalry cut them down. Many of these loyal followers of Henry lost their lives in later struggles. The last of them were hunted down by Lord Montague. At the Battle of Hexham in 1484, the Duke of Somerset, Lords Roos and Hungerford, deserted by their levies, were captured. They were all executed. Lord Roos meeting his fate two days after his capture on Sandhill, at Newcastle -on-Tyne. He had ceased to be Lord of Turnham Hall before his death for an Act of Attainder had been passed upon him on the fourth of November, 1461. This Act which could be carried out without judicial process, took land and civil rights away from a person sentenced to death for treason or felony. Edward IV gave the manor to John Pilkington as a reward for his loyalty. Over twenty years later, when Henry VII, of the House of Lancaster, was on the throne, the Attainder was reversed in favour of Edward Lord Roos.

Many more battles, intrigues and murders took place before this Henry, the first of the Tudor monarchs, was on the throne of England. Edward IV survived various plots to remove him. When he died suddenly in 1483 his young son's claim to the throne was disputed by a number of people. The disappearance and death of Edward V and his brother is still a subject of much research and controversy at the centre of which is their uncle, who, in 1483 became Richard III of England. He had only been in power for two years when another claimant to the throne landed in Wales. This was Henry, son of Edmund Tudor, who many years before had been forced to flee to France. Aided by French naval and military support, and joined by the few remaining Lancastrians, he marched into England. At the Battle of Bosworth, Richard, who received little or no support from those he had summoned to his cause, was defeated and killed.

Henry VII married Elizabeth of York, Edward IV's daughter, but despite this there were uprisings against his rule. Serious revolts broke out in Yorkshire in 1489 but the king won the goodwill of the people there when his opponents allied themselves with the Scots, the long-standing enemies of northern Englishmen.

Hostilities between the Scots and the English had continued throughout the battles for the throne. During one of these periods Edward III had given Selby Abbey a licence to crenellate their church and other buildings. The battlemented parapet flanked the two towers and extended over the entire front. A. Hutchinson in his booklet on Selby Abbey Church remarked that the buildings matched a description applied to Durham:

> *Half church of God*
> *Half castle 'gainst the Scot*

.
The king had also had given Drax Priory and Convent licence to add battlements to the upper part of the walls of both their church and their bell-tower to help defend themselves against any marauders.

The numerous uprisings against the various monarchs, the continuous warring with the Scots and the presence of roaming mercenaries, robbers and vagabonds in the woods surrounding places like Selby must have required constant vigilance. In 1431 Henry Botson was awarded 6s8d. by the monks of the abbey for:

> *...his pains in arresting Richard Legiard and his companions coming to Hillam in war-like array about the feast of the Nativity of John the Baptist, and giving them over to the sheriff of Yorkshire.*

It was an offence for anyone to help or harbour Scots. Robert Brown of Cow Lane in Selby was fined 3s.4d. at the Manor Court for receiving Scots and other suspected people into his house. As the hostilities continued many people found it necessary to have a certificate to prove that they were *"trewe Inglissemen"*. In 1476 John Richardson who had been accused of being *"a Scottes man borne in Scotland"* obtained a certificate stating he was a true *"ligeman to the king of England"*. It was witnessed by ten men made up of esquires, gentlemen, yeomen and husbandmen. They vouched that John had been born in Crossby near Carlisle and gave details of his two godfathers and godmother. The copies of the certificates in the York Records Office include another addressed in 1447 to John Tong, mayor of that city. It concerned John Colyn who was accused of being a Scot *"and no Ynglysman"*. The witnesses on his behalf included Master Robert Symson, dean of Darlington and Sir Robert Clerk, priest.

Despite the wars with France and Scotland, when Henry VII died he left his surviving son a united and peaceful realm. This situation did not last for soon the ministers were fully occupied finding new sources of revenue to cover the immense expenses incurred by an ebullient and athletic young king intent on making England a strong and powerful kingdom. An uneasy peace with Scotland grew progressively more fragile as the Borderers continued to cross the Tweed to attack their enemies and steal their cattle and goods whilst the English devastated the country's small navy.

Matters came to a head in 1512 when Henry VIII joined the Holy League of the Pope and Emperor Maximilian in their war against France. The French appealed to the 'Auld Alliance' between them and the Scots but the Pope threatened to excommunicate the Scottish king, James IV, if he broke the treaties made with England; treaties that Henry had already broken. In 1513 France appealed again for the Scots to invade England. James therefore, delivered a defiant ultimatum to Henry in Flanders but this was summarily dismissed and three days later the English put the French to flight in a battle that heralded the petering out of hostilities there. James by that time however was moving towards the border with England at the head of the largest and most magnificent army a King of Scotland had ever led. An equally large English force met the Scots on a lonely north-eastern spur of the Cheviots where three hills of Flodden make a natural fortress. It was here, facing their homeland, that the Scottish King halted his army. On the 9th.September 1513, during a fierce and bloody battle James IV, many of the aristocrats of Scotland and thousands of their countrymen died fighting with extraordinary obstinacy and ferocity. The body of James IV on its way to London, was put on display in York where, as late as the seventeenth century, a citizen would sue for libel anyone who called him "a Scottish foundling". It is known that, on the English side, the noblemen who survived the Battle of Flodden included Sir Brian Stapleton, knight, of Carlton, whose grandfather had been at Agincourt; Sir George Darcy of Temple Hirst and Sir John Everingham of the manor of Birkin. The Bishop of Durham was also present but no evidence has been uncovered to show whether the Abbot of Selby or his proctors, were there. The number of leaders representing the region around the town suggests there would have been a feudal muster of local men.

Having survived the ferocious onslaught at the Battle of Flodden, Sir Brian Stapleton was present at the most staggeringly expensive and lavish encounter between Henry VIII and Francis I of France. An affair which was supposed to bring an end to the long period of hostilities. The meeting took place near Guisnes in France in June 1520 in an area known as the 'Field of the Cloth of Gold'. A tournament took place there that is said to have been the last display of medieval chivalry. Henry spared no expense as he attempted to outshine the French king with the splendour of his tents and the glitter of his trappings. The colourful pageantry impressed all who witnessed it but the flamboyant event failed to bring peace between the two nations.

The Last Abbots

Little information has been found concerning the abbots who officiated over Selby Abbey during the long years of conflicts with France and Scotland. John Cave became abbot after William Pygot. His family had originally been awarded lands by William the Conqueror in North and South Cave and they lived in Yorkshire for many centuries. Some of their relations resided at Stanford where the abbey had extensive possessions. John Cave was abbot for only seven years but his successor, John Ousthorp held the abbacy from 1436 to 1466. It was during these years that the eastern aisle was added to the north transept. This was made possible by an endowment for a chantry there by John Lathom. Pious and wealthy persons had begun a practice of building small chapels called chantries which they endowed with rents or lands. The monies arising from these gifts were used to make sure that one or two priests were daily employed saying mass in the chantries for the souls of the founders, their relatives and other benefactors. The custom lasted until Edward VI dissolved them by Act of Parliament and the endowments taken by the crown. John Lathom who endowed the chantry in Selby Abbey was an ecclesiastic holding high office in the diocese of York. In his will he ordered a pipe of wine to be distributed amongst the abbot and his brethren at Selby at the solemn celebration of his death. He also bequeathed them money to continue to *"celebrate for my soul"* in the Perpendicular chantry which can still be seen today on the opposite side of the choir, and to the east of the north transept. Chantries already referred to were, one founded at Hambleton by William Hamelton in 1307 and another at Gateforth by John Lacy.

The abbot from 1466 to 1486 was John Sharrowe but all that is recorded regarding him is that he was present at the famous banquet at Cawood held in January 1466 to celebrate the induction of George Neville as Archbishop of York. There is even less known concerning Lawrence Selby who followed him and was abbot for 18 years. His successor, Robert Deeping was the first monk for more than a century and a half to be chosen from another monastery. He came from Croyland Abbey and, sometime between 1504 and 1518, he had its arms carved on beams in new rooms that were being added near to the abbey gateway. The pattern of the tracery in one room was described as being extremely delicate and exquisite in design whilst on the north side were 'painted in' frescoes, single figures in compartments, which formed a feature of considerable interest. Thomas Rawlinson and John Barwic each served as abbot for four years. John Barwic, John Shireburn and Lawrence Selby are the only three abbots whose tombstones are still to be seen in Selby Abbey Church. They are all in urgent need of conservation. This work is to be carried out by Cliveden Conservation at a cost of ten thousand pounds; the finance being covered by the Selby Abbey Trust. In 1526 John Barwic was succeeded by Robert Selby, alias Rogers. He was the last Abbot of Selby.

During the period the last few abbots were at Selby the English Benedictines moved gradually away from the renunciation of the world, a concept that in earlier years had brought the black monks admiration, influence and their numerous benefactors. Material comforts played a greater part in their lives than either strict self-discipline or religious fervour. People of influence were concerned about the standards of religious life practised in its institutions. Henry V who had been sympathetic to the monks made efforts to introduce some reforms but there was a general unwillingness to reverse the trend away from the strict Benedictine rules. When Henry VIII came on the throne the monks' influence for good was in decline. At Selby they were no longer attaining positions of importance outside the abbey and little teaching was being done. Religious houses were still receiving endowments through their continuing vigilance at the bedsides of the ailing rich and they had also appropriated nearly all of the country's church patronage. Eighteen churches contributed to the upkeep of Selby Abbey. Continuing prosperity tempted the monks and friars of many religious houses to stray from the godly life they had led, towards a more comfortable and idle existence; an inactiveness that helped to make them more susceptible to evil thoughts and deeds. Examples of how monks at Selby Abbey broke their vows have already been described.

This departure from lives of piety and christian zeal had an effect on the people living in and around Selby. Estates were neglected, jobs lost and the guidance and teaching once given by the monks had to be sought elsewhere. Selby had grown, by medieval standards, into a town of modest size. It continued however to be dependent on the abbey for many things and was still answerable to the Abbot of Selby in his position as lord of the manor. Courts were held where offenders were punished and rules laid down as they had been for centuries. For example at the Great Inquest, 25 October Henry VIII (1533) it was ordered, amongst many other things:

That no man, or other person cast any carrion in the dam. That none from henceforth fish or fowl in the dam, or in the lordship and liberties of Selby, or hunt without licence of my Lord Abbot of Selby. None harbour vagabonds from henceforth. That no brewster sell any ale above a penny a gallon. That every baker make good bread and wholesome for man's body, and sell according as they buy. That the cordwainers sew well their shoes, that the miller grinds the Lord's tenants afore other men.

These familiar instructions show that life had changed little for the common people but what was different was that Selby, along with other richly endowed abbeys and monasteries was attracting hostile publicity and, as Archbishop Scrope had feared, people were beginning to question their right to so many generous endowments and lavish gifts.

Pilgrimage of Grace

Apart from the battle at Flodden Field and the king's excursions abroad the early years of Henry's reign had little impact on the north of England. It was not until 1529 when the king, declared himself head of the Church of England that his northern subjects showed signs of unrest. This pronouncement which destroyed the power of the Pope in England was followed by further actions which caused the north to erupt into open rebellion.

In 1515 Cardinal Wolsey, royal councillor to Henry VIII, had obtained grants enabling him to raise revenue by closing a number of monasteries. The houses chosen to help finance the building of Christ Church College, Oxford, were described as being small places with low incomes where neither God was served nor rules obeyed. Following his downfall from favour and subsequent death in 1530 Wolsey's place was taken by Thomas Cromwell who, within four years, held the high position of King's Secretary. Cromwell committed to making drastic reforms in the Church became Vicegerent, giving him the powers of Royal Supremacy in religious matters. In this capacity he pointed out to his sovereign how by closing more monasteries the king could increase his royal revenues and, at the same time, punish those abbots who had not supported his divorce plans. The Abbot of Selby was one of those who in 1530 did sign the letter to the pope in favour of Henry's divorce from his queen, Katherine of Aragon.

Royal commissioners made visitations to selected monasteries and after vigorous enquiries declared the conduct and behaviour of the brethren had not improved despite earlier warnings concerning their irregularities. In 1536 an Act of Parliament was passed which authorised the closing of all religious houses with revenues under £200 a year. The annual available income of Selby Abbey at its peak may have exceeded £1000. The number of suppressed monasteries totalled 376; their combined annual revenue came to £32,000 and the goods, chattels and plate confiscated were valued at £100,000. Henry took most of this but he gave various valuable articles to chosen subjects to make them aware of what was available. The commissioner continued with visitations to other houses where they tried to induce the monks and friars to surrender to their inevitable fate. People in the north of England were already nursing grievances against various social and economic changes that had been recently made by Henry's government. This, coupled with the resentment and fear growing concerning the interference in religious matters and the treatment of the monks, brought about an uprising in the north that became known as the 'Pilgrimage of Grace'.

Trouble first flared up in Lincolnshire where Cromwell's commissioners were busy assessing the size and prosperity of certain religious houses and seizing many of their assets. Warned by their vicar of the forthcoming visit of the commissioners to Louth the church's valuable treasures were hidden away and the townsfolk prepared to meet Cromwell's men. In October 1536, armed with pitchforks, staves and scythes, they crowded into the market place and successfully dispersed the unwanted visitors. The rebellion spread to towns all over the county and spilled over into Yorkshire. Henry's treatment of the monasteries was felt more keenly there for, despite their lapses, the people still looked upon the monks and friars as friends involved in a great part of their lives. It also made more of an impact because of the greater number of earls and nobles in the county who patronised the religious houses. The monasteries served them all, not only for the service of God but as shelters for their aged relatives and unmarried daughters and the provision of lodgings when travelling in wild, lonely districts.

The rebels eventually gained control of nearly all the north-east of England as far as the Scottish border. Five hostages had been taken at the uprising in Louth. They had been forced to write a letter to the king which outlined the pilgrims' wishes. These included no more suppressions of the monasteries, the restoring of Papal supremacy and the return of religious observances and customs, an end to taxation during peace-time and the tenth paid by the clergy. They also suggested a Parliament at York or Lincoln where northern grievances could be settled on the spot. In all correspondence with King Henry during the uprisings the rebels insisted the quarrel was not with their sovereign or the nobility but with the government, especially Thomas Cromwell and others like him who they charged with manipulating affairs for their own ends. A copy of their demands was sent to Lord Thomas Darcy at Temple Hirst manor, once the home of the Knights Templar and not more than six miles from Selby. Lord Darcy held offices of trust but had lost favour with the king when his strong religious convictions had prevented him from fully supporting Henry's divorce. He was later restored to favour and, among his duties, was made supervisor of all the royal castles in Yorkshire. When rebel movements began in the county Lord Darcy informed the king of seditious talk around Sedbergh. This prompted Henry to order Thomas to move from his home in Temple Hirst to command the castle at Pontefract. As the number of uprisings increased over 140 people of property, including the Archbishop of York, sought shelter in the castle. Lord Darcy, a deeply religious and honourable man was unhappy with the continuing suppression of the monasteries but felt strongly about his duty to his king. That position was played upon by the leaders of the Pilgrimage of Grace when they sent him a copy of the requests written out at Louth and in subsequent meetings with Lord Darcy when the castle was under siege.

These meetings at Pontefract took place during the pilgrims march southward through Yorkshire. They were making their way towards London, gathering support from the many towns on their route. There were many groups with their own leaders but the main one to emerge was led by Robert Aske, a lawyer, whose family lived at Aughton, near Bubwith. After he had been reluctantly drawn into the fray, Aske sought out men of authority to help the revolt succeed. These included Lord Darcy at Temple Hirst and Henry Percy, 6th. Earl of Northumberland residing at Wressle Castle, situated on the east bank of the Derwent, around 5½ miles from Selby. However, Aske soon discovered both men had moved from their residences to Pontefract Castle. The latter, unlike his brothers, Sir Thomas and Sir Ingram, did not join the rebels at any stage of the rebellion. Supporters of the pilgrims' cause were called to a muster on St. Wilfrid's Day, 12th. October, at Skipwith Common. It is reported that the supporters from in and around Selby met on Riccall Common adjacent to the moor. Thomas Maunsell, vicar of Brayton was pressed into attending the muster. At first he had been as reluctant as Robert Aske to join the rebellion but eventually he swore the oath to enter the Pilgrimage for no profit for himself but suppression of the heretics. Maunsell quickly became a willing and very capable recruitment officer.

After more meetings at Market Weighton the groups divided and soon the towns of York, Hull, Pontefract, Wakefield and Doncaster were in their hands. Thomas Maunsell was instrumental in gathering supporters in the last three towns for, after the capture of York, he had been sent ahead by Robert Aske to reconnoitre Pontefract Castle and, as recruiting sergeant, to muster the inhabitants of the local towns to join the Pilgrimage of Grace. As the main groups marched towards Pontefract Castle many country families with their retainers, and a few Yorkshire abbots swelled the ranks of their supporters. A troubled Lord Darcy, in command of a poorly defended castle, whose pleas for help were being ignored by his king, sent a steward out to ask Robert Aske for a full statement covering their grievances. A meeting was then held in the castle attended by Lord Darcy, Sir Robert Constable, who had fought for the king at Flodden Field, around fifty other notables and Robert Aske, supported by Thomas Maunsell. The outcome was that the king's men were given 24 hours in which to consider the rebels' requests and to surrender the castle. When the time elapsed all those who had not fled the refuge took the Pilgrims' oath. This included Lord Thomas Darcy and Sir Robert Constable.

When Henry VIII received news that the rebels were over-running the north he sent the Duke of Norfolk to deal with them ordering him only to negotiate if it appeared that the king's men might suffer an embarrassing defeat. At the end of October the Duke facing an army four times the size of his troops was forced to agree to a meeting of leaders in Doncaster. There it was decided that representatives of the rebels should travel to London to put their case before Henry. The delegation believed that their requests, similar to those appealed for in Louth would be accepted. However, deliberate delays on the part of the king during which he plotted and bluffed whilst increasing his army, meant it was well into December before the pilgrims received any promises from Henry. Promises that persuaded Robert Aske and others to ask their supporters to continue with the truce begun in November.

After Lord Darcy had taken the pilgrims' oath the manor at Temple Hirst became a council chamber where representatives from both sides met and leaders of the rebels received hospitality. At one stage during the truce, whilst the intrigues and manoeuvring continued, it appears that Robert Aske stayed in Selby. At one point a message was sent there asking him to join Lord Darcy at Temple Hirst to view some suspect letters brought by the king's men. There also exists a letter written from Selby by Robert Aske. During the troubles both sides had plundered the deserted monasteries for anything to help their cause whilst many of the religious houses that still existed sent what they could to assist the rebels. The priory at Wotton was one of the latter. The following letter written to the prioress by Robert Aske is to be found in the Records Office:

> To the sub-prior and his bretheryn, and to the lady prioris and all hir covent lady of Wotton, be this dd. 1536
> Right wel-beloved I hertly do recommend me unto you advertising you that I have rescyved the spice plate by th'andes of Mr. Prior of Ellerton, for the whiche I hertly thanke you for the same and you shall always be assured of me to do you pleasour unto dethe take me. I never entended to be a suppressor of religious, but always a preservatour and maynteynour of them ,and therefor hertly pray you be merry and think not that I wold hurte ne harme your house, for of southe my mynde is to preserve you all.

From Selby the xviith day of Novembre and who soever wold do you any displeasure shall doom the same.
       Your captan
ROB ASKE

The letter does not reveal whether Aske was enjoying the hospitality of Selby Abbey but there would have been many inhabitants of the town willing to give shelter to the rebels. Records reveal that there were many ardent supporters in nearby Snaith. The movements of the monks there had already been curtailed by the king. On the 12th. October 1535, an order had been issued from the manor court at Snaith forbidding the prior, sub-monk, and all the priests of the church from leaving their own houses or the house in which they dined together after eight o' clock in the evening in winter and ten o' clock in summer on pain of forfeiting to the king, 6s.8d. for each offence. When the following year the rebels were marching on Pontefract Castle they were joined by the town officials from Snaith. In November, following the agreement of a truce between the king's men and the rebels Robert Aske took the opportunity to ride to Wressle Castle to meet with the Earl of Northumberland, who was still refusing to aid the rebels. He found the earl low in health and further troubled by the fact that two chests of clothes coming to him from London had been stolen by some rebels from Snaith. When Aske managed to retrieve the full chests and return them to their owner the earl was so impressed that he presented the goods to the miscreants' leader.

Robert Aske and Lord Darcy were amongst those who were trying to keep the truce intact but there were many on both sides who acted differently. Darcy received news that some royal troops had been seen gathering together in a woodland near Snaith where he had another residence. It was also reported that Sir Brian Hastings, Sheriff of Yorkshire, and steadfastly loyal to the king, was with other notables and 5000 men heading that way intending to take him prisoner. Darcy, normally a peaceful man, reacted angrily by warning that if the Sheriff so much as put a spark to Snaith he would burn every house Sir Brian possessed.

William Nicholson, a tenant farmer, and John Hallam, a yeoman farmer, were members of the Pilgrimage of Grace. They laid no trust in the king's promises and planned to take the Duke of Norfolk as hostage to force Henry to keep his word. It is reported that in 1537 rebels from Snaith joined these men and others in what turned out to be a fruitless attempt at a second revolt in Hull. Nicholson and Hallam were executed in the town in February of that year. Sir John Constable, a kinsman of Sir Robert who had joined the rebels, presided over the executions.

As the executed men had feared, Henry VIII had no intention of carrying out the pilgrims' wishes but fully intended to punish those who had led the uprisings against his government. Systematically, using intrigue or force the main participants in the rebellions were apprehended and executed. The Brayton priest, Thomas Maunsell and Sir Richard Tempest were amongst those who had tried to keep the peace whilst awaiting the implementation of the king's promises. Thomas's fate is not known but Sir Richard, accused of double-dealing, was put in the Tower where he died of the plague. Sir Ingram Percy was another captive who did not emerge alive from the Tower. Heads of religious houses who were known to have taken part in the Pilgrimage of Grace were executed. The king had wanted Lord Darcy, Robert Aske and Sir Robert Constable to be executed in or near to Doncaster, but the Duke of Norfolk pointed out the dangers of another rebellion breaking out if Darcy should be taken back to the north. Lord Darcy died on Tower Hill on the last day of June 1537 and his head displayed on London Bridge. At the king's insistence, Aske and Constable were taken north. Robert Aske was brought to York where, like so many before him, he was dragged on a hurdle through the city to the scaffold at Clifford's Tower. The execution took place on market day to ensure the greatest number of people would be there to witness the king's punishment. Aske was beheaded, his body dismembered and the remains hung in chains on Clifford's Tower. Sir Robert Constable was executed in the same manner on market day in Hull and his body hung in chains on Beverley Gate.

One of the positions Lord Darcy had held was that of High Steward to Selby Abbey. There were a number of stewards responsible for the administration of the monks' properties but this title was held by a member of the nobility appointed to support the monastery in times of need. The position lay in abeyance with the death of Darcy and was not re-established until 1974 when Brigadier Kenneth Hargreaves, CBE, Lord Lieutenant of the West Riding, was appointed High Steward of Selby Abbey Church.

The possessions of Lord Darcy, Sir Robert Constable, Nicholas Tempest and many others whose lives had been so savagely taken, were amongst those awarded to, what the king ruled as, more worthy persons. In 1538, Sir Marmaduke Constable, knight of Everingham and kinsman to Sir Robert, received in thanks for his loyalty to Henry a grant of the site of Drax Priory with a great deal of land belonging to it.

The End of a Monastery

Robert Rogers, the last abbot of Selby Abbey escaped the reprisals that followed the failure of the Pilgrimage of Grace. In April 1539 he and the Abbot of St. Mary's York, showed great courage as mitred abbots by taking their seats in Parliament. An Act legalising actions already being taken to close religious houses was passed. It confirmed the dissolution of all the remaining institutions, including Selby Abbey. Out of the 186 greater monasteries left, only 38 were wealthier than Selby. It is reported that none of the twenty mitred abbots present in Parliament voted against the Bill.

Later that year a panel of commissioners, led by Walter Hendle, the Solicitor of Augmentations, came north to complete the suppressions of the monasteries. For part of the time they stayed in Selby from whence this letter was sent:

> *The Commissioners of the North to Thomas Cromwell.*
> *After meest humble commendacious to your good lordship. pleaseth it the same to be advertiesed, that we have altered Burton-upon- Trent, and accordinge to the kinges highnes commission and instructions we have dissolved the house of Hampole, Sancte Oswaldes, Pountefracte, Fontaunce, Sancte Maries in Yourke, Nonappleton and Selbye, and also altered the house of Sancte Leonerdes in Yourke, after suche ordre and fassion as we trust shall appeir to your lordship to be the kinges honour and contentacion*
> *At Selbie, the viijth of Decembre,*
> *Yours at commandement,*
> *Waltere Hendle, Richard Layton, Thomas Legh, Rychard Belassys, Richard Watkyns.*

Dr. Thomas Legh, Dr. Layton (afterwards dean of York) and their assistants had been the ones concerned in a visitation to Selby, the details of which were later destroyed. Morrell states in his *"History of Selby'* that surviving documents which include letters passed between the commissioners and secretary Cromwell were, in 1867 held by the British Museum, (Cotton MS. E4, fol. 242). Selby Abbey and many other religious domains, were accused of the lapses from grace as alleged by the enemies of the monastic system, but there were no special charges brought against them.

The Last Monks

Following the dissolution of Selby Abbey on the sixth of December 1539, the monks were awarded annual pensions. In line with many of the other religious houses the abbot received one hundred pounds per annum, the prior eight pounds, the 22 remaining monks received pensions ranging from between five and just over six pounds and two novices £2.13s.4d. To help them augment these pensions, Abbot Rogers and his brethren were given dispensation in March 1540 to accept any church living offered to them. What happened to most of them after this date is unknown.

Tradition has it that Abbot Rogers fled to France taking with him as many valuables and documents as he could carry. This has not been verified but documents from the abbey have been discovered in France. As late as 1968 the original manuscript of *"Historia Selebiensis Monasterii'* was found by Monsieur Pierre Janin in the French Bibliotheque Nationale. Many other valuable abbey documents which may never have left England are now housed in the Brynmor Jones Library at Hull University. What is proven is that in 1543, Robert Rogers and his chaplain were living in a house on Gowthorpe. It was there that he gave an unnamed person the original volume of the Selby Chartulary or Coucher Book, in which were recorded, amongst other relevant matters, particulars of the lands granted to the abbey over the years. This volume, now in the British Museum, has the following statement written in it;

> *This bouke was dlyvered to me by Maister Robert Rogers uppon Friday the xxvith day off July anno regni regis Henrici vllj xxxv (in the thirty fifth year of King Henry VIII's reign) at his house in Gowthorpe in Selby, Sir George Goode being present, his chaplyn.*

The abbot's chaplain, Sir George Goode, was a native of Barlow, near Selby, who after the dissolution, appeared in records as a priest at Haddlesey. 'Sir' in this case indicated that he was an ordained priest and had some literary education.

The Ancient Parish of Snaith

Rogers finally moved from Selby to live in retirement at Rawcliffe manor in the ancient parish of Snaith. At the dissolution the head of Snaith Priory received a pension of six pounds. Its last priest, James Lay, ended his days in the vicinity of his church, most probably carrying out his duties until his death, sixteen months later. The churches that had been under the jurisdiction of Selby Abbey were divided into two distinct peculiars except for Adlingfleet which reverted to the Archbishop of York. Being Peculiars meant that both were exempt from being ruled by the Bishop in whose diocese they lay. Brayton was joined with Selby whilst the chapelries of Airmyn, Goole, Hook,

Rawcliffe, Swinefleet, Whitgift and Carlton became part of Snaith Peculiar. The two divisions remained unchanged until the nineteenth century.

Sharing out the Land

Selby Abbey remained in the hands of the king until 26th. August 1541 when its remains, the manor and a large portion of its property in the immediate neighbourhood of Selby were granted to Sir Ralph Sadler, knight. Sir Ralph was asked to pay a lump sum of £736 and a yearly rent of £3.10s.8d. The annual values of the lands and properties were recorded by commissioners in 1540. The moated site of the monastery with its buildings, dovecote, horsemill, orchards, and an area described as *"Little Park, overgrown and full of nettles"*, covered about ten acres. Its annual value was recorded as one pound. Near to 200 acres of land around the monastery, much of it described as being often over-run with the waters of the Ouse or *"overflowed the most part all winter with water, charged with a sewer"*, were stated as being altogether worth up to ten pounds a year. Other possessions valued included the Abbot Staithe described as *"waste ground in the town of Selby, lying upon Ouse bank, for to lay wood or other stuff that might chance be bought or sold or delivered to or from the said water of Ouse"*. It was classed as worth sixpence a year. The mansion house in Selby known as the Vicarage, together with its tithes and offerings from the parish church was noted as £6.6s.8d., which included the salary of the curate.

A most valuable item on the commissioners' list was wood. An estimated one hundred and sixty oak and ash trees were quoted as being part of the timber trees grown within the moated area of the monastery. Five, six and nine year old trees growing on 120 acres of land which included Staynor Park, Elyston Hagg and Robert Croft were estimated to be worth £36.6s.8d. In Selby Out-woods 1,300 sturdy oaks were valued at sevenpence each. The four Haggs with herbage worth 13s.4d. a year contained, besides different varieties of timber trees, acres of oak from three to nine years old. The sum total value of all the trees was set down as £117.19s.4d.

Individual items were sold or leased out. The fishing rights on the Ouse were granted to Richard Kryke for an annual fee of 13s.4d. Haystede in Wistow Ings that had always been reserved for the mill-horses was let in 1539 to a Robert Goode. The four corn mills 'under one roof' were let to Robert Beyley of Selby for ten pounds. Selby ferry boat was let to Robert and Thomas Heryson for the same amount.

The last abbot of Selby died in Rawcliffe: An entry in the ancient burial register states:

> *AD 1558 Jan ltm xxvj th day Robert Rogers Clark*
> *who was lait abbat of Selby..........Roclif*

There was only a poor chapel-of-ease at Rawcliffe. In the seventeenth century it was recorded as having a dilapidated roof of thatch. The Abbey church at Selby would by that time have been well plundered so it is extremely likely that the body of Abbot Robert Rogers was interred in the Priory Church of Snaith. To reinforce this belief there can be seen today in the sanctuary of Snaith church, within its altar rails, an extremely large marble grave slab. Cut into its upper surface is the representation of an ecclesiastic, complete with mitre and crozier.

When the last abbot died all that was left of the monastery were the partially destroyed Gateway with its adjoining buildings, and the Great Tithe Barn, which continued to be used by the people of Selby for many years. Towering above them, however, was the Church of St. Mary and St. Germain which was to fulfill its new position as Selby Abbey Parish Church.

CHAPTER 6

LIFE WITHOUT THE MONKS

The Lords of the Manor

Sir Ralph Sadler, awarded Selby manor after the dissolution of the monasteries, was a distinguished statesman of the time. Born in Hackney, Middlesex, in 1507, he became a servant in the household of Thomas Cromwell, Earl of Essex. Henry VIII employed the loyal and industrious Ralph in various political issues eventually appointing him Secretary of State. During a confrontation with the Scots in 1547 Ralph Sadler was made a 'knight banneret'. This was an order of knighthood given on the field of battle for deeds of bravery. It was conferred by tearing off the points of the recipient's pennon - a swallow-tailed flag carried on the lance. There were very few such orders bestowed after the reign of Elizabeth the First.

Hostilities with the Scots and the French had increased when the death of James V of Scotland left his week old daughter as his only legitimate heir. Henry quickly claimed Mary, Queen of the Scots, as a bride for his son and heir but this was resisted as the child's French mother started negotiations to marry Mary to a French prince. Peace was made with the French before Henry's death in January 1547, but the differences with the Scots rumbled on.

Edward Seymour became Lord Protector of the young Edward VI. Under his new title of Duke of Somerset he led the English in a defeat of the Scots at the Battle of Pinkie. This action, during which Sir Ralph Sadler received his banneret took place on the 10th. September, 1547, near Musselburgh, just east of Edinburgh.

Sir Ralph received many rewards at the dissolution of the monasteries but did not seem to have cared to keep Selby. In 1541 the year he was awarded the monastery he leased the site to Oswald Sysson, an inhabitant of the town. Then, in the same year, with the king's permission, he sold the monastery site, the little park of ten acres and the manor of Selby to Leonard Beckwith and his heirs.

Leonard Beckwith was another enterprising individual who elevated his social position and increased his estate from the ruins of the monasteries. In the 1530s he was already the abbot's steward in Acaster and his native Stillingfleet; he also held the same position for the Liberty of St. Mary's abbey in York. Beckwith was involved in the survey of the lands of several northern abbeys and used his position as the county receiver of the Court of Augmentations to make some opportune, many say fraudulent, investments in the property market. Lands previously owned by the monks at Byland and Fountains made up part of his estate.

The new lord of the manor of Selby continued to increase his possessions in that district. By the end of 1541 Leonard Beckwith also owned the lordships and manors of Brayton, Thorpe and Fryston. In 1553 Robert Twist conveyed three acres of land in Selby to Francis Grant which a year later was conveyed to Leonard Beckwith. At his death in 1557 his estates were yielding him an income of at least £360 per annum. These lands passed to his son, Roger who continued to increase the family's assets. For instance, he procured an award confirming his right to 'willows and sallows' in the Dam Carrs. In 1577 the lord of the manor of Selby conveyed a large amount of his possessions to his servant, Alice Petty. This consisted of Staynor Grange and chapel which, with 316 acres of land, was to be rented after his death to his servant for 99 years, at an annual rent of ten shillings. Also Thorpe Grange, all his town of Thorpe Willoughby, his water mill and soke there, and the tithes payable out of these lands to Selby and Brayton churches, were to be given to Alice at five shillings per annum. These conveyances were temporary measures for in 1579, Selby, Staynor and Thorpe were conveyed to William Beckwith of Clint.

Why did Alice Petty, described as a "single woman of Selby, servant to Roger Beckwith," feature so prominently in his conveyances of land? The answer lay in the records of the Archbishop's visitations to Selby during the sixteenth century:

Bishopthorpe 1581
Roger Beckwith to do penance in a white sheet with a white wand in his hand in the churches of Selby, Cawood and Brayton, confessing that he unlawfully married Alice Petty in a private chamber in his house and lived with her at bed and board. Performed penance and fine commuted to near fifty pounds. Money to be shared-£6.15s.0d to poor of above parishes, £25 to officers of court £20 to making the causey between Cawood and Shereham.

That same year the manor of Selby passed into the hands of the Earl of Shrewsbury. He gave some of its land and acres at Pontefract as a wedding present to his youngest son, Edward Talbot. The earl's second wife was Elizabeth Hardwick, better known as 'Bess of Hardwick' who had acquired great wealth from four successively richer husbands, and whose ancestral home was in Derbyshire. It is believed that she provided for her relatives out of the Selby estates.

Edward Talbot the youngest son of the Earl of Shrewsbury, owner of Selby manor, survived all his brothers but after only holding his father's title and lands for a year, he died. There were no male heirs so the estates were dispersed. Sir Thomas Walmsley, one of the Justices of the Court of Common Pleas became the next owner of the Selby estates. A member of an honourable family from Sholley in Lancashire, he became a Justice in 1589 and was a judge for twenty five years. He received his knighthood during the reign of James the First. A document listing the steward's accounts for the period 1608-9 reveals that the net return to the owner of Selby manor that year was around four hundred pounds. Some of the income of just over eight hundred pounds came from rents and sales of timber. The Michaelmas rents yielded £451.12s.10d., wood out of Staynor Lordship brought £52.1s.4d. whilst trees from the Outwood sold for £20.10s.0d. Expenditure items included the annual payments of forty pounds for the steward's work and ten pounds for the vicar's wages. Other expenses were similar to those incurred by the monks. The repairing of the lead on the Selby chancel and the windows there came to £4.10s.0d., repairs to the wooden staithes and the stone staithe cost almost eight pounds and replacing decayed posts at Thorpe Hall a further four shillings.

When Sir Thomas Walmsley died in 1612 he was succeeded by his son of the same name. At his death in 1640, Charles, his only son by his second wife, inherited the

Selby property. When Francis Walmsley, the last person to bear the family name, died in the early eighteenth century the Selby estates passed to Catherine, his only sister. This heiress married Robert, 7th. Lord Petre of Writtle on the 17th. March 1711. The Petre family were lords of the manor until 1854 when their estates in and near Selby were bought by the first Lord Londesborough. Up to this date the lords of the manor rarely visited the town or its neighbourhood. Unlike the abbots of Selby Abbey they played a minor role in the lives of the local inhabitants.

The Reformation

The dissolution of the monasteries took place at a time which saw the emergence of new movements of progressive Christianity and the creation of Protestant and Anglican churches. When Henry VIII was on the throne he did demand obedience to his wishes but saw no need to change the faith or even the rituals to which his subjects had been born. However, by the time of his death more determined forces were at work. The Duke of Somerset, guardian and uncle of the child-king, Edward VI, and Thomas Cranmer, Archbishop of Canterbury, were in the forefront of a religious revolution. Cranmer had worked with Thomas Cromwell to spread the English Reformation and he became the chief instigator of religious changes during Edward's reign. The Book of Common Prayer was written in English and accepted by Parliament in 1549. Four years later a second prayer book and the Forty-two Articles were produced. These Articles, the principles of the Church of England, modified to thirty-nine, were also approved by Parliament. Edward VI surrounded by Protestant sympathisers, accepted these changes and even agreed to the dissolution of chantries, where masses were sung for the benefactors. The form of services was altered and the physical appearance of most churches changed to conform with orders issued by the Privy Council. Effigies of saints and other images were removed and altars replaced by communion tables.

Many people paid lip-service to the changes whilst secretly holding on to their old faith. In his will Sir Leonard Beckwith made it known that it was his wish to be buried at York *"in our Lady queare wher they singe messe"*. This is believed to have been behind the high altar in York Minster. Another lord of the manor of Selby, Sir Thomas Walmsley, was suspected of not being fully committed to the changes. The family stayed firm believers in the Roman Catholic faith and Thomas's children were brought up in that persuasion.

Mary, the daughter of Catherine of Aragon and Henry VIII, succeeded Edward in 1553. When news of the new Catholic queen reached York there was great rejoicing all around the district. The Reformation was put into reverse; Mary did her utmost to turn England back into a Catholic country. During her time 45 heretics were prosecuted in York. Mary dismissed Robert Holgate, the Archbishop of York, who was the main instigator of the Reformation in the north. His possessions were taken, sold or destroyed. The description of the goods and chattels that were not vandalised makes interesting reading for it gives some idea of the magnificent style in which an Archbishop of York lived. From Cawood alone, in addition to ready money totalling nine hundred pounds, and articles of silver and gold, the list of possessions included a hundred beasts, four hundred mutton, two thousand five hundred sheep and around one hundred horses. There was also good harness and an artillery sufficient for 140 men.

Elizabeth, daughter of Anne Boleyn and Henry VIII, had been in a perilous position whilst her sister reigned but evidence was never found to connect her with the

Protestant conspiracies against Queen Mary. Immediately on her accession to the throne in 1558 Elizabeth sanctioned the restoration of a Protestant church settlement as it had been before the death of her brother, Edward VI.

The valley of the Trent marked a divide between north and south. To the north changes were more slowly absorbed. Throughout the 1560s a large minority in Yorkshire were still using Catholic forms in their wills. Allegiance to the Catholic faith, though hidden in most parts, was especially fervent in Richmondshire and parts of the northern vale of York. To weaken the strength of the old feudal families in the north which included, the Percys of Northumberland, the Nevilles of Westmorland and the Cliffords of Cumberland, Queen Elizabeth deprived them of their positions. These posts were given as rewards to some of her more trustworthy supporters. Elizabeth also insisted that the earls spent long intervals at Court which proved very expensive for the struggling northerners. Another irritant to the earls was that the queen steadfastly refused to name Mary Stuart, Queen of the Scots, 1542-67, as her successor.

The mild responses to calls to arms made during localised outbursts of revolt against the queen and her government did not worry those in power unduly until the rebellion that became known as the *"Northern Earls' Rising"* took place in 1569. The Duke of Norfolk was the central figure in the uprising. A second cousin to the queen he symbolised the conception of nobility those in the North wished to retain, but one which the Tudors were intent on destroying.

The revolt was an attempt to overthrow Elizabeth's government in order to restore Catholicism and put Mary Stuart on the throne of England. The Catholic Mary had presided uneasily over an ever-increasing Protestant majority in Scotland until she was deposed in 1567. After escaping from prison she fled to England provoking a crisis and becoming a long-term problem to Elizabeth and her followers. It was at this stage that the northern earls, who resented the spread of Tudor power determined to carry out the planned uprising, an event that was to culminate in Selby before falling apart. The earls were awaiting the signal to take up arms when the Duke of Norfolk was summoned to court. Made aware that the main conspirators were under surveillance he quickly withdrew from the plot. The duke pleaded for a royal pardon but to no avail for in October 1569 he was sent to the Tower. The Earls of Northumberland and Westmorland had been awaiting his signal to rise and when it did not come they returned to their homes. A month later, however, when they too received a summons to court, fearing for their lives they rose in revolt. Unfortunately for them the delay cost them the support of other leaders; the expected aid from Scotland and the Continent also did not materialize. They did not generate the popular response from the tenants that the *'Pilgrimage of Grace'* had received, many having to be threatened or bribed before they joined the rebels. But to their relief thousands of the common people did rise up as their forebears had in 1536 in a mass condemnation of the new way of life and new method of government.

Meanwhile Elizabeth had sent the Earl of Sussex as "Lord President of the Council at York", instructions to warn all the justices of the peace in Yorkshire and other northern counties to keep a good watch wherever people gathered together. York, Hull, Pontefract, Knaresborough and other towns were put on the defensive even though Sussex did not fully believe there was to be a rising. He made Cawood his base whilst he arranged such matters as the mustering of troops and secret searches throughout the shire. Sherburn became one of his depots where the mustering took place and where an artillery house was established.

Early in November Sussex, having received conflicting messages regarding a possible rebellion, requested the presence of Percy and Neville in York. However, before the messenger had even left Percy's residence at Topcliffe, church bells were sounding the tocsin-signal for the rebellion to begin. Sussex ordered a general mobilisation of the armed forces of the North which may have included men from the Selby area. The earls who had already gone with their followers, in armour, to Neville's castle, were denounced as traitors. Two days later the rebels entered Durham where they trod the new prayer books underfoot and then celebrated Mass. Sussex could not drum up enough support to defend the whole county so concentrated his troops around York; the opposing forces mustered at Clifton Moor were reported to have had sixteen hundred horses and four thousand foot. The earls, adding to their forces on the march seized the towns of Richmond, Ripon, Knaresborough, Wetherby and Tadcaster. On the 22nd. November they entered Sherburn and held it for two nights whilst they secured the surrounding countryside.

Sir Ralph Sadler, the first secular owner of Selby Abbey estates, served Elizabeth as faithfully as he had her father. Acting as her agent he informed the royal troops moving up from the south that, because the rebels lay at Tadcaster and Sherburn, messengers could not pass that way to York but must go from Doncaster via Hull to reach the north. It was believed that the earls and their men were trying to get as near as possible to Tutbury in Staffordshire, to attempt a rescue of Mary Stuart who was held prisoner there. Sir Ralph and Lord Hunsdon reported this news to Elizabeth and emphasised how serious the position had become. They substantiated the claims Sussex had expressed over the difficulties he was having against such heavy odds.

The progress of the rebel army southwards indicated that the fears expressed by the queen's agents were correct. From Sherburn the earls moved onto Cawood and then Selby. In each place they entered these upholders of the Catholic faith made a point of burning the translations of the Scriptures, overturning communion tables and celebrating Mass. Many of the troops were not averse to plundering the premises. They entered Selby on the 24th. November, filling the streets with their mounted men and foot soldiers. The Abbey Church was treated in the same manner as other places of worship and the town was ransacked. Selby proved to be the southernmost limit of their march. Records do not show whether any attempt was made from the town to launch a quick raid on Tutbury, fifty miles away. It is a fact that on the 25th. of that month Mary was moved to Coventry and by the 30th. the mass of rebels were back in Richmond. The increasing number of royal forces massing in the south and those streaming into Yorkshire, compelled the insurgents to retreat. They fled to safer refuges in the wilder regions of the north amongst a more sympathetic population. By December the Earl of Sussex and other royal commanders were in Sherburn and two weeks later the revolt collapsed.

A cry went up that all in the West Riding were traitors and deserved punishment. It was proposed that in places where the bells had rung for rebellion only one bell was to be left intact. Despite efforts by the Earl of Sussex to prevent the appalling waste of livestock and other cruel acts on a poverty stricken land, the southern army spoiled vast areas from Doncaster to Newcastle. Selby and the area around it must have suffered some of this devastation as the troops drove the cattle before them, seizing lands, goods and leases. In some cases they even ransomed off the poorest of the poor. Hostages were taken and executed in the main meeting places. In Selby this would have been in front of the market cross. Sixty-six petty constables who carried out many duties in the towns, were executed. There were reports of from five hundred to eight hundred of the common people being hanged as a warning to them all.

The earls, who had accepted defeat at Durham on the 15th. December, moved further north. They disbanded their weary, bedraggled foot soldiers and fled to Hexham and across the Pennines. Evading the queen's forces at Carlisle they sought shelter in Liddlesdale where in 1346 Walter de Selby and his sons had fought so valiantly to defend Liddell castle against the Scots. The Scottish border families gave the earls protection until Neville fled to Flanders and Percy went into Scotland. The hostile attitude of the Scots prevented the handing over of Thomas Percy until 1572 when he was ransomed to Elizabeth for two thousand pounds. The rebel Percy was beheaded in York and his head displayed on Micklegate. The rising threat of English Catholicism had been demolished and Protestantism more firmly established.

Roman Catholics

It is believed most of the congregations in Yorkshire followed the government's orders although there were many parishioners who remained untaught and ignorant of religious changes. They continued to worship passively in the manner traditionally practised in their local area. In 1570 the Archbishop of York, Edmund Grindall had complained *"they offer money, eggs and other articles at the burial of their dead; they pray on beads...so as it seemeth to be, as it were, another church rather than a member of the rest"*. In the Visitation Records for 1575 it was noted, *"Selbye- the yowthe do not repaire to the mynister to be taught in the Catheisme"*. Recusancy - a refusal to attend Church of England services, increased after Elizabeth's men gained control of the patronage of the north following the collapse of the *'Northern Earls' Rebellion"*. Recusants in Elizabethan times were, like the troublesome Borderers, offenders who needed to be punished.

The inhabitants of Selby must have been amongst those who followed the government's orders with regard to religious matters for there were very few Roman Catholics in the town during the course of the Reformation. This was despite the close proximity to devout Catholic families such as the Babthorpes of Hemingbrough and the Stapletons of Carlton. The Stapletons had kept a chapel at their family home, Carlton Hall, since about 1380. The district around it soon became the centre for Roman Catholics. It is known that Richard Stapleton was a recusant and before his death in January 1584/5 he kept a catholic priest in his house. Between 1583 and 1590 there were other priests of the 'Old Faith' in the area. One was based at Carlton in order to serve the Osgoldcross wapentake, another was centred at Osgodby, maybe at the Old Hall belonging to the Babthorpe family, whilst a third was stationed near Bubwith Ferry. The last was possibly residing at an old house of the Vavasours at Willitoft. Around this time Sir John Duckate, curate at Carlton, was reported to have married *"certain persons unlawfully being strangers"*. This may have been because the couples did not recite the Catechism; one of the rules of the Protestant church directed at the curates was: *"ye shall not marrye any persons which before were single unless they can say the Catechisme by hart and will recyte the same to you"*. Fifteen recusants were also noted at Carlton including the wife of Richard Stapleton. This lady and others were accused of not going to church *"but the curate goeth to their hall to do service"*.

In 1585 a Statute was passed which made it a felony to give relief to a priest. Under this Act the priests were forbidden, under penalty of death, to remain in England.

This was the cause of many executions. The Catholic Mary Stuart, after great pressure was put on Elizabeth to agree, was executed in 1587. By this time the number of Roman Catholic recusants was slowly increasing; twelve were noted at Carlton; by 1603 this had increased to 17 plus seven noncommunicants. Thirty-four years later the number was twenty-nine. In 1606, three years after James I had ascended the throne he made it law that Roman Catholics had to take an Oath of Allegiance to the Crown. Failure to do this resulted in the loss of property and life imprisonment. The wording of the oath made it totally unacceptable to the priests.

The Stapleton family continued to stand out against going to Church of England services. In 1616 Gilbert Stapleton paid three hundred pounds in fines for 15 months' non-attendance at the Protestant Church. He married his second wife, Elinor, daughter of Sir John Gascoigne of Barnbow, near Leeds, in 1618. Sir John had taken the Oath of Allegiance to the Crown in 1607 but Gilbert managed to hold out until 1624. Gilbert and his wife brought up their family in an old hall on the Quosquo Estate, situated about two miles west of Camblesforth. The family steadfastly adhered to the old faith even though they were often crippled by the heavy fines incurred because of failures to attend the Protestant services.

Gilbert's recusancy roll, fourteen feet in length and made up of parchment receipts stitched together shows that between 1616 and 1649, Gilbert and his wife, Elinor, paid £1748 in fines.

Selby Abbey Church

Before the Dissolution of the Monasteries the Abbey Church at Selby had had an average annual income of £700. The steward's accounts for 1608 show that from 1540 the curate at the Abbey Church received a fixed income of only ten pounds, a situation faced by many of the parochial clergy. For a number of years they were scarcely distinguishable from husbandmen and the lowest of the yeomen. Some undertook other occupations to supplement their incomes. In Elizabethan times a few kept ale-houses but soon found themselves presented to the archbishop's representatives for this offence. In 1600 the curate at Rawcliffe was reported to Snaith Peculiar Court for such a misdemeanour

Curate seldom wears surplice at celebrations of communion. He keeps an ale-house, says it is his wife's mother who keeps it.

The vicar at Selby did not have his stipend increased until the 20th. March 1618 when the Abbbey Church was formally established, by royal letters patent, as the parish church of Selby. The following year James I gave grants to the poorer parishes which included Selby because *"the parish consisted of about 3000 souls, who for want of a preaching ministry had lived long in ignorance"*. The king granted thirty pounds to the curate and his successors for ever. Even then the post of curate was difficult to fill and the congregation relied on visiting clergy who were paid a shilling to preach a sermon. This eventually led to the pew system, the rents of which became an important part of a minister's stipend.

When the monks departed there was no-one to supervise or cover the expenses for the maintenance of the church or the highways. There were people, however, who like their predecessors, gave grants or left legacies for the church but now they included other agencies. In 1547 Roger Beckwith bequeathed two closes covering just over seven acres, known as Wistow Lane Closes, the rents from which were to be used to repair the highways, the parish church and its steeple. This is believed to be the first endowment to be controlled by the Feoffees Charity which still exists today, though in a different form and whose history will be discussed in more detail in a later chapter. Fifteen acres of land given by Robert Anby, a draper, was to be used to keep a 'Ring' of bells in the church and repair the church windows, whilst an extra rood was added for the provision of butts for archery practice. It was still the custom for men to be levied for military service, as during the *"Northern Earls Rising"*, and practising at the butts was compulsory.

Thomas Cromwell had prepared the Mandate in 1538 that ordered every parish to have a secure chest in its church, complete with two keys, one for the minister and one for a churchwarden. The minister had to enter into a book every christening, marriage and burial at which he officiated; this register had then to be kept secure in the newly acquired chest. In 1563 the Roman Catholic Church also ordered the recording of marriages and christenings. Parish records for Selby going back as far as 1579 are stored in the Borthwick Institute at York. The earliest ones are fragmented. The more complete records of marriages begin in 1583.

> *1583*
> *-Thomas Clyfe and Kathleen Wilsonn*
> *maryed the xiiijth of September.*
> *John Mendall and Dorythe Colson*
> *were maryed the xxixth day of September.*

> *1594*
> *Thomas Smyth of the Cyttye of York, merchante and … of the diocese of York*
> *weare maryed within parish of Selbie on ffrydaye being xth. of maye 1594.*
> *They weare maryed about the howers of ix and tenne the fore none the same*
> *day by virtue of a lycense directed unto me Thomas Thomlingson, Clerk Curate*
> *directed bearing dayte the 9th. of maye …*

David Nutt and Anne Lawton were married in July 1586. The following were in the baptism records:

> *1587-William Nutt the sonne of Davye Nutt baptised the 14th. of November.*
> *1589-Marye Nutte the Daughter of Davye Nutte Baptised the 8th of September.*
> *Also…1593-Robtie Barton the sonne of Elizabeth Barton a Bastard Baptised the*
> *vijth of October. Richard Ebbatte fraunt (servant) unto Mr. Dalleson of*
> *Lawghton in Lincolnshire certyfied to be the supposed ffather by the midwife.*

Note that the name of the mother of a child was not recorded unless her baby had been born out of wedlock. This custom continued well into the eighteenth century and beyond.

> *York Herald, May 1799*
> *On, Monday se'ennight the lady of the Hon Harvey Hawke was safely delivered*
> *of a son at his house at Womersly*

Godparents were not listed at that time but any person wishing to take on that role had to have received Holy Communion and be able to recite before the minister the articles of the Christian faith in English. Holy Communion could not be received by anyone unable to say by heart the ten commandments, the articles of faith, the Lord's prayer and the Cathechism.

The first entries in the burial section of Selby Abbey Church's register were brief but later ones were a little more detailed:

1581-WyIla Watson sonne of Rychard Watson was buried the iiij daye of August.

1596-xxixth of Maie one male childe was buried, beinge left (by the mother thereof a pour ganrill or wanderer) at John Hoggs doore, or entire into his house and kepte by the chardge of the Inhabitants of Selbie at nursinge till the day of the buriall.

John Hartley the sonne of Anne Hartley, beinge a bastard begotten in adultery by Thomas Loinshoppe buried the same day

1604 Elizabeth Roseby a young virgin was buried sixth day of October.

1608- Being an infant, new borne infant, a young twin, Alexander, son of JohnTomson drowned by misfortune in his 'minositic'.

Customs and Traditions

Many traditions lingered on into the sixteenth century. In Tudor times the English nobility, especially in the north, still retained much of the living style of their medieval ancestors. Families like the Percys of Northumberland continued to celebrate Christmas in the old traditional manner. When they were at Wressle Sir Henry played host to the *"Lord of Misrule'* and was visited by the boy-bishops of York and Beverley just as the Abbots of Selby had been before the dissolution of the monasteries. The entertainments continued to include nativity plays, minstrels and musicians.

The powerful northern barons who had for centuries often been a trial and threat to their sovereigns also fell out amongst themselves causing long-lasting feuds. One such quarrel led to the enactment of another old custom that had been introduced to this country during the eleventh century, that of 'Trial by Battle'. On the assumption that God would protect the person in the right, the two people in conflict arranged to begin to fight one another at noon; to prove his case the accuser had to fell the defender before the first star appeared in the sky. George Darcy, the younger son of Lord George Darcy, whose tomb lies in St Wilfrid's church, Brayton, was challenged to this type of combat in 1557. A feud existed between his family and that of Sir William West's from Wales, a village near Rotherham. The main agitators were the two sons from each side.

The animosity came to a head when John and George Darcy met the West boys at Rotherham fair on Whitsun Monday, 1556. A fight broke out and Lewis West was killed. Flight must have followed this action but in May a letter, which is preserved in the Foljambe family's memoirs, was sent from the Darcy household containing the message *"....eldest son sore hurt and offers to surrender himself to Sir John Foljambe or Lord Darcy will provide bail...".* A compromise was eventually agreed upon in November regarding John but exempting George. Sometime after this the latter took sanctuary in Westminster and, on the 16th. December, he was publicly whipped and did penance in a white sheet. However, this was not the end of the matter for on the 10th. February, 1557, he was accused at the bar of the King's Bench and challenged to combat. Whether he endured the Trial by Battle and saw that evening star is not known for his fate is lost in the past. The brothers' father, Lord George Darcy died in 1558 and was buried in Brayton. He had spent his childhood in that neighbourhood, his father having land at Temple Hirst and he himself, at some time, being the owner of the Gateforth Hall estate. His eldest son and heir, John, inherited the family seat at Aughton, near Rotherham. During the rebellion by the northern earls in 1557-8, Sir Ralph Sadler had placed John Darcy in control of Doncaster. His son, Michael, predeceased him so it was his grandson, John, the fourth Lord Darcy, who eventually succeeded to the estates. He was a private individual but, despite this, in 1616 he was challenged to a duel by a George Markham. John did not accept the challenge and Markham was subsequently censored by the Court of the Star Chamber at Westminster. Duelling persisted as a way of settling differences. In 1669 George Aislabie of Osgodby elected, unwisely, to settle his quarrel with Jonathan Jennings by challenging him to a duel in York. The ringing of the prayer bell at the Minster was used as a signal for the confrontation at which George lost his life. His son, of the same name, rose to become Chancellor of the Exchequer in 1714 but fell into disgrace at the time of the bursting of the South Sea Bubble. It is to his credit, however, that he was responsible for beginning the creation of the beautiful Studley Royal Gardens that were eventually merged with Fountains Abbey.

People in the Selby area continued to attain high positions in society after the monks had left the town. In 1556 Sir Richard Dobbs a native of Cliffe, became Lord Mayor of London and four years later, John de Cawood was appointed Master of the Stationers' Company and Printer to Queen Elizabeth I. In 1628 George Montaigne of Wistow was Archbishop of York. Admiral Sir Jeremiah Smith buried in Hemingbrough church was not a native of that place but had bought Osgodby Hall, former residence of the Babthorpes. It is believed he also resided at the Prior's House in Hemingbrough. As Captain Smith, he gained commendations for his brave and daring conduct in a sea battle during the Anglo-Dutch war of 1665-67 when acting as second in command to George Monck, the first Duke of Albemarle. Samuel Pepys recorded details of the engagement in his diary. He described how during a confrontation with the Dutch on the third of June, 1665, Captain Jeremiah Smith of the *Mary* put his ship between that of the Duke's and the *Urania* 76 guns and 400 men. Its captain named Seaton had vowed he would board the Duke's ship, the *Royal Charles*. Captain Smith took the Dutch ship after the death of its captain and 200 men. All the officers on board the *Mary* save Captain Smith and a Lieutenant were killed and 99 men lost.

The Manor Courts

Many aspects of the feudal system also lingered on, for, though Benedictine abbots no longer ruled over the Selby estates the people were still beholden to a lord of the manor and answerable to a Manor Court or Court Leet. These meetings were held in a room above the abbey gateway. In Dr. Burton's description of the abbey written in 1758 he states that; *"The barn, with part of the granary and chief entrance, or great gateway, facing the north, are yet remaining. On the side of the latter is the porter's lodge, over there arched with stone, are two chambers, in which the abbots held their courts, and transacted business; and the same use they are applied to at this time"*.

In these rooms, on the 15th. October, 1581, a *"woman called Ledell"* and three others were fined for not paying the swineherd's wage; William Beilby for not making his fence between the fields and William Beckwith, for not *"scouringe his water sewers"*. Michael Clarke was penalised for cutting down trees belonging to the lord of the manor and for providing lodgings for vagabonds. The laws and the attitude of the inhabitants of Selby manor towards them had undergone little change.

An innovation was the compulsory payment of rates by the parishioners to four groups of officials- the Overseers of the Poor, the Constables, the Surveyors of the Highway and the Churchwardens. The creation of the office of Overseer of the Poor had been established by the Poor Law Act of 1597/98 and became binding in 1601. At least two people, with the approval of the justices of the peace, were appointed annually by each vestry. Their duties included the collecting and distributing of a poor rate. The money was intended to relieve the distress of the swelling number of poor who were moving into the towns. Old standards had been overthrown; labourers were mainly free men who worked for hire but, whereas under the feudal system they had been able to pay their landlords in labour it was becoming very difficult to earn money for rent by doing outside work. The landowners had cut down on cultivation as the grazing of sheep increased thereby halving the labour force needed on their estates.

It has already been noted that in Selby, as in other places, rich and benevolent residents had begun to leave legacies to help the poor and the church, but not all the wealthy inhabitants of the town were so generously minded. At the beginning of the seventeenth century Selby was a small but thriving market town with many well-to-do inhabitants. However, this gradually changed as more and more people, mainly jobless and poor, were attracted to Selby. The place became so crowded that by 1614 many houses in the town were being shared by four to five families. A number of the wealthy residents left Selby for the country rather than be imposed upon to pay towards the relief of the poorer tenants. Those who remained complained bitterly to the courts that the town was being brought to ruin and decay. Their misgivings were aired before the justices at the General Sessions of the West Riding held at Pontefract. They gained a sympathetic hearing. The Overseers of the Poor with the Churchwardens, were ordered to make a new assessment for the relief of the poor of the parish. They were to assess such persons having, or wishing to have tenants in their homes or tenements, so that more support was given to the poor by these landlords than by any other persons. That is, the rent given by the poor tenants was to be added to the landlords' assessment until such time as they avoided having too many needy in their houses.

To prevent further burdens on the inhabitants of Selby it was also ordered that no person was to receive any strangers or 'forreners' into their house or houses who may, through having children or for other reasons, become dependent on the parish for their upkeep. This was unless the incomers could offer good and sufficient security to the Overseers of the Poor and other officers that they would not become a burden on the parish of Selby. If anybody broke these rules they were to be brought before the next justice to be proceeded against and punished.

Fortunately there were charitable people living in the town at that time. This is illustrated by the manner in which they dealt with fire victims. In one case inhabitants of Selby, Brayton and other places nearby, went to the court in Pontefract to give support to William Greaves and his family who had been made homeless by a *"fearful and lamentable fire"*. They described Greaves, from Bucton, in the then parish of Brayton, as an honest, labouring man, diligent in his vocation and with a wife and four young children, the eldest not above ten years of age. It was agreed by all that he had maintained his family well until the fire which consumed his house, its contents and all his hay and corn, leaving them destitute and homeless. Greaves swore in court that this was so and that his loss amounted to fifty pounds. The court therefore entreated the ministers and curates of the several parishes in the West Riding to publish the details concerning William Greaves in their churches and other places. They also ordered that the officials at Selby and Brayton should organise the collecting of the gifts until they had fifty pounds for the destitute family.

The Churchwardens had many duties ranging from the extermination of vermin, the caring of parish arms and soldiers' pay to ensuring that their parishioners attended church regularly; the poor were educated and offences committed within their jurisdiction were presented at the church courts. This was a parish post of great antiquity and some of the many duties were specific to a particular period of history. Two to four churchwardens were elected by the vestry, usually on Easter Tuesday.

The post of Surveyor of the Highway was created by the Highway Act of 1555. He was an unpaid official appointed by the parishioners. This was altered in 1691 when the justices chose a name, usually by rotation, from a list of eligible landowners. The surveyor was obliged to survey the highways three times a year and to organise the 'volunteer' labour force to repair the roads. Every able-bodied householder was bound to do this work for up to four days each year. Cawood and Wistow had byelawmen whose duty it was to fix the days when their villagers should fulfil the obligation. The Surveyors of the Highway for Selby called this duty 'Common Day work'. In their accounts for 1725, expenses included fifteen shillings for "drink and diners" for the three days this work was carried out. The following was listed in the Disbursements column:

Collected of the Inhabitants not coming to Common Day works £12.18s.11d.

A case brought before the court at Pontefract during the early seventeenth century clearly illustrated the state of one important road leading into Selby. Many inhabitants of the town and other places adjoining *"Hambleton Causey"* had petitioned the court concerning this route, it *"being the high road way from Halifax, Bradford, Leeds and Wakefield unto the market town of Selby and the town of Kingston upon Hull, which causey is two miles in length and so extraordinarily broken and decayed with carts and carriages that the said inhabitants thereabouts are not able to repeir and maintain it"*. The justices ordered that Edward Stanhope, esq. and Gervase Hamond. esq., two of his Majesty's justices were to view the said causey and examine the defects there and certify what, in their opinion, needed to be done to repair it. They were also to report on the abilities of the adjoining parishes to undertake the work, so it all could be lawfully carried out.

The Constable or Petty Constable was a post that is thought to be more ancient than that of Churchwarden. At first he was appointed by the Court Leets but later this was taken over by the justices of the peace. The position was not popular with many of the parishioners when it became their turn to carry out the duty. Several paid other people to take their place. Their numerous tasks apart from keeping the peace, included caring for the parish bull and collecting various taxes. The last duty made them very unpopular. In the early 1600s Richard Poskitt, Constable for Birkin petitioned the West Riding Court because several of the inhabitants within his constabulary refused to pay assessments legally imposed upon them for his services. The Court ordered that any who would not pay would be bound over to appear at the next sessions. Richard also joined Thomas Wayte, Constable for Selby, in a further complaint to the Court that some parishioners would not pay their taxes. Sometimes it was the Constables who rebelled. Those at Wistow, Hillam and Burton Salmon, along with Richard Poskitt of Birkin, were reported by the High Constable for refusing to pay rates imposed upon them for the relief of the poor in Hipperholme and other places near Halifax.

The Constables of Selby also received these instructions:

You are to make pursuit of Hue and Cry as at all times when demanded of you with the assistance of such persons as you choose to call upon by day or night.

The system of 'Hue and Cry' was introduced in 1285 and allowed a person wishing to make an arrest to call on others in the parish or manor to assist him. Everyone was obliged to join the 'Hue' and to cry out loud to attract other helpers. When in 1723 Joshua Toplass and Thomas Toplin were the appointed Constables they claimed expenses of two shillings for *"making pursuit of Hue and Cry"* three times in one quarter of that year.

The Courts and the Mills

A feudal rule that was in force long after the departure of the monks from Selby was centred around the four mills they had had built near the Dam. These were still known as the 'Soke Mills' and were under the jurisdiction of the Lord of the Manor, which meant all the inhabitants of Selby manor were legally obliged to have their grain ground there. This was a very restrictive practice for the millers were not all trustworthy folk. In the early seventeenth century a farmer from Elmswell in the East Riding, recorded that he found differences in the grinding of two bushels of corn; he received one and a half pecks more of meal from one mill than he had from another. This farmer was free to change mills if he found the millers taking too much grain for themselves. He could also have his corn collected from the farm and delivered back before ten in the morning the next day, for some millers worked through the night if so needed. The carriers were paid fivepence a day by the miller for carrying up to 18 bushels on their horses. It is therefore not surprising that during the sixteenth century and those that followed the townsfolk of Selby lodged complaint after complaint about the millers' behaviour and the compulsory grinding of their grain at the mills. In the seventeenth century townspeople were openly defying the ancient right of the Soke and grinding their produce elsewhere. An action was swiftly brought against them by the Lord of the Manor and it was decreed that the inhabitants of Selby were still bound to use his mills.

The townspeople continued to break this law. In 1617 a suit was instituted in the Court of Exchequer against Thomas Marshall and others who had broken the rules of the soke. They were ordered to conform with the ancient tradition. In 1726, Lady Catherine Petre was owner of the manor and mills of Selby. Court cases were recorded in 1730 and 1813. When the soke was ignored in the last instance, the Trustees of the Honourable E.R.Petre sued Robert Myers, J. Bradley, maltsters, W. and S. Walker, Bakers and Flour Dealers, all living on Ousegate, and John Cape, a brewer from Gowthorpe. The townsfolk won that case but in 1820 they were again sued for disobeying the soke.

Much legal wrangling went on at the last two trials which were held in York. At the first it was argued that the old custom did not prevent the defendants from buying and selling on their premises flour produced from corn ground at other mills. At the next trial it was stated that the Lord of the Manor had pulled down one of the mills and had left another to decay; the townsfolk declared they were bound by law to use four mills thereby they held the Lord of the Manor had suspended the custom. The defendants won both of these cases and by the end of the nineteenth century all the soke mills had disappeared. A custom that had bound the people of Selby manor to their Lord since the monks built the mills in the eleventh or twelfth century had come to an end.

In his notes the Elmswell farmer mentioned some of the foods made from the grains that formed part of the staple diet in those days. In winter time his family ate bread baked from two bushels of mixed corn. The grain was ground and then made into the finest flour by putting it through a coarse hair sieve. They also ate brown bread made from equal amounts of rye, barley and pease (crushed dried peas). It was explained that before these goods were ground the farmer instructed the miller to take a besom and sweep the place before pouring the crops onto the floor and blending them together with his hands. Only after this was the miller to take a scuttle and scoop the mixture up to be ground. Pie crusts for such as the farmer were made from the best wheat, lesser folk used mixed grains, whilst the poor mixed rye with a smaller amount of pease. The chief ingredient for puddings, consisting mainly of types of flour boiled in a bag, was barley, except for the poor who generally used pease. However, at harvest time, the workers were given puddings made from wheat.

It was not surprising that the people shunned the corn mills of Selby for in 1817 their flour had been described as being expensive to buy, even though it was of the poorest quality. So bad was the flour that even a loaf made from the best of it might be shaken and the inside heard striking against the sides within, like a kernel in a ripe hazel nut. George Lowther, a well-known figure in Selby in the nineteenth century, recollects that when open it resembled a lump of birdlime.

The Town of Selby

After the destruction of many monastery buildings, small changes took place in the lay-out of Selby. The archaeological digs of the 1990s confirmed the existence and alignment of Kirk Dyke, as shown on the medieval map of Selby, and dated it from as early as, or before, the twelfth century. It had been used as a waterway by both monks and local inhabitants until the time of the dissolution of the monasteries. Excavations revealed that for some time after this the dyke was allowed to silt up until it was replaced by a narrower channel in the seventeenth century. This was back-filled during the eighteenth century and then superseded by a brick culvert that followed the same alignment. It was, maybe, when the dyke was silted up and did not form a barrier that Finkle Street was formed. No references to the street have been found in the available account rolls of the monks but it is referred to in the Manor Court Rolls of 1570. The records detail the transference of one messuage of land in Finkle Street from one owner to another. The development of the leather industry and the increase in other trades, in an area between the market place and where the Griffin Hotel lies today would probably have necessitated the making of a passage-way from Gowthorpe to Micklegate. It has also been supposed that Finkle Street was laid out to follow the land highest above the frequent flooding.

Another bye-way, of which no record was found in the account rolls was Water Lane. The first reference found occurs in the Manor Rolls of 1568. The storage buildings or warehouses at the north end of Micklegate, now mainly used as garages, also received no mention in the translated account rolls. As described in Chapter Three there are many references to money being paid out by the monks to the men and women of Selby for carrying goods from the staithes to the abbey gates or the turf house and tithe barn within the monastery grounds; there were none that referred to any store houses near the River Ouse. As regards the staithe, the impression gained from the archaeological surveys is that it was located near to where the stone warehouses now stand. The archaeologists also conclude that the staithe must have been on a bank of high ground adjacent to the river, behind which the ground fell considerably and quickly. It was described thus in the following item from the monks' 1404 accounts:

Likewise the same person accounts for the service of twelve men for one day digging and throwing earth upon the abbot's wharf and raising the same, with food (being provided)...4s.

It can be supposed that the warehouses were built later as trade increased, using stone from the disused abbey; there is little evidence of any other buildings in Selby having been made from the enormous amount of stone that must have been available. A new passageway to Ousegate would have been formed by the side of the warehouses which, if it is so, appropriately became known as Water Lane. The 'digs' carried out in Micklegate uncovered a series of ditches which were used as boundaries or as drainage channels during the frequent and catastrophic flooding that occurred. The 'finds' also suggested that in the sixteenth century this was an open area with leather-work, smithing and open stabling which increased during Tudor times. For example, Irwin's Yard progressed from use as a disposal area during the time of the monks, to light industry. Clay floors and evidence of hearths and charcoal were uncovered. The size of the hearths implied much heat had been involved as in metal working. Evidence of a later construction of a large stone building suggests the industry may have expanded and become more organised. Excavations were carried out in the vicinity of 16, Gowthorpe; that is the area on the north side where today can be found the 'Birthday' card shop with a passage way next to it. What was uncovered there led to the belief that properties had been laid out on the street since not long after the Norman Conquest. Masonry structures, dating from the fifteenth or sixteenth century when a major expansion of urban economy occurred, were found on the site. Here also were uncovered signs of a workshop used in late Medieval times for smelting or processing metal.

Cloth Markets and Fairs

The ports of Selby and Hull grew in importance during the Tudor period. By Elizabethan times products of the West Riding woollen industry were being carried to the Low Countries and the Baltic whilst flax and corn were being imported. Coasters were bringing in foodstuffs, coal and miscellaneous goods and returning to London with lead. York which had slipped from first provincial city in the land to sixth, with a population under eight thousand, had begun to grow again. The York inhabitants found the clothiers in places such as Leeds, Halifax and Wakefield, with their access to cheaper materials and labour and an abundance of water mills too competitive for them. During the late sixteenth century however the revival of trade helped the merchants and tradesmen of York to prosper. Selby's geographical position on the River Ouse proved an asset for coastal trade and for the West Riding manufacturers. Their woollen goods were conveyed by packhorse and wagon to the inland port to be taken by water to Hull. Much of this traffic used the two mile long Hambleton Causey.

The markets and fairs flourished with the increase in trade. When Leonard Beckwith became Lord of the Manor of Selby in 1541 he was granted a charter to hold a yearly Michaelmas Fair and a weekly market in the town. He was also accustomed, like the abbots before him, to take tolls and other charges at these affairs. Towns and villages near Selby such as Cliffe, Duffield, Pocklington, Hemingbrough, Osgodby, Riccall and Pontefract also held charters to hold fairs and markets. To these were soon added Howden, Snaith, Sherburn, Cawood, North Duffield and Whitgift. Many clothiers patronized these markets and fairs but some, usually the more wealthy traders, instead of relying solely on the Yorkshire markets, annually took their cloth to London to be sold at the St. Bartholomew's Fair. The trek to the fair must have felt like a great adventure, especially to the first time travellers, but often, as the northerners approached Smithfield, close to where the fair was held, feelings of uncertainty overwhelmed them. This was because, in an age when the laws defining the length, breadth and weight of cloth were always changing, it was difficult for those living as far away as Yorkshire to keep abreast of the latest changes in the Statutes. William Lunsdale, an inhabitant of Selby was caught up in such a dilemma in 1558. A number of clothiers, including Lunsdale, arrived at St Bartholomew's Fair that year, bringing with them a large amount of kerseys and cloths. However, when they entered the fair they refrained from opening their bundles in front of the officials for they were not sure if their cloth conformed to the laws set for that day. The Privy Council was made aware of their predicament and to allay their fears called a selection of the northern clothiers, which included Lunsdale from Selby, to appear before them. The Council conferred with the traders; they discussed the state of the Cloth Acts with them and generally did everything they could to put their minds at rest. When the clothiers from the north were confident they would not be penalised and lose their cloths they happily set out their wares.

This incident showed that there were still clothiers in Selby though the main industry had become centred around the expanding West Riding towns. Articles were still being made using flax. Though a great amount of the material was being imported, the crop was still being grown in the Selby area. In the details of a twenty-one year lease granted to William Babthorpe, knight, in 1571, amongst the tithes he was to receive were hemp and flax from Barlby, Cliffe, South Duffield and Osgodby. The steward of Selby manor listed in his expenses for 1608-9, the cost of six stone of hemp and six stone of cord.

The Plague

Further outbreaks of the 'plague' and other illnesses threatened the growing prosperity of many towns during the sixteenth to seventeenth century. In periods of marked deterioration in the climate that resulted in poor harvests there was much malnutrition, exacerbated by the demands of an increased population upon limited resources. This same situation existed throughout Europe and was made worse by epidemics of fever and infectious diseases that swept through the lands decimating the expanding population. In England, more than in other parts of Europe, it was these diseases, rather than the dearth of food that proved a killer. As the inhabitants of Mill-gate had suspected when they blamed their recurring 'shivering' attacks on the water-wheels, Selby was especially prone to epidemics and a sweating sickness, now believed to have been a kind of influenza. This was mainly due to the vast amounts of water which, due to poor drainage in the neighbourhood, collected in numerous stretches of wet woodland, known as carrs. During the 1550s heavy rains ruined the harvests and the plagues and 'flu' took their toll. The 'plague' which was more prevalent in the towns than the countryside must have been present in Selby in 1570. In June of that year, the Corporation of York ordered that a vigilant and continuous watch be kept at the city gates to prevent *"any suspect persons"* from Selby entering the town.

In 1604 the plague which had been raging through London the previous year spread as far as Northallerton. It swept through York killing 3,512 people, about thirty per cent of the population. To help curb its passage, markets were forbidden in the city. Stone crosses were erected on the roads leading to York where country folk could leave their wares for the citizens. One of these crosses can still be seen at Fulford by the A19 York to Selby road. It is believed that Selby followed the same pattern. A temporary cross, serving as a focal point, was believed to have been erected on a slightly elevated piece of land on a lane leading out of the western side of Selby. Modern maps show a Cross Hills Lane continuing west from Flaxley Road.

Thomas Wentworth, President of the Council of the North, took drastic precautions in 1631 to protect York from further outbreaks. He demolished the squalid shanty town, populated by the poor, that had developed round the walls of the city. This isolated the city and may explain why York escaped the epidemics suffered by Bristol and Hull and the fierce one that later raged through London in 1665. Trade with the metropolis was forbidden that year and fairs banned in many places. In August 1665, a King's Proclamation stated that Howden Fair and others in the County of York were forbidden and that no Londoners were to go to them or any other fair because of the plague.

Despite all efforts Selby, and many other places, suffered recurrences of the illnesses that periodically swept through the land. There were no real answers to epidemics that could swiftly empty a village within a year or the less publicised stomach and bowel disorders that killed off one third of children under five. Population recovery from these illnesses was usually marked by high marriage and birth rates.

More Conflicts with the Monarchy

The failure of the northern earls' rebellion, the dissolution of the monasteries and the results of the Reformation marked the end of the Middle Ages. Elizabeth I placed trusted supporters in positions of power in the north. Edmund Grindall was made Archbishop of York and Henry, Earl of Huntingdon, became Lord President of the Council of the North. From the middle years of Elizabeth's reign a strong Tudor government contributed to the decrease in feuds and lawlessness in northern counties. It also brought about an increase in the growth and prosperity of Yorkshire and the nation as a whole.

At Elizabeth's death in 1603, James VI of Scotland became James I of England. He had taken the crown of Scotland in 1567 after the removal of his mother, Mary, Queen of Scots. His right of succession to the English throne was through his great-grandmother Margaret, daughter of Henry VII. James accepted the Established English

Church which disappointed the Puritans who had petitioned the king for church reform. The only good result for them was the agreement to undertake a new translation of the Bible which became the *'Authorised Version'*.

James's lack of support for Roman Catholics led to the decision of a small group to blow up their persecutors during the formal opening of Parliament.

An annual commemoration of the failed attempt to blow up Parliament, known as the 'Gunpowder Plot' is held on the fifth of November, the day Guy Fawkes was discovered in the cellar. Traditionally, bonfires are lit, fireworks ignited and effigies of Guy Fawkes are burnt. For many years after the event it had also been used as an occasion for anti-catholic feelings to be demonstrated in the burning of public hate-figures.

Selby did not miss out in the celebrations all those years ago. In 1727, the Constables expenditure accounts for Selby listed the following:

5 November: to Bonfire and drink...six shillings.

Troops in Selby

Charles I became King of England, Scotland and Ireland in 1625. He had become the heir apparent to James after the death of his elder brother, Henry, in 1612. Charles soon caused anxiety throughout the nation by his attachments to ladies of the Roman Catholic faith. This increased when he married the Catholic French princess, Henrietta Maria. Difficult relations soon developed between the new monarch and Parliament over financial, political and religious issues. By 1629 Charles had ceased to call Parliament. He continued to cause anger by his actions such as allowing the lands of English landowners, who had settled in Ireland during the sixteenth and early seventeenth centuries, to be recovered for the crown and the Established Church. These landowners were mostly Protestants and known as the New English. The king was particularly insensitive to the Scots and their Scottish pride. For example, he used the English style religious ceremony when worshipping in Scotland.

Apart from brief outbreaks of insurgency the monarchy had enjoyed supreme authority over the nation for over a hundred years. Its strength had been in relying on laws and customs rather than military force so that when Charles I tried to rule alone he did not have an army to subdue unruly subjects. For eleven years the king had no funds to pay for a military force, the lack of which was a major weakness during the struggle for power between Charles and his government.

The absence of a standing army was particularly felt by the king when in 1637, together with Archbishop Laud, he attempted to impose on the Scottish Calvinists a new prayer book, based on the English Anglican version. The Scots signed a National Covenant binding themselves to protect their religion. They also quickly raised an army placing Alexander Leslie, an experienced soldier, as its Commander-in-Chief. Charles now had to find a military force to face this foe. As part of the levies men were ordered to meet at Selby by the 1st. April 1639. The king was in York at that time where he had summoned the kingdom's nobility to assemble. During Easter week he travelled to Selby where an army of six thousand men and as many foot soldiers had gathered. Sir Henry Slingsby who kept a diary of events, wrote:

On Wednesday in Easter week ye king's majesty went to Selby to vew his troops yt lay there.

The lack of attention and previous failures in funding the armed forces became evident. When in 1639 the northern militia assembled at Newcastle, the twenty thousand foot and twelve thousand horse were made up of indisciplined, untrained and ill-equipped men who showed no enthusiasm for fighting to impose Anglicanism on the Scots. Other troops under the Marquis of Hamilton, sent with a fleet to menace the Scottish coast were equally untrained; only about two hundred of them were able to fire a musket. The first encounter with the Scots, known as the "Bishops' War" ended inconclusively after an English force had bolted when faced by a Scottish detachment led by Alexander Leslie. A treaty was signed at Berwick giving many concessions to the rebels.

In 1640 Charles again tried to assert his authority over the Scots. He made efforts to create a professional army by raising militia from many countries but lack of money dogged his attempts. The continuing lack of enthusiasm by the English for the fight also led to mutinies, desertions and plundering on a grand scale. Soldiers were billeted or ordered to enlist in many places including Selby. The state of the king's troops at that time was illustrated in a letter sent from the town to Newcastle on the 10th. July, 1640. In it, Sir Jacob Astley, a staunch Royalist Commander wrote that he had orders from his Lord General to send four to five thousand men to Newcastle. He complained that not a great number had arrived in the town and those that had had neither colours nor halberds and were in need of drums and other equipment. Sir Astley wrote that he was now under further orders to receive *"all the arch-knaves in this kingdom, and to arm them at Selby"*. He added that before he arrived in the town some five hundred men had been brought there by Lieutenant-Colonel Ballard. The undisciplined recruits had beaten up their officers and the local country folk, opened up the prisons and generally caused havoc. Another regiment under Colonel Lunsford had come to Selby on the eighth; they had also been guilty of fighting with their officers and plundering the place.

The attitude of the troops and some collusion between the Scots nobility and English aristocrats helped to bring about a miserable defeat of Charles' men in the "Second Bishops' War". At the Treaty of Ripon, in August, 1640, the Scots were granted a massive indemnity of over four hundred thousand pounds and occupancy of land, mainly in Northern England, as security.

There is evidence that not all the soldiers billeted in Selby behaved in the manner described in Sir Astley's letter. In March 1640, the presence of some recruits in the town averted a terrible disaster. At the West Riding Sessions that year, Isabel Hodgson, widow, and Richard Ibbotson, blacksmith, both of Selby, petitioned the Court that upon the 26th. March, a *"fearfull and lamentable fire"* in both their dwellings had spread upwards and along five other houses. The other homes were only saved, they claimed, because there were soldiers billeted in Selby who went to help and prevented the whole town from being consumed in the flames. The result was that Isabel and Richard were the only two to lose their homes and outhouses with all their contents to the fire. The Court, as on previous occasions, ordered the churchwardens and the overseers of the poor to raise funds to help the unfortunate victims.

Selby Prior to the Civil War

Whilst events were building up towards a confrontation between Charles I and Parliament, life in Selby and its neighbouring villages carried on almost unchanged. Benevolent people continued to leave legacies to help the local inhabitants. In 1632 Ralph Lodge died. His family, it was said, lived in a house on a plot of land in Barlby, locally known as 'The Island'. It was on the site of an ancient manor house which most probably had had a moat surrounding it. Ralph Lodge requested he be buried in the church at Hemingbrough and willed five marks to the poor people there and twenty shillings for the poor in Riccall. He also left twenty shillings towards the mending of the causeys between *'Barle Croft yate and Lyd yate"* with any money remaining to be used on roads along the town towards 'Mabb pole'. Forty shillings was allowed for Barlby chapel *"if others will do the same"*. To his son and heirs he bequeathed the messuage where he had dwelt in Barlby and other lands he owned in the township. Ralph also left in trust for his younger son, some freehold land in Riccall. The executors were to receive the rents during his minority and use the same to maintain the boy at university.

Less affluent people willed what they had to their families. John Mendall, senior, a joiner in Selby died on the 30th. December, 1634. He left his son John, five shillings and a suit of clothes, his daughter, Maria, a sack of malt whilst her husband was bequeathed twelve pence. William, Edward and John, sons of John junior, were to receive ten shillings apiece when they came of lawful age; Petronell their sister, when she came of age, was to receive forty shillings. This was maybe to provide her with a dowry; Thomas Lund, cordwainer, left ten pounds to his daughter to inherit when she was twenty-one or getting married. Elizabeth Lund, a widow of Hambleton, left clear instructions. To one of her many grandchildren she left the *"bed that I lyeth in and bedding, puter chamber pot, long settell and thirty shillings that Robert Ledsam oweth me"*. Two of her daughter's children were to share equally, ten pounds owed to her by Urias Turner. The widow left many gifts but stipulated, *"It is my will that the legeses aforesaid that I have given to my grandchildren, four Palmers, shall not come to William Palmer, their father's hand, noe part nor persill of it"*.

In the Constables' expense accounts for the year 1723 there was the following item; *"For carrying a vagrant to the Cripple Cart ... 7 shillings"*. The Constables may, in this case, have been moving the disabled vagrant out of their parish so he would not become a 'burden' on the inhabitants' taxes, or they may have been carrying out a custom that seemed to have prevailed for a number of years, that of providing 'transport' for disabled people. In 1640 there were several meetings held during the Pontefract Sessions concerning this ancient custom of carrying disabled people. Two routes between the towns of Ferrybridge and Doncaster were under discussion. At one meeting it was ordered that the inhabitants of Skelbrooke, Campsall, Norton, Womersley, Stapleton, Burghwallis and Smeaton Parva were to continue to observe the ancient custom of conveying disabled people between the two towns. Skelbrooke inhabitants refused to acknowledge this order for they vowed they had not received notice of the meeting and so had not attended. They were commanded to carry out their duty until another meeting could be held. An argument then took place over which of two routes should be the official one. People from Darrington, Wentbridge, Aldwick and other places near the alternative way joined in the many quarrels and deputations that followed. In the end the Court appointed four justices of the peace to examine each highway, to listen to the villagers' concerns and then to make a decision agreeable to everyone! Until the matter was settled those concerned were commanded, on pain of retribution, to obey the previous order. In October the Court confirmed that, as everyone had been saying, both routes were of a similar length. They declared, however, that the most convenient was the more ancient way from Ferrybridge to Knottingley, then Cridling with the Park, Womersley Stubb, Walden, Norton, Campsall, Burghwallis, Skellow and so to Doncaster. The justices stated that the villagers of Darrington, Wentbridge and Skelbrooke were not to be troubled anymore with the carrying or conveying of disabled people but should contribute an annual payment of twenty shillings to the cost.

Ferrybridge and Doncaster were important to Selby in connection with other customs that had developed over the years. Edward III (1327-77) is said to have begun an inland postal service which was improved upon by later kings. Relay posts were organised to enable a single horseman carrying state messages to travel at quite fast speeds with fresh mounts every twenty miles. It was Henry VIII who appointed the first "Master of the Posts" in 1516. The nearest major road to Selby was the Great North Road passing through Doncaster. During the reign of Elizabeth this town became Post Stage No. 13 with Stage No. 14 at Ferrybridge. A royal proclamation in 1609 imposed the Crown Monopoly over the letter post and when in 1635 Charles had a postal system set up, all inland private systems were abolished. In 1669 Selby was one of ten market towns listed as receiving its letters from the Post Stage at Ferrybridge. Two hundred years after Charles imposed the Crown Monopoly over the post Selby was still receiving its mail through Ferrybridge by horse post.

Crimes and Punishments

By the seventeenth century indictable offences were being referred to the General Sessions held in Pontefract and Wakefield. John Inchbald, gentleman of Drax, was charged at Pontefract with enclosing and obstructing with hedges and ditches, in a close at Drax called Brandhurst, a common horse way between the town of Airmyn and Selby. His actions prevented other people from travelling on a right of way. John was not present in court but Edward Jacques was recorded as the chief witness against him. Three months later, in July, 1640, John Inchbald admitted to the offence at Wakefield. He paid a fine of sixpence to the sheriff but was also ordered to *lay open the old ancient way forthwith so that his Majesty's subjects may pass unhindered as they have always done, upon pain of xxxxs"*. In 1639 John Brayshawe, husbandman of Hambleton, was charged with assaulting and maltreating John Middleton. Elizabeth Middleton appeared as a witness. The offender paid 3s.4d. to the sheriff. Two years later Geoffrey Wright, a labourer from Selby, was charged with a similar offence on one Francis Pothan. Having confessed he was fined ten shillings. Two gentlemen named Thomas Bambye and John Willan with Thomas Leadall a glover, all of Selby, were accused at Wakefield with breaking into the free chase of Thomas Walmsley, esq. lord of the manor and with unlawfully chasing deer there, killing one with a gun before taking it away. Two witnesses Alice Walker and Richard Hurst testified to this crime. All three men were bound over to keep the peace but no fine was recorded.

At a Court held in Doncaster the money paid by one offender was put to good use. John Moseley was fined twenty shillings for keeping *"an Ale-house or Tiplinghouse"* without the consent of the justices at Shepley. He was also fined sixpence for assaulting one Edmund Haigh in Whitley. The money received was ordered to be given to the poor. There were many unfortunate culprits who could not pay their fines so other forms of punishments were arranged for them. Deborah Middleton a spinster of Hambleton, was accused at Pontefract of stealing five hens, value eighteen pence, and one capon valued at eightpence, the property of Robert Lund. Deborah pleaded guilty and was fined tenpence but having no chattels she was whipped. Luke Middleton of Monk Fryston also appeared in court for harbouring her after the offence. Another offender who could not pay his fine was John Beck, a Selby labourer. Accused of stealing three quarters of malt valued at 3s.4d., he pleaded guilty and having no possessions was burnt in the hand. Robert Parkinson, husbandman, Anne Newton, wife of another tenant farmer and Mary, wife of John Dawson, miller, were all charged with harbouring John Beck.

Other miscreants must have had good friends or associates to give them shelter for many reported cases ended with the words, *"At large"*. Ratcliffe Barnaby, a widow of Selby, was one of these when accused of stealing a black cow in the town in October, 1640. The owner of the cow, Richard Spicer appeared in court; but the widow was "at large". It is interesting to note that whilst the cow was valued at 70 shillings, a maidservant hired, at that time, to milk animals on a farm would have been paid between 24 and 28 shillings, annually. Another lawbreaker recorded "at large" was a confidence trickster named William Pothan, a Selby yeoman. In October 1639, posing as the Bailiff of Marmaduke Langdale, a knight and Sheriff of Yorkshire, he unjustly exacted fifteen shillings from William Dodgson of Stanley.

Civil Wars

Following the disastrous Bishops' Wars Charles was forced to recall the English Parliament to raise the money promised to the Scots and to pay his army. He made sweeping concessions to pacify his opponents but within two years his more devious actions, coupled with his determination to regain royal supremacy, brought confrontation with Parliament. The crisis came in 1641 over who should control the army needed to suppress an Irish uprising triggered by resentment over the increasing number of English and Scottish settlers taking land in Ireland. What had started out as a rebellion in 1641 became Civil War the following year when in August, Charles raised his Standard in Nottingham.

In the months leading up to this event the king had been plotting and scheming to outwit those wishing his downfall. With the seizure of Hull in mind the king travelled north and held his court in York. Whilst there he gave out commissions to trusted supporters, and in return received considerable amounts of money. However Parliament forestalled Charles's plan to take Hull by making one of their members, Sir John Hotham, Governor of Hull. In this way they secured the town for Parliament, and the arms and ammunition stored there. Civil War was inevitable but in Yorkshire the two sides were so evenly matched that, in order to save unnecessary bloodshed, their leaders agreed to a treaty of armed neutrality to keep the county free of military action for as long as possible. Signed in September, 1642 its effect did not last long for soon the county became involved in the nationwide conflict. When Charles rejected a proposition that it should reign in his name Parliament commissioned the Earl of Essex to raise and lead an army of ten thousand men. Anyone remaining loyal to the king was declared a traitor.

Charles had the support of those of the gentry and aristocracy who bore a natural loyalty to the crown, and nearly all Catholics, and those fearing what the radicals in Parliament might do if in power. People from the richer, urban and commercial parts of the country, such as the clothiers in Yorkshire, joined by the majority of Puritans, gave their allegiance to the members of the Commons. The feelings of Selby people concerning King and Parliament were referred to in a letter sent from Hull in June 1642. It contained reports of *"great stirrings in York"* concerning an anti-Parliament petition which many there refused to acknowledge. The writer went on to say those in Selby were believed to have generally been of the same mind.

Selby and the Civil Wars

Selby had already been involved in the strife caused by the activities of Charles through the billeting and gathering of troops there during the Bishops' Wars. The town and other places in the district were destined to suffer much more pain and disruption as the events of the Wars unfolded. The battles and movements of troops that took place are too many and too involved to recount in their entirety but those that occurred in the vicinity of Selby are recorded. Fighting around the town began in 1642. When the king moved from Yorkshire to Nottingham, Sir John Hotham, who had refused Charles's entry into Hull, left the town to search for those who had supported the monarch. Meeting up with two more companies of foot on the way, he led an attack on the archbishop's castle at Cawood held by Royalist troops. The garrison, commanded by Captain Gray, was chiefly made up of local townsmen, the majority of whom, being offered favourable terms, soon surrendered to Hotham's soldiers. It is said the archbishop left the area for his native country of Wales. Hotham then marched to Selby where Captain Gray had had his outpost. He garrisoned it with two companies of infantry under his son, Captain Hotham. The Parliamentarians now had a secure line of communication between Hull and the towns of the West Riding. With Sir Thomas Fairfax in Tadcaster and the Hothams controlling Selby and Cawood they were in a good position to carry out a constant harrying of the Royalist stronghold at York

Throughout November, Lord Ferdinando Fairfax and his son, Sir Thomas Fairfax assisted by Captain Hotham continued to gather their forces, whilst a net was being drawn around the Royalists holding York. At the end of the month Sir Thomas was centred at Wetherby whilst his father had made Tadcaster his base. By this time the Earl of Newcastle was advancing into Yorkshire from the north with a Royalist army of six thousand men. Captain Hotham, following several victories over the enemy was holding the medieval bridge over the Tees at Piercebridge, but Newcastle successfully took the bridge before moving on to relieve York.

Their first clash with the Fairfaxes was at Tadcaster. The large Royalist army was driven out of part of the town by a smaller Parliamentarian force of nine hundred men. Some details of the battle were described in a letter written to a cousin by Sir Henry Foulis, Baronet. Sent from Selby on the 17th December 1642, it began with an apology for not writing more regularly. A fault blamed on the *"troubles of our Country"*. Sir Henry bemoaned the fact that Cleveland had turned into a wilderness where his wife and children were the *"sole Governours"* others having fled through fear of the fighting or because of their religious persuasions. Sir Henry stated that his goods were at Hull whilst he and his troop of horse were at Selby. They had, he said, lost contact with a regiment of foot near the walls of York but, Sir Henry bitterly remarked, even if they came to Selby, one musket report and they would all run away, just like the troops had at Yarum. At that place, he continued, five hundred had quickly been reduced to two hundred after just one encounter with the enemy, then quickly dwindled to eighty.

Sir Henry described how he came to Selby via Knaresborough, Wetherby and Tadcaster. They were waiting at Wetherby to encounter Newcastle's troops when the enemy was spotted upon the moor, about a mile out from Tadcaster. The horse troops of Sir Thomas Fairfax, Sir Charles Wray and the writer gathered in a field near to the moor, a ditch forming a barrier between them and their foe. The fighting lasted about three hours. The Parliamentary forces only had one demi culverin, a cannon using shot of about nine pounds whilst the Royalists had five culverins, long cannons using an eighteen pound shot. But, wrote Sir Henry, the guns did little harm for their fire was spent before it reached its target, the horse troops. When hostilities ceased the Royalists had lost thirty men and had twenty taken prisoner; Fairfax's dead consisted of three common soldiers and Colonel Lister. Sir Henry reported how Newcastle had stayed with the wounded all night but even so at least five hundred men deserted him. The writer then explained how, even though their small army had beaten the Royalists they were unable to hold the town through lack of ammunition and food. For twenty four hours, he added, not even the Commander had eaten, much less a common soldier. Therefore, whilst the enemy were regrouping and tending their wounded Fairfax and his troops stole away from Tadcaster. They were now at Cawood and Selby in order to refresh their men. They would however, Sir Henry assured his cousin, fall upon the Earl of Newcastle if he came that way despite missing two leaders and fresh men to relieve their wearied troops.

The Parliamentarian troops had fallen back to Selby because it lay on their route to Hull and was not too far from York. On the 9th. December, 1642, Sir Thomas was sent, by his father, into the West Riding with five companies of foot and two of horse to bolster their forces there and try to secure Leeds and other clothing towns. The enemy's forces were so heavily present in the region that Fairfax had to retreat back to Selby. He had planned to reach Bradford via Ferrybridge but found the crossing place occupied. On his way back to Selby his troops had a small skirmish with some Royalists they chanced upon at Monk Fryston. Information given by the five prisoners they took there illustrated how poor was the intelligence of the Parliamentarians or Roundheads, as they came to be known. Sir Thomas had been informed that the Earl of Newcastle and his troops were moving slowly and had only reached Sherburn-in-Elmet. In fact, as the prisoners disclosed to him, Newcastle was at Pontefract and had left eight hundred men guarding Ferrybridge.

The younger Fairfax was determined not to stay couped up in Selby so decided to give his men some action by joining Captain Hotham in a raid on a small detachment of the enemy supposedly quartered at Church Fenton. Finding the place empty of troops they moved towards Sherburn-in-Elmet intending to give the troops there a fright. Not being able to find cover in the flat, open country-side, they were spotted and some two hundred horse came out from Sherburn to obstruct their passage. What followed next has been described by many as an almost perfect cavalry raid. Fairfax, eagerly supported by Hotham, led his cavalry in a charge on the group of Royalists. They pursued them so closely they were able to enter the town with the fleeing horsemen. They ransacked the soldiers' quarters before returning to Selby and Cawood with prizes that included many prisoners and the enemy's best horses.

One of the *"King's Pamphlets,"* No.85, 1642, which according to Morrell is held in the British Museum, consists of a letter written by Sir Thomas from Howden in December, 1642. It describes how he lost only two men in the raid then returned quickly to Selby for Royalist troops were at both Ferrybridge and Tadcaster. Sir Thomas described how his father, Lord Fairfax, had almost finished his trenches at Selby which, when completed, would make the town a place of great strength. He had also cut down Tunbridge and sunk all the boats on the river, the only drawback being the lack of food. Tunbridge, in this case may have been Turnbridge, on the old River Don.

Selby was still occupied by the Roundheads in February 1643 for in that month the Earl of Essex addressed a dispatch to the Fairfaxes there. They were, however, forced to withdraw in April 1643 when the tide of war turned against them. On the 29th June 1643 they suffered a defeat at the Battle of Adwalton Moor, near Bradford, which forced the Fairfaxes to retreat from this area. A message was then received from Hull with the good news that the beleaguered Parliamentarians would be made welcome in that town. However, Hull was sixty miles away with the country in between controlled by the Royalists. Ferdinando made his way to Leeds but Royalist prisoners broke out there and seized the magazine so he had to press on towards Selby. His son, left in Bradford with only eight hundred foot and sixty horse had no choice but to abandon the town to the enemy. Accompanied by his family, Sir Thomas also headed towards Leeds but on route was challenged by a party of Royalists. In the skirmish that followed his wife was taken prisoner. Leeds was in a turmoil when they arrived and those who were lucky to escape decided to try to dodge the enemy cavalry and make for Hull. The Royalists would have dearly loved to apprehend either of the Fairfaxes so it was a very relieved party that, after twenty four hours non-stop hard riding, arrived at Selby.

Sir Thomas was informed that his father was about to use the town's ferry to cross the Ouse and that the enemy now holding Cawood, were set on capturing him. He gave the following account of the next events.

> *My father being a mile before with a few men, getting over the ferry, word came to us that he was in danger to be taken; I hastened to him with about forty horse, the rest following in some disorder. He was nearly got into the boat when the enemy with three cornets of horse entered the town. I drew up in the market-place, directly before the street they came down; when they were almost half come into the market-place they turned to the right-hand. With part of my troop I charged them in the flank and divided them; we had the chase of them down the long street that goes to Brayton. It happened, at the same time, that those men I left behind were coming up the street, but, being in disorder, and discouraged with the misfortunes of so many days before, they turned about; and gave way, not knowing we were pursuing the enemy in their rear. At the end of this street was a narrow lane which led to Cawood. The enemy strove to pass that way, but it being narrow, there was a sudden stop, where we were mingled one among another. Here I received a shot in the wrist of my arm, which made the bridle fall out of my hand...our men laid me on the ground...my surgeon came and bound up the wound and stoppd the bleeding. After an hour's rest; I got up on horseback again. The other part of our horse had beaten the enemy back to Cawood, the same way they came first to us. Thus by the goodness of God our passage was clear; some went over the ferry after my father; myself, with others, went through the levels to Hull; but it proved a very*

*troublesome and dangerous passage, being often interrupted by the enemy,
sometimes in our front; sometimes in our rear:*

On the 4th. July after a close encounter with Royalist troops, a ship carried them over to Hull, battle weary but alive and free.

For the rest of 1643 the Parliamentary forces were too depleted to strike against their enemies in the area around Selby. During this time, however, more and more men were finding their way to Hull where Lord Ferdinando Fairfax was now Governor. When his son had gathered together a new force he moved out to Beverley to harass the Royalists at places such as Stamford Bridge. The Earl of Newcastle was moving south but changed direction when he found his men would not leave their home county whilst the enemy was attacking there. The earl, therefore, deployed them to besiege Hull. This action began on the 2nd. September, 1643; sixteen days later Oliver Cromwell arrived in the district with his troops; four days later he was in the town. Sir Thomas Fairfax then accompanied Cromwell to East Anglia where they joined up with the Earl of Manchester. The Parliamentarians were victorious in that county and in Lancashire and Cheshire. Whilst the leaders were helping the troops in those areas the Earl of Newcastle, after some severe fighting, abandoned the siege of Hull and in October withdrew to York.

Earlier in September, whilst all this fighting was taking place, Parliament formed an alliance with the Scots. It was known as 'The Solemn League and Covenant' which incorporated a covenant previously signed by the majority of the Scottish nobility which rejected Episcopacy in favour of Presbyterianism. The signing opened the way for the intervention of those Scots opposed to the king. In January 1644 a Scottish army crossed the Tweed. Newcastle now had to deal with this new threat whilst dealing with Ferdinando's activities in the North and East Ridings of Yorkshire. Sir Thomas, by that time in Lancashire was having trouble raising levies for, like Newcastle, he found men were reluctant to move out of their own county to fight and wished to remain to protect their own homes; others, with spring approaching, had dismissed themselves and gone to follow the plough!

The Royalists held the upper hand in Yorkshire but with their commander committed further north in the snows of Durham and Northumberland, Parliamentarian resistance began to grow. Incursions were made again into the West Riding and other places. Sir William Constable slipped out of Hull on several occasions on successful forays against the enemy.

John Belasyse had been made governor and commander in York on the death of Colonel Sir William Saville. He was aged around thirty and was a prominent Catholic Royalist with considerable military experience. It became his responsibility to keep the Royalists in power in Yorkshire. It is not clear what orders he had been given but he set out to consolidate the garrisons and reorganise the field armies, setting up headquarters in towns such as Leeds and Halifax. He prepared himself to fight a short, defensive campaign against Parliamentary leaders such as Colonel Lambert, in order to prevent them reopening the line of communication from the West Riding to Hull.

The Royalists made an attempt in early March to oust the Parliamentarians from Bradford but were beaten back by Colonel Lambert and his men. A second attempt was made from Selby on or around the 25th. March. The town had been chosen by Belasyse as a base from which to move against the enemy. Selby was seen as being in a better position than York for it stood four-square between Lambert in the West Riding and

Hull. It is also believed that Belasyse had intercepted a letter containing details of a Fairfax plan to unite their scattered forces at Selby before marching north to assist the Scots near Durham. The York Governor gathered together an army of five thousand foot and fifteen hundred horse at Selby; a George Porter was amongst the leaders of the troops sent to assist him. Belasyse came from York with six pieces of cannon and a train of attendants, to command the forces at Selby. He made a bridge of boats over the River Ouse to help communications with the East Riding. In the second attempt to seize Bradford Belasyse sent one thousand foot and five hundred horse from Selby, including George Porter and his troop. During the long fight for the town George Porter's cavalry were scattered and the main Royalist army forced to fall back towards Leeds. Porter went back to Nottinghamshire to, as he argued, recoup his losses. It was his duty to return to Selby but his dilatoriness in doing so is said to have contributed in no small way to the outcome of the battle that took place in the town.

The Battle of Selby, April 1644

The conflict at Selby was the result of the consolidation of two Parliamentary forces which Belasyse could not have foreseen and which he was ill-equipped to defeat. In March, 1644, Sir Thomas Fairfax was back in Yorkshire with two thousand horse. He met up with his father, as arranged, at Ferrybridge. None of their troops could cross the Ouse because the Royalists held the ferry at Selby, a key crossing point. Ferdinando Fairfax, therefore, had avoided the town and with some difficulty taken his men and carriages over the river, ten miles further downstream in Marshland. It had taken two days for his two thousand horse and dragoons with two thousand foot to make the crossing before marching onto Ferrybridge. Sir Thomas had previously received orders to take his horse and dragoons to Northumberland to support the Scots against Newcastle, but when he learnt that his father had come from Hull with plans to attack the Royalists' base at Selby, he joined him in that enterprise.

Belasyse had little option but to stay in Selby and face the combined Parliamentary forces. If he had retreated to York he would have effectually abandoned a large area to the south and west and given the enemy the direct line of communication between the West and East Ridings they so wanted. The Parliamentarians also needed to remove Belasyse to allow them to join forces with the Scots, especially since it was known that the Earl of Newcastle's obstructive warfare against them was becoming less effective. On the 10th. April 1644, the Fairfaxes and Sir John Meldrum, marched their troops towards Selby. In response to a summons from Lord Fairfax to deliver the town up to the Parliamentarians, Colonel Belasyse replied that he would keep Selby as long as he had a drop of blood in his veins. Chancing upon a party of Royalist troops they chased them back into Selby taking a few prisoners on the way. The day being almost spent Lord Fairfax quartered his men for the night in the region of Thorpe Willoughby. Next day they drew their forces close to the town. Sir John Meldrum deployed the foot around the outskirts of the town, ready to storm the barricades. Sir Thomas' two thousand horse were ready to support them. The bulk of the troops were concentrated at the south end of Ousegate, the west end of Gowthorpe and down New Lane which led the way to Brayton.

The Royalists put up a long and strong resistance against their attackers but were gradually beaten back. The fighting at the barricades continued until Lord Fairfax's foot regiment broke through defences near the river and the horse were able to get into the narrow confines of Ousegate. Here the attackers encountered the defenders' horse but after one charge at them the Royalists began to flee over the boats towards York. Belasyse then led a countercharge but in the crowded fighting soon found himself isolated in the midst of the enemy who killed his horse from under him. The Royalist governor was shot at with pistols and slashed at with swords from which he received wounds in his arm and head. Belasyse was carried to Lord Fairfax who sent his 'chirurgeons' to dress his wounds. Sir Thomas was also unhorsed but his cavalry continued to drive the Royalists back. The Parliamentary foot entered the town to support the horse. Those of Belasyse's men who managed to reach the bridge of boats fled towards Cawood or York. Others making for Pontefract were pursued as far as Ferrybridge. The bodies of the dead were strewn along this route and for up to four miles in the direction of York. Nearly five hundred of Belasyse's men were later captured near Hemingbrough and confined in the parish church overnight. It is believed in the confusion and in their hurry to reach York they mistook their way.

Heavy losses were sustained by the Royalists at Selby and many prisoners taken. There were few men left in Colonel Sir Walter Vavasour's cavalry and Colonel Belasyse's York Infantry who had fought so well in 1643, were almost completely destroyed and ceased to exist. It was reported that sixteen hundred men were captured in the town including four colonels, four majors, twenty captains and one hundred and thirty 'inferior' officers. Two thousand arms were collected, all the soldiers' bag and baggage and many ships. Most of the prisoners were marched to Hull. The common soldiers were most probably freed on condition that they took no further part in the fighting. Colonel Belasyse who remained a prisoner for ten months was taken to London before he was exchanged.

The defeat of the Royalists at Selby was chiefly blamed on two factors: the failure of George Porter to appear with his troops and the cowardice or betrayal believed to have taken place at the barricade down Ousegate. In her autobiography a Mrs. Alice Thornton recording events in April, 1644, related how her mother, Lady Wandesford, was taking her whole family, from Snape, near Bedale, to live in York to be with her sick son, Christopher. Halfway to the city she was met by a kinsman, who had ridden post haste from York and who warned her not to go there *"for the Parliamentary forces had met with the king's and they were all betrayed ..... and York would be besieged"*. This may have been referring to a claim by the Royalists that the enemy gained entry to Selby through the treacherous actions of a Captain Wilson who it was known had been manning the Ousegate barricade. This belief was supported by the contents of a private letter written in December 1644 by a Major William Vavasour of Colonel Sir Walter Vavasour's horse. The correspondence was sent from Holland where the major was living in exile. In it he declared that as far as he was concerned the Selby affair was not down to disobedience or ill-conduct but to the cowardice of some foot officers. Also, it was stated by Sir Thomas Fairfax that his troops had entered the town at a point where they had previously failed to make any impression. Other evidence in support of this treachery was the fact that Captain Wilson was shot by order of the Council of War, either on the field or later in York.

Reminders of the Civil Wars

There are reminders of the Civil Wars to be found in or around Selby today. Records of some of the soldiers who fell in the town or its suburbs are recorded in

Morrell's *'History of Selby'* and in registers kept by the Borthwick Institute, York. Twenty-six deaths were recorded in the burial register for 1642, but pages were left blank during the periods in the following two years when Selby was occupied by the Royalists. It is believed the Abbey Church was used for storing equipment and stabling horses. Howden Church suffered severely at the hands of a troop of soldiers from Hull who were making their way to assist Fairfax in his attack on Selby.

Articles discovered in the district during the twentieth century are believed to date back to the time of the hostilities. Two young boys found a cannon-ball in Chapel Street, Hambleton. Jason Embling and Mark Hollebon took it to York Museum where they were told it was most probably a relic from the Civil Wars. It is surmised the cannon-ball could have been fired from a gun known to have been used at Tadcaster. Previously a jury sitting in Selby Court House had to make a decision as to the owner of a hoard of coins dating from the time of the wars. Robert Newton from Brayton turned up some of the coins when working at Thorpe Hall Farm. He was using a tractor plough and trenching to a greater depth than usual to undermine a crop of thistles. With the help of Mr. R. Chambers, the owner of the farm at Thorpe Willoughby, more coins and a broken earthenware jar containing a large collection of them were unearthed. The hoard contained a James I gold piece, 107 silver half-crowns, 1140 silver shillings and 1431 silver sixpences issued during the reigns of Elizabeth I, James I and Charles I. Mr. Sinclair, manager of the National Provincial Bank, was of the opinion that the money had been deliberately buried. When the site was excavated a depression in the clay was found four inches deep and twelve inches wide. It was suggested that the jar had been placed there sometime between 1642 and 1644 when fighting was rife in the district. There were no banks at that time so it was common practice to bury one's valuables when danger threatened. The owner in this case may have become one of the many casualties of the fighting between the two opposing forces. Sixty to seventy fragments of the jar were uncovered and examined at Hull by the director of the Municipal Museums there, Mr T Sheppard. He believed they came from a sixteenth century filter. There was a hole near the base of the vessel almost one and a quarter inches across which was for a tap. The filter had probably contained charcoal or other matter to cleanse the drinking water. The jar was partly glazed outside but well glazed on the inside. It would have had an opening at the top large enough to take the coins, with a small handle on either side.

Because it appeared the money had been stowed away the jury in Selby counted it as treasure trove which, in 1939, meant that Mr. Newton was the true finder. It also implied that the money belonged to the Crown and would go to the Keeper of Coins at the British Museum. A law passed in 1931 ruled that the keeper was allowed to retain any coins of special interest. He was duty bound to pay Mr. Newton their full monetary value and return to him all the coins not kept by the museum.

Thomas Johnson

The names of the majority of people from Selby and the surrounding villages who died in the Civil Wars are not known. However, one Selebian did have his name recorded when he died fighting for the Royalist cause far away from his home town. His name was Thomas Johnson famed as a herbalist, editor and translator before becoming a royalist soldier known for his exceptional bravery.

The date of his birth is uncertain for the Selby Abbey Church registers record two marriages under the name Johnson and the baptism of two Thomas Johnsons. At some time he moved from Selby into Lincolnshire. Well educated, he later went to London, became an apothecary and before 1629 was running a business on Snow Hill where he had a physic garden. A Dr. John Argent gave Johnson some unusual specimens for his shop. The keen plantsman always wrote down detailed accounts of his samples and described the doctor's gift in these words; *"...they all hang their heads downwards, have rough and uneven ends and are five cornered...".* Thomas Johnson was in possession of the first bunch of bananas ever to be exhibited in a London shop.

After many years of apprenticeship Johnson was admitted to the Society of Apothecaries as a free brother. As custom required in those days he was presented with a spoon. Investigations of British plants made him famous as a leader in this field, his travels in search of specimen plants taking him as far north as Durham. It is known that Johnson visited York, Pontefract, Guisborough, Pocklington and Roseberry Topping on his tours. He recorded how he found many examples of the plant; *"Giant Bellflower (Campanula latifolia),* on the banks of the Ouse as he travelled from York to visit his home town of Selby. Johnson also noted *"Wilde Basills (Calamintha acinos) - a little this side of Pomfret".* In 1629 the apothecary had a short account of one of his botanical excursions published. It was the first local catalogue of plants published in England. Before 1641 Thomas Johnson produced many more books recording the plants he had found on his tours of England and Wales. His most important work came in 1633 when he amended and enlarged upon the herbal, *"The History of Plants,"* written by John Gerarde. Johnson added over eight hundred new specimens found during the 36 years since the book's first publication. In the 1970s when the scriptorium of Selby Abbey Church was being cleaned several precious books were found. They included a Geneva Bible, sometimes known as the Breeches Bible, and John Gerarde's 1597 herbal, *"The History of Plants";* both books are often on display in the Abbey Church.

When the Civil Wars broke out Johnson joined the Royalist cause in London before moving to Oxford. There, partly due to his loyalty and partly because his published works illustrated his learning and industry, Thomas Johnson was made a bachelor of physics then a 'Doctor of Physick". Johnson also gained recognition for translating out of Latin the work of Ambrose Parey, chirurgeon, which was, for a long time, used as a working guide by English surgeons. It was re-issued in 1649, 1665 and 1678.

Parliamentary papers stated that Johnson had lost his great esteem in London when he openly professed himself an enemy of their cause. Ignoring this, in 1643 Johnson went with Colonel Rawdon to Basing House in Hampshire. He took an active and heroic part in its defence rising to the rank of lieutenant-colonel to Sir Marmaduke Rawdon, governor. The following year the Parliamentarins resolved to take the castle by starving out its occupants. Again Johnson performed many deeds of valour in Royalists' attempts to break the siege. However, during one fierce skirmish, involving a detachment of troops led by Colonel Richard Norton, Johnson received a shot in the shoulder *"whereby contracting a feaver he died a fortnight after".*

This soldier respected for his valour and conduct on the field of battle was the best herbalist of his age in England. His botanical works were collected and edited by T.S.Ralph in 1847. The name Johnsonia now belongs to a genus of Lilaceae. Johnson Lupulia and Johnson Pubescens are grassy type plants from Western Australia.

In Selby, Johnson Street off Flaxley Road, commemorates the genial, modest and brave man who was born in the town but lost his life far from it in the Civil Wars.

The Siege of York

Parliament in London made the 23rd. April a day of Public Thanksgiving to mark their significant victory at Selby. A service was held at St. Margarets, Westminster, for the members of the House of Commons.

The outcome of the battle of Selby had alarmed the Royalists in York where only two garrison regiments were left. Urgent messages were sent to the Earl of Newcastle to hasten back there. He marched to York with a Scottish army not far behind him. When the Royalists reached the city on the 16th. April, the Scots were at Thormanby. Next day the Scots had branched off to Boroughbridge on their way to link up with the Parliamentarian forces around Selby. They met with cavalry at Wetherby and Tadcaster. On the 22nd. April the troops remaining at Selby began to move along the east bank of the Ouse, probably crossing the river using a bridge of boats at Cawood. By the following day the two forces had advanced on York and taken up siege positions.

The Earl of Newcastle wrote from York to the king concerning the merging of the two armies. He warned, "unless there is some speedy course taken to give us relief, and that with a considerable force for their army is very strong.....We shall be distressed here very shortly". The Parliamentarians also had concerns. They doubted whether they were well enough equipped to maintain the siege of the city and then news reached them of the possibility of at least four Royalist armies advancing from the west or east. At one point the Earl of Leven and Sir Thomas Fairfax took their cavalry back to Selby then to Ferrybridge to cut off some Royalist horse they had been informed were heading there from the direction of Knaresborough. The Royalists were successfully intercepted and prisoners taken. It was learnt from them that because of an insufficiency of forage in York, Newcastle had risked sending some of his cavalry to join the king's forces in the Midlands.

During May, whilst the siege continued, the Parliamentary cavalry made many forays against isolated enemy strongholds. Near the end of the month Lord Manchester came to the city ahead of his army which he had left marching towards Thorne. He stayed overnight then rode to Selby where his men had joined the troops already there. Manchester remained in the town for three days during which time he went into the neighbouring villages to check on the state of his soldiers billeted there. It is known that places as far away as the Haddleseys had troops quartered in them. At a meeting of the commanders at Escrick, it was decided all the troops from Selby and other billets should move to York. On the first of June, the day the armies advanced, an intelligence was received from Selby which ended with wishes for the success of the venture. Messages were constantly sent between York and Selby. Christopher Foster, who was the Constable for the Holy Trinity, Goodramgate parish, in April 1644, recorded in his accounts that he had spent two shillings and twopence for a horse *"that went post to Selby"*.

The most damaging practice carried out by both sides during the siege and at other times, was the billeting of troops on private citizens. Commanders were often promised money from their headquarters that was either late or never arrived. The householders on whom the soldiers were billeted were, therefore, given promissory notes. It is uncertain whether the unfortunate holders of such tickets ever had the notes honoured. Lord Manchester, who had not wanted to delay his army at Lincoln where he had been awaiting funds, had pressed on nearer to York. Regardless of the fact that he was without money he had quartered his men in Selby and the neighbouring villages.

Food was hard to find for by the time of the battle at Selby the countryside around the town was much wasted. Armies had found they could not stay in one place long without facing starvation. In the worst weather, horses died and men weary of struggling, especially in the winter months of frost and snow, would not suffer it any longer and ran away. Troops of both sides suffered tempestuous rainy weather well into June during the months of the York siege. Lists of supplies sent periodically from London for the Scottish armies illustrate what was eaten and used. Peas, oats, oatmeal, biscuits, butter and cheese were recorded; boots, shoes, and twenty thousand pounds, were included in one shipment. The people living in the neighbourhood of York complained that during the siege the soldiers, especially the Scots, wasted their corn, took beans, oats, barley intended as seed, ate their animals, stole their sheets and bedding and even took hostages for money.

By the beginning of June the Earl of Manchester was at York with more than six thousand men whilst Royalist troops were advancing towards Yorkshire gathering recruits on the way. The end of June found the people in the city desperately short of provisions whilst the besiegers were in danger of being trapped between the defenders and the advancing Royalists who were then at Knaresborough.

On the first of July the Parliamentarians marched out to Long Marston to defend the road leading from Knaresborough to York. The Royalists tricked this force by leaving a cavalry screen on Marston Moor whilst the rest of their troops went via Boroughbridge, approaching the city from the north and not the west. York was relieved. Most of the Parliamentary armies fell back towards Tadcaster thinking the enemy would march for Newark in Nottinghamshire. Cromwell, however, remaining with his cavalry on Marston Moor was made aware of the Royalist horse increasing in number and speedily summoned back the rest of the Parliamentary forces. On the second of July the biggest battle of the Civil Wars took place on Marston Moor. The Parliamentarians won a resounding victory. The York garrison surrendered on the 16th. July. Apart from small pockets of resistance the whole of the north was in their hands.

To prevent the seizing and holding of castles in the north the House of Commons resolved:

> "That the several castles of Thickhill, Sheffield Knaresborough, Cawood, Wressle, Sandall, Bolton, Middleham, Hornsey, Mulgrave and Craike, in the County of York, being inland castles, be made untenable and no garrisons to be kept or maintained in them."

Most of Cawood Castle was demolished including the roof and crenellated parapet of the Gatehouse. Much of the stone was used in other buildings; in the eighteenth century large amounts of it were shipped to York to become part of the Archbishop's palace. Wressle Castle was made untenable in 1650, but the whole south front survived with its square towers and circular turrets. For a long time an iron pan of a beacon, with its framework, was preserved on top of one of these. Royal Assent had to be given for the erection of these warning stations. Stacks of wood were used before the reign of Edward III but were soon replaced by pitchboxes. The beacon at Wressle had been used to signal such events as the arrival of the Spanish Armada.

The end of the first Civil War came in September 1646 with the total defeat of the Royalists. Charles surrendered to the Scots but was handed over to the English Parliament when he refused to sign the Scottish Covenant. In August 1647 he escaped to the Isle of Wight. Early the following year the second of the Civil Wars began when there were uprisings in support of the return of the king. Many people had wearied of the harsh laws set by Parliament. The rebellions were soon quashed but it was realised that the king had to be permanently removed. On the 3rd. January 1649, King Charles I was executed.

His son was rightfully proclaimed King of Scotland. He gained the people's support there by eventually accepting the Covenant. Parliament was once again at war with the Scots. Cromwell with other leaders, including John Lambert and George Monck (later 1st. Duke of Albemarle) determined to remove the monarchy once and for all. The last battle of the Civil Wars took place in 1651 around Powick Bridge, near Worcester, the scene of the first encounter between the opposing forces. After fierce fighting the Parliamentarians were again victorious. Charles II made his escape and fled to France. Cromwell, a great military leader and a fervent Puritan became lord protector; a position giving him great powers in association with Parliament and the Council of State.

The Aftermath

The successes of the Parliamentary forces at Selby, where the enemy's cavalry were overwhelmed and the foot regiments were utterly broken beyond repair, weakened the King's forces, and were instrumental in bringing about the siege of York and the eventual defeat of the Royalists at Marston Moor. After the battle the town continued to be occupied by Parliamentary troops, sometimes made up of Scots. It is not clear when the town was eventually freed from billeting troops but it is known that repercussions from the fighting were felt by the townspeople for many years. A huge number of non-participants became impoverished through the constant demands of the troops for food and shelter. Many who took part also had to help finance the actions against their enemies. Those with property gave money to help feed and arm their troops when aid did not arrive in time. When the fighting began in the north, Captain Robert Howe, a Royalist supporter from Sherburn, was commissioned to raise a company of volunteers for the Regiment of Foot under Colonel Sir William Pennyman. It was said of him that *"he did his best to complete it"*. In August 1660 when the fighting was at an end, he applied for the post of Thames Water Bailiff, where it emerged that as a lieutenant and then a captain, Howe had often been imprisoned and *"later impoverished himself by buying arms and necessaries by royal order"*.

The Parliamentarians demanded aid from Royalist sympathisers. In 1644 they were in dire need of funds to pay the Scottish troops so conceived a scheme for extracting money from known supporters of the Royalist cause. By 1645 a committee had been formed with the authority to summon anyone they believed had aided the enemy and to sequester their property. The person chosen had to send a petition to the committee with particulars of his estate and a certificate showing he had taken the National Covenant before an approved minister. Any concealment of property resulted in the offender paying four times the yearly amount decided upon and the forfeit of his estate. The committee, having read the petition, prepared a report of the offences, a valuation of the culprit's property and a proposed fine. The recipient was ordered to pay part of the fine immediately but was given time to find the rest.

A report on William Myers, a Selby draper, accused him of living in the enemy's quarters and supporting their cause against Parliament. In August 1644 Myers repented of his actions before a full congregation of his neighbours in the parish church.

He was the first person to stand up and swear his allegiance to Parliament in Selby Abbey Church. The draper's property included lands in Selby, Cawood and Kelfield; he also paid rent on other holdings. Creditors owed him just over fifty-eight pounds and his debts totalled two hundred and seventy pounds. In his defence Myers prayed the committee would consider that, during the siege of York, he furnished Lord Fairfax with four beasts worth £22 and that during the battle for Selby he lost to the soldiers cloth, goods and personal estate worth five hundred pounds. At the bottom of the report on the draper were the words, "6 *Feb. 1646 No Fine*". John and Richard Wilkinson, husbandmen of Cawood were both charged with assisting the enemies of the Parliamentary forces. They had lands seized and fines to pay.

Voluntarily coming forward to confess one's sins lessened the punishment. Nicholas Raynard, yeoman of Wistow, had been a petty constable during the wars and was forced to execute warrants sent to him by the commanders in the king's army. He approached the committee to settle by mutual consent; his estates were temporarily taken from him.

Robert Marshall, a gentleman living in Selby when the troubles began, was charged with deserting the town and moving to York whilst it was garrisoned by Royalists. Robert argued that he never took up arms against the Parliamentarians but, being an old man, had *"for his quiet"* gone to York. The report on him listed his possessions as including lands and tenements in Wakefield, Skipwith, Selby, Wistow and Brayton. The yearly value of this property before the fighting began was recorded as £78.12s.0d., out of which he paid twenty pounds in taxes, fee farm rents and quit rents. The last paid to the lords of the manors of Skipwith and Selby excused a tenant from carrying out the usual manor services; a custom not abolished until 1922. It was noted that a house in Wakefield belonging to Robert Marshal had been destroyed. Amongst his payments it was shown that he annually gave the lord of Skipwith one quarter of rye valued at £1.6s.8d. whilst Charles Walmsley, lord of the manor of Selby received 2s.3d. for two houses in the town and one cock, one hen and fourpence, equal to 1s.8d. in money, as tax on a house in Brayton. The report confirmed that Robert had taken the Covenant before the minister of his parish and at the bottom were the words, *"18 June 1646. Fine £116"*.

Charles Walmsley, the lord of the manor of Selby lived at Staynor Hall during the Civil Wars. A Royalist and a Roman Catholic, he did not escape the attention of the committee for some of his estates were sequestered by Cromwell's ministers.

Confiscated lands were offered as a reward to those who had actively supported Parliament on condition that they advanced half the value of the property to the committee in ready money. Three recipients of such lands who handed money over to the hard pressed committee were Tempest Milner, who in 1647 was given Wistow for £1873, and Richard Warner and Henry Carnish who, a year later, for the sum of £5,080 gained most of the manor of Cawood.

Religious Persecution

Many loyal Church of England clergy suffered indignities, pain and poverty at the hands of the Parliamentary forces. They were not only driven from their homes but many of the larger, ancient residences were turned into dungeons to supplement the jails already overflowing with ministers and gentry. Cawood Castle became one such prison. During one of the battles for Leeds a vicar named Henry Robinson was captured as he fled from the Parliamentary armies. His sympathies were not entirely with the king but after a series of misfortunes he was imprisoned in Cawood Castle, under the authority of Captain Hotham. His troubles did not end there for during his confinement the upper part of a tower fell upon him. Miraculously the minister only sustained a broken arm. His wife, imprisoned with him, told their captors of the calamities that had befallen her husband and they were released. Henry Robinson later became the rector of Swillington where he died in 1663.

The rector of Wressle church was cruelly treated in the castle. He had the added indignity of being forced to watch whilst his church was burnt down to prevent its use as a shelter by any raiding parties. Robert Thornton, the rector of the impressive Norman church in Birkin was relentlessly persecuted by the Puritans for his unyielding loyalty to his faith. He was expelled from his living and deprived of all his possessions on more than one occasion. Finally, frustrated and angry that they could not shake this brave man's beliefs, his tormentors tied him to the tail of a horse and had him pulled all the way from Birkin to Cawood Castle prison. Happily Robert Thornton survived this ordeal to enjoy a much pleasanter future. He was restored to his church when Charles II regained the throne and was succeeded as Rector of Birkin by his son and grandson. An inscription in the church commemorates this stalwart man.

Many ministers were driven out of their livings, especially after Hull was garrisoned by Sir John Hotham and his Parliamentary forces. Some sent petitions to the Earl of Newcastle beseeching the Royalist commander to write to the Chancellor begging him to recompense them for their losses by putting them in the possession of livings deserted by Puritan incumbents. One of these petitioners came from Selby. He was William Langley who declared that he had been expelled from his living *"By the rage and fury of the rebels"*, due to his loyal support of the king. He beseeched the earl to ask his Majesty's favour in procuring for him the living at Croston, in the county of Lancaster. The vicar there, he declared, *"is now in actual rebellion against his majesty, being at this present with the rebels preaching seditious doctrine and animating the rebels in this unnatural war"*. It is not known if William Langley ever received that living but it is recorded that the vicar at Croston, one James Hyatt, was not ejected until 1662.

Selby gained some benefits, for the curate at Selby, the vicar at Brayton and the preacher at Barlow all had their stipends increased by fifty pounds. A happy condition for them that only lasted until the restoration of the king. Parliament altered many religious practices during the years they were in power. Church weddings were replaced by civil contracts witnessed by a magistrate; the unions were then recorded in registers by appointed officials. John Oddingsells of Rest Park, magistrate for Wistow, recorded that George Briggs and Mary Bateman of Wistow were the first couple to be *"married before me ye 18th April. 1653, in witness whereof I have set my hand ye day and yeare before written"*. For around six years the civil marriages at Selby took place near the market cross.

Despite all the changes in religious practices in the seventeenth century people were still expected to honour the Sabbath Day and attend the local church. Visitations from church officials continued and complaints taken before the Peculiar Courts. The state of the buildings, the behaviour of the communicants and the officials were all noted. During an Ainsty Deanery visitation that took place in 1637 the communicants at Drax lodged a complaint against their churchwarden, Robert Wilkinson. They grumbled that when the consecrated bread had been used he pulled a loaf out of his pocket, cut it and administered it to the great offence of the people. Also there was never enough wine; many went away from communion without its benefit. John Sawle, clerk at Hatfield, solved the lack of wine by replacing it with beer; he was suspended! Absentees from church were called to account. At Cawood, John Hall, baker, was charged with sitting in the street during sermon time. His defence was that he had been left looking after the baby. In Selby three men were accused of being drunk on the Sabbath, one of whom had gone into church to sleep off the effects during prayer-time. James Natherer was in trouble for entertaining card players at tables in his house when they should have all been attending Sunday morning prayer-time. Thomas Tweed of Whitgift was summoned for buying a rake in prayer time. Complaints were lodged against eight butchers for killing and dressing meat in Selby on the Sabbath. Reluctant church-goers disrupted the services. Francis Stevenson of Whitgift was accused of walking and talking during prayer time whilst John Pinder of Swinefleet had profaned the church on Easter Day by leaping over the stalls. Also at Whitgift, Christopher Wressle of Reedness was summoned for striking one Holdenby in church during divine service. Other misdemeanours were also brought before the courts. George Lambert of Snaith was in trouble for pulling up church boards which he had vowed he would have, despite the Churchwardens. Comments on the state of the buildings included the fact that Airmyn chapel was strawthatched and its seats were not uniform, Snaith choir was out of repair whilst Hooke chapel needed its roof, windows and stalls refurbishing. In 1640 an enterprising Selebian faced being disciplined for taking down the church fence, uprooting graves and converting part of the church-yard to his own use. What punishments were suffered by these offenders is not known but Robert Fawcett of Wistow accused of *"attempting the chastity of Catherine Ratcliffe and Anne Br...pall"*, was excommunicated - a severe punishment for anyone at that time. It was recorded in 1640 that Thomas Easingwold repeatedly attended prayers at Barlby chapel and would not leave even though he had been excommunicated.

The curate of the Abbey Church suffered disturbances at his services before the Civil Wars spread to Selby. They were not caused by religious differences but over who had the right to appoint a minister at the church. When it was made Selby's parish church, James I had also granted the Archbishop of York thirty pounds per annum for holding services there and given him the right to choose the ministers to officiate at them. Many people in the town believed it was the right of the lord of the manor to appoint the curates and in 1642 made their feelings known by disrupting services officiated over by persons chosen by the archbishop. At the Pontefract Sessions Thomas Ayre a gentleman, William Parker a barber, and Thomas Grunnell a skinner, all of Selby, were charged with *"unlawfully and riotously assembling on Sunday 13th March, in the church there and disturbing John Johnson, clerk and preacher of God's Word"*. Thomas Godsey tanner in the town, was charged that two weeks later, in the parish church he *"openly and publicly said the scandalous words 'I care not for the king nor his lawes'"*. All these offenders were recorded as being 'at large'. Paul Hammerton clerk, and Henry Watson cooper, both of Selby, did not escape their punishment. They put themselves on the grace of the court at Wakefield in July and were each fined twenty pence. Their crime was that in April they too had disturbed John Johnson whilst he was taking divine service.

The matter did not stop there for early in April a petition, from around two hundred inhabitants of Selby, was sent to Charles the First. They explained to the king how Selby was a great parish where Mr. James Waide, appointed by the lord of the manor, Charles Walmsley, had been in quiet and peaceful possession of the church until Easter Day. This was when Mr. Johnson *"under pretence of having the right to serve the cure there, and whom some people, being facetious, do comply, entered the church"*. He was accompanied by Sir Henry Cholmley, justice of the peace, who, although not of the parish, commanded Mr. Waide to permit Mr. Johnson to read the prayers and officiate at the service. The petitioners reported that Mr. Waide was threatened and told he would be bound over to keep the peace if he refused. It was said, he ignored Sir Henry and carried on with the service, at which, a constable who had been sent for, treated the curate as if he was a malefactor. He was ordered to provide sureties and to appear before Sir Henry at the next sessions at Pontefract. This caused such an uproar amongst the parishioners that it was decided to appeal to the king to bring calm back to the town. All could be settled, the petitioners agreed, by his Majesty commanding Sir Henry Cholmley and John Johnson to forbear from further molesting Mr. Waide, and leaving him to carry out his duties until such time as he was succeeded by a new curate. They also asked for him to be freed of the recognizances by which he was bound, for doing no other than his duty.

The king replied that he was offended by any disturbances at divine services and wished to have his subjects left in peace to enjoy that which by law was their right. The king commanded that the petitioners' requests be granted but he also demanded that he be sent a true account of the affair as seen by the justices.

Their verdict was that all the charges against Sir Henry Cholmley were without cause. A letter accompanying the verdict described how false information had been sent by the petitioners and that Sir Henry had done nothing beyond his duty. More details were given concerning this involved affair. It appeared that earlier, Thomas, father of Charles Walmsley, had through misinformation from certain parishioners, appointed Paul Hammerton as curate of Selby Abbey Church. This was quickly revoked when it was discovered that Hammerton was not fully qualified to act as a minister. As related, he was later fined for disrupting a service in the church. The Archbishop of York then legally appointed Mr. Johnson to the post and the new curate made a point of having his position acknowledged by the lord of the manor before beginning to officiate at the church. This was when the services began to be interrupted by parishioners who did not agree with the method of appointment. It was further disclosed that the offenders also misled Charles Walmsley when he became lord of the manor. They had persuaded him to appoint Mr. James Waide as curate in opposition to Mr. Johnson.

The controversy was resolved when Mr.Waide willingly resigned and all charges against him, Mr. Johnson and Sir Henry Cholmley were dismissed. The principle movers in the plot to go against a Royal edict were bound over to keep the peace. Mr. Johnson was left to officiate until he was legally replaced.

CHAPTER 7

THE RESTORATION AND A DIVERSITY OF RELIGIONS

After the Parliamentarians were victorious, a government with a repressive religious policy was put in power. Pleasurable activities such as dancing and acting were looked upon as sinful. When Oliver Cromwell took on the office of lord protector he ruled increasingly by decree. His attempts to govern England well proved difficult following the events of the Civil Wars. It had been a terrifying time to live through for both sides had believed they were right.

On the death of his father in 1658 Richard Cromwell, an amiable and hard-working man, found himself in the role of lord protector. His tenure in office was soon disrupted by financial chaos and fierce disputes between the government and the army. He was forced to dissolve Parliament in April 1659 and was out of office the following month. Amidst the mounting confusion of that year, George Monck, First Duke of Albemarle, opened negotiations with Charles II and was instrumental in bringing about the king's restoration to the throne.

Charles returned to England in May 1660. In contrast to Cromwell he enjoyed all kinds of sport and entertainments, especially the theatre. During his reign women were first seen on the stage and his court became notorious for its loose morals encouraged by a king who entertained many mistresses.

When proclaimed king Charles made conciliatory promises to his government regarding religious liberty but such freedom did not last long for many dissenters. The Church of England was restored with all its bishops and other clerics. Statutes were passed handing back to the Crown and Church land that had been confiscated by the Commonwealth.

Royalists were given the right to retrieve their land through petitions or the process of law, but those compelled to sell land because of crippling fines received no compensation. Charles Walmsley, lord of the manor of Selby, was one of the fortunate owners who recovered his property after 1660. A Mr. Danby, who had owned Cave Castle, near Market Weighton, appears to have been one of the unfortunate ones who received no compensation. He had supported Charles I in the Civil Wars and for this was heavily penalised by Parliament. To pay the fine Mr. Danby was forced to sell his estates. Much of the land he sold came into the possession of Mr. Henry Washington of Selby. There were others who lost their land and did not regain it all because Cromwellian officers and Puritan merchants would not part with property bought so cheaply before 1660.

Dissenters continued to suffer intolerance and persecution during the Stuart period. James, the other surviving son of Charles I succeeded his brother to the throne. Before his succession there had been widespread alarm at James's religious convictions which increased in 1660 when, as Duke of York, he converted to the Roman Catholic faith. Parliament tried many times to exclude him from the line of succession but by the time he was crowned king in 1685 opposition had subsided. However, two years into his reign James II angered Parliament by putting forward pro Catholic policies. When the birth of a Catholic heir threatened the future of Protestantism, prominent personalities invited William of Orange to lead an army into England. So unpopular was James that the majority of the people deserted him and he was forced to flee to France. He died in exile in 1690 after launching an unsuccessful campaign from Ireland to regain the throne.

The crown was offered to William of Orange and his wife, Mary; they were cousins and were both descended from Charles I. Both were of the Protestant faith which was a great relief to many of their subjects. They ruled together until Mary's death in 1694, her husband then reigned as William III. A Declaration of Rights aimed mainly against the actions of James II, gave, amongst other things, free elections and free speech within Parliament and increased its meetings.

When William died, Mary's younger sister Anne became queen, the last Stuart sovereign. During her reign, after much debate, an Act of Union brought England and Scotland together under one British government. Anne had received a Protestant upbringing which led her, in 1704, to set up the *"Queen Anne's Bounty"* a fund for the relief of the poorest Anglican clergy. A large amount of money for this charity came from taxation of the churches; a custom which the Pope had begun in the twelfth century to help the Crusades to Jerusalem. Before becoming queen, Anne had agreed to the Act of Settlement which secured the succession of a Protestant to the throne. On her death in 1714 the stronger hereditary rights of the Catholic Stuarts were ignored and the crown given to the nearest Protestant claimant, George, Elector of Hanover (1688-1727), the great-grandson of James I of England. Despite being a Protestant the first Hanoverian monarch to rule Britain did not gain the support of his subjects.

Quakers and the Established Church

Selby witnessed the growth and struggles of several religious groups after the Restoration. The people were expected to attend the Abbey Church and be communicants there. Laws were passed to reinforce the position of the established church and to restrict the activities of dissenters. A set of these Acts passed between 1661 and 1665 became known as the Clarendon Codes. Further laws called the Test Acts, intended to exclude Catholics from office included the ruling that all who refused to renounce the Covenant, to take sacrament in a Church of England place of worship, or swear allegiance to the crown, were not to be allowed to hold any civil or military position.

In Miss Richardson's work on local history she notes that in 1745/46, John Baynton Adams of Camblesforth who wished to take the oaths to become a justice of the peace, availed himself of the necessary documents. Adams produced a certificate which showed he had previously been witnessed receiving the sacrament at Drax parish church and also evidence that the property qualifications were covered by lands he held in that parish.

Selby Abbey Church and the churches in the district where the national religion was practised were still subject to visitations and summons to the Peculiar Courts. Church services continued to be disturbed for a variety of reasons. In 1674 George Bucklesin of Snaith was brought before the Peculiar Court for disturbing a man and refusing to let him sit in his usual seat in time of divine service. A nonconformist group known as the Quakers and later as the Religious Society of Friends, used other methods to disrupt services in parish churches.

The group was founded in the 1650s by George Fox. It is said the members were given their nick-name after Fox told a judge to tremble at the name of the Lord. The Quakers' precepts that provoked most trouble for them were as follows: a refusal to pay tithes for it was not in the Gospels, a refusal to pay rates towards building or maintaining places of worship other than their own; an unswerving determination not to take any kind of oath even though this led to imprisonment, banishment or sometimes death. Many laws were directed against the Quakers. It was made an offence for more than five nonconformists to meet for worship except in an authorised place. The Five Mile Act passed in 1665 banned their preachers from living in, or even visiting any place where they had formerly held worship. These measures were mainly activated through fear that the dissenters' meeting places were the most likely venues where plotting against the king might take place. This was contrary to the beliefs of the Quakers for they testified openly and publicly against war and violence. They refused to bear arms or hire substitutes to take their place. In 1664 Sebastian Ellithorp of Holme-upon-Spalding-Moor had goods taken from him to the value of five pounds for refusing to contribute towards the cost of the militia.

The Quakers also spoke out in streets, market places and in churches of national worship against the preachings of the ministers and what they saw as vice and immorality. These activities brought retribution upon the heads of many Quakers including some in the Selby area. As early as 1652 William Sykes, a merchant in Knottingley, who was not then fully committed to being a Quaker but who was convinced of the unlawfulness of paying tithes, was severely punished for speaking out about the issue. He so incensed the priests that they compelled the magistrates to prosecute him. Sykes was committed to York Castle prison on the 14th. August 1652 by warrant of four justices of the peace. In September he was indicted for not paying any tithes, for publicly proclaiming it, and for speaking out against maintaining the ministers by such methods. He was found guilty and fined the excessive amount of £66.13s.4d. for which non-payment he was returned to prison. William Sykes lay in the dreadful surroundings of the Castle prison in York until his death in October of that year.

John Leake of Selby was one of many who in 1665 were committed to prison for not paying their tithes. The expenses incurred in taking the offenders to prison were recovered by the seizing of goods valued well above the actual debt, from their Quaker prisoners. This was also the case when collecting to cover the cost of unpaid tithes. Corn, hay, lambs, cows and horses were taken in amounts and numbers greatly exceeding what was required. Such maltreatment was repeated at a later date, when its victims again included John Leake of Selby, in company with Joseph Arnold, John Walker senior and John Walker junior from Brayton, William Cuttorth, Timothy Jessup and Thomas Whitside of Rawcliffe, Mary Hemingway and Richard Ward of Hillam. William and Richard Walker of Heck and Azariah Williams of Fishlake were also listed.

Samuel Poole of Knottingley was fined twenty pounds a month and then put into Pontefract prison for not attending national worship. In 1683 the Archbishop of York was informed, "There is none that absents from the Church at Selby but Quakers that are already presented and are prisoners at York and are under bayle when they come to Selby". Three of these dissenters fined a total of £5.l0s.0d. for not attending their parish churches were Germaine Canby of Selby, Joseph Walker of Brayton and Robert Scott of Staynor.

Many of those who did attend divine service could not refrain from speaking out loudly against what was being preached there. Thomas Goodair was one of the earliest Quakers in Selby to have been prosecuted for staying firm to his beliefs and speaking out about them in church and elsewhere. He spent a great part of his life in prison. From 1661 to 1672 he was confined in Warwick gaol for refusing to take any oaths. He died in Selby in 1693, a true and loyal member of the Society of Friends. Mary Fisher, a maidservant in Selby, became an early convert to the Quakers' beliefs. Like Goodair she fiercely advocated civil and religious freedom and constantly argued with ministers and judges. She was often imprisoned for speaking out loudly and aggressively against the preachers in the churches. In 1652, the same year William Sykes lay dying in York Castle, Fisher was sentenced to fifteen months imprisonment there for shouting out against Richard Calvert, the minister of Selby Abbey church, during divine service. Her harangues against him included, *"Come downe thou painted beast, thou art but a hireling and deludest the people with thy lies".* In a later incident, overwhelmed by frustration and anger, Mary Fisher threw a stool at the minister. For this she was flogged. After suffering six more months in prison for *"declaring the truth in the steeple house at Pontefract",* the undaunted maidservant lost her freedom again for repeating the offence in the same town.

When not in prison she travelled round the country vehemently putting forward her beliefs. During these travels she stopped at Cambridge to preach to a group of students but her fierce, belligerent manner offended many of them and officials were called to apprehend her. Mary was dragged to the market cross where she was publicly whipped. The unrepentant Quaker would have been hooted at and pelted with unsavoury missiles on the way before being stripped to the waist and flogged.

Though the Quaker maidservant from Selby must have been reviled and mistreated in many places she was not deterred from her mission. Mary Fisher eventually left Selby to travel abroad and during her journeys visited Istanbul, then known as Constantinople. There she tried, but failed, to convert the Grand Turk, Mohammed IV.

The Quakers were possibly the earliest non-conformists in Selby. Following the passing of the Toleration Act in 1691, which gave many dissenters more freedom, a meeting house was registered in the town by six trustees, including a Zachariah Canby. In 1785, a new meeting house was built which was enlarged upon forty years later. Traces of the building can still be seen today at the back of No.23, Gowthorpe. A narrow passageway between the shops on the main street leads to a small piece of land backing onto what was once the meeting house. This was the Quakers' burial place. In 1785 it was recorded in their building expenses that the cost of erecting a wall around the 'burying ground' was six pounds. The land was later left to the people of Selby to be kept as a garden forever. In 1973 five gravestones from the Quakers' Summercroft burial ground at Drax Abbey farm were placed in the little garden. The inscriptions on them are now hard to define but the clearest one reads, *"Hic Jacet Johannes Hodgson, Medicinae Doctor, qui Mortuus est 12 die Februarii Anno Domini 1681".*

When the Rev. Geoffrey Rishton (1700-1721) made entries in the Abbey Church registers he recorded the births and deaths of some dissenters. The babies were not brought to be baptised at the church but to obtain the advantages of a legal registration:

14 December 1700 Stephen, son of Robert Adams, house carpenter, quaker, was *buried at quaker burial place.*
1702 Marmaduke, son of Marmaduke Storr, tanner and quaker, was born 3rd. april.

Sir Jonathan Hutchinson

The names of many Quakers appeared as householders in parish lists and as defaulters reported to the Ecclesiastical Courts for the non-payment of church rates. As late as 1862 it was recorded in the local paper that John Webster, churchwarden for the parish of Brayton, had applied for warrants of distress against two Quakers, Jonathan Hutchinson, merchant of Selby, occupying land in Brayton, and William Hutchinson of Thorpe Willoughy. This was for nonpayment of church rates at Brayton and for disobeying an order made by magistrates at the Petty sessions. The warrants were issued after the non-appearance of the men and gave the officials the right to seize goods to the value of the money owed to them. Jonathan Hutchinson was the partner of Thomas Proctor, a flax merchant and member of a wealthy and industrious Quaker family. Jonathan Hutchinson had been drawn to Selby because of the growth of its industry. He became a middleman between the farmers and the Leeds manufacturers who purchased flax for making linen. His large family of twelve lived in an old red house in Ratten Row on the banks of the Ouse. The old medieval buildings nearby were adapted as warehouses for storing such goods as flax, linseed and cheese.

The second son of this family was born on the 23rd July, 1828. Named after his father he grew up to be an eminent surgeon and pathologist in London. The family employed governesses to educate their children before they attended a school kept by a Mr. Beilby. He remembered Jonathan as a domineering boy both at home and school. Jonathan Hutchinson expressed a desire to become a doctor and in 1845 he was apprenticed for five years to Caleb Williams of York, apothecary and surgeon, whilst he attended the York School of Medicine and York County Hospital. In 1850 Hutchinson went to London to further his education. At each hospital where he worked he added new material to the knowledge of clinical medicine and dental defects in children; he also made important contributions to other studies including that of leprosy. Hutchinson went on to hold every office in the College of Surgeons whilst still continuing his studies and taking time to teach. It was said, he was the best clinical teacher of his time, excellent with undergraduates.

In July, 1856, Hutchinson married Jane Pynsent West, daughter of William West, chemist, who founded Reynolds and Bramson Ltd. of Leeds. They had ten children who their father never stopped educating, even at mealtimes. Even so he still found time to cultivate his consuming interest in educational museums which set forth contemporary geological, biological and historical knowledge by specimens and illustrations. Hutchinson came back to his home town to open a museum and also to give short lectures, for he believed that *"a museum without a lecturer to explain it was like having a church without a minister."* In 1898 he purchased the building in Park Street now occupied by the Salvation Army. Public Rooms had first been built there in 1839. When it became a Mechanics' Institute in 1861 it was furnished with a reading room and a well-stocked library. Members of Selby's Young Mens' Institute and the Scientific Society used the rooms for lectures. Charles Dickens is believed to have given one of his 'Penny Readings' there. Jonathan Hutchinson also gave a lecture on the premises in

1865. When he later purchased the building he gave the contents of the library to the town and refurbished the lecture rooms. He also roofed over the adjoining disused swimming pool and floored it over to make it into a museum.

Hutchinson was breaking fresh ground in Selby for by that time the inhabitants only knew him by repute. He encountered some violent opposition to the subject matter of his lectures which covered such topics as the thickness of the earth's crust, probable age of the world and lessons to be learnt from whales. His forward looking talks were not well received by the local churches; sermons were preached against their contents in both the Abbey church and the Wesleyan chapels. The *Selby Times* newspaper carried a leader after the third lecture which read, *"When the very foundations of our faith are called into question, a very grave responsibility faces us. We have therefore abstained from noticing the lectures at length"*. Hutchinson had a faithful group of followers and sometimes his lectures were well received. Despite this, in 1904 he again received a very bad press. Letters poured into the newspapers and the *Selby Times* ran another article condemning his ideas.

In 1906 Hutchinson lectured on *"Museums and what they teach"* to try to raise more interest for the one in Selby. His museum may have been neglected by the majority of the townspeople but it became of great use to many of them in the October of that year when their beautiful Abbey church was almost gutted by fire. Sir Jonathan Hutchinson, as he was by then, telegrammed officials in the town to say that the Museum Hall was at their disposal during the catastrophe.

This eminent surgeon died in 1913. The flags of the church, the town hall and the museum were flown at half-mast. The *Selby Times* which had so often been opposed to his thoughts and ideals wrote one of the truest obituaries ever to be composed.

"He made Selby think and second thoughts were best."

In 1983 the Greater London Council put a plaque on a house in London where Sir Jonathan Hutchinson had lived from 1874 to 1907. Near Johnson Street in Selby, which commemorates the town's celebrated botanist, is Hutchinson Street, a reminder of another famous Selebian.

The Presbyterians

The first Presbyterians followed the established religion of the land. Some officiated at services in the national church. Thomas Birdsall was the incumbent at Selby Abbey church from 1658 until he was ejected for his non-conformity upon implementation of the Act of Uniformity. Passed in 1662 it required all clergy to be ordained according to the rites of the Church of England. Amongst other preachers similarly ejected were Mr. 'Anty' Fido at Hemingbrough, Mr. Bovel at Monk Fryston and Mr. Robert Sherburne at Cawood. Robert Sherburne went to join his father who, as the preaching minister at Brayton, had conformed. It was a rare occurrence when the ejected son was allowed to preach in his father's church.

Some non-conformist clergy made their way to Selby. The Reverend James Duncanson was ejected from the curacy of Sand Hutton but by 1672 he had a licence to preach in a large house in Selby he shared with Robert Moorewood. The Reverend Robert Stretton also had a licence which allowed him to preach in the house of James Richardson in Cawood.

Around 1660 many Presbyterians were meeting in Millgate. They were helped in their worship by Noah Ward of York, a non-conformist minister whose beliefs had caused him much suffering when at university. Ward preached every third Sunday in York and at other times visited various places in the district including Selby. Just before his death in 1699 he became one of the trustees of a Presbyterian chapel in the town. The site for this had been conveyed to the group by Alice Barstow of York when carrying out the wishes of her late husband. It is not clear when the first chapel was founded on Millgate but in the indenture made on the 11th. May, 1699, it was stated; *"all that messuage or tenement or Chappell commonly called Saint Michael Chappell in a place or street called Mill Gate ... late in the tenure of one Richard Robinson"*.

The Reverend John Travers was the first pastor at the chapel. He is recorded in the parish registers as having baptised one of his congregation in 1699, although it was another eight years before the chapel received its official licence. This was granted at the quarter sessions in Halifax following an Act of Parliament which exempted from the penalties of Sunday Law, those Protestant subjects dissenting from the Church of England.

The principal supporter of the Presbyterians in Selby was Mrs. Beatrix Bacon, a wealthy and caring widow who endowed the trustees with over four acres of land, made up of a field in Thorpe Willoughby and one between Selby Dam and Leeds Road. A further four acres were added at the time of the enclosure of the common in 1805. As late as 1867 the minister's salary was being paid out of the rents from these fields. By this period many of the Presbyterians had embraced the principles and title of the Unitarians.

Millgate Chapel began to be in need of repair and by the 1880s some services and Sunday school were held in the nearby Chamberlain Trust schoolroom. A few years later the room also housed a congregation from Ousegate. These Unitarians had been worshipping in an old iron chapel brought from Ossett when it was no longer needed there. *Slater's Directory* of 1887 records a Rev. Joseph M. Pilkington as minister of the Unitarian chapel on Ousegate. The congregation found the building uncomfortable and cold, especially in winter. When the land on which it stood began to subside towards the Ouse, the chapel was quickly sold for forty pounds and the worshippers moved to Millgate.

It had been advised as early as 1889 that the Millgate chapel, then in a dilapidated condition, should be sold and the congregation move elsewhere, but this was opposed. In 1903 the present chapel with seating for over a hundred people was opened on Millgate. Gradually over the years the number of worshippers declined. In 1925 the Sunday collections rarely went above five shillings. A shortage of preachers, lack of music and facilities for visitors eventually forced the chapel to close in 1965. Today the building has become a domestic residence in line with the old and new houses on Millgate.

Leonard Chamberlain

The schoolroom used by the Presbyterians in Millgate in the nineteenth century had been built using money from a trust bequeathed by Leonard Chamberlain in 1716. He was a woollen draper from Kingston-upon-Hull who left extensive estates for the support of many charities. A devout member of a dissenting chapel in Hull he left much of his money to be used to assist various non-conformist churches including Millgate chapel, Selby. The rent from fields that he owned around the town, including one near Millbridge was used to provide the town with a dissenting minister, a schoolmaster, a schoolroom for twenty of the poorest children of any denomination, and homes for six of the poorest widows receiving no parochial relief.

The schoolmaster, who was often also the minister, and the six widows lived in a building on land near Millbridge, bounded on its sides by Selby Dam, Millgate, Holme Lane and Holme Dyke; almost opposite to where the Selby Soke Mills once stood. They had use of a croft, a garden and an orchard. In 1716 the schoolmaster received four pounds a year which was given to the widows if the post was vacant. Over a hundred years later this had increased to twelve pounds with an additional pound for pupils' books and a share of two more pounds from the rent paid by a Mr. Wilson for his use of charity land. The widows' stipend remained at two shillings. It was, however, increased in times of excess profits but cut accordingly with the master's wages, if insufficient funds were available. In 1865 the widows benefiting from Chamberlain's Trust were recorded as Ann Clark, aged 70, Elizabeth Hunt - 65, Jane Brown -72, Mary Towning and Ann Fryer, both aged seventy-three. The almshouses were rebuilt in 1899 as a two storey block with three apartments on each floor. Each room contained a bed, pantry, recess, coals fireplace and living space. There was one water closet upstairs and one downstairs.

The number of children attending the school varied greatly. In the early 1800s it rarely exceeded ten because of the smallness of the population and the sufficiency of other centres of education. The state of the building also affected attendance. In 1850, Mr. Westwood informed the Trustees by letter that he had removed the children to a better environment because of the dreadful state of the schoolroom. He was threatened with dismissal and ordered to bring the pupils back to Millgate. The following year a separate school was built nearby. The cost of £110 was shared by Mr. Westwood who was then allowed to use the old room as part of his house. In the new premises twenty boys were taught reading for no fee but had to pay half towards the cost of instruction in writing, arithmetic and other subjects. There was also, during one period, six paying scholars, including a girl; they paid sixpence a week to be taught the three 'R's or threepence for reading alone. A list of schools drawn up by the School Attendance Committee showed that in 1885 there were 59 children attending at Millbridge. Despite this good number the school closed in 1895 when G.C. Pearson, who was both minister and schoolmaster, eloped and no replacement was found.

The premises were used for many purposes after this. As late as 1934, Selby Urban District Radio Relay Service situated at 47, Brook Street, was allowed to make a small 'fixing' on the property in Millgate, for the purpose of Wireless Service. For this they paid an annual peppercorn rent of a shilling postal order. Another small annual rent of one shilling revealed that in 1920 the Salvation Army had premises very close to the property in Millgate. They had been allowed to lay a water pipe across the almhouses' yard to their place of worship.

Over the years some of the Trust's land was sold and parts of the property were destroyed but it was not until after 1969 when the local authority bought the estate in order to widen the roads around Millgate that it all disappeared. The draper's legacy still continues however, for in 1970, funds from Leonard Chamberlain's Trust were used to build a two-storey block down D'Arcy Road. Known as Chamberlain Court it provided accommodation for widows or spinsters of pensionable age. Today the Trustees are involved in building twelve bungalows. Four are fully equipped for use by disabled persons, the others only partially. To help the tenants remain in their homes for as long as possible all, save one bungalow, have two bedrooms, to enable carers or relations to be accommodated if necessary. The bequest left by Leonard Chamberlain almost three hundred years ago is still being used to enhance the lives of people in Selby.

Roman Catholics

For over two centuries the owners of the Selby estates and their stewards followed the Catholic faith; despite this the number in the district was never large. In 1680 there were eight in Selby and three in Brayton. Twenty-six years later there were only five recorded in Selby which included Francis Walmsley, lord of the manor. Carlton Hall still played a major part in keeping the Roman Catholic faith alive in the area. Excerpts from Sir Miles Stapleton's household accounts as noted by Miss Richardson, reveal that a new chapel was built in the gallery of the Hall. Built in 1668 it also contained a bed chamber and two closets. Like the monks of Selby Abbey, Sir Miles made sure he had a good supply of wine, wafers and wax for candles. It is interesting to note that his mother, who lived at Quosquo, kept bees in straw skeps in the garden and the orchard there. Her son paid her at a rate of one shilling for each pound of her beeswax.

Sir Miles also used local men to create his lovely chapel. Cornelius Barker of Selby went to Howden to choose the right timbers for the building and did much of the carpentry. The wood was brought by water from Howden to Carlton Landing. Edward Clough of Airmyn and Joseph Rodger of Carlton were plasterers who used hair, lime, laths and nails on all the partition walls including those of the closet for the resident priest.

Another person brought in to help with the woodwork was listed as a nameless 'Quaker of Selby' who without doubt would have been trusted to keep his own counsel about what was being done at Carlton Hall. This was very important for the lives of Catholic priests and those who harboured them were still in jeopardy. It was noted in the accounts for 1676 that two shillings had been given to Christopher Ward, constable for Carlton, for not revealing the names of known Catholics at the Wakefield Sessions. Money was also given to John Sotheby for accompanying Ward to make sure he kept his promise! The search for priests intensified during the reigns of Charles II at the time the Duke of York, the future James II, was showing his support for the Catholics. Rumours of plots against the king and the Protestants were rife. In 1679 Sir Miles Stapleton was accused with his uncle, Sir Thomas Gascoigne, of being involved in such a plot. Mr. Robert Bolron who, five years earlier, had gone to live with the latter as his steward at the coal-pits, spoke out against them both. Sir Thomas Gascoigne was in his eighty-fifth year when he was tried and acquitted of high treason at the King's Bench, Westminster.

Sir Miles was taken to York where he was also acquitted. He had energetically defended himself and produced many witnesses of note to throw discredit on the evidence of informers. Nine years later when William of Orange was being put forward as the next Protestant ruler of the country, Sir Miles Stapleton was again in danger because of his harbouring of priests. In December he paid Ann Barber, a member of his household, to slip away with a message to his brother-in-law, Thomas Osborne, at York. In it Sir Miles told him of his fears of being molested and asked for protection. Thomas Osborne, Earl of Danby, had recently seized upon York to raise support for the Prince of Orange and was busily encouraging the cry of "no popery". He offered no protection to his brother-in-law. Two days later a large mob burst into the house at Carlton and failing to find a priest, carried off Sir Miles and his retainers. Mr. Hugh Taylor of Coates led the search; there was an old Coates Hall just off Temple Hirst Road. Assisting him were John Taylor of Newland, Alexander Clarke, John Lamb, John Barnes and John Haworth of Rawcliffe supported by around sixty other searchers from Rawcliffe and Newland. Most of them spent the night in the house consuming vast quantities of bread, cheese and meat washed down with half a hogshead (210 pints) of wine and as much ale. Meanwhile, the prisoners had been taken to Ferrybridge and released. They had to spend the night there which Sir Miles Stapleton noted cost him almost five pounds.

The Venerable Thomas Thwing

Many Catholic supporters suffered dreadfully during this period of rumours and deceit. Thomas Thwing was one of the unfortunate people accused of being involved in a 'popish plot', a fictitious plan to assassinate Charles II, massacre the Protestants and form a Catholic ministry. Titus Oates (1649-1705), who had become a Catholic in order to move in their circles, was one of the main inventors of the plot of 1678. Opponents of the Catholic Duke of York, the future James II, helped to spread the false rumours until belief in the existence of such a plot became widespread. When later, inconsistencies were found, Oates was convicted of perjury. He was pilloried, flogged then imprisoned. This was not before, however, around 35 supposed plotters were executed, including Thomas Thwing.

He was a relation of the Stapletons and came as a priest to Carlton in 1660. Thwing was also the headmaster at the Quosquo school. In 1680 he stood in the dock at York accused with Mary Pressick of Barwick-in-Elmet, of intending to help carry out the aims of the 'popish plot'.

The chief witness against them was Robert Bolron, the steward of Sir Thomas Gascoigne who had also implicated Sir Thomas and Sir Miles Stapleton in these crimes. At some time during the 1670s Mr. Bolron had become a practising Catholic. He said he had been questioned by Thomas Thwing and others concerning how he stood regarding the Roman Catholic faith and whether he was willing to stake all for it. He said there had been a meeting at Barnbow Hall, home of Sir Thomas Gascoigne, at which the accused and Sir Miles Stapleton had been present and where all there had agreed on a plan to kill the king. He confessed that whilst he had given ten pounds towards the funds it had enabled him to see the list of other donors. He quoted Mrs. Pressick as saying, *"The king was an asse and not fit to govern, that what money the parliament gave him he spent on whores and concubines"*.

In summing up the judge declared that there was enough evidence of High Treason, but if the jury did not believe what the servants and other witnesses swore with regard to Thomas Thwing being agreeable to the plot and in gathering supporters, they were to acquit him. Mary Pressick was released but Thomas, the chaplain to the Stapletons was found guilty. The judge did not listen to Thomas Thwing's protestations of his innocence but instructed him that;

> *The law doth command and the court doth award, that you be carried from*
> *hence to the place from whence you came, that is the prison, and from thence*
> *you are to be drawn to the place of execution; you are to be hanged by the neck,*
> *you are to be cut down before you are dead, and your intrails are to be taken*

out of your body, and thrown into the fire before your face, and your head is to
be parted from your body and your body seperated into four quarters, and your
head and your quarters are to be disposed of according to the King's pleasure:
And the Lord have mercy on your soul.

When the National Catholic Congress was held in Leeds in 1909, on show were the Mass Vestments used by Thomas Thwing. It was noted that he was the last of the English Martyred Priests *"who suffered under the law".*

Saint Mary's Catholic Church

These dreadful executions did not put an end to the continual harrying of the Catholics even during the reign of George I. In Selby the constables' accounts for 1723 show that they were paid five shillings for riding two days with Mr. Marshall in search of arms and horses belonging to any Catholics. They claimed funds for documenting at Tadcaster the presence of such people and sixpence for the warrants to hold the suspect inhabitants.

The few Catholics managed to stay faithful to their beliefs and by 1783 their number had begun to increase. Father Edward Leadbitter, who had taken charge of a chapel at Stourton in Leeds, began to say Mass in Selby on alternate Sundays. The first chapel in the town was provided by the ninth Baron Petre, lord of the manor of Selby and grandson of Lady Catherine Stourton. It was in the large upper room of his steward's house on Ousegate. These premises were used by the Catholics in the town for nearly fifty years until the house became the property of the railway. From 1834 when the Leeds to Selby railway was opened, to around 1885 it was lived in by the station masters.

About three years after they had lost their meeting place the Roman Catholic congregation moved into a new church on the corner of Brook Street and Gowthorpe, provided for them by E.R.Petre, lord of the manor. It was built in 1837 during the time the Rev. George Best was chaplain. The devastating potato famine in Ireland, 1845-50, caused immigrants to pour into England, those settling in Selby greatly increasing the Catholic congregation. Despite numbers being diminished by the terrible cholera outbreaks in the late 1840s the church in Gowthorpe was overcrowded. By that time there were 41 English and 443 Irish Catholics worshipping in the town. The owners of the Selby estates came to the rescue again. In 1856, the Hon. Laura M. Petre, widow of the Hon. Edward R. Petre, had a new church built. The handsome Gothic church, St Mary's, seating five hundred persons, has a residence for a priest and is situated at the west end of Gowthorpe. When the Staynor Wood estate was developed in the early twentieth century worshippers there found it a long way to go to St. Mary's so a Chapel-of- Ease, St Patrick's, seating two hundred and fifty people was opened in the 1950s at the junction of Petre Avenue and Volta Street.

The old church was eventually demolished. In 1913 a senior school was built on the property fronting onto Brook Street but the sacristy remained as part of the infant school. Today the pupils go to St Mary's R.C. school in Brayton before moving up to the Holy Family R.C. in Carlton. The fate of the old disused buildings on the corner of Gowthorpe and Brook Street, including the little sacristy is yet in question. It is possible they will be demolished to make way for a housing complex.

The Methodists

In the eighteenth century the Catholic, Quaker and Presbyterian worshippers in Selby were relatively few in number and offered no serious challenge to the established Anglican church. The impact made by the Methodists, however, was much greater.

The term 'methodist' appears to have first been used in the seventeenth century as a nickname for those leading extremely well-ordered, devotional lives. This included members of the 'Holy Club' established in the 1720s by a group of Oxford undergraduates, of which Charles Wesley was a member. His elder brother, John, joined this club and very soon dominated it. Eventually the name was used exclusively for people influenced by John Wesley. Their ministry began in 1738. The only hostility they appeared to sustain came from the Anglicans who objected to their open air meetings and their evangelical enthusiasm. Soon local societies were formed and an annual conference established. The rise of Wesleyan Methodism in Selby began shortly after the group was formed. It gradually expanded until it had a large congregation in the town, averaging between six hundred and seven hundred members at its height.

A visit to Selby by the early Methodists was referred to in a collection of doggerel verse published in 1751 by William Darnley, assistant to John Wesley.

Like wise to Selby we do go
God's mercies to proclaim.

John Wesley became an Anglican minister and for many years Methodist Societies remained within the Church of England. In his journal the minister recorded six visits to Selby. One was in April, 1759, when he wrote, *"I set out for Selby the congregation obliged me to stand in the garden though the north wind was exceedingly high"*. The garden is believed to have been between where the park entrance is today and the market place. Another visit occurred in June 1788. On this occasion Wesley had been told by the Rev. William Potter that he was welcome to preach in the Abbey Church. The vicar, however, changed his mind before Wesley arrived so the Methodist preacher took a service in the town's chapel, ending with a blessing of the children. This had become a custom over the years; Mrs. Samuel Staniland, member of a prominent Selby family at that time, often spoke of being one of the children receiving this blessing.

The chapel visited by John Wesley was in Millgate. When Selby first became part of the York circuit, services were held in a small cottage in the yard of the Leeds Arms Inn, Micklegate. Methodist preachers often delivered open air sermons in the front of the adjoining premises until in 1785/6 a chapel was erected in Millgate. The foundation stone was laid by Mrs. Samuel Staniland. Members attended morning service there at half past nine then went in large numbers to the one being held in the Abbey. This Millgate chapel was in regular use for about thirty-two years before the congregation moved to James Street. In the nineteenth century the vacated chapel was used by a Mr. Adams as part of his flax mill. On a valuation list of 1857 it was described as being *"No 133, flax mill, with engine and boiler house"*. Number 133a was listed as the Friendship Inn beerhouse, occupier James Jinks. In the 1900s the chapel was used as a marine store warehouse by a Mr. Cardis and described as being in the yard of the Friendship Inn. The public house is still there today but there are no remains of the chapel in the modernised Millgate.

In 1813 Selby had become head of the circuit with a congregation of 444 people. The Millgate chapel became so overcrowded it was decided to erect a larger building with a preacher's house in James Street. The land was presented to them by the lord of the manor, E.R.Petre and the new chapel was opened in November, 1817. The continuing rise in the congregation numbers made it necessary to enlarge the premises on more than one occasion. By 1864 the chapel had acquired a gallery and had seating for a thousand people. In the 1860s the town worshippers numbered 412, the villages 674, there were three stationed ministers, 42 local preachers and 68 leaders.

The Methodists supported the Missionary Society and in 1814 a branch opened in the Millgate chapel. It received generous contributions from the townspeople. At a time when the Wesleyan society was active in promoting the abolition of slavery, two members of the society, William Dowson of Cawood and William Clough of Selby went as missionaries to the West Indies; a venture that involved considerable risks.

A group of Primitive Methodists were introduced to Selby in 1818 by Rev. Mr. Clowes. Their first meetings were held in a room in Micklegate. A chapel was erected in 1844 in Mr. Morley's yard on Gowthorpe, which was described as being near to Foster's Printing Works. This soon became inadequate for the growing number of Primitive Methodists attending the chapel. Twenty-two years later a much grander building was erected on land sold to them by Lord Londesborough then lord of the manor. Situated on Gowthorpe at the junction with Brook Street, almost opposite the Catholic buildings, it contained a chapel with seating for 460 people, vestries and schoolroom with a house adjacent for the minister.

Not long after the Primitive Methodists began to worship in their new chapel, another use was found for it. In January 1863 leading figures in Selby decided that an evening class would benefit the community, one where *"instruction might be imparted in writing and arithmetic, and other kinds of useful knowledge on terms adapted to the means of the humbler classes"*. Everyone agreed that the new chapel was the ideal venue. A course of instruction was begun by a Mr.W. Allison and was well attended. To celebrate this success, over 130 members were invited to a tea followed by a meeting at which the guests were entertained and intrigued by various experiments carried out on an 'electrifying' machine. They were then delighted and mystified by striking views of distant objects produced by the use of a magic lantern.

Eventually the two Methodist groups merged together and in 1956 the Primitive Methodist Chapel, noted for its beautiful decorations and carvings, was closed down. It was used for a time to accommodate the town's clinic until one was opened in Raincliffe Street. The building was then occupied for many years by a Motor Tyre Company. In 1992 it was bought by the Town Council, and four years later, following renovation, it became Selby's Town Hall. All the business connected with the Town Council is carried out there. It is also used sometimes for Coroners inquests and as a Polling Station. Groups such as Local Family History and the Workers' Educational Association make use of the rooms available for hire. The Town Hall is also host to the well supported Arts Centre.

The Methodists continued to worship in the chapel down James Street until the 1980s. They had, however, found the building too large for their needs and parts of it were put to other uses. In 1939 a Public Library and a Post Office shared the premises. The library eventually moved into rooms above a Doctors' Surgery in Abbey Yard. In March 1984, a new library was opened in Micklegate and in January 1993 the doctors moved to the new Beechtree Surgery down Doncaster Road. The first official Post

Office had been in Micklegate from 1892 until 1909. It then moved onto the next site once occupied by the Albert Hotel. It was from there that it moved into the vacated school part of the Methodist building. This was supposed to have been a temporary move whilst a new Post Office was being built but World War II halted the work and it was not until 1962 that the new office opened on Micklegate, next to the Griffin Hotel.

The Methodist congregation made use of different parts of their premises until the buildings were demolished on the redevelopment of the area. During this time they shared services with other religious groups including St James' the Apostle Church, Audus Street. Finally, the Methodists moved into their new, smaller and more modern building in Portholme Road.

The Congregationalists

Another non-conformist group was formed in Selby in the early nineteenth century. John Clapham of Leeds and William Bowden of Hull, well-known Congregationalists, travelled the country to introduce the foundations of independency in villages and small towns. They came to Selby in 1808 to help some like-minded friends to establish a Church and build up a congregation.

Such dissenters as these had been in existence since the sixteenth century. They too clashed with the authorities after the Reformation in England when, as it has been shown, the monarch was regarded as head of the church and the process of reformation proceeded according to royal dictates. The earliest Congregationalists, or Independents as they were often called, declared the Reformation must be undertaken according to the words of Jesus Christ, as written in the Bible. They declared that no monarch, pope or bishop had the right to direct them in their beliefs as they only followed one leader, Jesus Christ. Along with the other groups of dissidents, they suffered persecution. Two of their leaders, Robert Browne and Robert Harrison were forced to flee to Holland for a time. Robert Browne was imprisoned over 32 times when he returned to England. Two of his friends were hanged for 'crimes' such as circulating the writings of Browne and Harrison. Many suffered long years of imprisonment in the cruellest and most infamous gaol in the country, Fleet Prison.

The first preachers to come to Selby used a hired room for their services. These were the Rev. William Kent of Gravesend and the Rev. Andrew Reed. The latter then held services in a converted barn on Gowthorpe, owned by a Mr. Shipton, a tanner. On his first visit Mr. Reed, subsequently Dr. Reed, appeared to be ignorant of the existence of other Christian groups gathering members in Selby for he described the place as a market town of three thousand to four thousand inhabitants lacking instruction in the gospel of Christ. He was invited to preach in the commodious Assembly room of a hotel. It is thought possible that this was the hotel which is now known as the Londesborough Arms situated in the market place, in close proximity to the Abbey Church. It would explain the objections that were lodged after the first services, attended by 120 to 220 people, were held there. The group were refused further use of the room. Undaunted, they continued to employ the bellman to advertise their presence in the town, and soon their new venue on Gowthorpe was filled to overflowing.

New premises had been urgently needed for the expanding congregation. In 1801 a Christopher Twist bought land in New Lane, Selby, from the trustees William and Richard Osbaldeston. Seven years later he sold almost 194 square metres of it to the Congregationalists on which they built a chapel. It opened in March 1809 and the first minister was the Rev. Thomas Pinchbeck. Old records belonging to the church show that baptisms took place there. Catherine, daughter of John and Sarah Harrison born on the 12th. June 1811 was baptised there on the 12th. July.

As with other dissenters' groups the chapel was often in need of alterations and enlargements. A major rebuilding took place in 1865 but in the early twentieth century it was proposed that a new church should be erected elsewhere. Over the years many sites were considered including the former Primitive Methodist Chapel on Gowthorpe, but by 1957 no decision had been made. None of the plans put forward were acceptable and in the end the church was challenged to refurbish its own buildings in New Lane. On the 17th July, 1977 a Service of Thanksgiving was held in premises which had been modernised in places but which had still kept many of its old features. During the 1960s a union between the Congregational and the Presbyterian Churches in England and Wales was proposed and in the following decade the place of worship in New Lane became known as the Selby United Reformed Church.

There was always a bond of friendship with the Methodist groups which by the twentieth century resulted in the sharing of some services. In 1959 a Selby Council of Churches was formed at which the Protestant churches in the town could discuss local and national matters. This had not been possible before the Reformation when people had little choice in where they wished to worship. In Selby and district the people were all expected to attend the churches owned by the abbey and practise its religion. This began to change when the monks departed. Their old faith was almost obliterated during the course of the English Reformation which allowed, as we have seen, many new religious societies to be formed. Today, the Selby Times Citizens' Guide lists ten religious venues in the town, many of which are continuing to strive to work together and to share resources.

7. Hull to Selby Railway Bridge

8. Selby Town Hall

9. Rifle Armoury and Drill Shed, 1865

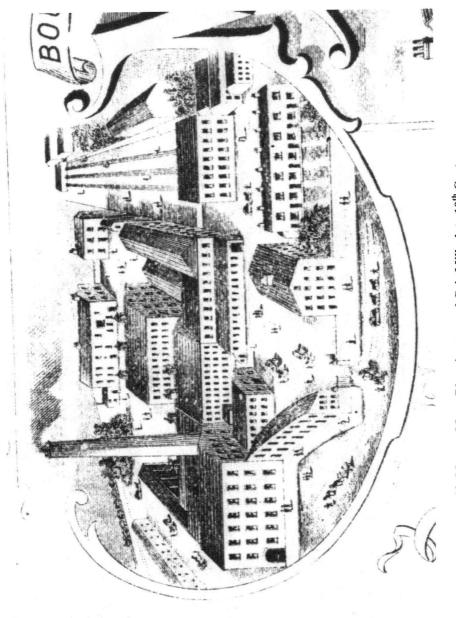

10. Messrs. Moss, Rimmington and Co's Mills, late 19th Century

11. Demolition of Abbey Tythe Barn around 1896

12. Selby Local Board Offices

13. Selby Union Work House

14. Ernest and Percy Whisker

15. Gas Lighting in Selby Market Place at the beginning of the 20th Century

GG170. SELBY, OLD TOLL BRIDGE FROM EAST.

16. Selby's Wooden Toll Bridge

17. Last Toll paid on Selby Toll Bridge, September 1991

18. Selby Abbey 2004

CHAPTER 8

THE EIGHTEENTH CENTURY

The Hanoverian Monarchs

Three Hanoverians reigned as kings during the eighteenth century. George I was as much concerned with Hanoverian affairs as he was with the happenings in England. A shrewd and diplomatic man he left the administration of the country to his ministers. He showed restraint when anti-Hanoverian feelings were roused and supported religious toleration.

His only son succeeded him as George II and reigned from 1727 to 1760. He was opinionated and assertive which caused friction between him and his ministers. Eventually he withdrew from active involvement in politics but as a keen soldier became the last British monarch to appear in battle. He acquitted himself bravely in 1743 when leading his troops against the French at the Battle of Dettingen near Hanau, in a war brought about by disagreements concerning the Austrian succession.

He was succeeded by his grandson whose long reign lasted from 1760 to 1820. The first Hanoverian king to be born and bred in Britain, George III tried to exercise royal powers over his government but eventually had to recognise the reality of party politics. His involvement declined during the 1790s but he continued to successfully oppose Catholic emancipation. It was not until 1829 that an Act was passed allowing Roman Catholics to sit in Parliament and to take many public offices. The Act of Settlement preventing a Catholic succeeding to the monarchy has not been repealed.

The Growth of Education

Besides the growth of many religious groups during the reigns of the three Georges it was also the time when people did more to educate the poor. During the Elizabethan period the mass of the people had been illiterate or had been half-taught to read by 'dames' - impoverished old ladies trying to earn a living. When secular canons became administrators of monastic cathedrals in places like York, Beverley and Lincoln, they put more emphasis on the need for education. Schools were maintained and bishops gave certain people licences to teach. Many unauthorised persons tried to earn a living by teaching. In 1600 Robert Browne, a lame man, was summoned to Snaith Peculiar Court for teaching children in his house without a licence. When dissenters were excluded by law, or custom, from gaining a higher education at the established schools and universities, they opened their own academies for all age groups. The Anglican churches followed their example and founded charity schools not only to educate the poor but to teach them the principles of the Church of England. In 1666 the licensed schoolmaster of the Free School at Fishlake was brought before officials for not taking the children to church. Hundreds of charity schools were opened during the reign of

Queen Anne and they were sorely needed for the state provided no education for the poor. Ordinary parishes had no endowed schools so it had been left to the dame schools and unlicensed persons to teach the needy.

Education was in the minds of many people when a parent died. In 1652 Margaret Eshley of Selby, a widow, was bound (obliged) to administer the estate of William Lewys of Selby, her son deceased, and to educate and bring up her grandchild William. After the death of Henry Scowcroft, of Thorpe Willoughby, in1664, it was recorded that Edward Hopkinson was bound to bring up and educate Thomas, Edward and Alice Scowcroft, Henry's children.

The records of the parish officials in Selby show that there was a Free School in the town in the early eighteenth century. The cost of repairs to this school were recorded in the Churchwardens' accounts. In 1722 Thomas Brearley was paid 9s.8d. for glasswork done to the premises. Four years later, ten men working from three to six days to repair the school were paid £4.2s.1d. whilst Robert Adams received 10s.6d. for providing a desk. In 1727 the Overseers paid sixpence to James Turner, which represented his quarterly school wages.

Blue Coat School

The charity school movement tried to excite local interest in the setting up of schools instead of relying on wealthy founders such as the generous non-conformist, Leonard Chamberlain who enabled one to be opened in Millgate. Small shopkeepers and traders were encouraged to subscribe, collect donations and to take a personal interest in the activities and success of such institutions. Around 1745 a group of people began to meet 'amicably' in Selby. They became known as the Amicable Society and, aided by subscriptions and endowments, opened a Blue Coat School where at least twenty of the poorest boys could be clothed and educated. For example, in 1775 a legacy of one hundred pounds was invested in five acres of land down Wistow Lane, known as Mile Stile Close. In 1778 Mr. John Herbert gave one hundred pounds for investment; it was to go to his heirs if the society was dissolved. The school was given the use of a wooden floored room in the upper part of the sacristy adjoining the Abbey Church. It is not clear where the Free School had been and it is possible it had used the same premises. The Blue Coat one at Selby was run on lines similar to those previously used by the monks. Besides receiving an education the pupils were trained as choir boys and had to attend church three times on a Sunday and several times in the week. The name 'blue coat' came from the uniform worn by the boys. It consisted of a blue jacket and knee breeches, both adorned with brass buttons, and a pork-pie hat. Vacancies for the school were advertised by the bellman; hopeful applicants appeared before the subscribers and the most needy selected. In 1785 public donations enabled the opening of a Grey Coat School for girls. Mary Waud, a subscriber to the boys' school, willed two hundred pounds to the vicar and the Feoffees, the interest from which was to be used to teach eight poor girls reading, writing, accounts and understanding the catechism. This was run by the ladies in the town on much stricter lines than the boys, but it always had a waiting list of poor girls wishing to be educated.

The Treasurer's accounts for 1830/31 reveal that the annual subscriptions from the Amicable Society members to the Blue Coat School had gradually increased from three pence a year to thirteen shillings. During that period when Isaac Butler, the schoolmaster received an annual salary of £22, the boys, numbering 22, were each provided with two pairs of shoes valued at five shillings a pair. They were also given two pairs of worsted socks at 1s.5½d. a pair. A suit of clothes was made for each boy at a cost of five shillings whilst a neck band for each child came to ten shillings. Other expenses included £1.11s.6d. for school dinners for the boys and their master and 1s.6d. paid to the bellman for *"crying six vacancies"*. Some income for the school came from church collections and from special sermons preached to raise money. Other funds came from rented lands, the interest on money held for the charity, and legacies. The subscribers for the year 1830/31 included such well known Selby names as Staniland, Hawdon, Weddall and Audus.

Other benevolent people left funds to help educate the poor. In 1780 Joshua Raynor left one hundred pounds to be used to purchase land stipulating that the profits from it be used to educate six poor boys and to instruct them in the church catechism. However, if the funds were misused they were to go to his heirs. In his will, dated 1669, Charles Read left funds to help in the education of all the poor children in the parish of Drax. Edward Atkinson of Camblesforth bequeathed six acres of land near the river at Newland-on-Aire, the rent from it to be used to provide a master or a mistress to teach the children of Camblesforth.

Homes and Employment

Much information concerning the lives of individual members of the community around Selby may be gained from a study of inventories of goods valued during the seventeenth and eighteenth centuries. There were many farmers, yeomen, husbandmen working on the land, whilst in Selby people followed the occupations carried on in the town since medieval times. These included tanners, curriers who dressed the tanned leather, fellmongers who prepared the hides for the tanners; linen websters who wove flax, mercers who dealt in textiles and small wares, cordwayners who made shoes, tallow chandlers who sold candles, whitesmiths or tinsmiths and wine cowpers who made wine casks. More familiarly named craftsmen included joiners who charged sixpence to make a coffin. Shipbuilding was also becoming an important part of Selby life, providing jobs for many people.

Labourers worked on the land whilst others went as servants and lived in large farmhouses such as Dyon House near South Duffield or Whitemore farm which lay close by it. These houses had five rooms downstairs, including a dairy, and four or five chambers upstairs, including a garret. The most common crops grown on these farms at that time were wheat, rye, oats, barley, rape, winter corn, potatoes, peas and beans. A rarer crop, teazles, was grown in Biggin, Stillingfleet and Camblesforth. In the 1750s, William Newham at Whitemore farm, grew most of the above crops and also had three horses, three cows, three calves, a bull, two pigs and some poultry.

Hiring Fairs .

The workers employed on these farms or those who maintained large houses in the rural towns or country, were usually hired at the 'sittings' at Martinmas time. In Selby they gathered around the market cross or waited in the church-yard hoping to have a master seal their contract with the gift of a 'fastening penny'. Known also as a 'luck' or 'godspenny' it varied in value but was binding to both parties and if infringed, the master could be fined and the servant imprisoned. The custom flourished after the passing of the

Statute of Artificers in 1562/3 when it was laid down that the justices were to assess wages, and able-bodied men between 12 and 60 were to work in the fields, if required, whilst unmarried women were to do domestic work. Servants were to be hired for at least a year and apprentices to serve seven years; hours of labour were to be 12 in summer and all daylight hours in winter.

For a great part of the seventeenth and eighteenth century the chief constable in an area was in control of the hirings. He would notify his petty constables beforehand when he would be 'sitting' in their towns to give them time to collect a list of masters and servants intending to be present. This was during two or three days around Martinmas, set aside for the hirings. The officers in Selby in 1723 claimed expenses "*To going about to see what servants stayed*". No servant could be hired unless the chief constable was present. When arriving at a place, like Selby he asked each master, on the lists, if they were setting their servants at liberty. It this was so, the chief constable gave each servant a ticket for which they, in return, gave him twopence "for his pains". When a servant was hired the new master sometimes reimbursed his new employee. The chief constable also received a penny from every master who kept a servant for another year. Despite many efforts by concerned people to change this custom, hiring days continued until the start of World War II.

During Georgian times, servants would put on their best clothes, have an early breakfast and leave for the 'sittings' long before the hiring began, not returning until after dark. They were bound to give their old masters up to three days notice but, those who could, stayed with friends intent on enjoying their freedom and the Martinmas fairs.

When hired, many male servants hoped to be given an old suit and a hat, a pair of breeches, and maybe a pair of shoes, whilst the maidservants desired an apron or smock, or both. In return a hired foreman was expected to be efficient at mowing, sowing, stacking pease, ploughing, and trustworthy enough to go to the markets. The produce from the farms was sold direct to the customers at the local markets until the appearance of the middleman who bought up the goods and sold them at a greater price at the big fairs. At a time when a pair of shoes could cost five shillings the foreman was given two shillings and sixpence as a 'godspenny' and an annual wage of around 60 shillings. A good ploughman earned 35 shillings whilst maidservants who were good milkers received a shilling as a 'godspenny' and 18 shillings annual wage. One farmer at that time however, complained, "*But now of late we cannot hire a good lusty maidservant*".

In the early 1800s complaints appeared in the local newspapers concerning the Hiring Fairs. One person wrote, "*whole masses of uneducated beings are called together on hiring day, some in a beastly state of drunkenness. Turned loose for up to a week they go from market to market...commit all kinds of wanton damage*". There were also complaints made concerning the stalls, shows and unsavoury characters attracted to the gatherings.

Similar letters were being received in 1855 when it was said that the labourers came to Selby mainly for pleasure rather than to seek a master. Pickpockets were also out in force at these hirings. Ten of them were apprehended at the Selby fair; three women and four men were later committed to Wakefield House of Correction to do three months hard labour for their crimes in the town. Another pickpocket who received two months imprisonment was Sarah Mann of Hull. She stole £1.11s.6d. from Mary Chattam of Drax, who was selling hampers of apples. The amount stolen was equal to a months pay for some people.

Complaints about the hiring fairs continued through the years but there were also those who considered the plight of the labourers. One meeting to discuss improving hiring days for everyone was held in 1857 in the Red Lion at Howden where the vicar of Bubwith was the main speaker. It was resolved at the meeting that the chief constables of Goole, Howden and Selby be asked to comply with their requests. One was that servants should only be allowed to go to one statute fair each year for some masters had complained that their servants went from one to another without any intention of seeking new employment. Another request was that all servants should be given character references to help them in their search for good positions, a custom that was beginning to gain favour.

Matters did improve in Selby for in 1872, on a very cold and showery hiring day, the Public Rooms were opened for the benefit of masters, mistresses and servants. A temporary Register Office was run by Mr. H. Staniland where engagements were ratified and registered. Mr. Staniland must have been given his 'tuppences' for it was said he received enough funds to almost cover the cost of the room. It was also reported that there was the usual assortment of shooting galleries, peep shows, roundabouts and other side shows in the town.

In the Log Books for the Selby Wesleyan Day School, closed in 1928, is the entry,

1900 November 14th. Half holiday-STATUTE FAIR. This relic of bygone days is still maintained in this part of England.

On such days crowds of young people dressed in their best clothes gathered near the cross waiting to be hired. At their feet were wooden or tin boxes containing all their worldly belongings, whilst in their pockets they had a year's wages waiting to be lost to thieves, squandered in joyful activities at the fair or carefully saved towards a better future. Many of the older servants carried distinguishing trademarks. Shepherds wore a tuft of wool in their hats whilst wagoners sported a piece of whipcord in their headgear.

In 1872, a foreman on a Selby farm was receiving twenty pounds and a ploughman nine to twelve pounds. At Driffield in 1893, milkmaids were being offered ten to fourteen pounds a year. During the 1920s-30s, some farmworkers in the area received one or two shillings a week plus food and essential clothes. If they were in need of any extra money it was taken off their wages at the end of the year.

In the 1980s a resident of Selby remembered how sixty years previously she had to stand at Wetherell's, at the corner of Finkle Street (now a travel agents), with her tin box full of aprons, frocks and personal things, waiting to be hired. Hating the idea of leaving home she often avoided being hired by hiding, with other reluctant fifteen year olds, under bushes in a nearby field. She was taken on, in one instance, by a farmer from Holme-upon-Spalding-Moor but hated it so much she ran away. The farmer traced her to her home in Eggborough but when the tears ceased to flow he left her there – but not before retrieving his 'fastening penny'! Mrs Ruby Smith of Kellington remembered, around the same time, being fascinated by the Martinmas Fair where rides on the roundabouts and swings cost twopence. She quickly spent all her 'fastening penny' of ten shillings then returned home. Her mother allowed her to stay but she was forced to work very hard pulling an acre of turnips for five pounds enabling her to repay her hiring money.

Houses and Furniture

Many people lived in timber framed houses. To provide the raw materials to make these dwellings Wistow tenants were allowed to take wood from the lord's forests. Some ancient half-timbered houses survived in Selby until the early twentieth century. One stood at the west end of Gowthorpe near the traffic lights, in a space now taken up by a hoarding. In 1668 William Pothan, an influential gentleman, lived in a house containing sixteen rooms. It had a hall house, study, cellar, great and little parlours, kitchen, back kitchen, garden parlour, dairy, and a 'Matthewer House' which accommodated his animals, brewery vessels and other tools. There were six rooms upstairs of varying sizes and a closet. In those days the principal living room of a typical tradesman's dwelling was referred to as the house or hall whilst the parlour sited nearest to the street, usually contained the best pieces of furniture. This was where business affairs were discussed and private talks held. The number of parlours in Mr. Pothan's residence reveals he was a wealthy man. A tax imposed in 1696 on the number of windows or 'lights' in a house, also indicated the size of an abode. This tax, which trebled during the French Revoltionary Wars, proved unsatisfactory for windows were boarded up or blocked out. In 1755, out of 289 houses visited in Selby, 252 householders paid the window tax totalling £51.10s.6d. Other houses were empty or the residents too poor to pay. The majority paid two shillings and others paid from seven shillings for ten windows to £1.7s.0d for 25 windows. The last was paid by Mrs Mary Waud, a benefactor of the town.

Good, solid furniture found in these homes were sometimes referred to in the inventories as "heirlooms for ever". Mr. Pothan's 'Great Parlour' was furnished with a large table, twelve embroidered set work chairs, four Dutch chairs, two carpets, three stools, one map in a frame, one 'seeing' glass, two window-curtains and seven pictures. Carpets were often used to protect the boards of large draw-leaf tables. Iron ranges were rarely found in the average home but Mr. Pothan had four the one in his great parlour being adorned with brass knobs with shovel, tongs and poker also finished off in brass. Beds were to be found in most of the rooms in any houses. Small, narrow beds suitable for children, humbler people and servants, were known as stand or truckle beds; they could be stowed away or rolled up. Pothan's 'little parlour' had a stand bed with tester, curtains, valance and furniture belonging to it and a truckle bed with its furniture. Five of the rooms upstairs all known as 'chambers' had stand beds in them including the Great Chamber which also had a grand bed, most probably of the four-poster type. The linen for the house including table clothes, napkins, curtains, 37 pairs of sheets, fine and ordinary, with pillow cases and towels, was valued at sixty pounds. Besides the beds the Great Chamber had four high chairs, four low chairs, four stools, a couch chair and a footstool. There was also a cabinet, a four leaved screen, a range, eleven pictures and a dirty water voider. The contents of the room were valued at £15.5s.0d whilst the furniture in the servant's chamber, over the kitchen, was valued at one pound - the same figure as the manure left in the garden!

Articles in the lists made in 1760 concerning the household furniture belonging to the late Nicholas Stapleton of Carlton Hall illustrate the choice of beverages then available for the upper classes. Amongst the furniture listed was a mahogany fret tea table. It had become the fashion for ladies of leisure to entertain their friends to afternoon tea at which the hostess took pleasure in serving them herself using her best china. In Carlton Hall this included tea-cups and saucers, two milk pots and a sugar pot all of Dresden china. Large and small tea-kettles were kept in the kitchen. There was also a silver sugar basket and a tea chest for use by the mistress. The latter was very important for tea was expensive and needed to be locked away. In 1799 green tea cost 4s.8d. a pound (the same price as a pair of children's shoes) whilst a pound of sugar was sevenpence. High prices did not deter even the poorest people who bought the cheapest blends as England became a nation of tea drinkers. The presence of a chocolate pot, chocolate cups and coffee mugs on the lists at Carlton Hall shows what other beverages were also enjoyed.

Self-sufficiency

Many rural people living in the seventeenth to eighteenth century were sturdily independent and self-supporting. With all the goods they produced or displayed and sold in their front shops or back-yards, the crops grown in the nearby fields and the produce of their own animals and birds, they could, in all probability, have kept themselves and their dependants from starvation. Not a great amount of cereal was produced for many householders stored theirs in an upstairs chamber. Mr. Pothan kept brewing vessels, rye, wheat and hay in his corn chamber. The inventories showed that many Selby homes held an ample supply of yarn and hemp, retted or unretted for future use. Some houses boasted at least three spinning wheels used for making linen thread. The item *"One loume with all its geeres and woule-whelle"* confirmed that the art of spinning and weaving of wool was also still being engaged in the home. This was important at that time for laws had been passed in 1667 and 1678 declaring that the dead could only be buried in articles made from wool. The laws were intended to help the wool trade. Strictly enforced after the second act they were not repealed until 1814. The expenses incurred in the burial of a Hambleton man were listed as: ale and meat eight shillings, cheese- 4s. bread-13s., John Parat for flannel to wind him in 4s.3d., to widow Burne for winding him and the satisfying of the justice of the peace that she had done so - eight pennies. A penalty of five pounds would have been imposed if the widow had not had her actions certified by the officials.

Pothan's inventories showed that he had one cow, a heifer, one mare and three fillies, three pigs, chickens and four beehives, which all helped towards making his household self-sufficient. Pigs were the most common domesticated animals kept by the townsfolk and strict laws still existed concerning their rearing. During the eighteenth century pigs were free to roam the extensive woods near the town under the protection of a person known as a swineherd, appointed to his office by the Manor Court. One particular swineherd was remembered by many from his habit of walking around the town sporting a hat decorated with rabbits' tails and brightly coloured jays' feathers, set jauntily on his head. He flourished a long whip and was never seen without his badge of office - a cow's horn. Every morning at break of day the swineherd began his duties by giving a blast on his horn at the corner of every street in Selby. At the sound of the horn, out of all the yards in the town came the pigs! Like the enchanted children following the Pied Piper of Hamlyn, the pigs followed the swineherd out of the town, along the lanes and onto the common. There they stayed snuffling for acorns under his watchful eye until the evening. Then the swineherd rounded them up with blasts on his horn and led them safely back to their yards in Selby.

Shops

Shops were on the increase in towns. They usually consisted of a single room level with the street and had a shutter which let down to form a counter. Many had a sign hung above to denote their trade. At first all the goods sold in a shop had been made in a room behind the shop or a back yard. This gradually changed until shops became places where goods were brought in to be sold.

Robert Watson, of Selby, described as a bookseller, died in 1688. His house contained seven rooms. Behind the shop were a parlour and a kitchen, whilst upstairs were three chambers and a little closet. The shop must have been full to overflowing with all kinds of interesting articles and different aromas. Besides selling psalters, horn books, ABCs and construing books he sold cards, ink, powder horns, white and coarse paper, mortar and pestles, sealing wax, red lead, blue starch, quick silver and 33 gallons of treacle. Spices and flavourings ranging from aniseed to turmeric were also on sale. Stockings made out of leather or wool could be bought there, and ribbons, pins, knitting needles, thread and combs.

A line of shops extended westward from the remains of the Abbey gateway in the market place. It was known as Middle Row or the Shambles where there were butchers' shops. In 1705 the widow of a butcher named Swan, left as part of her estate, one shop in the Butchers Shambles, valued at ten pounds. A list of rents for seventeen properties on Middle Row in 1716 ranged from ten shillings to £31.11s.8d. per annum.

Robert Watson may have supplied many people with bibles for the inventories show that various households had a 'Great Bible' often kept in a special box. Others were recorded as having 'parcels of books'. Thomas Nichols, yeoman, left his grandson Nicholas Tarboton, five books including the bible and one entitled "The Practise of Pietie".

Gifts of Clothes

Stockings, shoes and materials for making clothes were available at the shops in Selby and at the markets. They were apparently expected to last for many of these goods were left as legacies. Thomas Nicholls who had bequeathed his books to his grandson, left his friend, William Smith of Drax, his best blue stockings and a pair of shoes; Thomas Anbye of Hemingbrough received one pair of his white stockings and a pair of cut shoes. Gilbert Sharpus of Burton, in the parish of Gateforth, left his relatives his cloak, coat, best 'dublite' and best britches. Philip Wood willed to Robert Spencer a pair of green britches, a pair of hose and shoes; his sister, Barbara, received his wedding britches. John Hutchinson was given his brother's green coat, hat and a shirt. Ann Godbehere left her daughter-in-law, her best gown and petticoat. Agnes Watson willed her morning gown with silver lace on it to her sister. It was the fashion for the more affluent ladies to have dresses for all occasions which involved spending a great part of the day changing clothes. Agnes was obviously not as frivolous as many ladies of fashion for she left a friend an apron with 'a seam down the middle', a practical use of two oddments of material. A gift of a petticoat of white flannel was given to one servant whilst an older servant received all her shoes and stockings and the clothes Agnes had used for everyday wear.

Tax on Fashion

The use of hair powder was a fashion that reached its height in the eighteenth century when even servants had to suffer their hair being pomaded and dusted with starch or flour. Parliament saw it as a good source of revenue and placed an annual tax on it. At the beginning of April his Majesty's Commissioners for Managing Stamp Duty authorised agents in several towns to be available for one calendar month to give out the appropriate certificates after a tax of one guinea had been paid to them. Anyone wearing hair powder after the fifth of April without a current certificate was fined twenty pounds. The fashion must have been followed around Selby for there were three agents in the area, John Clough, a grocer on Ousegate in the town, William Jewitt, a wine merchant at Snaith Lodge and Francis G. Osburn of Ropergate, Pontefract. When John Clough completed his list of the people holding hair powder certificates, he fastened it to one of the doors of Selby Abbey Church. This was very useful to informers who received half the fines when the culprits without certificates were apprehended!

Another duty collected by John Clough was known as the Armorial Bearing Tax. Passed in 1798 to raise more revenue, it obliged anyone having heraldic signs, badges depicting their rank or insignias of office engraved or painted on articles belonging to them, to pay a tax. This varied from 10s.6d. to two guineas for the use of them ranged from carriage doors to servants' buttons. The list of those who paid this tax in Selby was also displayed on the church door.

Game Laws had been enforced ever since the harsh forest laws imposed by William the Conqueror to safeguard his hunting grounds. They were burdensome and a legal hardship for the working classes who were even forbidden to kill rabbits and hares to supplement their poor diet. Gamekeepers and all those wishing to hunt had to pay a Game Duty. Their names were not displayed on the church doors but were listed in newspapers. In 1795 the names of people issued with game certificates in the North Riding covered a whole page of the York Herald whilst the West Riding names took up four columns. Those paying the tax came from all walks of life. In Selby in 1798 these included Charles Weddall, gentleman of Ousegate, John Aaron, captain, of Church Yard, John Coleman, common brewer of Church Hill, Joseph Smith, grocer of Market Place, George Bennett hatmaker, and Mark Fothergill, surgeon, both of Gowthorpe and James Shillitoe, Senior Chief Constable. Two clerks, George Alderson from Birkin and Samuel Bramley of Rawcliffe with a labourer from Cawood, were also issued with certificates. Gamekeepers were appointed but still needed their certificates. John Wharrie of Cawood was deputed by William, Lord Archbishop of York, for the manors of Cawood and Wistow. James Blanchard was chosen by George Thompson Esq. of Barlow to be gamekeeper for that area.

Advanced warnings of the payments of all these taxes appeared in the newspapers alongside the many complaints and comments concerning them. It is reported that in 1786 one copy of the York Courant newspaper was seen in Selby. It was bought by John Halliday, a shoe-maker on Ousegate who regularly read it out to all those who chose to gather at his shop to listen. In 1790, the York Herald and County Advertiser began publication. It soon had a wide circulation from Glasgow and Edinburgh in the north to London in the south. Seventeen were delivered to Cawood, 35 to Howden, Pontefract 30, Sherburn 11, Snaith 10 and 29 were bought in Selby. The publisher calculated that an average of ten people read each paper, therefore some 290 inhabitants of the town availed themselves of the opportunity to keep abreast with what was happening in Parliament, abroad or near at hand.

For instance, in 1798, on the front page of the paper reserved for notices, was this information:

> CAWOOD FAIR—*Those graziers and jobbers who purpose to attend Cawood Fair are desired to take notice that it will not be held on Whit Monday but on Friday, 10th May.*

Graziers looked after cattle going to the market and jobbers hired out horses. Notices of marriages, births and deaths began to appear in the newspapers but at first they were mingled in with the local news. Early ones included the announcement that Mr. Joseph Smith of Selby, a merchant, had married in Leeds, Miss Smith, also of Selby. The Rev. Thomas Allen, a curate, officiated at the marriage in Ryther on the 8th October 1799, of the Rev. Matthew Baker, a curate at Sherburn and Fenton, to Miss Gill of Low Lead. The death in May of that year of Mrs. Fothergill, wife of John Fothergill, surgeon in Selby, was also noted. The Christian names of the females were still being omitted!

Sports and Pastimes

The papers reported on the sports and pastimes enjoyed by people in the eighteenth and nineteenth centuries. The markets and fairs continued to be important for trading but also as sources of entertainment. In the eighteenth century market day was held on a Monday, as it is today; three fairs were held annually, at Easter, old St. Barnabas Day, 22nd. June (new, the 11th.) and old Michaelmas Day. There was also a Flax Fair every Thursday from Michaelmas to St. Peter's Day, old date. In Selby the markets were still held around a cross in the market place which had been a neglected crumbling heap of stones until 1775 when Lord Petre had it replaced. This cross stayed in its position in the market place until 1968 when it was moved to the park to save it from the corrosive effects of the internal combustion engine. By popular request it was reinstated in the market place in 1986 but with new stones at its base.

Various kinds of entertainments were offered at these events and on other occasions, many not acceptable in the twenty-first century. Located in the market place at Selby was a large stone block with a massive bull-ring attached to it. The butchers in those days were obliged to have a bull publicly baited by dogs before it could be slaughtered. This way the townspeople were made aware of the imminent sale of fresh meat and were provided with some free 'entertainment'. The condition of meat for sale was still closely supervised; it was the duty of the constables to burn *"refusal meat"*. Other sports enjoyed by all classes of society included bearbaiting and cock-fighting when small to very large sums of money were quickly won or lost in bets. The gentry held organised cock-fights attended by all classes of folk. One cock-pit in Selby was situated down an ancient lane leading from Micklegate to the corn mills and known as Spears Yard. A flight of stairs led down to a spacious pit made from bricks with sufficient accommodation around it for many spectators. From around the 1790s some schoolmasters supplemented their income by the holding of cock-fights. It is reported that as late as the 1850s when a private school was opened in Corunna House on Ousegate, a cock-pit was built within the roof of the house to accommodate the 'sporting gentlemen' of Selby. The oak pillars and struts in the garret of the school were said to be of the strength and design to withstand heavy weights.

On such holidays as Shrove Tuesday the local people put on their best clothes and gathered in the parkland which at that time stretched up to the walls of the Abbey Church. They indulged in the popular dancing games of the day including using their handkerchiefs to practise morris dancing. Other pastimes included quoits, skittles, shieing at oranges, wrestling and foot races. Any kind of racing was an excuse for more money to be lost or won. Various kinds of foot races and horse races took place on Selby Common, which was north-west of the town and covered 800 acres.

Archery was still being practised in the seventeenth century. Land known as Tyne Croft was being rented out for butts at five shillings a year in 1623, and the constables recorded being paid for a pair of butts. However, forty years later, a *"parcel of land called Butt Land formerly given for maintaining archery"* passed into the possession of Hugh Davis, a gentleman of Selby. The introduction of gunpowder into warfare gradually made compulsory archery practice unnecessary. It was taken up again however when it became looked upon as a fashionable and pleasing exercise for the upper classes. Sir Aston Lever with a few friends formed the first archery society in England. Ten years later this had grown to over thirty, including one named 'The Yorkshire Archers'. Their meetings became great social events full of pageantry and colour where sometimes the level of conviviality overshadowed the archery contest. Some ancient societies flourish today. The Yorkshire Archers is no more but the York Archers, formed in 1833 still exists. Selby has its own society formed in 1976 with the assistance of the archers from York and Harrogate. The club's home has always been in the Selby Rugby Club grounds based down Sandhill Lane, off Leeds Road. For a number of years it operated an indoor range in an old Nissen hut. In 1994/5 this was demolished and the members moved into a new brick indoor range believed to have the finest indoor facilities for archery in Northern England. The club also has access to an outdoor range, soley for archery up to a maximum distance of 100 yards. The club has produced many Regional and National champions at junior and senior levels and has amongst its members the present (2004) Lady and Gent Longbow Indoor National Champions – the third consecutive year the Championships have been won by Selby Archery Club members.

The Mail Bag Robbery

People in the eighteenth century had many ways of gathering news concerning matters outside their own environment. Notices of current events were read out at church or pinned to its door. Coachmen brought news from as far as London and the town criers yelled out the headlines; other matters were read in the newspapers or in letters brought by the post. This still came via Ferrybridge; it arrived every day around six in the morning and was taken out about five in the evening. Much concern was shown with regard to the safety and speedy delivery of the Royal Mail. Mail carriers were threatened with hard labour in the House of Correction if they interfered with the fast arrival of the mail through loitering or letting other people ride their horses. They were also urged to be *"very attentive to your arms, that they are clean, well-loaded and hung handy"* for many kinds of robbers roamed the countryside.

Despite these warnings, one evening in February 1798, a post-boy travelling to York with letters from Howden and Selby destined for York and London, was stopped on the road between Selby and Riccall by a footpad flourishing a gun. The robber was said to have been stoutly built with dark hair and wearing a drab coloured jacket over a cloth apron. From his appearance it was suspected that he was a flax dresser or rope-maker. After he had forced the carrier to unstrap his seven bags of mail the assailant let the boy gallop away unmolested. The Post Office immediately offered a reward for information about, or the capture of, the offender. They then placed a notice in the York Herald quoting a figure of two hundred pounds over and above that *"stated by an Act of Parliament for the apprehension of a highwayman"*. Despite the large reward offered the culprit was not caught.

There was a strong suspicion that Selby people had been involved in the robbery. These feelings later appeared justified when, in 1876, on Church Hill, an old pouch was found in a derelict house that was being demolished. Discovered amongst some old clothing in the roof, the bag was fairly well preserved and had on it the name 'Selby' and a medallion bearing the letters GR, representing the Crown monopoly of the postal service. It seems possible that the robber had had other accomplices hidden nearby who had helped him spirit away the bags of mail.

Transportation

If the culprit had been apprehended he would have been executed for robbing the mail. In 1775 a man convicted of robbing the Whitby post was executed at Tyburn near York. In the latter part of the eighteenth century over two hundred offences were punishable by death. Stephen Robinson of Barlby, a labourer, was sentenced to death in 1798 for taking from the common, a cow and a year old calf belonging to William Ambler. This was later commuted to transportation to Botany Bay, Australia. The transporting of convicts to Australia was a move by the government to help ease the overcrowding in the prisons and the derelict sailing ships, or hulks, used to accommodate the ever increasing number of convicted prisoners. It was also a way of gaining a foothold in the South Pacific.

Richard Newham of Burn, had his sentence of execution stayed. It seemed to be the custom for a judge to pass many sentences of death during the Sessions, then to reprieve a number of prisoners at the end, thus appearing to be merciful.

Richard Newham's father had been born at Dyon House, South Duffield the house referred to previously in the Inventories of people's possessions. On the 7th. March 1801, Newham was accused of stealing three sheep and two lambs, worth seven pounds, from Robert Blanchard of Belby, near Howden, for which he received the death sentence. This was then changed to transportation to New South Wales for fourteen years. On the 28th. May, he was transferred by coach from York Castle to a prison hulk named 'Captivity', moored at Gosport, near Portsmouth. Newham was confined in this derelict ship with 514 male prisoners and was lucky to survive the outbreaks of diseases such as typhus, dysentery and smallpox that raged through the hulks. He embarked on the convict transport ship, 'Glatton' on the 8th September 1802; it set sail from Spithead fifteen days later with 280 male and 130 female convicts. On the 13th March 1803 the ship arrived at Sydney Cove, Australia. Newham survived the treacherous journey but behind him in England he left a wife, Mary, and six children the last, named Richard, being born in 1801 whilst his father was in prison in York.

Newham was assigned to a settler named Thomas Habby for whom he must have worked hard and caused no trouble, for in 1806 he was awarded a ticket of leave. This meant he was free to work for himself. Seven years later he was granted a

Conditional Pardon by the Governor of the Colony, Lachlan Macquarie; the only, but heart breaking, restriction being he could not return to England! This condition was omitted in later years for other pardoned convicts.

Many transportees committed bigamy because as Newham's experience shows, the chances of anyone returning to England at that time were slim. In 1807 Newham married Mary Ann Burnett, who had been transported for seven years for stealing a variety of small articles including a cotton gown, a cloak and a candlestick. Over the next thirteen years the couple had seven children and their family went on to have a happy and settled life in Australia. One of the children, Thomas, born in 1815, has at the present day descendants living in England.

Miscreants who were not hanged or transported spent years in the hulks or existing in equally dreadful conditions in prisons. Snowden Dunhill, a notorious corn thief, who lived near Howden, was sentenced to seven years transportation for one of his crimes. He spent the time in the hulks, returning to Howden in 1819 to find the rest of his family had been transported! He soon joined them there.

Many prisoners from the Selby area who were not transported or hanged, were incarcerated in York Castle prison or the Wakefield House of Correction. There were, however, many other forms of punishment. Examples have already been given to show how some accused of theft were burnt in the hand or publicly whipped. Other law breakers were put in the stocks or fastened in the pillory where they were ridiculed and pelted with missiles. In Selby these two instruments of punishment were situated in the market place near to New Lane. In 1723 the town constables recorded that they put two men in the stocks and paid others to attend to them. The officers later supervised the removal and repairing of the stocks. Other primitive implements including a ducking stool, a scold's bridle, whips and scourges, were all stored in the south-west corner of the nave of the Abbey Church. A recorded instance of the ducking stool being used in the town was in 1671 when Jane Farrett, wife of a Selby shoemaker, was charged at the Wakefield Sessions with being a 'common scold', annoying and disturbing her neighbours and generally causing a breach of his Majesty's peace. It was therefore ordered that the *"said Jane Farrett for the said offence be openly ducked three times over head and ears by the constables of Selby"*. This was looked upon by the populace as a justifiable punishment for being a 'scold'. There would have been many spectators witnessing her plight. Indeed, in those days, the more the public were out of sympathy with the culprit the more missiles were thrown or money paid to the wielder of a whip to lay it on strongly! The constables' accounts for 1723 reveal they paid ten shillings to have three vagrants whipped and then for attending to them for two days and nights. It is possible these vagrants were able-bodied men travelling from parish to parish avoiding work, which was punishable by law.

Maps of the period show ponds of various sizes near to the market place, the largest being known as the Abbey Pond. The longest side of this pond ran north to south down where James Street lies today; it was about 208 feet in length, whilst at its widest it measured 140 feet. Most probably it served as a drainage pool for the surrounding area and would have been a watering place for cattle; not a salubrious place into which to be ducked.

The poor of the parish sometimes benefited from the punishments meted out to some offenders, especially those brought to justice by a society whose aims included enforcing observance of the Sabbath Day. The "Society for the Prevention and Discouragement of Vice and Profaneness" also wished to stamp out prostitution and drunkenness. Cawood seemed to receive a lot of attention from this group. It was reported in the York Herald in 1795 that they successfully had a farmer in Cawood fined two shillings for swearing a profane oath. Soon after this the haler (hailer) there was fined five shillings for using bad language on five occasions. Leonard Button, another haler, was convicted twice for similar offences. A third Cawood haler, Stephen Green, paid the court five shillings for carrying out his work on the Lord's Day, whilst William Cousan, a shoemaker, paid the same penalty for being found drunk on the Sabbath. In each case the Reverend Thomas Elgin, justice of the peace, ordered that the fines be given to the churchwardens to be used for the benefit of the poor.

The Constables

Joshua Tophass and Thomas Tomlin, constables of Selby in 1723, had many duties to carry out besides that of seeing to prisoners. They were responsible for paying out money to people with 'passes'. Out of the funds for that year the constables gave five guineas to *"shipwreck seamen and soldiers, widows and children and others who had passes for relief"*. They took money to the Barlby constable for the relief of women and children moving to that place. Passes and licences were often forged. Tophass and Tomlin noted expenses of £2.15s.0d. incurred when a 'sturdy' beggar, caught with a false pass, broke out of prison and needed guards to keep a watch on him overnight before horses were brought and the beggar escorted to the House of Correction. 'Sturdy' in those days meant a person who was fit to work. The false pass held by the culprit may have been one for relief, a licence to beg given by justices to those incapable of work, or a certificate allowing him to move out of his own parish. The constables recorded escorting one man, his wife and child to Justice Adams to get them a Vagrant Pass - this showed the man was unable to support his family.

The constables were also responsible for the burials of certain people, such as *"Soldier sick, then died and funeral costs...16s"*. Suspect deaths were more complicated. From the short notes in the accounts it appears that the body of Jonathan Gregory was found and taken into the house belonging to John Smith. Smith and Elizabeth Hembrough watched over the body for two days and nights whilst the constables went to Pontefract for the coroner and to Cawood to see if Gregory could be buried there. He appeared to have no relations and perhaps this was his last known abode. The coroner gave the constables warrants to be delivered in Brayton, Wistow and Cawood; whether these were for searches or arrests is not clear. The town crier was paid to spread the news of what was obviously looked upon as a suspicious death. An inquest took place and then the constables paid the expenses for a coffin, four men to carry it to church and the burial fees. The whole affair cost them thirty shillings.

The state of the town's pinfold was also their responsibility. This was the place where stray cattle were kept especially on market and fair days. The animals were looked after and fed by a man known as a pinder who exacted a fee from the owners before the cattle were returned. In 1726 three shillings were spent on mending Selby pinfold with a further eight pence for repairing its gate. An 1891 map of the town shows a pinfold down New Lane, almost opposite to St. Mark's Square. This pinfold has disappeared but a stone built one can still be seen in Hambleton, set back on the north side of the A63. In 1984 a brick pinfold at Barlby was refurbished as part of the Selby Community Project. It is situated on the west side of the main road through the village.

The constables' accounts also reveal that the Abbey well was still in use. In 1723 a new bucket, hoops and tackle were bought for this well. The bucket was renewed three years later but was soon in need of repair. It was also noted that iron work and timber were purchased for the town's pump. Like other towns and villages in the eighteenth century, Selby's buildings were mainly made of wood with thatched roofs so fires were a major hazard. It was essential to have easily accessible supplies of buckets and poles, another duty carried out by the constables. The expense of mending the fire buckets and poles (used for pulling down the thatch) was noted, also the hanging of them in several places, including at the church. Jonathan Baldby and William Otty must have been grateful for the constables' vigilance that year for both their houses caught fire. Money and drinks were given to the men who carried the water or assisted in other ways at both conflagrations.

Churchwardens

The first duty of these officials was to look after the fabric and running of the church. The upkeep of Selby Abbey church had been neglected for many years and in 1690 the central tower came crashing down destroying the south transept. It was not until 1702 that the churchwardens were able to organise the rebuilding of the tower. This was possible through the generosity of some Selby townspeople, members of the clergy and a number of the gentry. The Reverend G. Rishton, incumbent from 1701-1720, could not afford to give as generously as others for the living remained at ten pounds. Like others before him he could only supplement this with the rents from pews allotted to him. His position improved however, when the Archbishop of York was made aware of his plight and gave the vicar of Selby church the good living of Brayton, which was forty pounds. The churchwardens had to find more funds during the 1720s when work was carried out on the rebuilding of the south abutments. This required the purchase of such materials as bricks, tiles, timber and six bushels of 'hare'.

The churchwardens had many responsibilities besides those connected with the church. They helped travellers in distress, gave aid to destitute men with licences to beg, and assisted the overseers in many of their duties. They were also responsible for the 'Perambulation of the Bounds', a custom known to date back to the ninth century. During Ascension week the incumbent, his churchwardens and many parishioners walked along the boundaries of their parish. An account was kept of each walk signed by the churchwardens and the town clerk. There were no public buildings at that time so the town's business was carried out in the nave of the church or in rooms above the Abbey gateway.

Some accounts of the walks were more detailed than others, especially the one recorded in 1762 when a disagreement between the parishioners of Selby and those of Wistow brought the perambulation to a halt. The walk began on the 19th. May and proceeded as follows: *"From the church singing psalms all the way through Micklegate to Ousegate to ye Clough..."*. Part of the walk took them along the riverside where they stopped for a time opposite Turnham Hall to sing a psalm. East Common was traversed and a break taken near a bridge at Staynor Hall where the gentlemen were given ale by Mr. Shillitoe. Arriving at Carlton Lane everyone rested and partook of ale and bread. Later, Longmans Hill Lane was reached and then Brayton Lane. A psalm was sung as the walkers approached Brayton Church porch where they stopped to hear the Epistle and a gospel read and everyone repeatedly cried, *"God save the King and the Lady of the*

Manor". Other similar stops were made at the far end of Thorpe Lane, John Nutt's Close, near a stile, and then just within the gate at Gilliver's (or Gilliner's) chapel, where the readings took place under a nearby sycamore tree. The only other reference found concerning a chapel with a similar name was in an early eighteenth century inventory. Amongst the articles belonging to the late John Leadall, tanner, was listed, *"the lease of the Gillin chapel...£50. Stored in it wheat and rye unthreshed, hemp rated and unrated, load of hay"*. The stop near the chapel marked the end of the first day. Ale, bread and cakes were served there before the walkers returned to the church via Gowthorpe, singing psalms all the way.

On the second day the boundary walkers set off singing psalms, through Micklegate and Cow Lane until they reached New Crosshill. There they followed the lane leading to Thorpe Hall, crossing fields to reach the bridge that went over the Dam. After the usual pauses for readings, they reached the Outwoods where the perambulation came to a sudden stop. A guide stoop that had stood about 40 yards west of the Selby boundary, and the remains of an old oak tree that had served as a marker for many years, had disappeared! In an earlier account, dated 1736, the walkers had stopped to have a gospel read at the old oak tree roots before moving on to the furthest corner of Elfhole Farm, Wistow. In 1762 the angry walkers discovered the guide stoop, about 300 yards within Selby Outwoods, thereby enlarging the portion of the Common within the Wistow boundary. There was no sign of the old oak tree. A long dispute took place between the Selby and Wistow parishioners. It was finally resolved when the gentlemen present agreed to a new post being placed half-way between the old position and the one where the Wistow folk had placed the marker stoop.

Overseers of the Poor

Examples of the many duties carried out by the overseers are to be found in their account books. In 1722, John Lofthouse, overseer, paid seven shillings for three months lodgings for Jane Roses and gave Elizabeth Fenteman, nine shillings for the rent owed to Mr. Rocke. He saw to the expenses for burying the Tabbott's child, including the grave and the coffin. Seven years after this Richard Otty, overseer paid out £2.16s.6d. to enable Widow Pendrill and her daughter to go to London to bury her other female child. Efforts were made in some cases to redeem part of the costs. The funeral of Mary Potter's daughter cost fifteen shillings; the sale of her coat, petticoat and shoes realised five shillings for the overseer. It appeared from the accounts that the officials helped the families of transgressors. John Smith had committed some undefined crime in 1727. Joshua Robinson, overseer, recorded the expenses incurred by the family. These included going to Wakefield with regards to Smith's wife, court charges, buying the wife a bed-stead, spinning wheel, pot, bolster, pair of blankets and a coverlet. Also clothes for their child and 4½ yards of canvas for Mrs. Smith.

There were many examples of the overseers buying clothes, mainly for children, and instances of medical care. In 1724, John Howson recorded, *"mended a child's scald head and provided her with two aprons, handkerchiefs, and stockings"*. Howson paid 7s.6d. for the treatment. Jonathan Morley received ten shillings from the overseer when he 'cured' Daniel Fenteman of a broken thigh. The official later noted down the gift of two shillings given to Fenteman *"because he was lame"*. Many places at that time, even hospitals, refused to accept pregnant women because the new borne babe might become 'a burden on the parish'. Some parishioners in Selby received better treatment. Money was paid out to enable Mary Broomwell to be cared for when she 'lay in' for one month at Nick Spence's home. A midwife was provided and the baby christened. Widow Graetin had no-one to look after her when she was sick so was given just over three shillings. This money might have enabled her to hire someone like Sam Sharp's wife who looked after Alice Bealby for a month for ninepence a week.

Besides the improvements in education the eighteenth century saw a slow progress towards better conditions for the poor and an increase in medical knowledge. The poor still suffered many hardships, the most humiliating being that of being 'badged'. This practise began after the Settlement Act of 1697 which obliged paupers to wear a capital 'P' on their clothing.

> *Selby Overseers' accounts*
> *1725...Badges – 1s. Setting on..2s.8d.*
> *1727...To setting on badges..3d.*
> *1729...For badging the poor..3s.*

The order compelling the poor to wear on their tattered garments such a cruel insignia of their poverty and wretchedness was still in operation in some places as late as 1801.

Workhouses in Selby

The expenses incurred by the overseers was mostly covered by the poor rate collected from owners or occupiers of houses and lands in Selby. In 1730 there were 496 taxpayers in the town-a third of its inhabitants. In 1777 the Poor Law Returns for Selby were £262.11s.7d. out of which £245.18s.7d. was spent on the poor. The workhouse which held twenty people at that time, was given just over twenty three pounds.

It is not clear where this workhouse was situated for it was not until 1785 that a hundred pound legacy left by Mary Waud was used to build a workhouse on Gowthorpe. It was situated on the north side of the thoroughfare, opposite Audus Street, where, until 2004, Whiskers had long had their greengrocer's shop. The existing accounts for the earlier workhouse date back as far as 1741. The parish had been made responsible for its poor since the early sixteenth century and the Poor Law Act allowed overseers to erect poorhouses at the ratepayers' expense. In the early eighteenth century parishes were encouraged to build or rent workhouses; those that were too small to support one were allowed a union with others. The early accounts for Selby were entitled 'Charity House' or 'Workhouse' and seem to have been a combination of the two.

Food and clothes were the main items recorded in the accounts dated 1741 and 1746. The provisions listed included wheat, rye, oatmeal, beef, mutton, potatoes, turnips, cabbages, onions and pease. Plenty of salt, treacle and flower of brimstone were bought in and smaller amounts of butter, sugar, eggs, pepper, vinegar, ginger and oil. Some tobacco and quick silver were purchased for individuals and yeast for bread making. In 1741 Mary Grayson received a penny for baking bread, five years later John Bennet was given eight pennies for the same task. Grayson was also paid five pence for doing the washing. James Bradbury was paid a penny for mending children's shoes that cost tenpence a pair to buy. Joan Wood received fourpence for sweeping two chimneys and someone was paid a halfpenny for fetching water from the river. The food provided was plain and monotonous and was accompanied by small beer and alegar - sour ale. A barrel of beer from Joseph Otty cost one and a half pence; the salary of the Master of the Charity House was four shillings and tenpence.

Relief was also given to the deserving poor who did not live in the Charity House. In 1742 this 'outdoor relief' was recorded as £2.19s.4d. The overseers were obliged to provide work for those receiving indoor relief. Oakum or old tarry ropes, were bought in for the inmates of the Charity House at Selby to pick and untwist so the pieces could be sold to be used for caulking the seams of wooden ships. Some of the oakum came from York and Bubwith. Mr. Bacon of Selby was paid eighteen shillings for oakum and just over seven shillings for old rope. This must have been quite a load for the price of an order of three stones of old rope including the cost of porterage came to one shilling and sixpence.

This kind of work did not appear to have been carried out in the new workhouse built on Gowthorpe. In 1803 the total poor rate for Selby parish was £1,247.19s.4d. Half of it was spent on outdoor relief for 48 adults and 18 children. Sixty four pounds was used to care for the ten persons, including some children, in the workhouse. The total money spent on purchasing materials to provide work for the poor was nil, as was the total earned by the inmates towards their maintenance in the workhouse. The number of children in 'schools of industry' in Selby was also nil. This was at a time when knitting and spinning schools were being opened to help keep girls off the streets and away from unscrupulous employers. Ladies set out to educate the poorest girls, and at the same time, teach them useful occupations such as knitting, spinning and running a home. These schools were opened by 'self-help' friendly societies that began to blossom because of the widespread sympathy growing amongst ratepayers for the genuine poor. The schools were opened mainly in towns where the need was greatest but self-help groups were also increasing in parishes like Selby which in 1803 had five friendly societies in the area with a total of 350 members. Subscription fees enabled the poorer members to receive money and care when they were sick and assistance even when they reached adulthood.

Apprenticeships

The churchwardens and the overseers were responsible for using the poor rate money wisely and for finding work for the children who survived long enough to become apprentices. The length of apprenticeships usually varied from three to seven years and were welcomed by the overseers as they relieved them of responsibility for the children. They, however, gave the children opportunities not otherwise found by the poor. One townsman who had taken on an apprentice from the workhouse remembered him in his will. *"To Henry Scholay, a poor boy, which was put as town's prentice to me – 10 shillings"*. William Stainley, a mariner of Selby entered into an indenture of apprenticeship between the officials at Pontefract and a poor child of that place, Joseph Bulmer. The boy was to be put out to sea service for seven years to the said William Stanley, to learn the business of a mariner. Premiums had to be paid by some to their masters, also the cost of the formal agreements. In 1741 the latter cost the workhouse one shilling and sixpence.

One apprentice, not from the workhouse, was willed his premium. Richard Wayde, a tanner, left William Robinson, his brother-in-law's son, the sum of eight pounds. Half was for clothes and to put the boy to a trade and half for when he reached the age of twentyone. Another townsman, Richard Hutchinson, stated in his will that he turned over to his son, Samuel, his apprentice, William Barley, to finish off his apprenticeship. Also, if he served his son well for the term of nine years, Barley was to be found clothes fit for a servant, an ordinary suit and ten shillings as his 'way gate' (end of service). Samuel Hutchinson, who was the ship's master of his father's keel was also to allow Barley to take four boules (8 bushels) of salt for trading purposes on each voyage he undertook as an apprentice.

The French Revolutionary and Napoleonic Wars – the Militias

There were many overseas conflicts during the reigns of the three Georges as countries changed their allegiances and trade became more competitive. George III was on the throne when Britain tried to assert power over its North American colonies. World-wide conflicts developed during the years 1775 to 1783, at the end of which America won its independence. Ten years later, after executing Louis XVI and becoming a republic, the French declared war on Britain. The French Revolutionary and Napoleonic Wars that followed continued until the Battle of Waterloo in 1815.

As relations with the newly established French Republic deteriorated and its leaders showed they were on an expansionist course, the king and government in Britain realised the need for a strong army and navy. The New Model Army of 80,000 men formed in 1645 under the control of Cromwell had been the first effective British land force. After the Restoration drastic cuts reduced this to five hundred men. Known as the Royal Bodyguard the numbers were increased before the death of Charles II but it was not until William III's reign (1689-1702) that a Bill of Rights put the army on the same legal footing that is still maintained today. The strength of the army varied according to hostilities. Before France declared war on Britain in February 1793 it numbered around 17,000, but then serious enlistment began and continued throughout the long wars.

The main army was sent abroad to fight the enemy so a second body of men was needed to protect the nation against a possible invasion. This was the militia. There had been riots and disturbances when the first militia acts of 1757 empowered the government to conscript all males of military age for three years service to ensure they received some training. During the earlier part of the century only propertied individuals had to provide and equip infantry men, but the new acts included all males between 18 and 50 years of age, with a few exceptions. The riots were especially fierce in Lincolnshire and Howdenshire. It is recorded in the calendar of York Assizes for the 13th. March 1758, that Richard Johnson, labourer of Howden, John Purden of Bubwith and Paul Watkins, tailor of Gilberdyke, were amongst many from around Howden who were charged with being part of a mob, armed with clubs and other dangerous weapons, that threatened the Constables. They were accused of forcing them to hand over money and, more importantly, the lists of the persons liable to serve in the Militia, therefore treasonably opposing the execution of the Militia Acts. Richard Johnson was indicted for High Treason and confined to the prison until the next assizes where he was acquitted. The others, found guilty of rioting were imprisoned for two months or until they could pay a fine of one shilling each. Similar disturbances broke out from time to time when further acts were passed during the French wars. The people of Selby no longer had the barons demanding their attendance at a muster, now it was the church wardens and other town officials who listed their names as men suitable for embodiment in the militia or to fill the quota demanded for the Navy. Act upon Act was passed by the government ordering the enrolment of men in the Militia, the Local Militia, the Supplementary

Militia and other fighting forces.

In November 1796 the Lieutenancy acting for the City of York, the County, and St. Peter's Liberty, met to consider lists of persons believed eligible to serve in the Supplementary Militia. After many hours of listening to appeals it was decided for example, that out of the 83 persons liable to serve in Tadcaster and the six in Oxton, eight were to be chosen from them by ballot. Those whose names came up for Tadcaster were Peter Dodgeson farmer, W. Scott and George Stelling innkeepers, George Cartwright labourer, William Hesslewood jun. cordwainer, Thomas Daniel basketmaker, and Thomas Shelburn, sawyer. Oxton asked to be treated separately and the unlucky one there was a labourer named George Holmbler. All other places were treated in the same manner.

Two years later men were summoned to attend a muster in their area *"for the purpose of a ballot to see who was to be embodied as His Majesty hath by His Warrant directed"*. Anyone not attending these musters was deemed a deserter. All who went to the musters took shirts, stockings and other necessities with them for as they were directed, *"It could not be known to whose lot it would fall to be embodied"*. Those who were not chosen were discharged from further attendance and given one shilling for every day they had been forced to be away from home. Those ordered to attend from the Selby area joined the Ouse and Derwent muster at Kexby. Men did fail to turn up at these meetings. In 1798 they included Sheircliff Smith, saddler from Pontefract, George Dawson, staymaker of York, and William Appleton, carrier of Selby. They were summoned to attend at the Common Hall in Beverley, to explain why twenty pounds should not be levied upon them. They were afterwards informed that no exemption from duty would be allowed.

Once the men were embodied there were many cases of desertion. Descriptions of some, or the capture of others, appeared in the newspapers. In July, 1793, the 'Leeds Intelligencer' reported; "Run away of Saturday last, from their master's service at Selby, George Harrison, born at Royston, near Wakefield; he is about 17, slender made, about five foot three inches high, yellow complexion and had light brown hair..." He was one of three runaway boys apprenticed to sea service, all dressed as sailors. Selby constable, Mr Edward Wilkinson, for their apprehension, offered a very handsome reward. In January 1794, as a party of the Inniskilling regiment of dragoons were conducting several deserters between Ferrybridge and Pontefract, one of them slipped off his hand-cuffs and escaped. Another in making a similar attempt was shot at by the corporal of the party and a bullet lodged in the back part of his thigh. This prisoner was then secured, and in what must have been a painful condition walked to Doncaster the following day.

As the war progressed numerous towns and villages formed their own volunteer corps to protect their area in case of an invasion. The approval of the Lord Lieutenant of the county was needed and an undertaking given that the men would be regularly trained. These corps served without pay and supplied their own arms and uniforms but were, at first, exempt from the ballot. They relied on subscriptions and the generosity of their commanders. York, Howden and Selby were assembly points for the West Riding volunteers. Howden Volunteer Infantry, under Captain J. Scholfield, was formed in 1798 and disbanded in 1801. Many groups folded when the government made it compulsory that anyone wishing to remain in the corps had to pay to be excused the ballot.

Selby Rifle Volunteers

The Volunteer Infantry raised in Selby in 1794 were, like many other groups, the forerunners of the present Territorials. Led by Major Foster, they drilled in the nave of the Abbey Church, most usually after a service, and stored their arms and ammunition in a chamber over the north porch.

A second volunteer corps was raised in Selby in November 1860. William Liversidge (1827-1918) a generous benefactor of both Selby Abbey Church and the town, became involved in the National Volunteer Movement in 1862. He assisted in the forming of the Selby Rifle Volunteers which soon had a membership of over a hundred. Liversidge became one of their leaders, a great agitator, he pressed for suitable premises for the corps. This resulted in Lord Londesborough providing a site for them. The drill hall and armoury opened by the lord of the manor in 1865 still stands today at the corner of Armoury Road, near to Brayton Railway Crossing. At this present time the building is being used as a tile warehouse. Liversidge further helped the corps by providing fifty of the uniforms needed by the volunteers.

The Selby Rifle Volunteer Corps marched to York for their regular inspections and on their return to Selby were greeted by crowds of spectators waiting to watch their progress through Ousegate, Water Lane and Wide Street on their way to the Town Hall on Gowthorpe. The Corps also paraded on 'Gala Days', through streets festooned with flags, their progress heralded by the sounds of a bugle. In the evenings crowds gathered outside the Londesborough Hotel to listen to the Volunteers' band as they played selections from various operas. However, as soon as the programme changed to a medley of dance music a space was cleared near the church railings and people performed stately quadrilles before changing to the more energetic polkas and old-time waltzes. A sight surely not to be missed on a warm summer evening!

The Selby Volunteer Infantry also found time for dancing. In June 1804, Major Foster and his officers, entertained the principal inhabitants of the town and neighbourhood of Malton to a ball and supper. The corps who had been doing their obligatory duty of twenty-one days in the area had arrived at Malton a few days before and were resuming their march to Selby two days after the ball. It was said that the well-regulated conduct of the privates, their attention to discipline, respect to their officers and steadiness under arms could not be surpassed by any of *"our Brave Volunteer Defenders"*.

There were several occasions during the fighting when the British people believed an invasion was imminent. In 1804, in readiness for such an event, those in charge of the West Riding defences split their volunteer and trained forces into three divisions. This was to enable them, if needed, to take three different routes to the East Coast. The northern division was to be centred at York, the southern at Airmyn and the centre, that was the wapentakes of Skyrac, Abrigg, Morley and Barkston Ash, at Selby. Boat bridges were to be constructed over the water at Barmby and Loftsome ferries. The cavalry when gathered in the town would then cross the Derwent at Loftsome then move onto Howden; the infantry would go via the boat bridge at Barmby with boats and rafts available at Hooke and Booth ferries for the southern division. Wagons were to be provided to run backwards and forwards carrying groups of soldiers over 12 mile stages until all the troops reached the coast.

Beacons set up on various high points were another defence against the French. The pitch, which had quickly replaced wood because it was easier to control, produced flames at night and smoke during the day. Twenty-five were ordered to be erected in the West Riding including ones at Brimham Craggs, Otley Chevin, Seacroft Moor Top and Brayton Barff.

Because of its strategic importance as an inland port Selby was also used as a depot for food and stores. The York Herald reported in 1804 that large quantities of biscuits were being shipped at Hull for depots of provisions being established in York and Selby.

The people of Selby and the surrounding district besides giving up their men to fight the French, also gave generously to various funds for the defence of the country and for the widows, wives and children of those wounded or killed. The assessment of some subscribers' taxes affected their generosity. Lists of donations printed in the newspapers revealed that Jocelyn Price Esq. of Camblesforth contributed fifty pounds but added another one hundred and fifty *"for his new assessed taxes"*. Other contributions included twenty pounds from Lord Carlisle's servants at Castle Howard, a guinea from Mr. T. Harwood of Gowdall and nine guineas from the parish of Cawood.

The Navy

Besides providing lists for the ballots and paying out bounties to encourage men to join the militia, the town officials had also to find volunteers for the navy. In the 1790s they made returns of such men enrolled at the petty sessions and the bounty agreed there. Churchwardens and overseers of the poor were subject to a fine if they did not raise the quota for their area as agreed upon by the navy.

The origins of the Royal Navy can be traced back to the ninth century when Alfred the Great formed a fleet to defend the country against Danish invasions. The navy, like the army, had to use various methods of recruitment. To fill the King's ships it resorted to the ancient custom of impressment. All eligible men of sea-faring habits between the ages of 18 and 45 could be pressed into service without notice. This rule was frequently violated and landsmen found themselves scooped up by ruthless press-gangs as they strove to man the ships of the Royal Navy.

No evidence has been found of press-gangs coming to Selby but they were certainly very active in Hull and even York. It is likely that many sailors heading for the inland port never got further than the coast or were even taken from their ships when still out at sea. Much misery was caused by this method of recruiting. The actions of press-gangs who entered people's homes, their places of work and entertainment in their search for victims, must have been known in Selby for a new society in the town protested against them. One of their rules stated, *"If any member of this society engage in the impress service or slave trade he shall be immediately excluded from all benefit from the society forever"*.

Formed in March 1792 it was known as the 'Duke of Clarence's Loyal Society', named after George III's third son, William Henry. He was a sailor and known to be very sympathetic towards the welfare of ordinary seamen. The society in Selby worked hard for the betterment of sailors' lives. In his book, *"History of Selby and Cawood"*, James Mountain lists twenty four leading townspeople involved in shipping in 1800. The first members of the society included three mariners, John Tate and William Altham from Wistow and David Aubore of Selby. Others from the town were Charles Hopkins hatter, Henry Savage and William Fielder cordwainers, William Emerson cabinet maker, William Pallister painter, Edward Sefton watch maker, Joseph Cheetham farmer, John

Woodcock schoolmaster and George Harris, a foundry worker. The first meetings were held at the Royal Oak, a public house on Church Lane, the home of their president, Charles Hopkins. He was a versatile man who later closed his tavern and instead, sold toys from the premises. Hopkins was also in great demand at local balls and entertainments for he was skilled in the playing of the violin and the pipe and tabor (drum).

Two years after its foundation Henry Savage became president. He also did more than one job for in the evenings he went around the streets of Selby selling milk. He carried the milk in two large tins slung on the sides of an ass. Other presidents included the farmer, Joseph Cheetham and Richard Precious, a mariner. The latter took over the Black-a-Moor Inn down Finkle Street which became the new venue for meetings. Isaac Butler, master of the Blue Coat School in the town was a member of the group and served it for thirty years. The Bay Horse in Micklegate was another venue for the society. This, and the Black-a-Moor are still functioning as public houses to this day. It is not clear when the society ceased to exist but it is reported they did have an annual dinner, described as 'a feast on a liberal scale' as late as 1866, where the president, Mr. John Shaw, was presented with a superb tea and coffee set, a gift from the members.

End of the Wars

The whole country suffered during the long French wars. Many menfolk were either fighting abroad, (more dying of yellow fever in the West Indies, than from battle wounds), or they were at sea seeking out the French fleets. The poorer people at home were slowly starving whilst the militias and the navy conscripted increasing numbers of their husbands, fathers and sons. The wars seemed endless, but in 1812, the tide turned. After his retreat from Moscow Napoleon no longer seemed invincible. An allied invasion of France the following year led to his defeat at Arcis-sur-Aube; Paris was entered on the 31st. March, 1814. Napoleon was banished to Elba. News of the signing of the Treaty of Peace reached York by coach on the 3rd. June.

The nation celebrated; all over the country there were illuminations, bonfires, feasts and dancing. On the 11th. June forthcoming activities in Selby were described in a notice on the front page of the York Herald. Many of the inhabitants of the town and neighbourhood had agreed to meet and dine at Mr. John Tomlinson's, the Sign of the Ship Inn, Water Lane. Before that event they were requested to do their best to raise subscriptions for the purchase of two fat oxen. One to be roasted whole in the street, the other to be cut up raw, and both to be distributed, with ale and bread amongst the inhabitants of the town. This was to enable everyone, but particularly the unfortunate prisoners of war, who had returned to their families after many years of confinement, to *"rejoice at a deliverance as unexpected as it hath been glorious"*.

The organisers put the following details in the paper to give their actions full publicity and avoid any misinterpretation. There was to be a dinner, dessert, malt liquor and wine, on the fifteenth instant, at a cost of l0s.6d. each. All parties were requested to join them in the undertaking of an act of benevolence and kindness. They most particularly wished to prohibit the firing of all pistols, guns, crackers and squibs at the celebrations as it was the determination of the peace officers to punish offenders with rigour. This was because it was the intention to amuse the public by the firing of great guns at intervals throughout that day. As the fifteenth was the day fixed by the majority of parishioners to commemorate the peace, it was desirous it be set aside for pleasure and rejoicing. The organisers did not wish to force this upon everyone but made it known they would feel much satisfaction if the inhabitants agreed by giving a holiday to their workmen, apprentices, servants and others. It was planned to illuminate as many houses as possible in the evening but left the choice of whether to follow suit to the individual. The organisers begged however, that there would be no disturbances to spoil such a joyous occasion. This last request was made because there had been much controversy on other occasions where illuminations had been used. Many protested that the money would have been better spent being given to the various funds for the wives, widows and children of those killed or wounded in the wars.

This in fact was not the end of the fighting but when peace finally arrived following the recapture of Napoleon after the Battle of Waterloo, the celebrations were much more muted.

A Prisoner of War

Thomas Giles was one of the prisoners who returned home at the end of the wars. He wrote of his experiences in what looks like a home-made exercise book which still survives today. This book also contains beautifully coloured fine drawings of Arras and Besancon where he was imprisoned. It is believed that Giles was from the Selby area for his diary turned up at Read School, Drax, where it has been carefully stored ever since.

He was serving on the Royal Navy frigate, 'Blanche' when it ran aground on a reef off Ushant, France, in 1807. It was a very dark and bitterly cold night, the sea was high and any boats launched were immediately overturned and many lives lost. The ship gradually broke up but somehow Giles and other members of the crew managed to struggle ashore. Inhabitants of the nearby houses appeared. They did not come to help but to abuse the men and rob them of what little they possessed. Giles records that sixty sailors died of sickness and exposure and the rest were herded together and marched to Ploughereau. From there the lower ranks were then forced to march to Arras prison camp. Giles kept careful notes of his time there and in other places, along with the distances he travelled in France.

Corrupt officials in the camps exploited the provisions Napoleon had promised to British prisoners. One butcher gave them three ounces of beef instead of their daily allowance of eight ounces, serving it with salt as black as soot and maggot-ridden broad beans. There was little in the way of clothing but if a prisoner was found trying to sell his he was put into the town jail for two years. The bedding provided was atrocious, the little straw they had was filthy and their covers were worn out blankets, cast-offs from the French army. The Continental prisoners fared even worse than the British; Giles, with others, took part in many dangerous attempts to feed these poor, starved and cruelly treated men. Things improved during the times more compassionate prison commanders were in charge.

Thomas Giles was 43 when his discharge papers were signed in June 1814, the month in which Selby inhabitants were planning their celebrations. His repatriation has been traced across France to London but then the trail peters out. It is believed that he came back to the Selby district at some time as his diary was found in Drax. When in France the prisoners received gifts of money from Britain. In 1808 Giles recorded in his journal that his group received the *"welcome sum of twenty-one pounds from the benevolent townsmen of Selby"*.

Smithson Tennant

Down Flaxley Road Selby, alongside the streets named after Thomas Johnson, the famous herbalist and Sir Jonathan Hutchinson, the medical man who gave the town its museum, is Tennant Street. It is so named in honour of a man whose brilliant scientific career ended abruptly in 1815, the year the Battle of Waterloo finally brought peace.

Smithson Tennant was born in the town in November, 1761. His father was the Reverend Calvert Tennant who was a curate at Castleford for a time, whilst his mother was the daughter of William Daunt an apothecary of Selby. Tennant went to grammar schools at Scorton, Tadcaster and Beverley where he soon showed an aptitude for chemistry. His earliest recorded experiment was when aged nine, he made some gunpowder for fireworks, from instructions in a book. Sadly by the year 1781 he had lost both his parents but though his education was neglected for a time he eventually continued his studies, going first to Edinburgh then Cambridge University. His fellow students at Cambridge described him as a happy-go-lucky fellow.

Tennant devoted himself to chemical research. In 1804 he received the Copley Medal from the Royal Society for discovering two new platinum group metals, iridium and osmium. His discovery of the densest metal, osmium, gained Tennant a place in the twentieth century 'Guinness Book of Records'. He carried out agricultural experiments and published a paper on the different kinds of lime used in farming. A partnership with W.H.Wollaston brought them both fame and fortune.

Tennant had always suffered from poor health which dogged his career. He had taken up horse riding to help improve it but never became a good horseman. Tennant often remarked to his friends that a fall from a horse would cause his downfall. Tragically this proved to be true. On the 22nd February 1815, Tennant was on holiday in Boulogne. Unable to sail from there because of strong winds he went for a ride along the sands with Baron Bulow to visit a memorial to Napoleon Bonaparte. Wishing to inspect a small fort they began to cross a fragile bridge. Unfortunately, because somebody had stolen the bolt which secured the bridge, it collapsed under their weight and they were flung into the ditch. Baron Bulow survived the accident but Smithson Tennant, the analytical chemist with a promising future, died later from a fractured skull in Boulogne Hospital.

CHAPTER 9

THE NINETEENTH CENTURY

The Monarchy

During the reign of George III, the monarch was suffering from the debilitating effects of an illness that has since been diagnosed as porphyria, a kidney disorder. His incapacity to rule resulted in his eldest son being made Prince Regent in 1811. Around this time James Watson and his father, both from Selby, became involved in important political events. James had been born in one of the old houses on Middle Row (Shambles) which were demolished in 1812 when John Audus had his fine houses built on the south side of the market place. Both father and son were indicted for high treason in 1817 for taking an active part with others in agitating for political and social reform. A brilliant counsel gained an acquittal for them all including their leader, Arthur Thistlewood. However, three years later many of them were in court again accused of inciting rebellion against the king, destroying property and conspiring to kill members of the Privy Council.

Known as the Cato Street Conspiracy, their plan was to murder the Cabinet ministers gathered at a dinner in Lord Harrowby's house, but they were betrayed. Their hideaway in Cato Street was invaded and thirty men found inside, surrounded by all kinds of weapons and ammunition. It is not known whether James Watson escaped from the fierce struggle that followed, but he was not amongst the five transported to Australia nor was he one of the four who, with Arthur Thistlewood, were later publicly hanged and beheaded at Newgate gallows.

George IV, selfish and vain, succeeded his father in 1820 and ruled for ten years. He was followed on the throne by his brother, William IV (1830-37). William made no impression as a king but during his reign slavery was finally abolished by law. The king died without a legitimate male heir so the crown passed to his niece, Victoria (1837-1901). Before the end of her reign this queen ruled over one quarter of the globe.

Enclosures

The development of more complex transport networks during the reigns of these rulers allowed Selby, along with some other market towns in the Vale of York, to grow rapidly, enjoying good land and water communications with larger towns. During the thirty years that followed the first national census in 1801, the population of the town grew from 2,861 to 4,600. From the 1850s it stayed around the 5,000 mark as the rate of growth of population slowed down.

Farming remained an important occupation around Selby. The industrial towns needed increasing quantities of materials and food for their workers. An 'agricultural revolution' took place alongside the 'industrial revolution'. New methods were adopted for growing crops which were difficult to follow using the traditional, long narrow strips in the common fields which had to go. An area of 400 acres which included Abbey Park and Stainer Hall Farm, was occupied by two hundred tenants. Large farms each managed by one owner took the place of smallholdings. Extensive areas, including common pastures and wastes were enclosed, the latter being drained and improved to make good, arable land. During the second half of the eighteenth century over 1,500 private enclosure acts were passed nationally, but a general enclosure act in 1801 cut down the expense and quickened the process. This resulted in the loss to tenants of the rights they had enjoyed on common lands such as free pasture, which was of great importance to the poor, many living at subsistence level. It has been estimated that within a century 5.9 million acres in England and Wales were enclosed by 4,000 Acts of Parliament.

In 1797 an Act was passed for the enclosing of the commons and waste ground in Selby parish. This included the Common covering 800 acres on the west side of town where the summer races had always been held and where people had grazed their animals for generations. Under the Act every freeholder, owner of a messuage or dwelling house, was entitled to a common-right, valued at 28s. a year. This was usually paid in kind, that is, an average of two acres of land, value £20, was given for each common right. Many of the poor or unskilled inhabitants sold their land to richer neighbours. The Act abolished the paying of tithes to the lord of the manor. Lord Petre was allotted just over 90 acres of land in compensation.

The people bitterly regretted the loss of the common lands with their abundance of birds, animals and fish. Their desires were ignored as more and more enclosure acts were passed. In 1799 it was reported in the *'York Herald'* that a *'Meeting of the Proprietors within the several manors and townships of Brayton, Thorpe Willoughby, Burton and Gateforth with Lund'*, was to be held at the George Inn, Selby on the 17th. April. The purpose of the meeting was to read over and sign a Consent Bill to be taken to Parliament. The Bill was for the dividing and enclosing of the common fields, commons and waste ground within the manor, and for making compensation for the tithes there. A second meeting was held in July at the house of John Robinson, inn-keeper in Brayton, in order to carry out a perambulation of the boundaries of the manors. Claims from owners of common rights were dealt with at a later date.

The numbers of labourers working on the farms in the Selby district in 1861 were 1,118 males and 98 females and 12 bailiffs. Farm servants working indoors numbered 185 males and 46 females. Amongst other occupations of the people of Selby, the highest numbers were labourers 233, females as general domestic servants 189, dressmakers 161, shoe or boot makers 149, followed by tailors 90, carpenters 80 and 68 seamen.

Trade and Transport – River Ouse

The woollen industry in Yorkshire was growing so rapidly the manufacturers needed better access to their markets. Many towns had no water transport within easy reach and land carriage was both expensive and dangerous. Wakefield clothiers complained they had to send their goods to Rawcliffe on the Aire which was 22 miles away by road. Sometimes everything was held up there for at least two months because the weather had made the roads impassable, causing carriages to overturn and their wares to be damaged or ruined. The cheapest form of transport was by water and many schemes were put forward to try to improve the waterways.

The upkeep of the Ouse had been the responsibility of York Corporation for around three hundred years. Surveying and dredging operations appeared to have been underway as early as the fifteenth century. In the York House Book kept in the City Archives it is recorded that a barge was provided in 1478 *"for to search the rivers"*. The ebb and flow of the tidal water which was sometimes beneficial to the captains of boats, eroded the soft, crumbling banks and resulted in a great silting up of the river.

In the seventeenth century York's interest lay in improving its own access to the sea via the Ouse. For some time ships had been getting bigger until a typical sea-going vessel was too large to reach York and the city was rapidly losing its port status to Hull. It took positive action in 1699 by requesting Sir William Robinson and Mr. Jenkins, the MP for the city, to send an engineer with all speed to 'view' the river Ouse with the aim of making it more navigable. Thomas Surbey, John Atty and Benedict Horsley were employed to carry out the actual survey. A boat was provided for them with two watermen to row it, a Master to sound the water for shoals and shallow ground, and a boy to attend to their needs.

The party set out on the 5th. May and at the end of the day had arrived at Cawood where they lodged for the night. The next morning after rowing against the tide they reached Selby at 9:30am and stayed there to dine. After sounding around Selby they recorded, *"Against Selby Ferry is a shoall about 5 feet under low water and here the tyde rises about 9 feet according to ye best account of ye ablest Masters of Ships and Others that we could talk with"*. They also noted that high water at Selby was around 11 o' clock and marked the presence of an island off Howdendyke not shown on Surbey's charts. This may give a rough date for the formation of Swan Island. On reaching Howden the boat was tied up; the Sabbath Day was observed and everyone spent the night on land. The next morning they discovered the boat had broken loose from its moorings which seemed to confirm the presence of spring tides or possibly an eagre.

On the return journey the party revisited Howden, leaving it on the 10th. May. When they arrived at Selby about one o'clock the crew assured the surveyors they could not row on to Cawood, *"thither this tyde"*. Therefore everyone went ashore to dine in the town, but the surveyors later walked overland to Cawood leaving the crew to row the boat there when conditions made it possible. On the 14th. May they were back in York ready to dine with the Lord Mayor and give him their report.

The chart, drawn by Thomas Surbey, is in York City Archives, (Accession 65). It shows Surbey was a surveyor of considerable skill, the quality of his work being unsurpassed for almost two hundred years. In their recommendations accompanying the chart, the surveyors stated that it was possible, either by deepening the river or by locks, to gain seven feet of water for half the price of clearing the shoals. They detailed the dimensions of a proposed cut through Naburn Ings to make the Ouse navigable for a ship of seven feet draught and drew details of a lock and a dam across the river. The first mention of a lock in operation at Naburn was in 1757. It was replaced in 1888 with a larger one having a depth of 13 feet 6 inches, the work being carried out by the Corporation in their continuing efforts to attract coastal trade to York.

Thomas Surbey surveyed many waterways. He added interesting comments to his notes as he travelled around the country:

27th. May Ferrybridge..then lodged at Bauterie. My hors was hobled with ye grypes. This town is remarkable for exporting Lead, Millstones and timber.

*29th. Nottingham. Saw them make fine glass ware for Drinking &
Earthern Mugs Beacons and Teapots. Here are but few marks of antiquity as to
Robin Hood but Sume prtest to Call a well (about a mile northwards) after his
name.*

Derby..Carpenters here paid 18d. to 12d. a day.

The Aire and Calder

Whilst York was trying to improve the navigation of the Ouse, there were
moves in other quarters to do the same on the Aire and Calder rivers. In 1698 a bill was
presented to Parliament to make these rivers navigable. As the bill was being prepared
York Corporation did everything it could to influence the outcome in their favour. In the
York City Archives Chamberlain Accounts (cc14f51a) it is recorded: *"11th February
1697 Ordered that what money is disburst upon account of petitioning that the Rivers
Aire and Calder be not made navigable may be reimbursed att the City's Charge".* The
following May, Alderman Thompson was sent fifty pounds to cover what he had used in
his "soliciting" about the two rivers. As a survey was being carried out in 1698, York
vied with the promoters of the Bill in their favours to the appointed surveyors, John
Clements, warden of Trinity House, and John Bromwell. The city accounts showed that
Jubb, a wine merchant, had been given almost four pounds for "treating" the people
surveying the rivers. Alderman Shackleton received ten pounds for his efforts. The Bill's
promoters countered this by entertaining the gentlemen from Trinity House at various
places along the banks such as Howden, Airmyn, Rawcliffe and Ferrybridge. Even so
they did not spend a tenth of that poured out by York to stop the Bill. The city's
generosity was all in vain for though the first Bill did not get through, the second
received Royal Assent in May 1699.

The proprietors of the Aire and Calder Navigation Company were given control
over the rivers from Leeds and Wakefield to the confluence at Castleford then down to
Weeland, (across the river Aire from Hirst Courtney). To ease the passage of vessels
they were allowed to clean and enlarge the waterways, strengthen courses and make cuts
through adjacent land, and make towing paths. They were also given the power to pull
down corn, fulling and rape mills and weirs that obstructed the passage of the ships. The
owners of many mills along the river Calder had opposed the navigation as they believed
it would stop their mills working whilst those in favour believed the improper drawing
off of water by the owners was a serious impediment because of reduced water levels.

When goods had been carried by packhorse and wagon, Selby had been the
nearest port on the river Ouse. Merchandise arriving there was loaded onto boats to be
taken up to York or down to Hull. After 1704, however, goods were transported down
the Aire and Calder navigation to the little hamlet of Airmyn situated near the
confluence of the Aire and Ouse. Airmyn prospered for seventy years as most of the
goods going to and from Yorkshire, and further afield, used the navigation. The owners
leased out the waterway tolls for an annual rent. In the first year the rent from these tolls
was £800; by 1774 it had risen to £8,500. The Aire and Calder Navigation profited to the
detriment of Selby. Trade increased as the manufacturing towns in Yorkshire,
Lancashire and Lincolnshire flourished but so did the complaints concerning parts of the
waterways. The chief grievance of the carriers was the lower, unimproved course of the
Aire, especially between the village of Weeland and Haddlesey locks. Hours were

wasted waiting for tides whilst navigation problems caused delays sometimes lasting up to a week.

Selby Canals

John Smeaton, an eminent engineer and builder of the Eddystone Lighthouse, was invited by the company to survey the waterways. He reported that the open river below Haddlesey lock was full of shoals and a vast amount of work would be needed to improve that stretch. Smeaton recommended the making of several new cuts to avoid the more difficult stretches. This suggestion met with a lot of opposition from landowners and failed to gain permission from Parliament. The proprietors' troubles were exacerbated by the knowledge that the Leeds and Liverpool Canal Company, encouraged by many merchants, was putting forward a plan for a canal from Leeds direct to Selby. This would have brought a swift end to the Aire and Calder Navigation's spiralling profits, but whilst they launched a vigorous opposition to the new venture, Smeaton evolved a new plan for them - a canal from Haddlesey to Selby which would bypass the tidal Aire!

Supporters of the Leeds to Selby project were overconfident and wasted valuable time, allowing the Haddlesey Canal Bill to be put forward along with theirs in 1774. The petitioners had been so certain Parliament would favour the Leeds canal even famous mapmakers of the time included the canal on their maps. Thomas Jeffreys detailed it on his map of the County of York, published in 1775 and John Carey had it drawn on a map of Yorkshire that came out in 1787. The route was surveyed by James Brindley, the engineer for the Duke of Bridgewater's canals and was favoured by many Yorkshire towns. The proposed canal was to go from Leeds to Methley where four river crossings were planned, with six land arches on a long aqueduct. From there it continued to Fairburn and the Great North Road, where a four hundred yard tunnel was to be constructed. It then went to the south of Hillam, crossed Hambleton Dyke to pass north of Hambleton and Thorpe Willoughby, before entering Selby to meet the Ouse at Holmes Lane, where, today, a new housing development is planned.

An intense struggle ensued over the two proposed canals. Opponents of the Leeds canal issued a document extolling the merits of their waterway and exposing the weaknesses, both real and imagined, of the other. To impress Parliament with their energy and enthusiasm they even ended the lease of the tolls on their navigation. However, time and money were running out for both sides when the Haddlesey to Selby Bill was voted in by 105 votes to 33. The chief advantage of the winner was its length - 5¼ miles as opposed to the more costly 23½ of the Leeds to Selby waterway.

Haddlesey to Selby Canal

There had been vehement opposition to this canal especially from people with interests in the corn and fulling mills. The Act did, however, accommodate some of their needs. For example, it made special provision for the water-level to be permanently two feet lower than the level of the Duke of Ancaster's land. With regards to flooding fears, William Jessop, given the task of building the canal, reported it was to have a double pair of flood gates at each end.

Construction of the canal began in 1775. Three years later, on the 29th April, a large crowd gathered at the eastern end of Ousegate to celebrate its opening. They witnessed the arrival from Haddlesey of several vessels, accompanied by the sounds of cannons firing, bells ringing and music playing. It was the beginning of forty years of prosperity for the town as Selby's coastwise trade was now linked to the rich, manufacturing interior of the West Riding. It made Selby the principal port on the river Ouse.

Development took place in Selby around the new waterway. Lady Stourton who owned much of the riverside leased the proprietors eight acres of land on the west bank, just near to where the canal locked into the river. Warehouses were built, a dry dock, counting house, crane, rigging and tarring houses, a sailmaker's shop, and a terminal depot for handling goods and the repairing of barges and ships. A place was also provided for the depositing of old ropes - maybe destined for the workhouses or the prisons to be made into oakum. Trade increased at such a rate that in 1788 the lock-keeper was given an assistant; two years later an extra clerk was employed. In the early nineteenth century a branch custom house was established on Ousegate. This meant that vessels were no longer compelled to stop at Hull to be cleared at its Custom House. In the 1820s the principal officer was Peter Passmore who had Joseph Peal and Michael Welburn, coast waiters, to help him and also Edward Popplewell, acting as an extra boatman.

Problems did develop with the canal because, with a depth of three feet six inches, only barges and keels up to 60 tons burthen could travel on it. It also had a two mile stretch of sandy banks which washed away in the rain and blew away in dry weather, causing constant dredging to be carried out. Even so Selby continued to prosper. Large vessels, some over 200 tons came up the Ouse. Schooners, brigs, sloops and Humber keels filled the river; the port had become the centre for Yorkshire's coasting trade. Apart from lighters going between Hull, Leeds and Wakefield, most goods at the port were transhipped from coaster to barge or vice versa.

This was done by way of a cut or 'handling dock' that ran parallel to the Ouse for about 80-100 yards. Barges could moor in this 'Lazy Cut' without going through the lock, whilst the sea-going vessels tied up adjacent to them on the Ouse. The goods were then lifted over the land from one craft to the other. At the turn of the nineteenth century, 369,780 tons of goods went through the port and 800 coasters came to the town. The manufactured goods of the West Riding, Lancashire and Westmoreland being sent all over the Continent of Europe, as well as London and other places along the British coastline, were transhipped at Selby. Imports such as cotton, linen, wool and yarn came to the port and were transferred into smaller vessels, with groceries, fir timber, oak, mahogany, beech and other woods, to be carried up the canal to Haddlesey and the river Aire.

In 1819 the Yorkshire Gazette published 'Selby Shipping' from the week ending 10th June to the 30th September. During that period 261 ships arrived at the port and 221 departed; of the number of ships docking at Selby, 103 were from London, 75 from King's Lynn, 29 from Wisbech and 23 had sailed from Boston. Of the other ten places listed, Rye was the furthest south and Newcastle the furthest north. London with 102, and King's Lynn with 70, were the most common destinations for ships sailing from Selby, followed by Wisbech with 11 and Boston with ten. The furthest port north was Newcastle but the furthest destination south for ships leaving Selby, was Chichester.

The Gazette named the ships that were at Selby during the week ending 8th. July. There were 11 arrivals and 13 departures. Three of the ships at the port that week were either built or owned in Knottingley. The *"Waterloo"* which left for Lynn was a

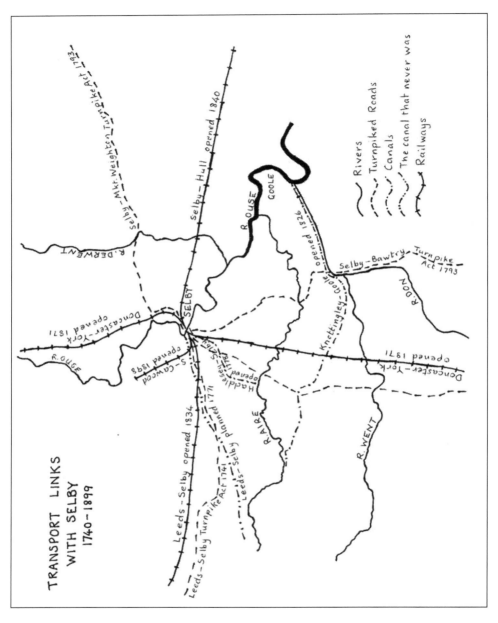

Figure 6. Selby Transport Links

sloop, burthen 49 tons, built in Knottingley in 1815 and owned by George Copley. *"John & Joseph"* sailing to London, was built by Joshua Vollans of Leeds in 1814 but was owned by Joseph Arnold and registered in Knottingley. An arrival from London, *"Lucinda"* was built in 1811 in Alkborough, Lincolnshire, but owned and registered in Knottingley by John Moon Jnr. and John Taylor.

Selby Prospers

The speedier and cheaper transport now available to the manufacturers and suppliers helped the growth of Selby. The population in 1574 was around 1,400; in 1801 the first census put it at 2,861, but by 1821 it had risen to 4,079. Corn milling increased in the area, as did flax dressing and linen manufacture. Baines' Directory for 1822 noted three flax and two spinners in the town, two hemp and flax merchants and three flax dressers and linen manufacturers; the Proctor family having interests in the last two. The export of stone down the Ouse had become an important industry. In 1822, Stephen Kay of Thornden Buildings was listed as agent for Mr Trueman, stone merchant of London. John Mowlem of The Crescent was also a stone agent.

Shipbuilding, an industry that had been carried on in Selby on a small scale for many years, enjoyed a boom period. Rope-making, sail-making, ironfounding and other trades associated with ships flourished in the town until a third of the population's occupations were connected with the canal and river. Baines' directory notes two block and mast makers, a sail maker and a ship rigger on Ousegate; a sail maker on Canal Side, four twine manufacturers and a baker, Michael Gibson, who specialised in ships' biscuits.

Fourteen shipbuilders or owners were also listed. Well-known Selby shipping families listed were the Stanilands, Standerings and the Weddalls. It was not just influential people who had interests in ships for as early as the seventeenth century men and women of Selby held shares in vessels which they passed on in their wills. In 1659, Alice Tuke of Selby left the son of William Gibson, a sixteenth part of Roger Ryley's ship, named *"Primrose';* the same in one named," *True Love"* and a share in a ship called *"Providence".* In 1678 John Wilkinson, a bachelor, left one half of his part of George Bell's pinck to a nephew, Leonard Wilkinson; he bequeathed the other half to his brother-in-law, John Wiseman. Pincks have been described as small sea-going vessels, masted and rigged and built with a round stem and bulging sides. One sixteenth of George Bell's pinck was left by a mother to her four daughters. They were to have *"the money that shall yearly accrue by the shipping".* Five years later, John Todd, mariner, left his son a sixteenth share of the keel, " *Caire-for All"* of which Samuel Bell was the master. The inventory of the goods of the manorial steward, Simon Spofforth, written in 1688, included *"one-eighth and one-two and thirtieth parte of a keele called Care for All".* The keel was almost like a flat bottomed barge with a mast, which could be lowered, and carried square sails. John Todd also left his son a sixteenth part of a cog boat; this usually referred to a small coaster or fishing boat, possibly with a mast and also oars.

Selby Shipbuilders

Mountain records that in 1800 Selby had a good shipyard where vessels from 50 to 800 tons burthen were built. He listed one ship builder. This was Alex Shepherd whose shipyard, situated at the far eastern end of Ousegate, was included on a map drawn from a survey of the Ouse in 1790. It is now the site of a new waterfront housing development. The next owner of the yard was Major John Foster, who died in 1845. He had been a banker, merchant, farmer, brewer and ship builder. Foster gave much of his time and money to help improve the lives of Selby people and held the commission of major in the Volunteer Corps during the French wars. Two launchings at his shipyard were part of the reason for some celebrations during the dark days of the Napoleonic Wars. The Jubilee of George III on the 25th October, 1809, was ushered in by the ringing of bells, firing of cannon and the launching of a fine ship, called the *'Jubilee'*. On the 5th October 1811, what the papers described as a *"remarkable handsome and good ship for Thomas Winter of Selby"* was launched from John Foster's shipyard. The vessel was intended for the Gun and Shot Wharf trade from London to Selby. Thomas Winter a 'Master and Mariner' living on Ousegate had had three vessels launched within a year which was the reason for him holding a celebratory supper.

Crowds had gathered on the foreshore at Ousegate on another occasion that year but for a very different reason. They were there to witness the approach of a ship's boat bearing the victims of a terrible disaster. A large, square-rigged brig, called the *'William'*, owned by the Stanilands and commanded by John Bateman, engaged in the coasting trade between Selby and London, had capsized in coming up the Humber, on Witton Sand. The captain's wife and their two children were in bed in their father's cabin and were drowned in their berths. Also drowned in her bed, was a lady passenger from Cawood named Mrs Rider, who was returning from London via Selby. The people gathered on the shore were moved to tears when the boat arrived but the greatest sorrow was felt by Peggy Harrison, the elderly mother of the captain's wife.

George Lowther accompanied his father to the scene. In his adult life Lowther held many positions in the town including being the bailiff for the manor of Selby and the sole steward for the Gateforth estate and house owned by the Rev. Richard Brooke. He started work however as an apprentice to Robert Staniland, joiner and cabinet maker in Church Street.

Samuel Gutteridge was listed in Baines' directory as both a boat and ship builder on Ousegate where it appears he took over Major Foster's shipyard. In 1824 Gutteridge built the *"Martha and Sarah"* which was registered in Knottingley by John Rhodes. The *"Two Johns"* registered in Knottingley in 1842 by John Lee and John Robinson, was also built in Gutteridge's yard. Ten years after this it was recorded in the Local Board's minutes that they had sent letters to Gutteridge regarding repairs to his property. He was given fourteen days within which to repair the footpath, that ran across his shipyard towards the lock on the canal, and to 'spout' the buildings abutting onto the same. He was only given seven days to make a drain to carry off the rainfall that gathered on the west side of the shipyard, near to the home of Joseph Bradley. In 1854 the Yorkshire Gazette recorded the launching of the *"John and Jane"*, 112 tons burthen, property of Turner & Co. of Hull, from Gutteridge's yard. A storm had prevented the original launch at New Year so it took place instead on the 23rd January. The paper said, *"A more beautiful launch never took place"*. Five months later the same paper reported on an inquest held on Samuel Gutteridge, aged seventy, a greatly respected shipbuilder in Selby for around 38 years. His body had been found in the canal.

During the time Gutteridge had run the shipyard on Ousegate, an apprentice, named William Littlewood, from Riccall, began work there. From the age of twelve Littlewood walked the 3½ miles to and from the shipyard. Work began at six in the morning to half-past five at night. He finished an hour earlier on Saturdays. Littlewood progressed to become a journeyman, then a skilled shipwright. He married a Selby girl named Ann Wheldrake but this was not until he had completed his apprenticeship for marriages before then were forbidden. Tragically he was killed when an anchor gave way and fell on him. Aged 67 he had been helping at the launch of a vessel named *"Concord"*.

Knottingley to Goole Canal

The prosperity enjoyed by Selby was short-lived. As trade continued to increase along its waterways the Aire and Calder Navigation Company realised they needed a more efficient and reliable route to the Humber. The proprietors, mostly from the landed gentry, had amassed fortunes as trade had continued to flourish on the Haddlesey to Selby canal. In 1780 dividends of £12,000 were being paid out and by 1810 these had risen to £48,000. Even so, as trade increased and bigger ships were built, the majority of the Company's owners did not hesitate to support a plan that would eventually render a huge economic blow to the interests of Selby. This was to construct a more serviceable waterway from Castleford direct to Goole, with its potential for a deep water port with spacious docks and warehouses.

The principal disadvantages of the Haddlesey canal were its shallowness and the presence of culverts under the canal to assist drainage, making it difficult to deepen the channel. It was also too narrow with no sufficient docks. Some landowners, led by the Hon. Edward Petre, opposed the plans for a new canal which was to go from Knottingley to Goole but it was strongly supported by almost all the South and West Yorkshire traders and coal owners. The increasing export of coal from the developing coalfields could not be accommodated at Selby. The act for a new waterway was passed and the Knottingley to Goole canal was officially opened on the 26th July 1826.

This had a serious effect on Selby as a port. It gradually lost its prime position in the coasting trade whilst Goole grew from an insignificant hamlet into a large river port. The Haddlesey canal was not abandoned for efforts were made to modify it under an act passed in 1828 for the improvement of the canals in the north-east of England. It was found a great deal of work needed to be carried out. The Company tried to pacify the worried townspeople by replacing the old, broken down lock with a new one and attempting to widen and deepen the canal. Further legislation for more improvements resulted in some widening and deepening of Selby Cut. Traders from York, Malton and other places near the Ouse and its tributaries asked for the canal to be further deepened: the waterway had shortened the distance between these towns and Leeds. Their requests were refused. Despite all efforts to make the Haddlesey Canal more navigable for the increasing trade, the Aire and Calder's Knottingley to Goole Canal became the focal point for the tremendous amount of trade coming from and through Yorkshire.

Road Travel

At the end of the seventeenth century the principal modes of travel over land were by horse, horse litter or on foot. Most goods went by packhorse and sometimes by cart. People travelled in groups because of the fear of attack by undesirables such as highwaymen. As trade increased, wagons and their loads became bigger and bulkier and the ruts and holes in the roads deeper and more numerous. There were no recognisable roads beyond the outskirts of Selby and the only crossings of the rivers were by ferry.

This did not deter Sir Miles Stapleton, as comments written by him in his accounts' book for the late seventeenth century show:

1663 Item. Given to Mr. Walmsley's coachman May 13th. when my wife and I went to visit them and borrowed a paire of their coatch horses and a pair of harnis because the ways were then very bad to Staynor. 2s:6d

1664 Given to Lady Downey's coatchman and footman when my wife and I went to see her and her coach met us at the ferry and conveyed us thither (Cowick Hall) and brought us back to the ferry. 3s:6d.

The Stapletons also visited Lady Yarborough at Snaith Hall, staying for two nights. In 1672 they travelled as far as Harrogate Spa *"to drink the waters"*. These were the early days of a fashion that was to become very popular. It being a long distance to travel Sir Miles took four coach-horses, two riding horses and two manservants. The family often made use of the Selby ferry. In July 1682 Miles Stapleton paid the ferryman 3s:6d. to cross with his coach and horses and ls:3d. for his riding horses. It is not known what kind of coach the Stapletons used. Many types were developed during that century as more and more roads were improved.

In her notes, Miss Richardson recounts two incidents from *"The Memoirs of Sir John Reresby of Thrybergh"*, (MP for York), which illustrate that crossing by ferry could be a hazardous affair. On the 10th September 1660, Sir John, on his way to York, came to the ferry at Selby. There a quarrel broke out between his company and others about who should first enter the boat. A scuffle followed during which Sir John Reresby was struck over the head with a cudgel. This spurred him to lay about his assailants with his sword. The people gathered there for the market took alarm at this and soon the minister, his two gentlemen friends and their servants, were in danger of being overwhelmed in the melee. After a long tussle, Sir John was pulled off his horse and was about to be, again, struck on the head when his 'Moor' dragged the attacker off him. The minister and his friends fell back until they found an *"honest"* householder who gave them shelter and protection until the angry mob quietened down and dispersed. Sir John Reresby suffered another misfortune in September 1680 when he used the Booth ferry. On this occasion he had successfully crossed the water on the ferry but, as he was leaving the boat, a horse on board turned suddenly knocking the minister off his mount. Sir John fell out of the ferry onto the shore, falling heavily upon his elbow. His shoulder was put out of joint but fortunately there was a 'bone-setter' in Howden who attended to him. The minister stayed overnight in Howden before returning homewards. It took a good six months for his shoulder to fully heal.

Surveyors of the Highway

In the eighteenth century the roads continued to deteriorate as the trade along them increased as the industrial towns expanded. Roads were ploughed up by the continuous traffic and repairs became increasingly expensive, especially where materials were not close at hand. The lords of the manors were no longer responsible for their upkeep since the Highway Act of 1555 had transferred responsibility for the roads to the parishioners and the Highway Surveyors.

These officials received money from the same sources as the Churchwardens and Overseers of the Poor. Selby surveyors for 1727 spent their income on some of the following things. They bought 24 slabs and 48 poles for the 'cause' in Ousegate Lane and paving for Brayton Lane. Other materials went towards the repairing of an old 'cause' in Bondgate and a new one in Wistow Lane. A 'cause' was a paved way raised above marshy or muddy ground. Sand, cobbles and gravel were also purchased. One expense recorded, *"To carrying cobbles out of boat and measuring them"*. Anby Chamberlain was paid for 31 'tunnes' of cobbles at 3s:6d. per hour. Stoops (posts) for foot causes cost two shillings to be brought over the Ouse by ferry. The surveyors paid men to work for them. The tasks included mending the gates at Carlton Lane, East Common and the Outwoods; also hedging the common and felling wood for the highways. As the monks had done before them, the men going into the forests to cut wood were the only workers given food and drink. Payments were also made for the opening of goatstocks in Wistow Lane and the repairing of goatstocks in Cow Lane, Brayton Lane and one in New Lane. According to the *Oxford English Dictionary*, 'goat' in this instance could be an alternative spelling of 'gote' meaning a channel of water and 'goatstocks' pieces of wood used to control the streams or drains. Men were also employed by the surveyors to open the water sewer dykes, fill up the ruts in the lanes and let out the water gathered in them.

Turnpike Roads

The compulsory maintenance of the roads was mainly concentrated in the inhabited areas for the parishioners were loth to work on trackways not frequented by themselves. However, as more and more traffic crowded the roads, the merchants agitated for better conditions. Parliament responded by legislating for the formation of Turnpike Trusts. These Trusts were often run by groups of interested, prominent men, who wished to raise money for the upkeep of the roads. They were allowed to place gates or bars across major highways in order to collect tolls from its users. The trustees hired out the toll-collecting for a set amount. It was then up to the toll-keeper to make a profit by collecting more money than he had paid out. Posts were advertised in the papers. One such advert in the York Herald in 1798 asked for "a *proper person as Collector of Tolls at the Bar"* for the Tadcaster to York road carrying with it an annual salary of fifty pounds and a rent free house.

A well integrated turnpike road network developed by 1770 in England and Wales. The first Turnpike Act in Yorkshire was passed in 1735 and was for improvements to the Rochdale to Halifax route via Blackstone Edge. By the middle of the eighteenth century 27 miles of roads in the East Riding, 138 miles in the North Riding and 252 miles in the West Riding had been turnpiked. The latter included a major road out of Selby, when in 1741 an Act was passed for *"repairing and enlarging the road from the town of Selby in the County of York to Leeds"*. Before the Aire and Calder Navigation provided better waterways, this road was the main transport route from West Yorkshire to the Ouse.

Nine years later a second act was passed to explain and amend the first. It stated that tolls were to be paid at a gate in Selby which ran across the road at the west end of Gowthorpe, near to Armoury Road, known then as *"Old Brayton Fare"*. The tolls were extremely unpopular; the townspeople strongly objected to paying where they once had free passage. It was reported in newspapers published as far away as Manchester that on

Friday, 8th. May 1752, Benjamin Wordsworth, common crier for Selby, rang his bell through the streets of the town exhorting the inhabitants to raise themselves and gather at midnight with axes and hatchets, and to join him in destroying the turnpike gates. Spiked bars had been added to many toll gates to discourage mounted horsemen from jumping over the bars to avoid paying the tolls - hence the name turnpikes. It must have been a strongly built barrier in Selby for the angry townsfolk had to gather on four nights before managing to totally destroy the gate. A reward of fifty pounds was offered for the capture of the bellman and his accomplices, with an extra twenty pounds added by the trustees of the road. The King's Pardon was promised to any of the rioters, except Wordsworth, who would help to bring him and the rest of the offenders to justice.

No record of their capture has been found. Their efforts however had not been in vain, for gates were never again erected in the town except on the road leading to Cawood. As more Turnpike Trusts were formed toll gates were erected on most of the approaches to Selby. There were several on the road from Selby to Leeds. One was situated at Hambleton, opposite to the Red Lion public house. If this toll house had been built according to the directions in the Turnpike Act of 1820, it would have been built at, or near the gates, with outbuildings and conveniences, an enclosed garden on the side of the road, not exceeding one eighth of an acre, with a lamp or lamps fitted. The Act also directed that should a toll-collector prove dishonest three Trustees were needed to discharge him. With the help of the constables, they had the power to remove any persons or possessions from the Toll House, if still there four days after their dismissal.

The whole contents of these Acts are too lengthy to be covered in this book but some items are noteworthy. In 1820, there were 184 trustees including Sir Thomas Vavasour, the Hon. Edward Petre, Thomas and William Proctor and Thomas Tennant. Five or more of these trustees were to meet regularly at places near to the road, including Selby, to deal with such business as appointing clerks, treasurers, collectors of tolls and surveyors. No person who sold ale, beer, wine or spirituous liquors by retail, was considered for the positions. Headed by the Royal Family those exempted also included military personnel and their goods, Sunday worshippers, and carriages carrying vagrants with legal passes. The Acts directed that foot causes be made on sections along the road, and ditches where needed, but the trustees were not empowered to use funds on repairing or mending the streets of Leeds.

The turnpike roads were initially financed by the trustees who invested set amounts at a fixed rate of interest. To ensure fair charges a 1754 Act had introduced the use of milestones. The Selby to Leeds Road was furnished with stones or posts set up at the side of the road at a distance of a mile apart. It was an offence to interfere with these signs, or to cause damage to the roads by, for example, allowing pigs to uproot or disturb their surfaces. Some milestones are still in evidence. One can be seen on the Selby to Leeds road (old A63 now A1238) on the south side of the highway opposite the Selby boundary marker. This milestone is one mile from Selby and 19 from Leeds. Another can be seen a mile further on, just beyond the junction with Fox Lane.

Market Weighton and Bawtry Turnpikes

Further turnpike roads were built from Selby. Two were authorised in 1793, one to Market Weighton and the other to Bawtry. The latter led to the opening up of Park Street in the town whilst Bubwith on the Market Weighton Road, gained a bridge over the River Derwent. This event was greeted with great rejoicing by the inhabitants. On the first Monday in August, 1793, the first stone of the bridge was laid by Edward Weddall Esq. of Bubwith, accompanied by loud cheers from a great multitude of onlookers. The mason's flag was then hoisted and the workmen, sporting colourful cockades made for them by the ladies in the village, paraded through the streets escorted by a band of musicians. They all sang "God save the King" with the spectators in full voice behind them. Celebrations continued all through that day and the next! Bells were rung, cannons fired, music played and everyone showed their delight at the new venture. The bridge at Bubwith was opened for carriages on the 23rd. September, when, it was reported *"there was general rejoicing at that place"*.

In 1796 the trustees of the Selby to Market Weighton turnpike road met at the New Inn, Bubwith, home of Mr. John Richardson. They had previously advertised that they would be there to publicly sell off eleven lots of the old road. Two of these were – *"All that piece of Old Road at the west end of Bubwith or the Ferry Lane, adjoining the premises of Mrs Barr, south and the Turnpike north and All that piece of the Old Lane, leading from the Common to Mr Brewer's gate, in the township of Barlby"*. The trustees were still holding their meetings at the New Inn in Bubwith as late as 1854 when they held their Annual General Meeting there.

Selby to Doncaster Turnpike Road

It was not until June 1832 that Royal Assent was given for the making of the turnpike road from Selby to Doncaster, most of which is now classified as the A19. It was said that the road would *"open a nearer, more level and better communication between Doncaster and the Port of Selby"*. Over a hundred trustees, ranging from baronets to clerks, were appointed. They included familiar names such as the Hon. E. Petre, Thomas Standering, James Audus, and Stephen, Samuel and William Staniland. One not so well-known name was that of William Hatfield Gossip. Their first meeting was held at the White Swan in Askern but thereafter they met alternately and at regular intervals, in Doncaster, Askern or Selby.

A map of the proposed road was displayed in the Clerk of the Peace's office in Wakefield. It cost the public one shilling to view the map and sixpence for every hundred words copied from it. The trustees were instructed that the road was not to deviate more than a hundred yards from any line on the map and an owner's consent must be obtained before destroying any property other than that already annexed under the Act. They were also, during the building of bridges, not to interfere with the passing of any craft along Selby and Goole canals, or the River Aire. Much property in the area of Selby where Brook Street lies today, and in the vicinity of the railway crossing, was annexed by the Act. This included many works, shops and warehouses such as John Twist's sawing pits and Messrs Gibson and Company's railway factory. Also listed to go were a subscription school occupied by its trustees and a pinfold owned by Lord Petre. Further from the town, a school house in Brayton, owned by Thomas Procter and lived in by John Sweeting, was on the list, as were the cottages for the poor in Burn, run by the overseers and occupied by some needy people. The trustees were empowered to build necessary bridges, banks and embankments, arches and tunnels. The Reverend George Alderson allowed around four acres of Haddlesey marsh to be taken for the new road to Doncaster. This resulted in a new three-arched iron bridge being erected over the Aire at Haddlesey to replace a wooden one.

The tolls were fixed by the trustees. Only half tolls were to be paid for any animal drawing a vehicle carrying lime, salt or sea sand to be used for manure; no toll was to be collected when the vehicle went through empty on its way to collect same. It had been found that narrow-wheeled vehicles, carrying ever-increasing loads, rutted the roads badly so a table of tolls was set for the Doncaster road which the trustees hoped would discourage this practice. The wider the wheel rims the lower was the toll. For example, a two-wheeled cart with wheel rims less than six inches wide and pulled by four horses paid 2s.6d. at each gate; whereas a similar outfit but with wheel trims over six inches wide only paid half the sum. This caused an upsurge of vehicles on the road with wider and wider rims. Additional horses were needed to pull the big, broad-wheeled wagons. However, because of the increased weight of the wagons their loads could not be made any larger. They were traffic-stoppers in narrow streets and often became stuck on muddy roads. The trustees were far-seeing for they also included this item on their list of tolls; *"Every carriage, moved or propelled by steam or machinery or by any other power Than animal....3s."*.

Many people tried to avoid paying the tolls but most were prosecuted. In May 1796, George Richardson, a farmer from Aughton Ruddings, was convicted before Henry Vavasour and Robert Denison, two justices for the East Riding, in the penalty of 40 shillings for evading the tolls at Bubwith toll-bar, which he paid together with the expenses. William Yates drove a carriage and four horses through the gate at Frees Hill Villa Bar, at Brayton, without paying the toll. The summons to appear at Doncaster Court in 1840 ended with the words *"Herein fail not at your peril"*. The toll house for this bar can still be seen today on the corner of Doncaster Road and Baffam Lane.

Selby Toll Bridge

The gradual improvement of the roads meant that the Lady of the Manor and other gentry, followed by such people as farmers' wives, could travel to the towns to buy the articles that were once made on the estates or in the local villages. In Selby, as elsewhere, craftsmen were gradually leaving the rural areas; self-sufficiency was coming to an end as even the cottagers bought from shops and markets in the towns. The major drawback for the Selby area was the lack of any bridge over the Ouse, south of York.

The only way across the river at Selby was by the ferry. It had operated since the time of the monks and after the dissolution became the property of the lord of the manor. There were other ferries at Newhay, near Hemingbrough, and at Long Drax. With the expansion of Selby as a port and the improvements of the Leeds to Selby road, the ferry was continually in use. Figures collected in the 1780s showed that an average of 11,795 persons used the ferry each month, 3,051 of them on horseback. During one month in 1789, led horses numbering 211 and 127 oxen, 66 hogs, 2,248 sheep, one coach, 15 chaises, nine single horse chaises, three wagons and 16 carts were ferried over the Ouse. The increase in traffic causing queues at the crossing, the turbulence created by other craft, the high and swift tides and fierce weather conditions that made it impossible sometimes for the ferry to be used, made people in the 1780s seriously consider the building of a bridge at Selby.

Therefore, despite the upheavals in Europe and threats of a possible war with France, supporters of such a scheme concentrated their minds and efforts in supporting a bill for a bridge over the Ouse. These included the residents of Selby, inhabitants of the surrounding villages and towns, the clergy who hoped for larger congregations, and merchants and manufacturers in Hull, the West Riding and as far afield as Lancashire.

William Jessop (1745-1814) a notable engineer, was appointed to survey and enquire into the practicality of erecting a bridge over the Ouse near to the ferry crossing at Selby. He was to especially look into what injury, if any, the navigation of the river, or lands adjoining it might suffer if a bridge was built there. The petitioners received a favourable report so an application was made to Parliament in 1789.

Opposition

Opposition was intense. On the 12th. January 1790, a general meeting was held in York where it was resolved that counteraction to a bridge at Selby be conducted as effectually as possible at the expense of subscribers. A committee of thirteen gentlemen was elected, headed by the Right Hon. Thomas Hartley, Lord Mayor. Two weeks later the York Herald reported it was happy the utmost exertions were being used by respectable people in York and elsewhere to oppose the building of a bridge at Selby. It believed the bridge would interrupt and damage the navigation to every place above the town and seemed calculated only to benefit Selby and a few individuals. The paper considered a bridge would be of no use to the *great public because there was not, nor likely to be, any communication of general use from there to the East Riding"!* The paper argued that if turnpike roads had to be made, materials would have to be brought a great distance thereby creating considerable expense for the people along those roads. The Herald believed the interruption in the tideway would certainly injure the banks, and overflows damage low ground. They insisted the ferry at Selby was one of the best and safest in the country and pointed out that a few years ago the town had objected to a bridge being erected at Langrick, Drax, which, it believed would have benefited more people than one at Selby. The paper noted there had been a considerable number of vessels lost at Goole and other places where bridges had been erected in tideways.

The following month a lengthy letter was published in the paper from a writer signing himself *"SCRUTATOR"*. He attacked everything Jessop had said concerning the bridge. The writer complained the engineer had been employed to inform the public about the possibility of a bridge at Selby but had exceeded that by becoming its advocate! 'Scrutator' argued that the proposed wooden bridge needed foundations as solid and strong as a stone one so disturbances to the water would be as great. He dismissed Jessop's calculation of not more than 150 large vessels passing above the bridge in a year, saying this concluded trade was not to increase or *"are we to prevent the possibility of it happening?"* The writer believed the hindrances caused to large ships trying to reach York would seriously affect the city's imports and exports. He was not surprised Selby wanted a bridge for it would make that town *"emporium of trade between York and rest of world. Selby will become rival to Hull; it will be made a regular port, custom houses may be erected there, and it will rise into greatness on the ruins of York, oldest city in England"*.

Amongst many other points put forward by Jessop and rejected by 'Scrutator' was the making of new roads. The writer discussed the improbabilities of making good turnpike roads to Selby on deep and flooded ground, void of any materials.

Other opponents asserted that a bridge would not induce even one more carriage to pass from Beverley or Hull by Selby southwards, whilst one at Langrick would have rendered essential service to inhabitants of these two towns and places further east.

The second reading of the Selby Bridge Bill was withdrawn and a proposal put forward that the different parties concerned should refer the matter to the opinions and decisions of three persons to be nominated by Earl Fitzwilliam, Lord Hawke and Lord Louvaine, the Earl of Beverley. Lord Louvaine declined to take part, being lessee of three down-river ferries. It was reported the citizens of York and others against the bridge were under the greatest obligation to Earl Fitzwilliam, Sir William Milner and Mr. Milnes, for the exertions they had put in on the opposers' behalf. Another meeting was held in York to hear a report from London. Apart from York citizens, those invited included anyone from Easingwold, Thirsk, Boroughbridge, Aldborough, Knaresborough, Duffield, Barlby and Osgodby. It is interesting to note the meeting was arranged for three o'clock on market day for the convenience of people living some distance away. At a well attended assembly, it was agreed to refer the business to three nominated persons, who were *"neither engineers nor mariners"*. In June it was announced they were to be Bacon Frank of Campsall, George Cooke of Street-Thorpe, and Fairfax Fearnley of Oakwell Hall. Cooke was found to have signed a petition in favour of the bridge so his place was taken by Charles Mellish.

The Survey

The three gentlemen placed a notice in the newspapers announcing they would meet on Monday, 11th. October, at ten in the morning, at the home of Mr. Hawdon, George Inn, Selby. They intended to proceed from there to examine the country, rivers, bridges, ferries and roads in the area. Their intentions were to adjourn to Mrs. Lowe's at Ferrybridge on Friday the 15th. to discuss the merits of the case, and to listen to the views of anyone who chose to visit them there. Two weeks later a short notice appeared in the paper postponing the visit. The investigators had been informed that the 11th. October was the day of Selby's Great Fair so, realising it was an inconvenient time to conduct their survey, their visit was rearranged.

They finally met in Selby on the 25th. October and five days later were sitting at Ferrybridge listening to evidence for and against the bridge. A week after this the men left to view the three bridges on the tidal Don, and its banks near Goole and Rawcliffe. On returning to Ferrybridge they remained there until the 13th. November listening to more petitioners. Consultations came to an end and the three referees departed to study the banks of the Ouse at low-water, at Selby, Cawood, Wistow and other places along the river.

On the 18th November, 1790, the three referees announced a verdict in favour of a bridge at Selby that, they said, would be of great and daily benefit to the public. One restriction imposed was the leaf (swinging section) should not be less than thirty feet and the bridge twenty feet wide for accommodation of passengers. The Selby Bridge Act of 1791 empowered a company to build and operate the bridge. It provided for finance and tolls, laid down compensation for the ferry owner and safeguarded the rights of the Ouse Navigation Trustees. Lord E. Petre and his heirs were to receive £25 per annum in respect of the ferry - a payment that took precedence over every other outlay. The ferry owner had been quite amenable to the arrangements provided he was given a share in the bridge company and received suitable compensation. The proprietors, including Lord Petre, were authorised to raise £7,000 amongst themselves in 70 shares and invite subscriptions up to £3,000.

Selby Bridge Tolls

It is not clear when the bridge was officially opened but a report in the York Herald points to it not being ready in July, 1793. On the last Monday of that month the large ferryboat at Selby overturned due mostly to the inexperience of the two men who had undertaken the management of the craft during the illness of the official ferryman. All but one man and his horse were saved. It was reported *"...the rapidity of the current carried the boat against the piles of the bridge erecting there."* Despite all the opposition and troubles connected with Selby Toll Bridge it became the best surviving example of a large timber bridge in England besides being one of the earliest swing bridges in Europe. An interesting feature of its mechanism was the early use, on a large scale, of ball-bearings, which facilitated the speedy opening of the 70 ton swinging span. It was not until the 1970s that the toll bridge was rebuilt and strengthened with iron.

The tolls for the bridge were leased out in the same manner as the turnpike tolls. In 1857 it was announced in the York Gazette that the *"Pontage and Tolls arising at Selby Bridge with the toll house and appurtenances thereto"* were to be let by auction at the Londesborough Arms, (formerly the 'George'). The highest bidder had to provide security regarding the regular paying of the rent and the opening of the leaf or swivel of the bridge.

When the bridge was first opened the tolls ranged from three shillings for a coach drawn by six horses to one penny for a cow. (It cost 1s.3d. for 20 cows to go through the Selby to Doncaster turnpikes.) Horses and carts carrying road materials were excused payment. At first pedestrians were charged a halfpenny but inhabitants of Selby and the surrounding villages were allowed to pass over the bridge free, once an initial daily payment had been made. This concession was changed eventually to all pedestrians because of the difficulty of enforcing the rule. It was not long before there were objections to the tolls and other matters concerning the bridge. In January, 1794, subscriptions of a guinea were collected to help fight the extra halfpenny the proprietors were claiming for every horse carrying bags; the collectors were to class them as laden animals. The guineas were deposited with Mr. Hardcastle, at the White Swan York, but papers for the signatures of persons wishing to subscribe were left at the Cross Keys Hull, Half Moon Howden, George Inn Selby, and at most of the travellers' inns in Yorkshire. The outcome is not known but in 1803 the Selby Bridge and Ouse Navigation applied to Parliament for leave to bring in a bill amending the first Bridge Act, which included increasing the tolls. Examples were, one penny up to 1½d. for each horse, ninepence up to 1s.3d. for a wagon and three horses. They also wished to impose penalties for supposed evasions of the tolls. An involved court case took place in 1862 concerning such a matter. The toll collector, Mr. Wheatcroft, was being sued by Thomas Silverside, a farmer from Riccall for illegally seizing sacks as payment for a toll. The plaintiff had passed over the bridge after paying the initial toll for three horse and carts - still allowed at that time for certain villages. However, on his third journey over the bridge he was accompanied by Mr. Dodsworth from Kelfield, a village not included in the Bridge Act of 1791. The toll-keeper demanded one shilling toll for one of the horse and carts claiming that Dodsworth was holding its reins. It was believed these had been grabbed by Dodsworth in an attempt to avoid paying the penny toll for pedestrians. Two sacks were seized from the cart when neither man would pay the shilling. The case had already been twice before the Escrick magistrates who had decided they had no jurisdiction. At Selby court, Silverside proved his right to exemption from the toll and was awarded the value of the two sacks. Dodsworth was given a severe reprimand for causing all the litigation in his attempts to evade paying the one penny toll as a pedestrian.

Changes in 1803 concerned vessels on the river. For instance, instead of expecting the leaf of the bridge to be opened to them as customary, craft not having middle decks or spars were to strike their masts and pass under the bridge unless prevented by floods or spring tides. The opponents of the Selby bridge had more meetings in York. They wished to raise £500 to help oppose the new bill. Within days the subscriptions added up to £1,327.15s.0d.

Toll Free Bridge

Controversies over the bridge continued throughout the nineteenth century culminating in a meeting in 1891 of representatives from the East and West Ridings, York Corporation and Selby Local Board. A resolution was passed that the wooden bridge be bought and a new toll free one be erected. An estimated figure of £17,000 put forward for the venture included £3,000 for purchase of the old bridge and £300 for demolishing it. Long and involved discussions took place amongst the different authorities. It was decided East Riding townships should be asked to contribute as they would benefit from a free bridge. Barlby promised to raise £245 by putting sixpence on the rates for three years, Osgodby £76 by the same method, Skipwith promised £58 if others contributed, North Duffield £30 from voluntary contributions, but, Riccall, Cliffe and South Duffield refused any financial support. The East and West Riding councils and York Corporation promised £4,000 each whilst Selby offered £1,500. At open meetings, chaired by Mr. Liversidge, the Local Board met with apathy from the townsfolk. Because of this and the exorbitant price of £4,350 asked for the old bridge by the shareholders, no further steps were taken, at that time, to have a toll-free new bridge at Selby. However, discussions, plans and arguments concerning the bridge continued well into the twentieth century.

Coaches and Steamers

In 1798 a poster advertising Selby Horse Show boasted, *"To those who are strangers, it may be necessary to observe, that since the building of good bridges over the Ouse and Derwent, all the danger and inconveniences of Ferries is removed and that a general communication to all parts is now opened by good roads'.*

The gradual appearance of straight, well-surfaced roads and the introduction of improved carriages, made travel by road more acceptable. Heavy, lumbering wagons were replaced by stage-coaches with fast horses. Inns, specially built to cater for these sprang up in the towns and along the turnpike roads; thus providing employment for thousands of people.

A state carriage built for the Earl of Rutland in 1555 was the first to be seen in England, but it took another hundred years before public stage coaches made their appearance. The first reference to one in Yorkshire was in April 1658, when a coach went from London to York in four days. The appalling conditions of many roads delayed any fast increase in coach travel but by 1683 there was a regular service from York, via Tadcaster, Ferrybridge and Doncaster to London. Leeds passengers rode on horseback to York or Ferrybridge to join the coach. Ferrybridge became a great coaching centre where private vehicles carrying Yorkshire's noblemen and gentlemen came to join the London coaches.

Steam Packets

Passengers had been carried on the Ouse as far back as records go but it was not until the 1780s onwards that any regular provision was made for them. Steam packets made their appearance not long after the end of the Napoleonic Wars and were soon in evidence on the Ouse and Calder Navigations.

In 1815, according to report, it seemed the entire population of Selby was thronged along Ousegate to watch the arrival of the 'Caledonia', the first steamer to be seen on the Ouse. That same year, the steam packet, 'Humber' began to ply regularly between Selby and Hull. Companies were quickly formed and more steamers introduced as they created an interest alongside the prosperous shipping concerns. Selby's position ensured it an important role in the transport of passengers as well as goods by water. Closer ties were formed with the expanding populations of the West Riding and Lancashire.

By 1822 steamers were sailing to Hull and back every day except Sunday. The number of coaches travelling to Selby increased. When it lost its status as the main trading port to Goole, the town remained a principal port of call for steamers. New jetties were built to accommodate the packets coming to Selby to connect with coaches from Leeds and other places. One of these was the 'Joanna' which left Selby for Hull and other places along the Ouse and Humber every Monday, returning on a Thursday if, as in every case, weather permitted. Journeys between the ports averaged about five hours.

The fare was two shillings but if the vessel provided food, male passengers paid an extra sixpence for each meal and females an extra fourpence. After a tiring journey on a coach the passengers could not always look forward to relaxing on the water. If the steamer became grounded they were expected to assist the crew to refloat it. Most aboard, for example, gave their weight to pulling on ropes looped around trees or prepared themselves to run from one side of the vessel to the other at a command from the captain.

The numerous coaches that ran from Leeds to connect with these steamers included a Selby coach named *"Blucher"* which operated from 1815-35. It left Leeds at five in the morning to catch the steamers leaving on the morning tide for Hull. The coach came to the town on Tuesdays, Thursdays and Saturdays. It returned from the *"George"* run by Tommy Hawdon, in Market Place, on the other three week days. By 1817 the *"Blucher"* was running a daily service between the two towns and was joined from 1823-34 by the *"Union"* which ran from the Bull and Mouth, Leeds, through Garforth, Fryston and Hambleton to the 'Petres Arms' on Gowthorpe, Selby. The *"Aire and Calder"* began daily runs from the 'Rose and Crown, Leeds in 1824. Now the site of the Queen's Arcade, the inn was a popular venue for cock-fights. From 1821 the *"True Blue"* ran every day from the 'Elephant and Castle' and 'Bay Horse' inns, Knaresborough, through Wetherby, Tadcaster and Sherburn to arrive at Selby half-an-hour before the packets left for Hull. Other coaches that arrived at Selby to meet the steamers were the *"Providence"* from York, to the Swan Inn, Ousegate; the *"Union"* which left Bradford at six in the morning for the Ship Inn, Water Lane, returning at seven in the evening, and the *"Union"* from Wakefield whose passengers alighted at the 'Rose and Crown', New Street.

The wharves where the steamers berthed belonged to R.Clay and J.H.Jackson. The *"Caledonia"* (seen in 1815), the *"Aire"*, *"Calder"* and *"Wellington"* berthed every morning between nine and eleven, their destination being Hull. Other craft coming to Selby included the *"Lowther"* a steam ship which left for Yarmouth every Friday with goods bound for Holland.

Carters

It was expensive to travel by coach. For example, in 1807 the *"Trafalgar"* a light post coach with room for only four inside passengers, charged its customers going from York to Hull, 15s. to travel inside or ten shillings on the outside. At that time a workman digging drains on the fens, near Boston, was earning 6s. to 7s. a day.

Wagons were still carrying merchandise from the industrial towns to Selby. White's directory lists York, Leeds, Manchester, Wakefield, Bradford, Sheffield, Pontefract and Snaith as places frequented by carriers. One haulier kept his horses stabled near his home on East Common. They were large draught horses used to pull long, low, heavily laden carts. Local carters took passengers to nearby villages and places as far away as Tadcaster and Thorne. Most of the carters operated on a Monday, market day, and left the town around three o'clock; the carter going to Tadcaster left at two. The people who could not afford the coaches used these carriers, especially for short journeys. Some inns in Selby favoured by these drivers were the New Inn, Market place, Black-aMoor's Head in Finkle Street, Grey Horse in Gowthorpe and White Swan in Micklegate. Travellers wishing to go to Leeds met at the Packet Office, Ousegate, whilst those heading for Pontefract met at five in the morning at the home of W. Golton, Millgate.

Mail Coaches

People travelling further afield brought back news concerning life outside their own environment. For instance, in November 1798, gentlemen arriving in York on the London coach brought news of the French Fleet which was passed onto the local papers. They told of a French corvette, with despatches for Bonaparte from the Directory, that had been taken by Nelson. It was said the captain of the corvette had thrown the important papers overboard but two British seamen observing this had leapt into the sea and rescued them.

The gentlemen from York had travelled on the Mail Coach. The newspapers were dependent on these coaches for most of their news but often the weather interfered with its delivery.

> *Jan.1 1798 Lack of news in this paper is due to Mail coaches being stopped by snow. Hull Mail Coach stopped by snow on Barmby Moor so mail brought on by man on horseback at two o'clock this morning. York Herald.*

Coach travel had improved so quickly that by 1780 stage coaches were completing their journeys faster than the mail service. Letters were still being delivered by relays of mail-carriers on horse-back who were frequent targets for highway robbers. John Palmer, a young theatre proprietor in Bath had introduced a regular service of post-chaises to carry props and actors between Bath and his new theatre in Bristol. He realised how his system could be used for the mail and eventually convinced a sceptical Post Office that it was workable. On a trial run a coach ran from Bristol to London in 16 hours; a journey taking two days using the mail carriers on their horses. By 1786 most letters and parcels were being transported all over the country by stage-coaches.

The guards and coachmen were armed, cutting down the number of mail robberies. They were also supposed to follow a rigid set of rules, any transgressions usually leading to dismissal. Four guards were discharged on one occasion, the first for going without his firearms and the second for putting the mail on the roof and using the official box for his own purposes - most probably to hide game sold to him by poachers on the route. William Joblin was dismissed for being intoxicated and J. Raper for leaving his mail-box (full of letters) unlocked when at Ferrybridge.

Selby still had its mail brought from Ferrybridge by horse post. In 1822 the letter carrier left the town for Selby and Howden at half past four in the morning. The first named postmaster at Selby was John Clough of Ousegate - the person who collected duties for such things as hair powder certificates. In 1837 Thomas Spivey was in charge of a Post Office in Church Yard. This was when the Royal Mail Coach came to the town on its Edinburgh to London run. A horse post left the town at nine o'clock in the morning to deliver letters to Howden, Goole, Snaith, Thorne and Ferrybridge. In 1840 Mr. Dickenson was paid £136 per annum for working the horse post between Selby and Thorne. Villagers in the surrounding district, some as far away as Hemingbrough and Haddlesey, had to travel to the town for their mail; letters from London cost them eleven pence. Francis Hutchinson of The Crescent, acting as postmaster, received £55 per annum.

London to Edinburgh

The coach that initially brought the mail to Ferrybridge for distribution to places such as Selby, started at London and finished its journey in Edinburgh. In 1786 it went from Doncaster to York via Ferrybridge and Tadcaster. In 1816 the Angel coaching inn at Ferrybridge was kept by Dr. George Alderson, the son of the vicar of Birkin. He was a doctor of medicine, coach proprietor and host at the Angel. Relays of horses for private carriages were stabled at the inn and postboys slept there. The latter were hired to drive or 'post' chaises from one inn to the next, often vying with one another for the fastest run. The Red Bear at Sherburn was another inn that provided the mail coach and others with fresh horses. Selby had no bridge at that time nor was there a decent road between the town and Doncaster. However, when the river was spanned and a turnpike road opened the mail coach went to York via Doncaster, Askern and Selby, thereby cutting three miles off its journey - a very important gain when speed was of the essence. The opening of the bridge for the passage of ships on the Ouse did not impede the progress of the mailcoach for the Turnpike Act of 1832 contained a special clause. It empowered the trustees to keep the bridge open for the mail coach during two specified periods of half-an-hour. This gave the Mail Coach precedence over vessels on the Ouse. Nothing in those days was allowed to interfere with the delivery of the Royal Mail.

The Last Delivery

The "Edinbro' Mail" ran without interruption from 1786 to 1842. On its best days the coach went from London to Edinburgh, including deliveries and changes of horses, in 42 hours 23 minutes. The 197 miles between London and York was completed in 20 hours and 54 minutes. On its route between Selby and York the Edinbro Mail passed Escrick Park, owned by Lord Wenlock. To mark its last run his lordship sent a footman to the park gates to stop the coach and to ask the driver, Tom Holtby, if he would leave the road and drive through the park to re-enter his normal route at the far end. The Edinbro' Mail left the road as requested and escorted by Lord Wenlock in his own outfit and Sir John Lister Kaye in his, was driven through the park. A huge black flag was hoisted from the coach roof and with Lord Macdonald holding the reins, the Royal Mail had a guard of honour all the way into York.

A Hitch-Hiker in the 19th Century

William Butterworth ran away to sea sometime in the early nineteenth century. After three years away he decided to return home to Leeds. On docking in London, William asked the captain of the *"Africa"* to hold his seafaring clothes for three weeks, and if he had not returned by then, to share them amongst his needy ship-mates. Having had no contact with his family whilst being away, the sea-farer was not sure of his reception. William enquired on the docks the best way to get back safely to Leeds. He was advised to go to the Gun and Shot Wharf where he might find some Hull and Selby traders. The runaway was very lucky to come across a sloop named, *"Unity"* which was bound for Selby the following morning. The master of the ship was Mr. Staniland, one of the distinguished captains and ship owners of that Selby family.

Mr. Staniland was very friendly and helpful to Butterworth and offered him a passage on his sloop. The young man boarded the *"Unity"* the next morning and five days later was in Selby. Butterworth now had to find a way to reach Leeds. He learnt it would take up to two days or more to travel the twenty miles to the town by the waterways. William Butterworth was 19 years of age and was too impatient to want to spend so long on a canal boat. Longing now to reach home he set out to walk. Dusk found him, footsore and tired, trudging along the track near Peckfield, twelve miles out from Selby. He was very relieved to be overtaken by a coach which an hour later dropped him in Leeds and into the happy and forgiving arms of his family. It had taken Butterworth around seven days to travel from London to Leeds using the transport available at that time.

Railways

Coaches and steam packets worked very well together until the invention of the steam locomotive and the building of railways. Coaching companies struggled hard to survive. Some prolonged their existence running in connection with the railways. During the 1830s the *"Celerity"* went from the 'Albion' in Leeds to Manchester by way of Huddersfield. It ran to connect with Manchester and Liverpool and the Leeds to Selby Railways. A coach running between Selby and Hull, completed a through connection from Hull to Liverpool.

Coaches running where no railways were laid survived longer but the ones that outstayed the rest were those taking the gentry on their seasonal trips to the fashionable watering places. The 'York Herald' published lists of lords and ladies attending such venues. In 1805 the gentry favoured Scarborough, Bridlington, Whitby and Redcar. When in 1840 the *"Celerity"* was no longer needed on the Manchester run, it became a 'season coach' making several runs a year to the fashionable Harrogate spa.

Wooden railway tracks first appeared in the coastal coal-mining areas of Northumberland and Durham where inclined tramways took wagons down to the nearby rivers and the sea. Cast-iron rails and then steam-powered locomotion were the next steps. In 1758 an Act of Parliament allowed Charles Brandling, the lord of the manor of Middleton, to build a wooden track from his colliery into Leeds, to connect it with the Aire and Calder Navigation. By 1812 rails replaced the track in order to try out a high-pressured steam locomotive. The experiment worked and the railway at Middleton became the first commercial user of steam locomotion. This was followed in 1825 by the Stockton and Darlington Railway, the first to provide public access for coal haulage.

Leeds to Selby Railway

Passenger services using steam locomotives began in 1833. The forerunner in Yorkshire was the Leeds to Selby railway authorised by an Act of Parliament in May 1830. As far back as 1802 "Mercator" a regular correspondent to the Leeds 'Mercury', had put forward the idea for a horse drawn wagon-way between Leeds and Selby. By 1816 several suggestions had been put forward involving the adaptation of the Middleton railway steam engines for use between the two towns. In 1821 a newspaper notice informed its readers that there was to be a meeting at the Court House, Leeds on the 24th. January concerning the *"Leeds and Selby Intended Rail Road "*. Many details were given in the notice including the following estimated figures: Leeds to Selby by water carriage - 16 to 18 hours, non-stop, at 14s. per ton; land carriage - 21 miles in one day at 26s.8d. per ton; and rail carriage - 5 hours at 10s. per ton. More meetings were held, during which time, at the request of Benjamin Gott, a Leeds cloth manufacturer, a route for the proposed railway was surveyed by George Stephenson. In 1829 the Leeds Selby Railway Company, consisting of one hundred and five members was formed. Its aim was to improve connections for the manufacturing centre of Leeds with the port of Hull; transport to the latter being provided by the steam packets operating on the River Ouse. Gott and his associates were not happy with the inclined planes and stationary engines Stephenson had proposed for the railway to Selby. James Walker, a civil engineer from London, was invited to examine the suggested line of the railway. In his report Walker recommended alterations to the proposed route that would ease the severe gradients of the original scheme allowing locomotive engines or horse power to be used without the need for stationary engines. The overall length of both routes was just under twenty miles. George Stephenson attended a meeting of the company held in Selby at which the revised line was voted in unanimously. Royal Assent was given to the scheme in May 1830. In July at a general meeting in Selby, the Hon. Ed. Petre and James Audus were amongst those elected as directors.

At first, stone from Monk Fryston quarry was laid on the track for the metals to rest upon; this proved unsatisfactory and wooden sleepers were introduced. The Leeds to Selby railway was partially opened on the 22nd. September 1834. One hundred and sixty passengers were accommodated in three first class carriages, painted yellow, and six second class open ones, pulled by the steam engine, *"Nelson"*. The guards were resplendent in green livery with shiny, brass plates denoting the company on their caps. After a short delay the train slowly steamed out of Marsh Lane terminus, Leeds, at 6:30 am. and continued at almost crawling speed for the first few miles. Frustrated spectators along the track urged the patrolling policemen to *"push her"!* One carriage was detached to try to make up the speed and by the time the train reached Garforth it was moving much faster. After the gradient fell towards Selby a terrific speed of 20mph. was reached and *"Nelson"* arrived in Selby minutes before 9:00am. The journey back to Leeds was done in one hour and sixteen minutes; the little steam train was welcomed there with salutes by a crowd of between forty to fifty thousand people. At first the morning and afternoon trains running from Leeds to Selby carried only passengers and merchandise. Horse power was used for minerals and heavy articles along the line. Short-stage coaches, forerunners of the omnibus, were allowed by an Act of 1832 to pick up and set down travellers in streets as well as at staging posts. One of these picked up passengers in Kirkgate, Leeds in time to catch the trains leaving Marsh Lane.

Going by Train

During the first four days of the railway's existence when only one line with passing places was in operation, 741 passengers were carried from Selby to Leeds and 779 the other way. The prices were sixpence for any person travelling up to five miles, one shilling up to ten miles and 1s.6d. for any distance exceeding ten. Trains stopped at Cross-Gates, Garforth, Roman Road and Micklefield, Milford and Hambleton. In 1835 they were leaving Selby at 8:30am, 5:30pm., and on arrival of the steam packets from Hull. On Sundays the trains left at 8:00am. and 4:30pm. During the summer 3,500 passengers were carried along the line.

At first there were no proper stations with platforms and waiting rooms. At Selby there were extensive train sheds on Ousegate through which the goods trains passed before crossing the road to the specially built jetties. They used the two pairs of outside lines, whilst the passengers who alighted in the sheds, were carried on the central lines. Tickets were obtained in the Superintendent's house next to the railway premises.

One coach connecting with the steam locomotives from the 15th. June 1835 was named *"Railway"*. It ran daily from the Elephant and Castle, Knaresborough, leaving each morning at five o'clock and travelling through Ribston, North and Kirk Deighton, Wetherby, Thorp Arch, Bramham Cross Roads and Aberford before arriving at Micklefield. There passengers boarded the train to Selby in connection with the steamers to Goole, Hull and Grimsby. The journey from Knaresborough to Hull on the oustside of the coach and the fore cabin of a steamer cost 6s. 6d; travelling inside the coach and in the best cabin cost 10s. 6d.

After two tracks were opened in 1835 a third jetty was built at Selby fitted with coal spouts. Not long after this the schooner, *"Audus"* shipped a cargo of coal to Rochester. The Audus family had invested in coastal trading when Goole began to take the inland trade away from Selby. All kinds of products, similar to those carried by the Aire and Calder Navigation were conveyed on the railway at competitive prices, and much faster. Tolls for horses, mules, asses, oxen, cows, bulls, or 'neat cattle' were ninepence each, under five miles, 1s.6d. under ten and 2s.6d. over ten miles. The toll for calves, sheep, lambs or pigs was sixpence each for any distance. Other charges added later, were a shilling for a dog, 15s. for a four-wheeled carriage, and half that for a two-wheeled one. The Company charged tonnage and tolls on other goods. For example, for every ton carried, the charges for lime, lime-stone, dung, compost, other manures and building materials for repair of roads was six shillings. The highest charges of 10s. 6d. per ton being for hops, tea, wines, spirits, vitriols, glass and other hazardous goods.

The railway between Leeds and Selby mostly followed a straight line but there were some slight changes in the gradient in places. These caused trouble on odd occasions for both engine and passengers. On one journey, after the bugle had sounded "all right" and the train left Selby, all went well along the level track to Hambleton Station, but when a gradient was encountered further on, the speed became noticeably slower. Spurting and groaning noises coming from the engine increased in intensity on the rise between Milford and Micklefield until the train finally shuddered to a stop! The guard quickly apprised the puzzled passengers as to what had happened. The heavy load was too much for the engine to pull up the incline! He asked the gentlemen if they would be obliging enough to leave their seats for a minute or two in order to lighten the load until the summit was reached. This they did with great alacrity and even helped to push the train up the hill. Then all jumped back in to enjoy the ride down the long incline into Leeds station.

There were many reports, even as late as the 1860s of animals taking fright at the sight and sounds of steam trains. The "Yorkshire Gazette" gave accounts of two in 1857. Mr. J. Wood a miller from Drax, was driving to Selby's Monday market in his dog cart when, as they neared the station, his horse took fright at the sudden appearance of a steam engine and bolted. The horse and cart struck a lamp post near the park wall. Mr. Wood and another gentleman were both thrown out with great violence. Mr. Hardisty, a joiner, narrowly escaped being run over by jumping over the wall. Neither gentlemen were too seriously injured but the dog cart was smashed to pieces. William Holdsworth, a news vendor of Selby, was not so lucky. He was carrying a pianoforte on a cart to Riccall when his horse took fright at a railway engine. Holdsworth was thrown off and dragged a considerable distance along the road. The paper reported he was in a very dangerous condition.

Whilst the railways were involved in cut throat competition with the waterways the turnpike roads were quickly losing revenue. The tolls collected for the Leeds to Selby road in 1820 amounted to £2,780. In 1834 they were £2,235, but two years after the opening of the railway between the towns they had dropped to £1,500. In 1888, most of the Turnpike roads were taken over by the County Councils, and the trusts dissolved.

Hull to Selby Railway

When the Leeds to Selby railway was opened in 1834 it inspired John Exley, a Hull Customs officer to suggest that it would be beneficial to many people if a line could be built from Hull to Selby. As the port's first railway, it would supplement the established waterways and links with the industrialised West Riding. Because of people's caution concerning the workings and advantages of railways nothing was settled until 1836. The Hull and Selby/Hull and Leeds Junction Railway Company was formed and a Bill for the track received Royal Assent in June. The line was to be 30¾ miles long and stations were planned at Hessle, Ferriby, Brough, Staddlethorpe, Eastrington, Howden, Bubwith Road and Cliffe. However, as the villagers objected to having a railway near their homes, the line was constructed outside the villages making it the longest straight rail track in England. The Hull terminus was close to the Humber Dock.

On the first of July 1840 the line was officially opened. Every building in Hull sported flags and ships in the harbour hoisted their colours. A grand procession had been planned but torrential rain caused its cancellation so to the sounds of Holy Trinity

Church bells the people hurried to the station. At noon a bell rang to warn lucky ticket holders that the trains were about to leave. At 12:15pm. the call "All's right" echoed through the station, the first engine *"Kingston"* whistled in reply and began to pull out on its journey to Selby. Five engines left Hull that day; the others were named *"Exley"*, *"Prince"*, *"Selby"* and *"Andrew Marvell"*, the poet and MP for Hull in the 17th century. The trains crossed the Ouse at Selby using the first railway bridge to span the river. It was twelve minutes past two when the first train entered Selby Station. The passengers were given two hours to explore the town and partake of a cold collation provided for them at the "George Hotel". The journey back took only one hour! There a cold collation of 750 dishes set out on 15 tables in the new warehouse awaited the dignitaries to help them celebrate the opening of the Hull to Selby railway.

The building of the railway bridge over the Ouse had been opposed by the Ouse Navigation trustees in the same way they had objected to Selby Toll Bridge. Fears were expressed over narrow passages for vessels but it was agreed any openings were not to be less than 45 feet and craft on the river were to have precedence over the trains. The first bridge was made of cast-iron with twin bascules lifting in the centre, similar to Tower Bridge. It was operated by hand and could be opened in one minute, as was proved at its trial opening in February, 1840. Fifty-one years later it was replaced, slightly downstream, by the present cast-iron bridge which turns on a pivot pier situated off centre providing one opening of 60 feet and the other of 54 feet. Only the former was for navigation purposes. The close proximity of the bridges over the Ouse at Selby caused difficulties for large vessels when there was an increase in the velocity of the tide.

Trains left Hull for Selby at 7am., 10am., 3pm., and 6pm.; only the earliest and the latest ran on a Sunday. It became possible for passengers to travel by rail between London, Leeds, York, Selby and Hull. Arrangements were also made for forwarding travellers to Sheffield, Derby, and Birmingham. At first, fares from Hull were as follows; 1st. class to Selby 4s.6d., 2nd. class 4s. and 3rd. class 2s.6d. To York and Leeds fares were 8s., 6s.6d., and 4s.6d. Remember the drain digger in Lincolnshire was earning 6s. to 7s. a day.

Selby to Doncaster

The number of railway companies increased rapidly and new tracks were being bid for all over the country, but the proposal that spurred the people of Selby into action was one for a line leading from Hull to Doncaster. In 1862 Hull was in need of a rail link with the manufacturing industries in South Yorkshire and the Midlands. Many companies applied for powers to construct a track from the Hull/Selby railway to Doncaster and all of them favoured Howden as a possible junction in preference to Selby. When it became known Parliament had rejected all plans because it was believed a bridge further down the Ouse would be both expensive and an obstacle to navigation, the people in and around Selby *"bestirred themselves"*.

Aware the North Eastern Railway Company was applying again for the authority to construct a line to Doncaster, an open meeting was held in the Public Rooms at Selby and two gentlemen were appointed to take a petition to the company. The case for a junction being at Selby and not Howden was clearly laid out in the report. It noted the presence of a bridge, that would reduce any engineering problems, and also the absence of strong opposition along the proposed route. Indeed the petition carried the signatures of inhabitants living in places that might be affected such as Selby, Brayton, Burn, Chapel and West Haddlesey, Hensall, Hirst Courtney, Temple Hirst, Whitley and Kellington. The company agreed to look at the proposed route from Selby to Askern along with other proposals they had received, but in the end it still contemplated having a junction at Howden. This greatly angered the people of Selby for they believed Howden's success could ruin their town but not vice versa. Howden's tradesmen realising the potential of having a railway junction in their town quickly formed an association to energetically support any Bill written in their favour.

All the plotting and scheming came to nought when the Engineer in Chief of the N.E.R.C. came and inspected the Hull/Selby line for a possible junction at Staddlethorpe and not Howden! He then 'posted' from Howden to the river bank near Hook to survey it for a possible bridge site! Howden's inhabitants were astounded at this complete change of route which, if forthcoming, would have the town three miles from the nearest station on the line and throw it completely out of the railway system. However, a few years elapsed before the companies renewed their applications and it was 1869 before a line was finally opened, with its junction at Staddlethorpe. Howden did not get its junction but in 1871 a main north-south line was opened that ran from Doncaster through Selby to York.

The London and North Eastern Railway Company had engine sheds in an area off Portholme Road, now occupied by a housing estate adjacent to the police station. The first roundhouse was built at Selby in 1871 and the second in 1896 to help house 46 engines. The buildings became known as 'Old Shed' and 'New Shed'. In 1912 a single track lean-to shed was added at the rear of the coal stage to house the railcars on the Cawood branch line. In 1914 Selby had 65 engines and employed 299 men. A Leyland bus, fitted with wheels was transferred from York to Goole and run on the Cawood branch. In 1926, it was accidentally burnt out. Between the wars the sheds had over 20 mineral engines engaged in bringing coal from various collieries to Gascoigne Wood. Today there are no sheds. At the end of the twentieth century coal excavated at Selby's mines was transported underground to Gascoigne Wood.

Cawood and Wistow Light Railway

When Selby grew in importance as a rail centre, a Bill was put forward in 1882 to extend a line from Wistow through Selby to Drax to join the Hull and Barnsley railway. It was abandoned as being both too expensive and poorly supported. A number of prominent people, including Captain Henry Liversidge, junior, J.P. of York, and Colonel Hawdon, J.P. of Selby remained interested in a local railway and in the 1890s they had a detailed survey done of the area which would be served by a line connecting Cawood with Selby. A Bill promoted successfully by Liversidge and Sebastian W. Meyer of Leeds resulted in the construction of the Cawood, Wistow and Selby Light Railway.

The line was sorely needed because of the poor state of the minor roads running through the agricultural areas. Cawood, Wistow and Ryther were surrounded by market gardens, smallholdings and fields upon fields of celery, potatoes, peas, grain and later, sugar beet. In Cawood there were brick, tile and pottery works. The village was also trying to increase the number of fishermen and visitors to the area.

The nearest railway was at Selby and it cost the villagers five shillings a ton to cart their wares to the station, so when the "first sod" was cut for the line by Mrs.

Liversidge, it was a very important day for everyone. On a hot day in July 1896, schools were closed, work suspended, decorations festooned about, and a flag raised on the top of the castle. Luncheons and teas were enjoyed and the Selby Rifles' band provided the music. The official opening of the railway took place on a bitterly cold and windy February day in 1898. The first engine *"Cawood"* left Brayton Gates Junction, near to the Armoury, and went along the four-and-a-half miles line, which crossed Leeds Road, where Court Drive is today, then over the Dam, past Flaxley Road and Selby Common before heading north to stop at Wistow and then Cawood. Going at no more than 25 miles an hour, it pulled two of the Company's coaches and five or six N.E.R. carriages, carrying the Lord Mayor of York, the Directors of the Company and some two hundred passengers.

In 1899 there were four trains each way every day except for Monday (market day) when there were five into Selby and six out. The fares were one penny a mile for 3rd. class and 3d. a mile for 1st. class passengers. This was until the N.E.R. took over the thriving railway in 1900 and applied their own prices. Sometimes special trips were run to Leeds for the pantomimes at a mere 1s.3d. return. There was a wooden platform, a shelter and a substantially built brick locomotive shed where the passenger trains stopped at Brayton Gates, (later known as "Wistow Junction" or "Selby West"). It was not until 1904 that the trains continued to Selby station.

The railway was the lifeline of the two villages until a regular bus service was introduced. Essential goods like coal, manures, soot and other fertilisers were brought in and the produce grown or made in the area taken into Selby. In the early 1900s twenty wagons of potatoes a day were put on the train. There were loop lines at the road crossings. Leeds Road loop became a distribution point for carters making local deliveries and a place for tank wagons of paraffin. All the road crossings were gated and had a gatekeeper's house.

The late Mrs. Agnes Cockerill of 'Ye Old Cottage', Wistow, now demolished, recalled the comings and goings of the little tank engines. Most memorable were the annual outings of combined parties of Anglicans and Methodists to the coast. For such a long run a heavier engine was needed but it was not allowed to go over the brick built bridge spanning Selby Dam. Therefore, the tank engine went to the villages to collect the passengers and on its arrival at Selby Station was replaced by a more powerful locomotive.

The line remained popular until road traffic increased. Up to 1953 sugar beet, potatoes and coal were still being carried but six years later a train only ran when required and in 1960 the Cawood, Wistow Light Railway was closed. Mr. John Woodall from Wistow travelled on that first train, *"Cawood"*, and was granted his wish to travel on the last one. Most of the buildings and tracks were removed over the following years. There is no trace of the Leeds Road crossing, new houses were built on the site of the Gatehouse and along the trackbed of the loop line. A large modern house was erected between Leeds Road and the remains of the brick bridge over Selby Dam. There are however some remnants of the railway left in Wistow. The station is now a bungalow but the weighbridge and the store at the end of the platform are still standing.

A Survey of Nineteenth Century Selby

The great developments in communications and trade that brought prosperity to Selby also altered the ancient lay-out of the town. Many changes took place along

Ousegate as the inhabitants enjoyed the fruits of a flourishing port. The shipyard business was booming and numerous dwellings were built for the accommodation of people involved in maritime activities.

The toll-bridge spanning the Ouse brought both trade and people to the town. At first, the only route for this traffic to and from the centre of Selby was by Water Lane, Micklegate and Finkle Street. This became a problem as the volume of traffic increased. John Audus, a Selby business man, came up with the idea of opening a way through Ousegate, to the west end of the bridge. He proposed that a street be laid leading from the market place and curving round the Abbey Church to the bridge. At that time the parkland on the south side of the town went up to the walls of the church and stretched along the back of Ousegate, being separated from it by Back Dyke. This land was owned by the lord of the manor and was not for sale. However, with characteristic determination, John Audus pursued the matter and obtained a 99 year building lease from Lord Petre. Audus modelled his new houses that followed the curve of the road on the Lansdowne Crescent in Bath. Today The Crescent, as it became known, has the Abbey Church on its north side and on the south begins at Wetherell's store on the eastern corner of James Street and finishes at the Albion Vaults on the corner of Thornden Buildings - named after Thornden Hall near Brentford, Essex, family seat of the Petres. From there to the bridge is known as New Street. It gained this name after The Crescent was formed. The boundary between the two seems to be where Back dyke ran along the edge of the lord's parkland. The dyke, which joined the Ouse near the canal, was put underground around this time.

The Shipyard

Morrell described the town as it was in the 1860s. His survey began where the canal met the Ouse. On the far side of the lock was a square of houses known as East Common, and on the west was the shipyard. In 1866 Mr. T. Green owned the business run for so long by Samuel Gutteridge. James Banks followed him but by 1887 it was being run by J. Burton. The Connell family became partners in the yard in 1887. Known as the "Shipbuilding and Engineering Company" it had another shipyard in York. Henry Connell began work there as a thirteen year old apprentice. He stayed with the yard to become foreman then owner. The largest ship built on the Ouse by this company was the S. S. Frithjof, with a gross tonnage of 1390, and a length of 231 feet. Mr. Connell claimed it was the first ship to generate its own electricity.

The company was liquidated in 1902 and "Henry Connell Ltd." was subsequently formed. A large and beautiful house was built for the Connells on the corner of Ousegate and Shipyard Road.

The last large vessel built at the yard was the barge "Selebian" in 1936. It was used as a balloon barge in the defence of Hull in World War II. When Goole's shipbuilding trade surpassed Selby's, Connell's yard continued to survive until 1958 by changing to the overhauling and refitting of pleasure boats, and by civil engineering which included the servicing of the toll bridges at Bubwith, Carlton and Selby.

In the early days when there were no trade unions or stewards to speak for the men, Connell had his own method for settling disputes in the shipyard. When any workers had a complaint to make they were invited into Connell's house to discuss the matter around his dining table. If a settlement was not reached in half-an-hour the meeting was not adjourned nor did the men call for an immediate strike. Instead Connell and the main complainant took off their coats, rolled up their sleeves and went outside on to the lawn to settle the matter with their fists. Defeat by either side was accepted and no malice borne afterwards by the combatants.

The Waterworks

In Morrell's time Selby's waterworks were situated behind Connell's shipyard, across Canal Road from the little swing bridge that spans the water. They were erected there by the Local Board of Health under the Public Health Act of 1848. Water was obtained from two artesian wells on land purchased by the Board. Two powerful engines of 15 horse power each, forced the water to a height of 85 feet into a water cistern capable of holding 155,000 gallons, housed in a massive water tower. The tower was a fine example of brick architecture which was sadly pulled down some time after the waterworks were superseded by Barff Water Works. When Selby's own water supply proved inadequate for the expanding town, Mark Scott, chairman of the Council had suggested boring on Brayton Barff. When the works were opened in April 1908, water was piped through to Selby; there was such a plentiful supply that some was sold to Pontefract and Leeds. Of course, paying water rates was unpopular. In 1864 W. Rawlinson and G. Watson protested at paying 8d. in the pound for something, they said, they did not use!

Ousegate to Millgate

Continuing along Ousegate in the direction of the toll-bridge Morrell noted on his right a packet wharf where a steamer still came daily, both up and down the river. Just before the railway bridge were the railway company's warehouses and staithes with accommodation for exchange of goods with the river crafts. Next to these stood the houses for the railway officials. In the 1871 census they were listed as, Locomotive Superintendent David Gibson and wife, Martha, Railway Station Master Edwin Storey, wife Margaret, two children and a sixteen year old servant from Fulford. Next to them lived the railway clerk William Paris with his wife, daughter and a thirteen year old servant from Knottingley. The good substantial houses they lived in are still in existence, as are the railway train sheds with their huge doors. A station was built on its present site after the Selby to Hull line opened.

The following notice was displayed in Selby's railway station:

In order to insure punctuality - no Passengers will be admitted through the Outer Door of the Railway Station after the clock has struck the hour of Departure.
Passengers too late to take their seats may receive half the Fare paid.

The tickets were bought from a clerk who painstakingly filled in date, passenger's name, destination and class of carriage, in a receipt book. He then copied these details onto a counterfoil before tearing out the ticket part against a thin steel straight edge. It is interesting to note that in 1872 the North Eastern Railways began issuing 3rd. class return tickets at a price some 50% above the normal single fare; a privilege long enjoyed by 1st. and 2nd. class passengers was *"extended to the working classes"*. Third class carriages were like cattle trucks, open and unprotected overhead, with hard board seats. Improvements were made to Selby Station in the 1890s including new offices and waiting rooms.

Continuing along Ousegate, past the toll bridge, the road led to Water Lane and the medieval warehouses where Mr. Foster and Messrs. Proctor and Co. stored their flax. Moving on into Millgate, besides an iron foundry, there were retteries for flax scutching. At that time flax was an important trade in the town. In 1861 there were 37 males and 7 females employed in the flax and linen manufacture. Six years later Ryder & Sons, flax spinners and manufacturers of patent shoe threads, shoe twines, sail and roping twines, employed 20 men, 32 boys, 43 women and 47 girls. These mills were at the southern end of New Lane, edged by Massey Street along the north side, Portholme Road to the east, up to where the Tesco supermarket is today. The houses now on Portholme Drive, follow the line of what was the Mills' ropewalk. The company was taken over by Messrs. Moss Rimmington and Co. and in 1887 they won the first order of merit for their sewing twine, shoe threads and shoe twine at a Jubilee International Exhibition held in Adelaide, Australia.

Mustard was also grown in the district. A mustard mill, managed by Cornelius Rimmington, occupied part of the premises down New Lane. It was taken over by Colmans' in 1912 and closed down. Described also as a commercial traveller, Rimmington owned a property on Gowthorpe, known as Mustard Yard, down which five families lived. 'Yards' were pieces of land containing workshops, homes and a large dwelling owned by a person who maintained the properties; the yard often carried his name. There were many of them off Gowthorpe and Finkle Street, forming little communities. Many flax workers lived in Massey Row off Massey Street, and Richardson's Buildings, off New Lane, whilst others lived alongside agricultural labourers and servants in the 27 houses down South Parade. Its name can still be seen on the side of Carol Winn's florist's shop on Gowthorpe but the yard is now a car park. Another yard, Precious Yard, nearby, was occupied solely by Irish immigrants. St. Johns Square, down New Lane was inhabited by railway workers such as labourers, porters and engine drivers.

Returning from Millgate to Wide Street, Morrell was faced, in the 1860s, by a number of quite desirable private residences. The 'Curriers Arms' for example was noted as a good specimen of Elizabethan architecture. Finkle Street, leading to the market place, was full of shops. In the 1841 census they were listed as milliners, straw hat makers, dress makers, drapers and one chaise driver.

Park Street, The Crescent and Gowthorpe

From there Morrell's tour took him back to the toll bridge and down New Street to Park House. Then into Park Street where stood the Mechanics' Institute. This institution, which aimed to improve the facilities for education, was founded in Selby in September 1846, and originally met in Abbey Place. The venue soon became unsuitable for meetings so funds were raised to move to a better place. In 1861 the members took possession of the Public Rooms on Park Street and adapted the premises for their own use. They had a newsroom and library, arranged classes in elementary education and sometimes gave lectures. The Mechanics Institute was eventually taken over by Sir Jonathan Hutchinson before becoming the meeting place of the Salvation Army.

Across the railway at the end of Park Street were the Gas Works. Selby Gas Company was opened on the 9th. March 1832, by a joint stock company. The minutes of the Local Board of Health record that in November an order was made for one hundred lamps to light the streets of Selby by gas. A three year contract with the Company was also prepared which included a stipulation that the lights would be put out on the first of May. Arrangements were made the following January to pay the first year's instalment and for a one shilling in the pound rate to be charged to all householders and occupiers of canals, railways or other such amenities.

Morrell came to the Market Place via Abbey Yard which ran parallel to The Crescent and connected Park Street to James Street. The monks' well was still in situ there and had not been long out of use. The Market Place was reached by turning right in James Street.

Across the square, near to the opening for Abbey Place, shaded by trees planted in the 1780s, was the Londesborough Arms, an old established hotel and posting house, known for centuries as The George. The name was changed after the purchase of the Selby estate for Albert, Denison Denison, 1st. Baron Londesborough, the first non-catholic to be lord of the manor. The Petre Arms on Gowthorpe, another old posting inn, changed its name to the George Hotel but, unlike the Londesborough, it succumbed to modernisation. In the 1980s much of it was destroyed, the part fronting onto Gowthorpe was converted into three shops with a passageway leading to a new shopping complex. George Bradley, who lived in the adjoining cottage when his father was ostler there, recalled what it was like in the 1920s before the advent of the motor car. Mr. Bradley looked after the horses and provided carriages, cabs and open wagons for any occasion. An old-fashioned glass hearse and carriages were used for funerals and open landaus for days out or rides into the country. The hotel ran a taxi service when needed and on Sundays took ministers out to their places of worship in the surrounding villages. On Market days it was very busy when farmers left their carriages at the George Hotel. Mr. Bradley stabled the horses and arranged the traps in order round the yard, ready for collection. He even, for a small fee, looked after bicycles. Weddings meant hard work as the carriages and horses were prepared for the big event. White satin went in the cabs, big bows of ribbon on the whips, and flowers in the carriage lamps. The horses were well groomed and their ears bedecked with white caps. When the use of motor cars increased it was the end of the horse and carriage business. Around 1931 the owner, Mr. Joseph Haynes sold the George Hotel.

Morrell described the shops surrounding the market place in the 1860s as being in the best business position in town. The first building on the corner of New Lane, and at the start of Gowthorpe, was the Town Hall, erected in 1825. Before this court affairs were carried out in the remains of the monastery and its gatehouse. Prisoners were confined there in a cellar. When the remains of the monastic buildings were removed, voluntary subscriptions enabled the building of the Town Hall on land given by the Hon. E.R.Petre. Until the 1850s the stocks were situated in front of it. The lower floor of the hall was used for the confinement of prisoners and the upper rooms for official business including magistrates' meetings. The Great Court Leet was still being held with a jury and the steward of the manor present. In 1832 their duties included appointing John Robert as the town's pinder and swineherd master and William Lowther as the town crier. They also dealt with numerous land settlements. For instance, at the time of his death Howard Nappey had held a tenement in Bondgate occupied by Samuel Lazenby. In his will he left the property to his granddaughter, Mary Wellburn, but she had to appeal to the court to be admitted as tenant in the property. This was granted.

Selby's early fire engine, which was in the care of the police, was housed under a high arched entrance down the side of the Town Hall. The horses used to pull the engine were stabled across the road at the George Hotel. Before World War I rockets were used to raise the alarm until they were replaced by maroons. A six to eight foot long steel tube was sunk into the ground and the maroon was dropped in to fire itself. A dangerous practice that was soon stopped!

The policy of keeping prisoners in the Town Hall on Gowthorpe continued until 1854 when plans were put forward for a 'lock-up' and a superintendent's house in New Lane. The Court House was erected at the expense of James Audus and magistrates met there every alternate Monday to administer justice. Magistrates still meet there, but prisoners are now dealt with in the new police station built on Portholme Road. The Town Hall, or 'Old Prison' as it was known, was rebuilt in the 1890s. During the late twentieth century it housed a bank and now, as previously stated, it is home to a drinking establishment, whilst the Town Hall occupies the fine old Primitive Methodists' building.

A wide variety of misdemeanours were dealt with at the police courts in New Lane. Examples from the year 1885 included a Hull labourer charged with trespassing in pursuit of game in the lord of the manor's woods at Selby. The culprit did not appear when summoned, but was apprehended on the following Saturday when recognised in the town, playing for Hull Shamrock Football Club against Selby's second team, in the third round of the *"Hull Times"* cup-ties. Also, a farmer from Barlby was fined £3.15s.9d. and costs, or one month's hard labour, for travelling from Leeds to Selby without a railway ticket. Three men from Leeds were caught gambling on the train between Selby and Milford Junction, the cards' owner being fined £4.19s.6d., the others two pounds less. A keelman and a labourer were fined over ten pounds each for using a stolen boat and net for taking salmon at Cawood - they had been observed killing a fish. A Hambleton farmer was fined 22s. for riding on the footpath there, whilst a poulterer was charged 19s.6d. for cruelty to a fowl. John Oxley, farmer's son of Thorpe Willoughby was put to one month's hard labour for being drunk and disorderly in Selby and a grocer from Drax paid a fine of a pound for being drunk in charge of a horse.

Banking

Also on Gowthorpe in the 1860s were the premises of the York City and County Banking Company. From the reign of Queen Elizabeth I to that of Charles II (1660-1685) tradesmen had produced their own coins or tokens, made from lead, tin, copper or brass. An example of one used in the town had the names Christopher Bacon and John Parrott on the obverse side and *"Of Selby, 1669, their half peny"*, on the reverse. A national copper currency was established around 1672.

Towns and cities in England also issued their own bank notes. John Foster produced them in his own name. An example, dated 1st. May 1815 was still in existence at the beginning of the twentieth century. Banks were formed by groups of merchants but the notes they issued could only be used in their locality. Such a bank was formed in Selby because it was difficult to obtain notes from London, and also it was easier and safer to carry paper than gold or silver. Two rare Selby Bank notes came up for auction in April 2004. Each of them, sufficient to feed a family for a week in the 1820s, would not have been owned by the average man in the street. One was issued by 'Selby Bank' in June 1823 and the other in December 1825. The town's insignia and a picture of the toll bridge are plainly discernable. Both notes feature the names of Scholfield, Clarkson and Clough. In 1823 these three bankers, with another named Coates, had a bank in Finkle Street, and were connected with bankers Spooner, Attwood and Co., in London.

One of the main commercial functions of Selby at that time was as an outlet for local agricultural produce. In order to service this trade the York City and County Banking Company rented premises in the town in September 1830 and opened an agency there on market days. James Audus who was appointed their agent later became chairman of the Yorkshire Banking Company. The private bank of Scholfield, Clarkson and Clough failed in 1831 and the York City secured its business in Howden and Selby. When the York City gained a licence to operate in the whole of Yorkshire it took over Scholfield and Co.'s last office, Bank House, on Gowthorpe. This site is now occupied by Woolworths.

From 1832 until 1867 the agency, which opened every day, was run by Robert Morrell. It was then taken over by his son, William Wilberforce Morrell who had been born in Bank House on Gowthorpe and began work in the Head Office at York when aged fifteen; a father and son employed in the same branch was unacceptable. The bank made steady progress and was able to move to larger premises in the Market Place, leased to them by Lord Londesborough. Business flourished in the more accessible offices and sub-branches were opened in Cawood and Sherburn. In 1901 the York City and County Banking Company moved into its purpose built premises on the corner of James Street. Eight years later it amalgamated with the London Joint Stock Bank and in 1918 was taken over by the Midland Bank. Around the year 2000 it became part of H.S.B.C. Bank plc., still on the same site.

James Audus

Past the bank and the old town hall on the south side of Gowthorpe was the Quakers' meeting place, set back from the road; today it is hidden behind a shop. Further along, in the 1860s, were the Primitive Methodists' chapel and premises belonging to the Roman Catholics. Further west were the almshouses in Feoffees Square and Audus Square. James Audus (1781-1867), responsible for the building of the second Square, was the son of John Audus, creator of The Crescent. He moved from Rawcliffe to live in the town after the opening of the Aire and Calder Navigation to Selby. Besides helping his father in modernising the market place and the new route to the toll bridge, James, a generous man with time, talent and money, took on many roles during his long life. He became the senior justice of the peace for the Liberty of Selby, presiding over many petty sessions at the Court he had had built in New Lane. For 25 years he held the rank of senior captain of the York and Ainsty local militia, consisting of 1,200 men, of which the Selby Volunteers became a part in 1808. He held many offices in the town including treasurer to the Feoffees. In 1833 Audus paid for ten small dwellings, for poor widows or aged persons, built on that charity's land on Gowthorpe.

Audus specified that an annual rent of £1.11.6d. was to be paid until his death, after which the occupiers were to live rent free. The interest from the accumulated funds, after deduction for repairs was to be distributed amongst the tenants. In 1871 the houses in Audus Square were occupied by eight females, one married couple and one widower, all over 60 years of age. The cottages in the adjacent Feoffees Square, built by the charity in 1823 to let at a low rent to needy old persons, housed five women living alone, three couples and a mother, daughter and grandson.

James Audus, in his eighties, was still being a benefactor to the town. Although a member of Selby Abbey Church he set his mind on having a church in Selby for ordinary people *"where no pew rents were paid or status in worldly terms important"*. To that end he had St. James' the Apostle Church built on his land between New Lane and the bottom of Audus Street. At the age of 85 he laid the foundation stone but sadly, he died in May 1867. The following September the church was consecrated. In 1871, the widow of James Audus enabled the 'Audus Memorial School' to be built near to the church.

Feoffees

As far back as 1664 the principal charities of the town were vested under the control of trustees known as Feoffees. Fifteen persons were nominated to use the funds accumulated from estates bequeathed over the years for the benefit of the town. Many examples have been given of these bequests left for the use of the church, the poor and the highways. The latter was the subject of much discussion after the formation of the Board of Health which claimed that it alone had the legally constituted authority to deal with roads and that no money had been received from the Feoffees. In 1867 a Charity Commissioners' inspector came to the town to help clear this matter and to look at the charity's accounts.

He found no faults with these but agreed that for many years no funds had been given to the surveyors or the Board for highway repairs. A spokesman for the Feoffees explained that this was because the roads were no longer in the deplorable state they had been when the charity was first formed. The trustees then described some of the ways they helped the poor. A list of recipients of alms was revised each year on the 21st. December when widows and other needy people in the parish of Selby could apply to the treasurer or other members for help. It was noted half of the average number of recipients were on parish relief. The largest amount given each year was five shillings but aid once given continued until the recipient died. Six penny loaves were also presented to those receiving gifts of money and to many who were not. Trouble often arose - some were accused of selling their bread and coming back for more. The loaves were bought from four or five bakers to ensure there was not a monopoly. St. Thomas's Day, formerly the 21st. December, is now celebrated on the 3rd. July. It was a tradition for employees to receive small gifts of money or eatables on the saint's day. The Commissioners' inspector in Selby disapproved of food handouts on just one day when there was a need for it throughout the year. He realised it was difficult to administer funds to everyone's satisfaction, but advised them to strive to avoid pauperism and increase their funds. Some of this could be achieved, he said, by both putting up rents and making savings by cutting down the amount of bell-ringing! He also recommended the building of baths and wash-houses which was vehemently opposed by one member.

Today the responsibility for these funds and the almshouses come under the auspices of Selby United Charities.

The Union Workhouse

As Morrell made his way back along the south side of Gowthorpe he came to Brooke Street, described by him as *"the new road leading to Doncaster"*. The street was named after descendants of Humphrey Brooke, who in 1564 purchased Gateforth manor from Lord D'Arcy. The Rev. Richard Brooke, who had taken his wife's name by royal licence on their marriage, succeeded to the estates in 1850. On his wife, Jane's tombstone in Brayton churchyard is listed the numerous gifts she gave to deserving causes, after the death of her husband, and others left in her will. The gifts ranged from £500 to as high as £30,000. They included £4,000 to aid the living at Gateforth and the poor there and at Brayton.

At the southern end of Brooke Street, (the 'e' was later dropped), near to the railway crossing was the Rifle Armoury and Drill Shed of the 38th. West York Rifle Volunteers referred to in Chapter 8. Diagonally opposite was the Union Workhouse built in 1837. The Poor Law Amendment Act of 1834 compulsorily amalgamated parishes into 'unions' to provide for the poor. The Selby Poor Law Union formed in February 1837, was comprised of 27 parishes and townships. The 1831 census put the population of these parishes at 14,782, ranging from Hirst Courtney with 117 people to Selby with 4,600. A Board of Guardians, locally elected, included three representatives for Selby and one for each other place.

The 1834 Poor Law Amendment Act almost entirely abolished outdoor relief (support given to the needy still in their own homes), at a time when there was much poverty in the district. Desperate labourers walked seven or eight miles a day looking for work. Compulsory labour on the roads had been abolished but the pay given to road workers was poor. In 1867 a claim for eight shillings a week for a man and his horse in a road gang was considered far too high. The average pay for this type of worker was around three shillings. Labourers on the land earned an average of 2s.6d. a day and paid from three to four pounds annually for a cottage without a garden. Policemen and railwaymen were regarded as having 'bread for life' jobs. Food had become a worse problem when access to the commons and woods had been taken away. In winter the poor survived mainly on potatoes, turnips and onions stewed up with fat into a watery mess known as 'lobs scouse'. During the severest winters soup kitchens were provided by churches and the officials in Selby. In the winter of 1854 hot soup and bread was served twice a day to over 500 hungry people in the town. On another occasion, the soup kitchen in Selby gave out 1,000 quarts of soup, 1,000 lbs of bread to the poor. Those who could not scrape a living went into the workhouse.

For many years families were segregated in Selby Union Workhouse which had four yards, one each for men, women, girls and boys. There were even separate schoolrooms. In 1854 the post of schoolmistress was advertised offering a separate sitting room and lodging room with an annual salary of twenty to thirty pounds depending on her ability. There was also a vacancy for a nurse offering rations and accommodation plus £15 a year. In the1871 census Mr. Ed. Pidd is shown as Master of the workhouse, his wife the matron; Hannah Umpleby was a nurse, and Richard Cass, a porter. No schoolmistress was listed. There were 45 males and 35 females, mostly from the local villages. Fourteen of the inmates were children. Amongst the other inmates 43 were classed as labourers.

The workhouse, enlarged in 1892, was still in use as late as 1925 when, in one week, up to 209 vagrants used its amenities. Selby Guardians complained of an increase in vagrancy. It had often been put forward that some method should be adopted to weed out the 'loafers' from the genuine needy persons. Most of those who came to the workhouse in the early twentieth century washed the dishes or chopped wood to pay for their bed and breakfast. Selby residents recalled how some of those wishing to be classed as 'in need' hid their money or valuables in a hedge across the road from the building. There it was safe from the workhouse officials but not the local children!

When the Union Workhouse was closed the buildings were converted into an elderly persons home, known as Brook Lodge. New premises were built for the use of Social Services on the site of the old workhouse. A Day Centre was opened facing onto Brook Street.

Today this caters for individuals or groups of persons over 18 in need of help or somewhere to meet. A place for elderly persons, Carentan House, was built behind the Centre, with its entrance in Union Lane. Social services still use the old board-room and casuals' block added in 1892.

New Schools and Old

After leaving the workhouse and returning along Gowthorpe towards the Market Place, Morrell turned down New Lane which once followed the boundary line of the monastery grounds as far as its old postern gate; from where tracks once led off towards Snaith and Brayton. Almost at the southern end of this lane, just before Portholme Mills, was the Subscription School. This was built in 1811 with funds mainly raised through the efforts of William Massey and James Audus. The short length of highway that runs along the side of the school still bears the name Massey Street. In White's Directory for 1838 the school was recorded as being attended by Wesleyans and Quakers, forty one children being taught there during the week. In his will dated June 1831, Stephen Staniland bequeathed £200 to the Feoffees for clothing and educating poor boys and £200 to the trustees of the Subscription School. A report in an 1896 newspaper stated that the premises had been used as a School of Art since 1876 and that for the past six years the £200 from the Staniland bequest had been lying unused in a local bank. The Urban Council recommended the money be vested in trustees for the benefit of the Art School. There was also a suggestion that scholarships be made available for children attending the elementary schools in the town. A report noted that Sir Gilbert Scott, engaged in restoring the Abbey Church had presided at an annual meeting of the art school and distributed the prizes.

Further up New Lane, on the opposite side of the road were much bigger and newer educational premises. Until the beginning of Queen Victoria's rule the government, apart from bestowing grants, still did not consider education as its concern. In 1839, however, it set up a committee to investigate how its money was being used. This education department became a Board in 1899, controlled by the government.

In the 1850s it was decided that Selby was in need of greater educational facilities and funds were raised to build three schools, boys, girls and infants, down New Lane. The Church of England Society and the Education Council both made contributions, the latter increasing its grants substantially over the following years. The premises, that became known as Selby Abbey National Schools, were opened on the 18th. January 1858. Fees were 4d. a boy, 3d. for brothers and girls, 2d. for sisters and infants under six; books were free but few in number. Those pupils in need were helped by the charities. Children were expected to attend every day except Saturday and to be punctual at 9am. and 2pm.; doors were locked five minutes after these times. The number of pupils attending the school the first year were 67 boys, 98 girls and 64 infants. Two houses were provided for the staff.

Returning to Gowthorpe Morrell continued through the Market Place and turned down James Street where parts of the Tithe Barn were still in evidence, being, at that time, occupied by a brewery and stables. The chapel and premises of the Wesleyan Methodists were also located down this street. By that time most religious institutions in the town provided some form of education for their congregations. The Methodist Sunday School was opened as early as 1834; nine years later during alterations a school building and a master's house were added. There was an infant and an upper school on the premises. The National schools were built in close proximity to the Methodist premises which sometimes caused confusion for both pupils and teachers. One entry in the Wesleyans' Admission Register, put in after a child had attended for only one day, read, "Admitted in error. (Got to wrong school)."

Interchanges of pupils went on for many years with some children leaving to go to a private school, or academy, as they were known in Victorian times. The number of these in Selby varied over the years. The 1871 census listed one next to the Primitive Methodist Chapel run by three Sisters of Charity and another down Brook Street which had eight scholars attending from as far away as Durham and Manchester. One academy opening in the 1850s and surviving into the twentieth century was situated on Ousegate, not far from where Morrell began his survey. Richard Taylor established a private school on Ousegate in premises that faced the river a few yards to the west of the toll bridge. This building later became known as 'Corunna House'. Believed to have been built in the early eighteenth century this fine house was the only one in Selby that Pevsner in his "Buildings of West Yorkshire" considered worthy of note. Today it is a grade two listed building.

Pupils attending Ousegate School in the 1860s expected to be taught "different branches of a sound literary and polite education", for fees ranging from six to eight guineas. At one period Taylor had one teacher and three servants to assist him in catering for 16 boarders, some from as far away as Staffordshire and Lincolnshire. Gregory Dent, "a severe but good teacher" took over the school in 1873. When he had two daughters he extended his curriculum to accommodate young children. One daughter later ran the school until its closure in 1926.

After the school was closed Albert Wales used the premises for a boarding house. From the end of the 1930s until the 1970s, Mrs Thornton and Mr. Simpson ran the Corunna Cafe there. After some renovations it became Garbo's Restaurant and more recently was used as offices. Today the owners are the proprietors of S.W.A.T. Security Company who have offices there. The barns at the back have been converted into dwellings.

Mr. Philip Milsom, Hon. Secretary of the Civic Society has spent some time investigating why 42/44 Ousegate became known as Corunna House. It was believed by many that relations of Sir John Moore owned or lived in the premises. Sir John was killed at Corunna in 1809 whilst leading the British forces against Napoleon in the Peninsular War. Philip Milsom found no evidence of any connection with Sir John or Corunna.

Cholera

Although Selby had entered the nineteenth century with a promising future as a trading port, it was a very unhealthy place. This was due to the increasing population, lack of sanitation, impure and inadequate water supplies, bad ventilation and plenty of dirt. The supply of clean, fresh water to the town came after it was placed under the Public Health Act in 1850, following an alarming increase in deaths caused by disease.

It was not surprising, therefore, that the town continued to suffer from diseases that for centuries had carried off many of its children. William Storr of Scalm Park, Wistow, kept a diary of events. He recorded marrying Elizabeth of Selby in 1688 and living in the town for seven years. The Storrs had ten children, some born in Selby. Seven of them died between 1689 and 1715, three of them under one year old, the oldest aged seventeen. At least two of them died of smallpox. In 1787 smallpox and putrid fever caused the deaths of 69 of the 114 mortalities in Selby.

Cholera, an acute infection of the small intestine caught from contaminated water, was rampant in many parts of the country between 1831 and 1832. Sunderland lost two hundred people to the disease within a few weeks. It spread through the ports, attacking sailors and other people connected with shipping. A justice of the peace who lived in an inland town free of the disease died from cholera. He had recently sailed in a vessel from Knottingley where the disease was prevalent.

Other places in the north affected by the disease included Hull, Goole, York, Doncaster, Leeds, Wakefield and Selby. Posters with the heading *"Cholera Morbus"* full of good advice regarding cleanliness were displayed around the town in 1831. People were advised to sprinkle their rooms with hot vinegar. Smoking tobacco was recommended but going out at night or drinking alcohol were discouraged. Despite this, Selby was very severely affected, 55 people succumbing to the disease. The deaths were so frequent that it was decided to suspend the continuous tolling of the 'passing bell' lest the terror already gripping the people was increased beyond control

During 1847 an epidemic of Irish Fever took the lives of many people in Selby and elsewhere. It was mainly brought about by the famine in Ireland but poor conditions in parts of Scotland and England exacerbated it. The epidemic in England was mainly typhus with some cases of the relapsing fever - a bacterial infectious disease with recurrent periods of fever. The contagion began to peter away in 1848 but just as Selby people were recovering from its effects, cholera appeared with a vengeance in the town.

The epidemic spread through the town during the latter part of 1848 and until February of the following year there was a respite until July when the disease became very severe again and continued so until November. It was prevalent in Millgate, Micklegate, Ousegate and Finkle Street. In the Union Workhouse there were 19 deaths from cholera and two from diarrhoea. Similar to 1832, a committee of health was appointed to help relieve the distress of the sick. A fund totalling £336.2s.1d. was quickly raised towards this aim.

The committee decided to have their meetings in the town hall on Gowthorpe, and to this end ordered the place to be thoroughly cleansed and made comfortable for them. Half a ton of coal was ordered and instructions given for a fire to be lit at 7:30 each evening. Many important decisions were made at these meetings. On the 18th. September, 1849, two nurses were appointed to the cholera hospital to replace the one who had fallen ill. Orders were increased for badly needed sheets, blankets and bedding. The next day the committee learnt that since their last report there had been 36 more cases of diarrhoea, a new case of cholera, one death and no recoveries. Also, eleven victims had been detained in the Union Workhouse hospital. At a meeting on the 20th. it was recommended that Kirk Dyke be flushed out. A report from the medical men pointed towards a slight improvement. The committee were given powers to purchase changes of bedding and linen to lend to the poor, and obtain necessities for the needy families who had suffered from the cholera, for which more money was collected.

However, the situation became so serious it was felt action must be taken to prevent the recurrence of such fatal diseases. The committee therefore deputed six gentlemen to take on the onerous duty of visiting the infected parts of the town. They were the Rev.George Best, Messrs. William Hawdon, William and Thomas Standering. John Linton with George Lowther acted as hon. secretary. Their report dated 25th.October 1849, stated they had visited 800 homes and supplied 358 families with the necessary goods and produce to ease their plight. The gentlemen directed attention to the alarming increase in the death rate in Selby which they attributed to the defective state of the drainage and sewerage; the main drain had not been cleansed for at least 45 years. Other contributing factors were the overcrowding of the parish graveyard, where internments were being made too near the surface, and the want of a proper supply of water. The latter was obtained from canal, river or wells and pumps around the town.

Health of Towns Act

At a meeting on the 1st November 1849 it was resolved that the town be placed *"under the provisions of the Act commonly called the 'Health of Towns Act'"*. On the 6th. March 1850 Selby was visited by William Lee, a superintending inspector of the London Board. His report clearly showed the disastrous state into which the town had fallen. This, despite the guidelines on the 1831 posters exhorting the scouring and cleaning of such places as drains, sewers and highways. The inspector's report revealed the average annual mortality had increased from 20 in the 1000 in 1841 to the alarming proportion of 40 in the 1000 in 1849!

The findings of the committee of six were more than borne out by this report which underlined the lamentable neglect of sanitary precautions and proper public works with the consequent prevalence of preventable diseases. It recommended that the building of a suitable water-works and an efficient system of drainage be carried out; the streets be improved to ease cleaning and the parish burial ground be closed. For this the parish was to be placed under the Public Health Act. It was ordered that a Local Board of Health with nine members be elected from gentlemen possessing real or personal estates of £1,000 and rated to the relief of the poor to the extent of £25 annual value. This took place in June, 1851. The six gentlemen, who during the worst of the epidemic had unselfishly jeopardised their lives in the interests of their fellow townsfolk, were elected alongside Jonathan Hutchinson, Joseph and Jonathan Richardson, James Audus and John Burkitt. Robert Morrell was appointed treasurer, George Lowther, clerk and John Linton, surveyor.

Selby's Local Board of Health

Over the years some of the actions of the Board were severely criticised but they did make many moves to improve the sanitary state of the town. It has been shown that a good water supply was obtained; this was in conjunction with an efficient drainage system. The parish burial ground was closed. When it had been realised that the graveyard around the church was too overcrowded to take the cholera victims, a space had been found for them in Abbey Place. This was also closed. In the late twentieth century the sad events surrounding this graveyard were recorded on a plaque, by the Civic Society, and placed on the nearby church railings. In October 1856, a piece of land off the Selby to Doncaster turnpike road was purchased from Lord Londesborough for use as a new cemetery. The whole cost was estimated as £1,200 which it was proposed could be borrowed and the repayments covered by an increase of one halfpenny in the pound on each poor rate. The new burial ground, situated at the junction of Longman Hills Road with Westfield Road, was consecrated by the Archbishop of York on the 21st. October 1858.

Extracts taken from the minutes of the Local Board for 1851-53 illustrate some of the other actions taken by its members in their efforts to improve living conditions for the people of Selby. Alterations and repairs were made to the roads and paths. For example, in 1851 a contract was drawn up with Captain Taylor for a barge of Spurn cobbles to be weighed at five shillings per ton for repair of the highways. Sea-gravel for this purpose was exclusively supplied by Mr. Wm. Standering, chairman of the Board; he was the only ship owner who kept vessels fitted out for this trade. Other materials ordered for the highways were two cargoes of white cliff stones and 50 tons of limestone. Roads repaired included Monk Lane, Scalm Lane, Finkle Street and Ousegate; the last using white cliff stones. The Board also undertook to widen the 'flagg' footpath in Park Street on condition the occupiers of the houses and premises there joined equally in paying the expenses. Three months later the committee requested a list of the sums of money collected from Park Street for the work recently carried out there. Flagging was ordered to be taken up from Mrs. Watson's in the Market Place to the Methodist Chapel down James Street, and redone the same width as at the front of her premises. It appears these flagged paths were pedestrian causeways, providing smooth walkways through the rough and cobbled roads.

Despite the competition from the railways the turnpike roads were still managing to operate. In April 1852 the trustees of the Leeds to Selby turnpike road requested £25 from the Board as a proportion of the expenses for keeping the highway in repair.

The accumulation of dust and debris on the roads and elsewhere was a constant problem. In 1852 the surveyor was given the authority to adopt measures for watering the streets and to have a pump fixed in the brick pond for supplying the water. Dust was still causing difficulties on the roads well into the twentieth century. In the 1930s a horse drawn water cart with a sprinkler bar on the back used to travel along Brook Street, Gowthorpe and Park Street; its gentle spray laid the dust for an hour or two but proved ineffectual when cars outnumbered horses. Their pneumatic tyres tended to suck out the binding medium used on the roads and create ever increasing dust clouds. It was not until tar was discovered to be a good sealant and highways were tar-macadamed that the water cart became obsolete. The 1850's Board of Health had a cart to collect dust, which included household and street rubbish. John Copley was paid eight pounds for a horse to pull the said cart. In many cases such dust was taken away free to yards on the outskirts of the towns where it was sifted through for cinders, bones, and anything else that could be of value. In Selby the street sweepings, including manure, were auctioned off, sometimes raising as much as £15 for the Board.

In the nineteenth century many by-products were put on the fields as fertilisers. A bone mill for the manufacture of fertiliser was founded in Whitley Bridge in 1828. The mill was well supported by local farmers who encouraged the owners to also construct a flour mill. This was done in 1852 and, at harvest time, many of the farmers paid for their fertiliser with grain. In the 1920s the flour mill was owned by John Croysdale & Sons Ltd. who made daily deliveries of flour to the bakers in Selby. The mill, which is still operating today, was bought by Jas. Bowman & Sons Ltd. in 1975; the bone mill had been demolished by that time but small remains of it can still be seen. It is interesting to note that in 1603 a Charles and Richard Bowman left property in Selby for use by a Thomas Bun and his wife, during their lifetime; all other lands were left for the use of the poor, the church and repairs to the highway.

Besides bones, other by-products used on the fields were ashes, dead fish, sludge, bracken, seaweed, soap ashes, hair from tanners, shoddy, lupins, and night-soil. The last item caused many a headache for the Board of Health. For example, George Wright, a farmer, was summoned for laying dung ashes and privy soil on the street in Ousegate. He was not alone, numerous people in and around Selby were summoned for "depositing" unsavoury loads on the streets of the town or for taking them through the streets, *"contrary to the Bye-laws"*. What 'bye-law' became clear when James and George Hebden with George Newsam, servants in husbandry to William Hebden of Wistow, were given notice to discontinue taking manure through the streets of the district between the hours of eight in the morning and twelve at night. The penalty for disobeying was five pounds. It was not made clear whether parts of the loads fell off as the wagons were being pulled along the uneven and rough roads or whether the culprits were illegally dumping their refuse.

The amount of night-soil requiring removal had increased since the committee, in their efforts to improve the sanitation of the town, had in 1851 passed the following bye-law: *"if at any time any house built before or after law, is without a sufficient water closet or privey and an Ash-pit furnished with proper doors and covering, the householder is to be given warning to provide same. If neglected, five pounds each default and forty shillings for every day after time given to do same".*

Mr. Linton, as Inspector of Nuisances was responsible for the control of vermin. He complained that the keeping of piggeries in the town, especially along Gowthorpe, was becoming a nuisance. Many people were ordered to discontinue keeping pigs. They included Widow Ann Obee on New Lane, Joseph Clarkson in the Ship-yard, and Peter Richardson and Thomas Wilson who were ordered to remove their pigs and pig-sty from the latter's premises in the church-yard.

Lodging House Rules

The Common Lodging Houses Act 1851 empowered the Board to pass many bye-laws regarding Lodging houses in Selby. This was at a time when many people were coming into Selby, including a great number of Irish immigrants escaping the famine in their land. Bye-laws set out for lodging houses in Selby aimed to stop the spread of disease. Examples of these are: the keepers were to thoroughly clean blankets, rugs and covers at least four times a year, in cases of fever or other infectious diseases or contagious disorders occurring the keeper was to notify the Inspector of Common Lodging Houses so he could inspect the same and direct any disinfecting process. Mr. Linton had this responsibility, besides being surveyor for the Board, and Inspector of Nuisances. For these duties he received an annual sum of seventy pounds. He instructed the keepers that, after the infected persons had been removed they were to clean any blankets and other things and fumigate the bedding. They were also to reduce the number of lodgers according to the inspector's orders.

Every lodging house was supposed to comply with the following rules: have a dust bin of a size to last for two weeks; a house with a yard to have a separate closet or privy for every 20 lodgers; water closet, seat, floor and walls to be kept free from filth and yards properly paved; floors, passages and stairs to be swept every day before l0am. and washed every Friday before noon; in April and October walls and ceilings to be cleansed and lime-washed; sleeping room windows, except in cases of sickness or bad weather, to be kept fully opened from 9am. until 11am. and 2pm. until 5pm; bedclothes were to be thrown back during this time to air the beds. Night workers only had to keep their windows open between 2pm. and 4pm.

The Local Board of Health fixed the number of lodgers for each house; lists were put up in each room. Two children under eight were counted as equal to one adult. There was to be no mixing of the sexes except for married couples, parent with child under 14 or children not yet ten. There was to be no sleeping in kitchens, sculleries used by lodgers or in rooms below street level. In January 1852, James Flynn and Dennis O'Connor of Spears Yard, Wide Street, were summoned for infringement of the Common Lodging House rules. Dennis Bradley, his wife and daughter, had been found sleeping in the same room. The husband was fined 5s. for not having registered. James Flynn and Francis Higgins of Precious Yard, were both fined twenty shillings for taking in up to eleven unregistered lodgers.

CHAPTER 10

THE TWENTIENTH CENTURY

Education

By the end of the Victorian period (1837-1901) the provision of education for the young had improved so much that most of the children in Selby and elsewhere were attending school. At first, only the '3Rs' were taught for it was thought by many that too much education would risk ruining the master and servant relationship. Attendance registers had been meticulously kept since 1862 when, for a period of thirty years, grants were paid to schools in accordance with inspection and examination results. Poor attendance was looked upon as a hindrance to good work. Even so there were many absentees. In Selby young boys went to work in the roperies whilst girls were drawn to the flax mills. Others, especially from many poor Irish families, took time off to weed corn and flax or hoe turnips. Jane Morley, aged thirteen, told investigators in 1868, she had been out for a year, mostly potato picking. The girl travelled a mile and a half to join a group of about twenty boys, some as young as ten, and a number of women, working from 8am. until 5pm. for ls.6d. a day. John Stead, aged ten, had been 'potato scratching' and weeding turnips in July and for two months in autumn, for three years. He said, some 'little girls' had worked with the boys; they were taken in a cart to the farm two miles away and paid ls.3d. a day.

A school attendance report for the 27th. January 1885 listed fourteen schools in the Selby area; the smallest being Gateforth with sixteen pupils and Langrick with thirteen. The Attendance Committee noted a thin attendance at Selby that day was due to a heavy fall of snow, and also that summonses had been ordered against parents who had ignored notices regarding absenteeism. An Act in 1876 had declared it was the duty of all parents to send their offspring to school but children continued to stay away well into the twentieth century, especially when the town crier informed everyone that it was time for such activities as "pea-pulling".

A year after the death of Queen Victoria, school boards were replaced by county council education authorities with the power to provide secondary education. In 1906, the local authority at Selby bought Gowthorpe House, set in four acres of land, at the western end of the town and, after alterations, opened it as a secondary school for girls. When the 1944 Education Act raised the school-leaving age from 14 to 15, notes were circulated to schools affected by it. The East Riding Education Committee informed its schools when the Act came into force in April, 1947. Those affected in the Selby area were Skipwith, Wheldrake, Thorganby, Elvington, Naburn and Heslington. Scholars of 14 to 15 were transferred to Fulford; Barlby Senior School absorbed pupils from Cliffe, South and North Duffield, Bubwith, East Cottingham, Foggathorpe and Ellerton.

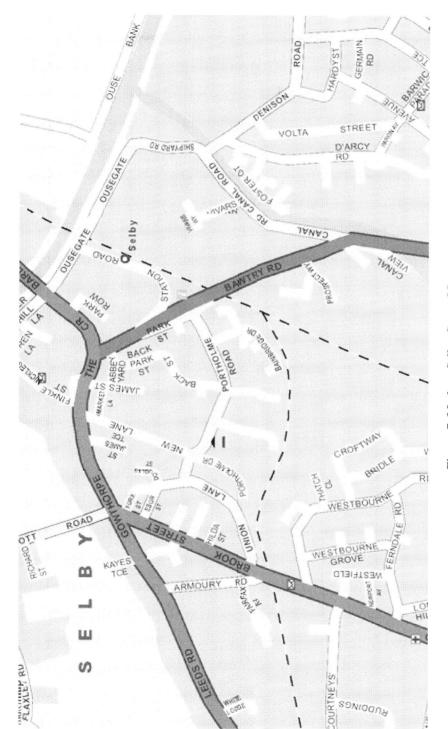

Figure 7. Modern Selby, Street Map

There were major changes in the 1960s when the secondary establishment at Gowthorpe House became a grammar school and admitted boys who had previously attended Drax Grammar School. This in turn became a private establishment. The Wesleyan Methodist School down James Street also underwent changes when Selby came under the authority of the West Riding County Council. In 1915 this body became responsible for finding other accommodation for the five hundred or so pupils in the overcrowded 'Council School'. Two years later it opened educational premises on the site of the present school on Flaxley Road. Twelve months later the new building was gutted by fire! It was almost a decade before the children were able to attend the present school on Flaxley Road. In the early 1960s the vacated Methodist building in James Street was used to house an overflow of older children from Flaxley Road, prior to the building of a secondary school on the Staynor Estate at Abbots Road.

Another place of education opened in Selby in the early part of the century was the Technical College, situated at the junction of New Lane and Portholme Road, on a site now occupied by Postern Gate Surgery. It provided instruction in subjects ranging from embroidery to painting and decorating. Evening classes were also held there for many years before the building was demolished in the 1990s.

Some of the Technical College's classes were taught in the Subscription School, across the road. This building is still fulfilling its purpose as an educational institute. It now houses "The 1811 Learning Centre" where tuition, much of it free, is given in the use of computers. Language courses in Spanish, French and German, have also been introduced.

The educational system underwent many more changes during the twentieth century including; the school-leaving age being raised to 16 in 1973; reorganisation in Selby and other places of secondary education on comprehensive lines in the 1970s, to end selection by examination/assessment and, in the 1980s, the increasing of parental choice of schools and participation in school life. Today in an area covering Selby and Brayton there are seven educational establishments catering for children up to eleven years of age, three for those aged from eleven to sixteen, and one further education college for sixteen to eighteen year olds.

Medical Care

George Lowther, in his memoirs of the late nineteenth century, wrote that there was no sickness fund at that time but money was collected by benefit societies and given as *"free gifts"* of ten shillings a week to members *"on the doctor's certificate"*. The subscription to the unnamed society was three pence. There was also a burial fund out of which ten pounds was given on the death of a husband and six on the death of a wife. Lowther may have been referring to Friendly Societies that existed in and around Selby. They were self-help organisations, providing insurance against sickness, infirmity or death; the money they expended came from a central fund.

Sickness amongst children in the late nineteenth and early twentieth centuries included such life-threatening diseases as scarlet fever, diphtheria and small-pox; outbreaks of whooping cough or measles were known to close schools for weeks at a time. There were many fatalities amongst young children. The vaccination of children against one of these diseases, small- pox, though compulsory between 1853 and 1948, was not accepted by all parents. In February 1872, during a serious epidemic of small-pox, William Clarkson, a book keeper in Selby, was summoned by the Local Board for disregarding a notice sent to him by Mr. A. Shipman, vaccination officer, calling for his son, Percy Allen, to be vaccinated in compliance with the regulations. Clarkson said he had refused on conscientious grounds, but the Board's chairman replied that Acts of Parliament could not be made to suit everyone's conscience and ordered the father to have Percy Allen vaccinated within seven days or pay a fine of one pound and costs. Despite this Clarkson steadfastly refused to comply. His possessions were gradually confiscated to cover the numerous fines imposed until finally, in October, having nine pounds to pay and nothing left with which to pay it, Clarkson was sent to prison for three months.

Dispensaries

When the inspector from the Charity Commissioners came to examine the Feoffees' books in 1867, he noted the absence, in Selby, of dispensaries that, with the help of subscribers, were able to give medical care to the poor. He suggested monies not spent on repair of roads could be used to finance one. Except in dire emergencies the cost of medical treatment kept all but the wealthiest away from the doctor. There were, however, some hospitals where the poor were accepted and dispensaries which gave medicine and surgical help to those in need. These institutions relied on donations and subscribers. In 1875 Selby gained its first dispensary, thanks to a bequest of two thousand pounds left for this purpose by Mrs. Jane Brooke of Gateforth Hall. When the workhouse on Gowthorpe had been demolished, two buildings were erected on the site and in 1875, the one facing Audus Street, became Brooke's Dispensary. In 1929 just over 700 patients were attended to at the dispensary. To be eligible for treatment sick persons were given tickets bought by subscribers.

Another dispensary for the sick and poor, "irrespective of creed or party", was opened in 1889. Situated in The Crescent, it was founded by William Liversidge J.P. of Millgate House. A generous benefactor to the town, he and his lifelong friend, Jonathan Hutchinson, had regularly taught at the Subscription School. Managed by the Wesleyans, the medical centre was much used and appreciated by the poor of the town. When, in July 1948, the Government set up the National Health Service, giving free medical treatment to all, the Liversidge Dispensary became redundant. However, its funds continued to accumulate until in 1982 the Charity Commissioners agreed to the formation of the Liversidge Charity. This continues today to give relief to those in need, through illness, in the form of apparatus, bedding, clothing, washing machines, and even televisions.

Hospitals

The Brooke Dispensary moved in 1901 to become part of a Cottage Hospital built down New Lane, on land donated by Lord Londesborough. The word 'Cottage' referred to an institute without a resident medical officer. Funds from the dispensary were used to erect the hospital and four years later a large donation from Miss Standering paid for further development. Miss Standering displayed great generosity in many ways. For instance, she covered the cost of a Parish hall for St. James', named Standering Hall in her honour. She also gave her time and money when organising Christmas parties for the poor in the Workhouse. The hospital gained the Mary Standering Memorial Ward for women and children, an operating theatre and a mortuary. Dr. George Todd was the Chief Medical Officer and Dr. Arthur Somers and Dr. Patrick Scannell were the Honorary Surgeons. Work casualties received treatment in the Cottage Hospital for which many employees paid weekly amounts into the Selby District Workpeople's Hospital Fund. Mr. Reg. Stamford who started work at the shipyard in 1915 remembered threepence being taken for the fund each week out of his five shillings wages.

An increase in the town's population after the 1914-18 War strained resources at the hospital and, at a public meeting, it was decided to have a new hospital built as a War Memorial. Public subscriptions enabled the necessary land to be bought on Doncaster Road and on the 4th. October 1927, the Selby War Memorial Hospital was opened by the Rt. Hon. Viscount Lascelles. The old Cottage Hospital was sold to the West Riding County Council who had it pulled down and Selby Technical College built on the site. In 1997, some years after this building was also demolished, the space was filled by the Posterngate Surgery.

Over the years innumerable organisations have raised funds for the Memorial Hospital. Galas combined with the Annual Trades Demonstrations were special occasions at which the public were very generous with their money. Sporting events also took place, the most popular being the walking race which always began when the Abbey clock struck five. The walkers then set off from the Bowling Green, to walk twenty miles through villages as far apart as Wistow and Temple Hirst. Help in kind was given by such groups as the Linen League who produced pillow cases, cushions, serviettes and covers for the hospital.

Since 1958 a volunteer group known as *"The Friends of Selby Memorial Hospital"* has provided both funds and invaluable assistance on the premises, allowing the nursing and other staff to give their full time to the patients. Supported by the generosity of the people in the Selby district they have raised about thirty thousand pounds towards the care of those in the hospital.

Although there have been many additions and improvements made to Selby Memorial Hospital it has recently been decided that the original buildings no longer provide adequate facilities for the twenty first century. A new hospital offering a greater number of services is planned for the near future.

Gateforth and Longwood

When Gateforth Hall, the home of the Brookes, was auctioned in 1896, Leeds Corporation bought the building and used it as a sanatorium for patients with tuberculosis. For a short period the small number of Anglican worshippers at Gateforth held their services in its chapel. In 1948 the Hall came under the control of the Leeds Hospital Management and for over twenty years it continued to provide care for patients with tuberculosis or other chest complaints. Since the 1970s the Hall has been used for various purposes, including a restaurant and an hotel.

In March 1893, a case of small-pox was reported in Selby, followed by others in Turner's Square, off Gowthorpe. This outbreak of small-pox helped the authorities to agree that a hospital for infectious diseases should be provided for Selby as soon as a site was found. The Selby Joint Isolation Hospital Committee was formed in 1898 and a fever hospital founded on Selby Common, off the Thorpe Willoughby to Cawood Road. A lady from Hambleton recalled how, in the 1920s, she and her sisters, suffering from scarlet fever, were taken to the hospital in a horse-drawn vehicle, driven by Mr.

Shepherd. Her mother cycled there every day but was only allowed to see her children through a little glass window in the door. All those at home had had to leave the house for a day during which time blankets were hung over the doors and the place was fumigated by council men. Harold Hill, who at 85 is still seen cycling around Selby helping others where he can, also remembers being taken by horse-drawn ambulance to the isolation hospital. He was five at the time and suffering from septic scarlet fever. He does not remember much about the following days for he was dangerously ill. Harold Hill survived to run a General Store at 85 Millgate, with a sixpenny library and Laundry Agency.

A report in 1945 on the isolation hospital described it as being good both structurally and in management, and capable of being extended to serve a wider area. At that time it had 17 beds and one ambulance. A sharp decline had begun in cases of diseases requiring isolation. In 1958, the premises, on a four acre site, were recorded as being used as a geriatric hospital, with 24 beds. Twelve years later, however, Longwood Hospital was closed down following the opening of Castle Ward in Selby War Memorial Hospital. The site was bought by Harris, agricultural engineers. Today, the site on Hospital Lane is occupied by a large dwelling house, whilst further back from the road other more modern premises are being used by various firms, including Pendant Glass.

Selby Abbey Church

Whilst great advances were being made in trade and transport during the 18th. and 19th. centuries, Selby Abbey Church was going through its worst period of neglect. The few who attended the services there, worshipped in the choir because the nave had been bricked up and was being used as a store and a drill room. Prisoners were confined in parts of its ruins and the Blue Coat School used the Scriptorium. A visitor to the town commented *"It is sad this beautiful church is not more reverently cared for. Some of its out-of-the-way corners seem to be treated as if they belong to a barn, not a church"*.

During the Anglican religious revival of the late nineteenth century alterations took place. The nave was opened up and extensive repairs carried out. To achieve this many fund-raising activities were arranged. One person instrumental in bringing about considerable improvements to the church was William Liversidge, a generous benefactor to the Volunteer Rifle Corps in Selby. He was one of three sons, Thomas, William and Henry, born to William Liversidge senior, who, in 1822 was living in Millgate House. In 1885 Thomas moved into a home built for him on Leeds Road, named 'Brooklands' but known locally as 'Jumbo Castle'. During the twentieth century it became an Art School and Technical Institute, and was used for adult evening and day classes. Today, after additions and alterations it serves as a care home for the elderly. Whilst Henry Liversidge eventually made his home in Sherburn, William took over the family home, Millgate House.

The brothers were brought up in a Methodist household but, early in his life, William transferred to Selby Abbey Church and soon became a devoted Anglican. By 1865 he was church warden and under his supervision considerable improvements were made to the fabric of the building. The whole exterior was excavated to the original floor line. The west door was restored and improvements made to the north entrance. Many other improvements including the present approach from the market place were initiated by Liversidge and paid for by voluntary contributions.

Not content with this, the churchwarden pressed for a complete restoration of the church. Plans were prepared by Sir Gilbert Scott; their fulfilment became the centre of Liversidge's life and he financed much of the restoration work. Extensive renovations were carried out on the choir and in other areas damaged by the fall of the tower, two hundred years earlier. Later it was discovered that the foundations were not able to support the weight of the main tower, which had to be reduced in height to decrease the load. The Abbey Church was regaining some of its former glory but on the 19th. October, 1906, all the fundraising, work and care lavished on the building were destroyed in one night.

The Abbey Fire

Shortly before midnight flames were seen pouring out of an Abbey window. Flames and smoke soon filled the sky with the central tower taking on the shape of a huge chimney as smoke billowed from its top. Selby's fire engine arrived on the scene but its usefulness was delayed by the fact that the town's water was turned off at night to conserve supplies. One of the York fire engines arrived by train, but a Leeds brigade was drawn by horses. The firemen driving the latter were uncertain of the way when they reached Monk Fryston railway bridge but were guided by the red glow in the sky seen by a fireman atop a telegraph pole! As daylight came a heart-breaking sight met all those who had gathered to help try to save the Abbey Church. Many spectators stood speechless whilst others wept as they beheld the smouldering ruins. It has never been conclusively decided what triggered off the disastrous fire.

Many tales of bravery have been told about the night as members of the congregation and others, strove to bring out valuables and artefacts from the burning building. There were also tales of souvenir hunters which resulted in the area being roped off and the church closed. This was when Sir Jonathan Hutchinson put the Museum Hall on Park Street, (now the Salvation Army Citadel), at the Abbey's disposal. Services were held there for a year.

The people of Selby certainly *"bestirred themselves"* following the disastrous fire at the Abbey. A restoration fund was quickly set up. All the religious institutions in the town offered their help and donated the greater part of their Sunday Collections. Thousands of sightseers came to Selby so sheets were held out at the south and west gates into which the majority threw donations. A national appeal was launched and contributions came pouring in from all parts of the country, demonstrating how the Abbey Church was renowned for its architecture and history well beyond the boundaries of the town.

Within one month there were enough funds to begin the restoration work. In 1907 the nave, which included Abbot Hugh's pillar was reopened; two years later the choir was ready. The craftsmanship throughout was of the highest standard with Tom Strudwick, the stone carver, maintaining the medieval style. A clock was placed in the tower and the bells rehung. In 1912, a donation from William Liversidge made it possible for the south transept, ruined in 1690, to be rebuilt. Stone for the abbey was again brought from Monk Fryston and Huddleston quarries, offered freely by their respective owners, the Rev. B Hemsworth and Col. Gascoigne of Lotherton Hall. The restoration was finally finished in 1935 when the upper stages were put on the west front using the original pinnacles.

Looking after such an impressive building is an endless task which is made more difficult at Selby because unlike many historical, religious buildings, it is a working parish church so its huge running costs have to be met by the parishioners. Funds are always having to be sought. In 1973 Government aid enabled the abbey to be thoroughly cleaned outside whilst public donations paid for the same inside. It was at this time, when the scriptorium was being cleared that the several priceless books were found, including the 1597 Herbal, *"The History of Plants"* by John Gerarde; the book was updated in 1633 by Thomas Johnson from Selby.

During the twentieth century the Abbey Church was visited by several royal personages, as it had been when the monks were in residence. In 1969 Queen Elizabeth and Prince Philip, marked the 900th anniversary of the Abbey's foundation by holding the Royal Maundy Service in the town. It was the first time the service had been held in a parish church. Seven years later the Queen Mother attended a service of thanksgiving for the restoration of the abbey church. In 1989, Princess Alexandria toured the church during her visit to Selby to open the town's new police station on Portholme Road. At the end of the twentieth century, after a tremendous amount of fundraising and work on the buildings, another royal visitor came to Selby. Hundreds of spectators turned out on the 31st. October 2002, to welcome Prince Charles to the abbey. Stone contractors, William Anelay, had spent much time restoring the west facade and the towers. It gained not only royal approval, for two months after the Prince's visit the Abbey Church was awarded a prestigious national building accolade at the National Stone Awards; a body that celebrated architecture using natural stone products. The monks would have approved.

The Abbey Vicarages

At the beginning of the twentieth century the abbey vicarage was located at the west end of Gowthorpe at its junction with Armoury Road. Mr. Grundy, undertaker, now occupies 145 Gowthorpe, still known by many as the 'Old Vicarage'. The premises were vacated by the church in 1907 when Park House, on The Crescent, was purchased, bringing the clergy nearer to their place of worship. When Canon John Kent retired in 1977 it was realised that future incumbents would not wish to live in such an old, rambling house. For a long time the abbey had owned a building on Church Avenue known as 'The Old Bottling Store', originally the property of Bentley's Yorkshire Breweries. These premises, near to the Hawdon Institute, were converted in a modern style to become vicarage number three. However, this was not to everyone's taste so in 1990 a new house on Leeds Road became the fourth and present home of the vicar of Selby Abbey Church.

Millgate and Hawdon Institutes

In the early years of the twentieth century the Abbey churchmen used the Millgate Institute for their meetings. This building, situated on the part of Millgate that leads to Bondgate was erected in the latter half of the previous century. The institute was the venue for billiards, snooker, whist drives and concerts. When the new school on Flaxley Road was destroyed by fire, it became a temporary primary school. It also housed one of the Abbey's Sunday Schools.

The military took over the premises during the Second World War. Millgate Institute was then bought by the scout and guide movement who still own the premises today. New facilities for the church were built on a site, known as Burton's Yard, that originally contained six dilapidated cottages, close to the north side of the abbey. The site, together with a gift of £1,500 had been given by Col. Hawdon. In July 1924, after further donations, the Hawdon Institute was officially opened by its chief donor. The amenities included space for billiards, table tennis and dominoes, a reading room with a regular supply of newspapers, and an upstairs room with a stage, for dancing and other parish events. Commandeered for use as a military canteen during the Second World War, it reopened in 1946 but now the viability of the place is under scrutiny as the need to adapt its rooms to suit modern requirements is recognised.

St. Richard's Church

When the large housing complex, known as Abbots Road Estate, was built on East Common shortly after World War II, Selby Urban District Council provided a site for a chapel and hall. Generous donations and the work of staunch church supporters enabled a temporary place of worship to be erected there for use until the permanent chapel was opened in 1962. The church hall and vestry were completed in 1975. Today, however, the members are facing a big problem for St. Richard's is in danger of collapse because the foundations are sinking into the soft ground.

Floods

When Prince Charles visited Selby Abbey in October 2002, Ernest Grace took his grandchildren to see the royal visitor. The ex-council worker told the Selby Times that the Prince had spoken to him two years earlier, at the time of the devastating floods that had affected large parts of Yorkshire. Mr. Grace had been part of a team which had worked to raise and strengthen critical sections of river bank along the Ouse, swollen by weeks of very heavy rain. He, and many others, worked twelve hour night shifts for eight days alongside more than 500 soldiers, laying 250,000 sandbags in successful efforts to prevent a threatened deluge. Chinook helicopters were scrambled in to airlift the bags that were being filled by volunteers of every age.

When the flood waters continued to rise, due to the incessant rain, the Environment Agency shipped over three of the world's biggest pumps from Holland. The pumps, seven metres long, three metres high and two metres across, and capable of pumping two tonnes of water per second, were set up at Millbridge in Selby and the ings at Chapel Haddlesey.

Emergency vehicles made their way to as many places as they could in the worst stricken areas of Selby and Barlby. A frozen food firm delivered groceries by canoe, whilst soldiers even used a flower decorated multi-terrain vehicle to ferry Anita Hudson, a stranded bride, and her bridesmaids from Barlby, across Bubwith bridge to the waiting wedding cars and her husband-to-be, Steve Alger.

Hundreds of people were evacuated from their homes during the dreadful floods of 2000. Some were taken in by volunteers whilst others were moved to rest centres at such places as Brayton High School and the Selby Leisure Centre; the army took over the Methodist premises on Portholme Road. As the waters subsided people returned to live upstairs in their flood-damaged houses or to stay in mobile homes whilst the long job of refurbishing their dwellings was carried out. Prince Charles visited some of these homes, the people who had been evacuated and many of the numerous volunteers who had worked round the clock to help those in need during the floods.

As the monks discovered before the Dissolution, the rivers in the Selby area are dangerously prone to breaching their banks. Examples from the last two hundred years include the events of 1794 when the Ouse burst its banks and within two hours the town was flooded. It was reported that the people of Cawood were in such distress that persons from Selby took boat loads of provisions to sell to those trapped in their homes. On the 17th. November 1866, heavy rainfall caused the River Aire to overflow and West Haddlesey lay under water. It then flooded the canal which overflowed into Selby. The villages hardest hit by this flooding were Selby, Snaith, Camblesforth, Hirsts, Haddleseys, Gateforth, Burn, Cawood and Ryther. The family of the late Mr. Prest, covered the losses of their tenants in Cawood and Wistow; they also made a 15% reduction on all rents.

Worse flooding was suffered in October 1892 when large areas of Yorkshire were under water. It was very serious at Selby. The canal had again overflowed its banks causing the stoppage of Great Northern Railway traffic, south of Selby. The Local Board of Health set a gang of men to cut a canal from the river at Ousegate to enable water to get away from the waterworks where pumping operations had had to be stopped. The Abbey well was reopened and used for domestic purposes. All that can be seen of the well today is a small rusty pipe at the bottom of a shed, at the rear of Wetherell's store, in Abbey Yard. In both 1866 and 1892 the canal water seeped into the retorts at the gasworks leaving the town without gas for more than a week. Houses on East Common and the old shipyard area were the worst hit even though the inhabitants had attempted to barricade their homes. Many works had to close. Selby Dam overflowed putting thousands of acres under water. Most stock had been moved to higher ground but Mr. Todd, a farmer at Birkin, lost 300 sheep. He hoped some had gone to neighbouring farms. Roads between Selby and Cawood and down to Haddlesey were impassable, causing havoc to the Monday market

The greatest floods to affect Selby in the twentieth century were in 1947. In March, after a long winter of snow, ice and rain, the only dry area when flooding began, was in the vicinity of Selby Abbey Church. There were floods all over England but, it was said, nowhere else were there so many houses rendered uninhabitable. Approximately 3,000 houses were damaged, 1,400 in the town. More than 200 had over three feet of water inside; the worst had it lapping against the picture rails. Oily water made conditions even worse for residents of Barlby Crescent. There was no gas, sparse electricity, works were closed, crops ruined and animals drowned.

There was no shortage of volunteers who struggled valiantly to help the town and villages. German prisoners of war were drafted in to help workmen repair the river bank at Hemingbrough. They used surplus 'D-Day' barges to help fill up the washed away banks. Soldiers from Brayton Camp helped to move people and goods around the stricken areas. Rest centres were set up but many people clung to their homes even though desperate officials warned them they were in danger of not being fed! Transport was a big problem but the military managed to get some R.N. 'ducks' (D.U.K.W.s) and, with the help of these, rowing boats and assault boats, of a small collapsible type, food was taken to the stranded householders. The crafts went from street to street, putting food, a little at a time, into baskets lowered at the ends of ropes from upper windows.

The clean-up following the flooding was distressing. As one distraught lady exclaimed, "I'd just cleared the last instalment on the furniture. And I'd just got my husband back after six years in the R.A.F. And now this". The council helped in every way possible. Mr. Fenton, an upholsterer, with premises next to Corunna House on

Ousegate, was allowed, (in a time of great shortages), as much material as he needed to repair damaged furniture. The council covered all the costs. Mr. Fenton also delivered food and clothes parcels with the furniture.

A 'Selby and Derwent Flood Appeal' was set up with Cllr. D.M.Cochrane as its president. Vouchers totalling £30,000 were given out to pay tradesmen and receipted accounts for goods such as furniture and carpets. Losses of personal belongings were great. These included shoes, consignments of which were sent to all areas. A booklet entitled "The Tragedy of flood-Stricken Selby and District" priced one shilling, was published to help raise funds. Complete with photographs it vividly describes the terrible devastation caused by the floods of 1947, and shows, as on other occasions, the untiring devotion of those who organise the rescues and help.

It has been said that emergency work carried out following the autumn 2000 floods will be incorporated into new flood defence schemes planned for the near future.

Cinemas

When the River Ouse burst its banks on the 22nd. March, 1947, the water overflowed into Millgate and crept towards the Hippodrome cinema where over 500 people were watching *"The Count of Monte Cristo"*. The water was already seeping into the auditorium, when the manageress, Mrs. Swift, advised by the police to vacate the premises, moved a reluctant audience out of the cinema and onto waiting buses. Selby's three cinemas, the Central, the Hippodrome and the Ritz, were all closed during the floods.

Selby's first cinema, the Globe, opened on Gowthorpe in December 1910. (Scott Road was opened up down the eastern side of the building in 1925). The manager was Mr. Albert Tuck who lived at 51, Brook Street. In the time of silent films the Globe used a gramophone and synchronised the sound with the picture. The cost of admission in the early days was one and a half pence and, sometimes, lucky patrons were given an apple or an orange. This was at a time when apprentices and labourers were earning from five to ten shillings a week.

After eleven years the Globe proved inadequate and was closed down. The rear part of the building was taken over by Mr. T Reed for his joinery and undertaking business. One of Selby's oldest family businesses, begun in 1908, it is still carried on down Scott Road, by Mr. Reed's grandson. He remembers how his father made a special handcart that would fit down the narrow passageways peculiar to old Selby. The Reed family is related to James Mountain, famous for his *"History of Selby, Ancient and Modern"* published in 1800. Pocklington Carpets now occupies part of the site once taken up by the Globe.

The second cinema built in Selby was the Central Picture Palace opened on James Street in August 1913. Proprietors, Richard & Son, auctioneers, estate agents and stock salesmen had the premises next to it. In the twenties it showed black and white films with music provided by a piano, violin and organ. Wooden seats at the front cost either threepence or fivepence. Red plush seats further back were ninepence or one shilling and twopence. The usherette in charge of the plush seats had the highest earnings! Amos Lund, who lived in a row of dwellings in North Duffield known as Seven Houses, had a bus in which he took farming people to the markets at York and Selby. On Saturdays, young people who put their names down were taken by the same bus to the Central cinema.

'Talking' pictures were first shown at the Central in September 1930. The cinema stayed open until the 1960s when audience figures slowly declined as gradually more and more people bought televisions or preferred the new craze for playing bingo. Its doors closed in August 1966, to be opened again within a month as a Bingo Hall. The hall and the premises next door were both demolished in 1988 when the site was redeveloped as part of Safeway's supermarket. In that redevelopment, however, a new Walker's bingo hall was built to the south of the supermarket. In 2004 Safeways was taken over by another supermarket chain, Morrisons.

Both Selby cinemas showed live acts between screenings until longer feature films were made. To accommodate these Mr. Tuck vacated the Globe for the Hippodrome Picture Palace built on a vacant space in front of Alma Terrace, once the site of a soke mill. Before the opening in February 1917 the management was dealt a blow in the form of a Government Entertainment Tax of one penny on all ticket prices - 25% tax on a four penny seat! Reviews, plays and even talent shows were put on at the Hippodrome. In the 1920s, Gracie Fields, one of the stars to appear at the Hippodrome, became stranded in the town because of some trouble on the railways. Arthur Friar, who ran one of the earliest taxi services in Selby, had also started a haulage business. Accompanied by his young son, Albert, he took Gracie Fields down to London in his removal van. She later sent the family a postcard from her home in Capri. Many years later the Selby Accordion Players were one of the turns at the Hippodrome.

The Hippodrome changed hands many times until around 1926/27 Mr.W.J. Swift became manager. The dwelling that once housed the shop where tickets were bought for its shows and films can still be seen on the corner of Alma Terrace and Millgate. This cinema closed its doors in 1955. After being used as a second hand furniture shop it was demolished in 1978 and the site later used for houses.

The last and largest picture house in Selby was the Ritz. Built at the corner of Flaxley Road and Scott Road, it opened in March 1939. During the 1940s an annual 'Miss Senior' and 'Miss Junior Ritz' competition took place. There were many years of arguments and soul-searching before, in 1962, the town's cinemas were allowed to open on a Sunday. However, the Ritz was the only one to actually open and it was also the first to accommodate bingo players.

Audiences for films gradually dwindled down to single figures and by 1982 its days were clearly numbered. Fate then played its part in the Ritz's future; on the first day of December, that year, a mysterious fire reduced the building to ruins. The site is still derelict and at the start of the twentyfirst century Selby has no picture house. However, films have been shown in the town hall using a mobile unit and meetings are being held to consider the possibility of having such equipment to hire out in Selby and the surrounding villages.

Recreational Activites

One group of people who enjoyed using flooded areas were the ice-skaters. As early as 1893 there was a Selby branch of the National Skating Association who, at a meeting, agreed steps should be taken to secure for the whole of the winter season, an extensive piece of ice at Bubwith Ings, where natural flooding took place. Skating was also possible some winters on a large frozen field on Bondgate, and on Carlton Lake.

The building, which later housed the Central cinema, was erected in 1909 to cater for those taken up with the Edwardian craze for roller skating. It was very popular in Selby where private lessons could be had from the manager of the indoor skating rink. Skaters also used facilities at Christies' Ballroom, next to the Station Inn on Ousegate.

In 1899 Lord Londesborough gave two acres of land, between The Crescent and Liversidges' saw mills, (now Travis Perkins, Builders' Merchants), to the council to be used by the town for all time. The park which was available to the townsfolk from the 27th. June was to have no buildings on it save some public baths. The only other reference to a baths hall was the disused one next to the Public Rooms which was converted by Sir Jonathan Hutchinson in 1898. The Baths Hall in the park, containing a pool measuring 25 yards x 10 yards and ten slipper baths, was formally opened by Lord Londesborough on the 9th. May 1901. A chlorination plant was added in 1936. Admittance and tuition fees for primary schoolchildren, in the 1900s, was one penny per head, including *"towels and drawers"*.

The Baths Hall was used for many other activities. Dancing was as popular as cinema-going. During the winter months the pool was decked over and the place converted into a hall licensed for 500 dancers. Harry Parkin's popular dances were held at the Baths on Saturdays and Mondays from eight until ten at night; tickets cost sixpence. Couples at a 'Bachelors' Dance in 1914 danced to the music of Messrs. Bartleys' band until three the following morning! Christies' Ballroom on Ousegate was another favourite venue as was Standering Hall on New Lane. Weekly dance classes took place there from eight until eleven with music provided by the Melodians - a musical quartet. From 1920 classes were also held, on a Monday evening, in the Museum Hall on Park Street, now the Salvation Army Citadel. Costing one shilling and sixpence, the music was again played by the Melodians.

Societies in Selby at the beginning of the twentieth century included the Temperance Friendly Society, Choral Society, Scientific Society, the Selby Philharmonic and the Operatic and Dramatic Society. The latter gave its performances in the three cinemas, then before the group disbanded, in the Baths Hall. On these occasions not only was the water drained away but the pipes were well plugged for the audience sat in the empty pool. As the floor sloped everyone had a good view of such performances as *"The Yeoman"*. The Philharmonic Society gave their concerts in the Museum Hall.

Selby was visited by various travelling shows and circuses. As early as 1835, Mr. Smedley, manager of theatres in Beverley, Pontefract and Gainsborough, came to Selby to sound out the possibility of having one opened in a town that was, at that time, growing in importance. The manager fitted up a temporary theatre on the premises of a Mr. Green in Escrick Street. His show consisted of a *"moral, instructive and awful tragedy"*, followed by dancing, comic soap and a farce. No permanent theatre was erected in Selby for the town was still being visited by travelling theatres in the 1900s. A portable canvas and wooden tented building was put up on a corner of the Recreation Ground off Portholme Road, by Mr. F.D.Albert, who showed motion pictures as well as live variety acts. His cheap form of entertainment came to a sudden end in June 1911 when the structure caught fire and burnt down. However, the generosity of the Selby people enabled him to open a new portable unit on the same site, a few weeks later.

The appearance of Edmund's Wild Beast Show, Bostock and Wombwell's Menagerie or Sanger's circus, was enough reason for schools to be closed all, or part of the day. Statute fairs and agricultural shows also merited this concession. The Selby, Tadcaster, Market Weighton Agricultural Association was formed in 1854. Its first show was held on the Recreation Ground in Selby and was attended by around 6,000 people.

The Association also hosted a winter show in the Public Rooms with a ploughing match taking place on three fields on Selby Common. Isaac Allison won the first prize of three pounds in the competition and H.Smith of Drax Abbey Farm was awarded the top produce prize for his ten swede turnips grown using guano. In 1857, the second meeting held in Selby took place on Leeds Road, in three large fields, owned by Mr. Armstrong of the Londesborough Arms. At this show the music was provided by a band of boys from the Workhouse. Serious cattle plague (rinderpest) that caused heavy losses in and around Selby in 1866, followed by disharmony between the committees caused the town to put on its own show, three years later. The inaugural meeting was held on the Bowling Green, off Portholme Road. The meetings ceased for a while then began again during the Second World War and continued well into the sixties. Band contests were held in conjunction with the shows and crowds flocked to the market place to watch their parading being judged.

Many of today's sports were equally popular in the first half of the last century and several clubs were founded. Boys organised their own football teams and raised money for clothes and equipment by doing odd jobs. This was also true of those who became scouts when that movement began. The Baths Hall accommodated many activities. In the 1930s professional boxing and wrestling took place there. Many years later wrestling was taking place at the Ritz in a joint promotion with television. Athletic Clubs were formed, their competitions often held in conjunction with the shows of the town's Horticultural Society and Flower and Stock group. In the town's council offices is a beautiful silver plated trophy won at an athletics show at Selby in 1889 by Samuel Bramley of Bradford, and returned to the town a hundred years later. During the twentieth century athletes from Selby represented Great Britain at the Olympics. S.Engelhart won the 220 yards race in the British Empire Games in 1930 then two years later represented his country at the Los Angeles Olympic Games. Another local boy, John Sherwood, won a Bronze Medal in the 400 metre hurdles at the 1968 Olympics in Mexico. His wife, Sheila, won a silver medal in the long jump.

In the early part of the twentieth century a small column in the Selby Times was allotted to sports news. Today the activities taking place in the town cover five pages. Sporting facilities have improved tremendously over the years, and whilst some activities, have lost their popularity, others like yoga, t'ai chi, badminton, ten pin bowling and skateboarding have taken their place. Facilities for these in Selby include a new Community Centre built in 1979, a Leisure Centre, opened in 1992, containing a swimming pool to replace the one in the park, and a recently acquired skateboarding park.

Industry

In the 1900s Selby had a timber yard with sawing and planing mills opposite the station, iron works on Ousegate, and a large tannery behind Gowthorpe stretching across where Scott Road lies today. Parts of it were utilised by the Globe and Mr. Reed's premises. Mr. Reg Stamford, remembered flax, mustard, clog and lace mills, and a cattle market that was situated down James Street. Mill owners were attracted to Selby because of the easy access to the town by river and the Aire and Calder Navigation; also the important L.N.E.R. junction with rapid connections, to all parts of the country.

In 1893 Lord Londesborough consented to sell a site in 'Cinder Walk' to the Local Board to be used for a cattle market. Cinder Walk appears to have been a track leading from James Street and along what is now Portholme Road. The owners of the Central Cinema premises ran the Selby Auction Market. Before the advent of mechanised transport the cattle were 'walked' to Selby and up the Cinder Walk from places as far away as Knottingley. By the second half of the 20th. century they were arriving at the Back Park Street entrance in transport ranging from huge cattle trucks to small trailers. The redevelopment of Selby town centre in the 1980s resulted in the demolition of the auction market, the Central, the Wesleyan Methodists' buildings, and Selby Bowling Club premises situated at the end of James Street. The Central disappeared, the Methodists moved onto Portholme Road and the Bowling Club to Brayton. The Auction Market reopened in spacious and up-to-date premises off Bawtry Road, ending the age old tradition of selling cattle in the town. Built on a four and a half acre site within easy reach of the new bypass, the new market has penning facilities for 400 pigs, 400 sheep and 300 cattle.

Selby's long tradition as a ship building centre came to an end in the 1990s. Cochrane and Cooper from Beverley had opened a shipyard to the east of the canal on Ousegate in 1898. The first ship built in the yard was the 'SS Volta', 102 feet long and weighing 168 tons. It was launched on the first day of February, 1899, by Lady Raincliffe. The same year Frank Bulling was apprenticed there to train as a shipwright and loftsman; he stayed with them until he was seventy eight. Reg Stamford began as an apprentice in 1915, aged fourteen. Both he and Frank Bulling had to sign indentures which bound them to work as apprentices for seven years beginning at five shillings a week with a rise of one shilling each year. The apprentices had to follow certain rules which included, serving their masters well and not disclosing the firm's affairs; not frequenting drinking premises, playing cards, dice or bowls, and not getting married before completing their indentures. Bulling's son, Henry, living in Hemingbrough, began work at Cochrane's yard in 1934. He had no indentures to sign but an apprentice's wage had only increased to eight shillings and ninepence a week. Harold Coward, at fourteen, started work about the same time in the quarries at Heck, he was paid four shillings and sixpence. It was also during the thirties that Reg Stamford bought himself a second hand Ford 8 car for fifty pounds.

The vessels made at Cochranes were launched sideways on to the Ouse, it being the only practical method for shipyards in Selby. Over the years the yard built many sizes and varieties of craft. The widest ship, launched in 1986, was the Sea-Link ferry 'Saint Cecilia' built to carry a thousand passengers, 142 cars and twenty roll on roll off trucks. The yard became a member of the Hull-based North British Maritime Group but this did not prevent the regrettable closure of Cochrane & Sons Shipyard in 1992. The owners pulled out of a depressed world ship-building market but it was a huge blow to the town; Cochranes had been a place where many Selby families had earned their living as proud members of a skilled workforce. The last ship built at the yard was the 'MV Forth Bridge', 5,800 tonnes and 96 metres in length. Its owners were Forth Tankers Plc. Edinburgh. The old shipyard owned by Henry Connell had closed in 1958 and when no formal offers were made for Cochrane's the town's historic link with shipbuilding came to an end.

Other firms that provided work for local people in the twentieth century have also closed. Danish Bacon Industries Ltd. and British Sugar Corporation are two examples, but many others have survived. Mr. William Lyall Kirby began milling flour in the town in 1890. He bought the old Abbot's Staithe Flour Mills site at The Quay, leading off Micklegate. After fifteen years he moved to the Imperial Flour Mills built on part of 24 acres of land he had purchased on the Barlby side of the River Ouse. In 1920 he retired and Joseph Rank bought the mills which are still trading under the name Rank Hovis Ltd., flour millers.

Kirby came out of retirement in 1933 and opened Yorkshire Ideal Flour Mill on the site of his old 1890 works. A site which was 'ideal' being near a tidal river which enabled wheat to be imported direct by barge and coaster, and near to good road and rail links to the populated areas of the North. W.L.Kirby's mill was the first in England to use electric power for its machinery. In 1962, when his grandson, R.J.Kirby, was working at the mill, the firm became part of Allied Mills Ltd., part of the Associated British Foods Group. Tug boats, barges and cob boats were used to bring the grain up the River Ouse from the ships berthed at Hull, the latter being used to manoeuvre the barges into position under the mill's elevators. Other mills paid casual labour to fill the buckets on the elevators but in 1933, the Ideal Flour Mill was using powerful pneumatic tubes that sucked the grain into the mill at a rate of 40 tons per hour.

Westmills Food Ltd., took over the site in 1990 for rice processing. In the 1960s river transport had been at its peak with up to 200 ships a year, mostly Dutch, German and Danish motor coasters, coming to Selby. However, most of the mills along the Ouse, and other industries in the area, have now forsaken the river for road and rail transport. Westmills is reversing the trend and utilising its proximity to the Ouse. The rice is loaded in Arkansas into distinctive yellow barges which travel down the Mississippi before being shipped to Hull and then brought up the Ouse to Selby.

A large part of the land bought by W.L.Kirby was sold in 1909 to Joseph Watson who, needing a steady supply of raw materials for his Whitehall soapworks in Leeds, built the Olympia Oil and Cake Company Ltd. on the site. There were oilseed crushing mills, a silo, refinery, storage places and offices. Before he sold the mills in 1919, Watson had three housing estates and the Olympia Hotel built for his workers. Steam tugs capable of pulling six empty or four laden dumb barges were used on the Ouse. The dumb (without an engine) barges were loaded at Hull from ocean-going vessels which had brought in maize, wheat, soya beans, palm kernels, linseed, fullers earth, copra and cotton seed. After many amalgamations the British Oil and Cake Company has become B.O.C.M. Pauls. With the construction of Selby bypass close by, the firm has submitted proposals to develop some of their land at Barlby. If accepted the project, which includes office units, a hotel and restaurant, could create around a thousand new jobs for the area.

Another long-standing Selby business is the paper processing plant down Denison Road. In 1936, its first owners, Rostrons, bought an old flax mill there because of its proximity to water. At first many of the employees worked in a roofless building and finished goods went by horse and cart to the railway station. However the firm grew and in the late fifties it was well established. In 1978 it was taken over by Rigid Paper Products which has continued to develop the site and increase its work force. This company, founded in 1907, currently employs 125 workers locally, but a new hi-tech factory now in process of being built on the East Common Lane site is expected to create 50 new jobs. The plant that mainly deals in buying waste paper and producing numerous kinds of packaging will have a factory that will be amongst the most modern corrugated manufacturing units in the U.K.

In 1823, during the early days of the British Chemical Industry, John Sturge founded a company in Birmingham that went on to produce citric acid from lemon juice. J & E. Sturge opened its plant on Denison Road, Selby, in 1939. Recently there have been many changes of ownership and it functions today as Tate & Lyle. The products from this company are used in industries connected with food and drink, medicine and cosmetics, detergents, organic chemical applications, metal cleaning and for numerous minor industrial uses such as the removal of cement incrustations. Another chemical business still in production, started life off Bawtry Road, as Yorkshire Dyeware & Chemical Co. Ltd. Today it is part of Clariant (UK) Ltd. which continues to manufacture industrial chemicals.

A food producing plant that has offered employment to people in the Selby area for many years, and was once owned by the Fletcher Sauce Company, is the Hazelwood Food Company. It is a sauce and pickle production plant, with a work force of around four hundred people. Another food plant was set up in Gateforth by Stanley Middlebrook in 1936. In 1988 Middlebrook Mushrooms employed around 700 staff and grew over 17 million pounds of mushrooms a year. Today, after several mergers it is owned by Monaghan Mushrooms and operates solely as a distribution centre.

Selby Coalfield

The development of the Selby Coalfield promised to bring people and employment to Selby for many years into the twenty-first century. In 1974 the National Coal Board applied for permission to mine coal at Selby in an area equal in size to the Isle of Wight. The four hundred million pound complex was opened on the 30th. October 1976. Two decades in the planning, it was the biggest deep mining project in the world with ten huge shafts sunk and 124 miles of underground roadways built to link the shafts to a main site at Gascoigne Wood Drift where coal was brought to the surface. Permanently coupled liner trains, known as 'merry-go-rounds', took the coal from this single outlet to the Central Electricity Generating Board power stations. These were at Drax, Eggborough and Ferrybridge where the electricity generating plants, especially the one at Drax with its cooling towers rising to 375 feet and its massive 850 feet chimney dominate the skyline. Many production records were broken during the life-time of this coal-field. In 1995 Wistow mine, operating for twelve years, mined a European record-breaking 200,743 tonnes of coal in a week.

Unfortunately, politics, the global price of coal, alternative fuels, geology and the environment have, between them, brought to an abrupt end what has been described as 'an almost invisible industrial wonder'. By the year 2000 U.K. Coal, decided the Selby coalfield, once hailed as a *"jewel in the crown"*, was too costly to keep open. Miners who thought they had 'jobs for life' have had to transfer to other mines or seek new employment through such agencies as the Regen Training Centre in Riccall. The sudden and unexpected demise of the Selby mines complex has also affected the working lives of people well beyond the pithead to the people who supplied the mines with the many necessary materials and equipment. The future use of the sites is still under discussion.

Two World Wars

The immediate causes of 'The Great War' 1914-18, which happened during the reign of George V (1910-1936), arose from the assassination of the heir to the Austro-Hungarian throne. Events following this resulted in declarations of war by the major powers in Europe, including the British one on the 4th. August 1914 against Germany and its allies. In the early months of that year the Selby Times had carried news of an aeroplane factory being built at Barlow. Two out of three air-ships were to be built at this Armstrong Whitworth works. It was proposed there should be an aerodrome there and 50 to 60 acres near the river be flooded to test sea planes.

The first local news relating to the war noted that it had caused Selby Bowling Club to cancel their match against Surrey. It was then reported that seven Germans working at the Oil and Cake Mills had been arrested and taken to York, but were later released on parole. The war must have become more real when Lord Kitchener's appeal for volunteers was posted on the market cross and a recruitment office headed by Mr.W.H.Latimer was opened at 4, Park Street. The number of tearful farewells at Selby Station increased as reservists and territorials answered the 'Call to Arms'. Local people flocked to the Globe for news of the war and were able to see a film of Selby volunteers training at Strensall, York.

As in other wars the people at home carried out all kinds of activities to raise funds for the forces at home and abroad. Children at the Wesleyan school collected 400 eggs and 25 shillings in one month for wounded soldiers, and joined with others in investing money in an aeroplane bank. Concerts were held at the Museum Hall for British soldiers abroad. One group of ladies gave out cups of tea and buttered buns to soldiers whose trains stopped at Selby Station. The 51 Squadron was formed for three years from 1916 to defend against raids by Zeppelins, large German dirigibles. In *"Hillam, A Village Remembered"*, Mrs. Freda Webster nee Heselgrave, recalls seeing a Zeppelin flying over the village. Soldiers were camped in Byram Park and regularly marched through Brotherton. Mothers gave them jam made from blackberries collected by their children. However, such things as this and War Relief Collections came to a halt in 1918 when a virulent Spanish 'Flu disease that had been spreading rapidly through the country, reached Selby. The 'flu, more deadly than the enemy, killed 25 million people in the world, 250,000 of them in Britain. The young were the most susceptible; the disease closed Selby's schools on more than one occasion.

Imperial Flour Mills, like other firms in Selby and elsewhere, surmounted many difficulties with supplies and transport, in helping the country's food supplies. There were five launching berths at Cochrane's shipyard. During the war an average of two vessels were launched from them every fortnight. These included trawlers, commandeered by the Navy to convert to minesweepers, tugs and small minesweepers.

The war ended when the armistice came into effect at 11am. on the 11th. November 1918. It was a market day in Selby so town and country people celebrated together through the streets. Schools were emptied, shops and works closed and decorations appeared as if by magic. The fire brigade set off its maroon rockets, followed by crackers, fireworks and squibs. The church bells rang out to be joined by the sounds of the newly formed Shipyard brass band. When night fell torches were lit and the shades taken off the street lights, as the people sang war songs.

Twenty years later the worst and only truly global war in history took place. The war in Europe stemmed from Adolf Hitler's attempts to reverse Germany's defeat in World War One and establish the supremacy of a greater Germany in Europe. In response to Germany's attack on Poland Britain declared war on Germany on the 3rd. September 1939.

Minesweepers, minelayers and dan layers to go on convoy duty and anti-submarine work in many parts of the world, were made at Cochrane's shipyard. Five hundred workers were employed, mainly launching at night because of war restrictions.

Cochrane's 'Assurance' class rescue tugs saved nearly 2,000,000 tons of shipping. The tugs played an important part in the 'D-Day' landings. They towed units of the prefabricated harbours known as 'the Mulberries' across to Normandy. Awards for outstanding service in rescue work during the invasion were given to officers in five tugs made at Cochrane & Sons shipyard.

The 51 Squadron was reformed in 1937 with some sections based at Snaith. Other airmen in the area included those of the 578 Squadron. Three units were based on Burn airfield for 14 months during the war. One of their members, Pilot Officer Cyril Barton, was the only Halifax bomber pilot to be awarded the Victoria Cross. He is remembered in Selby by a plaque in the Abbey Church and in the title of a housing estate in Brayton, known as Barton Garth.

It was a Halifax bomber that was involved in the most tragic event to happen in Selby during both wars. One of the aeroplanes, JB789, based at Rufforth not far from the town, had been taking part in a night time 'Circuits and Landings' exercise when it struck the spire of St. James' Church and crashed in flames, killing all seven crew members - five Australians and two British. Eight civilians including the night watchman were killed whilst many others were injured. St. James' Church has remained without a steeple since that day.

Members of the local First-Aid Mobile Units trained all through the war to help at such tragedies. The Railway First Aid Party practised in a sooty loco-shed belonging to the Cawood and Wistow Light Railway, at Brayton Crossing. One of the medical centres was set up at Carlton Towers and there was a Nursing Association in Cawood.

In January 1939 a 'Guide to Volunteering for National Service' had been delivered to every house in Selby. By August the town had 189 air-raid wardens, 101 special constables, 235 first-aid helpers and 21 boy and one girl messengers. On the 14th. May 1940 German forces were streaming across France and the Low Countries making an invasion of Britain terrifyingly possible. Volunteers were appealed for to protect the country. A quarter of a million men enrolled in the 'Local Defence Volunteers' which Churchill later named the Home Guard. Selby and Brayton units used the Armoury as a Drill Hall and Brayton Barff for field exercises. At the same time, around 120 air cadets of 15 and upwards were paying a penny a week to train in a hut belonging to Cyprus Mill down a yard on Gowthorpe.

Again, all sorts of fund raising activities took place for the war effort. In 1940, a suggestion by a Mrs. Simpson of Haigh Street, resulted in a 'thermometer' being set up outside the Londesborough Arms in aid of a Fund to buy a Spitfire. To help this fund a shot-down Messerschmitt 109 was put on display for seven days at Messrs. Watson and Mackays Garage, Gowthorpe. It cost sixpence to view it and another sixpence to be allowed to sit in the single seater fighter. With such fund raising efforts it only took a year to raise £3,366 to send to the Air Ministry.

Amongst other gifts, United Reformed Church members gave twenty pairs of badly needed socks to the men of the Royal Sussex Regiment billeted in the town. Many prisoners of war as well as soldiers were encamped around Selby. Thirty two buses, owned by Bullocks Bus Company were used to transport prisoners from their quarters at Riccall and the site of the mushroom factory at Gateforth, to farms scattered over quite a large area. The 504 PoW camp had its headquarters at Barlby Bridge School and the main camp in Holmes Lane between Millgate and Elston Place. After the war when minor floods preceded the deluge of 1947, prisoners were rehoused at Cowick Hall and Burn airfield. It was then, two years after the war ended, that the Salvation Army and other religious groups welcomed the prisoners to their services and at Christmas families invited them into their homes. Many of the prisoners were allowed to do this, and a choir of forty men from one camp was given permission to visit Naburn PoW Hospital in order to entertain their comrades.

In 2004 Hans Loffler, an ex-prisoner of war, brought his wife, Gisela, to see Selby Abbey Church. He told the Selby Times *"I, was here at a Barlby Camp from 1946 to 1948. Some of my time spent here has given me good memories, some bad"*.

Other visitors to Selby were evacuees. In one instance in 1939, over 1,500 children, with a few teachers and mothers, came from Hull to Selby as part of the evacuation of vulnerable cities. The children were taken in by both townspeople and villagers. Evacuees were advised not to return home but many unhappy and homesick children did. On the Barlby side of the Ouse, 813 children out of 1,774 quickly returned to their hometown of Sunderland.

The 8th. May 1945, was proclaimed VE Day, (victory in Europe), but the Allies remained at war with Japan. When this enemy surrendered on the 14th. August, the following day was proclaimed as VJ Day, (victory over Japan). There were numerous street parties to celebrate these victories. Thoroughfares were decorated, tables and chairs brought outside, then the people, dressed up in all kinds of finery, sat down to enjoy as much food as rationing would allow. During the celebrations that followed the end of the two wars, heartbroken people were receiving news of lost relatives. There are memorials to them including those in the churches around Selby and on Remembrance Sunday tributes are paid to those who lost their lives in the two wars and other conflicts.

Selby Today

Selby became an Urban District in 1888 and retained this status in the West Riding until the reorganisation of local government in 1974. The District of Selby formed at that time is the most southerly in the administrative county of North Yorkshire, and covers 280 square miles with a population of some 75,300. As the largest town, Selby is the administrative centre of the District with a purpose built Civic Centre, erected in1977 on Portholme Road. Although now part of a far larger area the town's historic traditions have been maintained by the creation of a Town Council with a Mayor at its head, whose first official headquarters were in the Community Centre on Scott Road. The town has also retained some prominence as a market town and local industrial centre. It lies amidst a highly productive countryside of mainly flat fields growing various crops including barley, wheat, potatoes, sugar beet and salads. Some of the power stations which give employment to many people in the area have diversified into growing market garden foodstuffs using water from the cooling system to heat the glasshouses.

Over the last twenty years the town of Selby has expanded as a shopping centre. It now has three large supermarkets. One is part of a shopping complex north of Gowthorpe whilst the other two are on either side of Portholme Road. Market Cross, a complex of smaller shops was developed south of the Market Place in 1985. A centre of larger shops has also been built down Bawtry Road, in easy reach of the newly acquired bypass. Selby still holds its markets on a Monday as it has done for hundreds of years. However, in 1933 the 4th. Earl of Londesborough sold all his rights, (held as lord of the manor), at the markets and fairs, to Selby Urban District Council, thereby ending an ancient custom.

The many yards that led off Gowthorpe and Finkle Street have disappeared during the different developments. Shops have been altered and a lot have changed hands several times. One shop, that has hardly changed is Mee and Parvins, a small tobacconists in Micklegate opened in 1886. There were also three family businesses that traded in Selby for much of the twentieth century. W.H.Whisker, (already referred to in Chapter three), moved into 28 Gowthorpe in 1932, extending into the adjacent shop after World War 11 . During this war W.H.Whisker was the sole distributing agent for Selby and the nearby military bases. All the other shops had to apply to him for their allocations of fruit and vegetables; everything was rationed, even potatoes. The 21st century saw the closing down of this family business.

G.S. Everatt, whose large furniture shop is at 47a Gowthorpe, first began work with his father, who had been selling second-hand furniture in various premises in Wide Street since 1919. He then opened his own shop in Brook Street in 1936, from where, like other traders of that period, he worked long hours pushing a cart bearing his wares all around the district. Three years later he moved into larger premises at 39 Gowthorpe but had to leave his wife, Freda (Swift) to run the business whilst he was serving abroad during the war. When hostilities came to an end furniture was scarce so, undaunted, Mr. Everatt set to and converted dozens of ex-army beds and wardrobes into children's bedroom furniture. His shop thrived and many years later he was able to buy a site further along Gowthorpe, on which were hoardings and old buildings. There at 47a he had the store built that is still trading today selling new furniture and carpets made by numerous manufacturers.

Another family business still flourishing at the end of the twentieth century is C.E.Wetherell & Sons Ltd., a large department store, situated at the corner of James Street. Charles Edwin Wetherell, whose father was a farmer at Cliffe, opened his first shop, near the toll bridge, in 1898. He had three children, one being Cyril Lucas who followed his father into the business. As with the other two family businesses, they moved into premises down Brook Street. The family later moved to The Crescent but were sandwiched between two shops owned by Cheesmans. All became classed as Drapers and Home Furnishers. However, the store thrived and today C.E.Wetherell & Sons Ltd. occupy the whole of the premises at the junction of James Street and The Crescent. In 1998, the business, which is now headed by Mark Russell Wetherell, celebrated one hundred years of trading in Selby.

Selby and Cawood Toll Bridges

Disputes concerning the fate of the Selby Toll bridge continued into the twentieth century. When the proprietors offered to sell the bridge to Selby Urban District Council for £6,300 the council did put forward £5,000 on condition the West and East Riding councils and York shared expenses and assisted in the building of a toll free bridge. However, whilst these authorities were dealing with other pressing matters, they were shocked to hear the bridge had been sold to Mr. James Percy of London! By 1910, traffic over the bridge had increased to the extent that concerned councils agreed to have another bridge built beyond the mile limit set down by the Selby Bridge Act of 1791. Local tradesmen opposed this idea so, consequently, the East Riding officials prepared plans for a new approach road on their side of the river. Any further progress was halted by the First World War and when peace came the councils were no longer co-operating with one another.

Matters were made worse when, at midnight, on the 30th May 1930, an oil tank ship named 'Agility' collided with the toll bridge, crashing into a leaf and then becoming jammed almost midway in the navigation channel. The ship was released with the fall of the tide but Selby was left with a damaged toll bridge and a massive traffic problem. Traffic over the river bridges at Cawood and Boothferry increased considerably. Cawood Swing Bridge had replaced the old ferry there in 1872. Its tolls had never exceeded those of Selby and, more importantly, with very little fuss, the bridge had become toll free in 1882. In Selby the L.N.E.R. quickly put on a regular weekday half hour service across the Ouse. There being no trains on a Sunday pedestrians, under the supervision of the railway staff, were allowed across the railway bridge. Just as promptly, Henry Connell, the shipyard owner in charge of bridge repairs, secured a ferry boat from Boothferry and was soon operating a service, using a rope strung across the river. It cost twopence to travel over by train or a halfpenny to brave the ferry crossing. It was the 19th. July before the toll bridge was reopened to the public. Cawood Bridge often served as an alternative route for drivers stranded due to the failure of Selby toll bridge or accidents involving craft on the river.

Many years were spent arguing over the fate of the bridge. Plans put forward included one by the R.A.C. and the A.A. for a high level bridge that would not impede the flow of river traffic.

The Ministry of Transport deemed this an ill-conceived scheme but did look at other suggestions concerning a Selby bypass. World War Two brought a halt to any plans for new bridges or roads.

The toll bridge had become known locally as the 'ha-penny' bridge when pedestrians still had to pay once a day. In the 1930s the toll gates were closed on a Wednesday afternoon, (pay day) so the toll keeper could collect a week's toll of three pence from the mill workers. People grumbled about paying tolls in the days of horse drawn traffic but when mechanised vehicles came into use, creating longer queues, there was even greater agitation to remove the tolls. This happy event happened on the 19th. September 1991, two hundred years after the tolls were imposed. To commemorate this long awaited event, Councillor Angela Harris, chairwoman of North Yorkshire County Council, came to Selby riding in a coach named 'Highflyer', that once ran between York and Leeds. Crowds of people gathered to witness the councillor pay the last toll at Selby Toll Bridge.

Selby Bypass

At the same time as people in Selby and elsewhere were clamouring for a toll free bridge they were also petitioning for a bypass that would avoid the traffic bottleneck at the bridge and divert many vehicles from the town's narrow streets. After decades of delay Selby bypass was finally opened on the 11th. June 2004. Running from the A63 south-west of Selby between the villages of Hambleton and Thorpe Willoughby, the six mile road takes a route south of Brayton and joins the A19 Riccall and Barlby bypass north of Selby, first mooted as far back as 1929. The route has a road bridge, two rail bridges, a Selby Canal bridge and a River Ouse swing bridge that takes 8-10 minutes ro open for river traffic.

In October 2002, a newspaper headline read *"National figures reveal Selby is fastest growing town in Yorkshire"*. It appeared that thousands of people have flocked from all over the country to live in Selby District, making it the top place in Yorkshire for inward migration. Census figures for 2001 showed that the District's population had leapt by 22.7% from 62,300 in 1981 to 76,500 in 2001. The opening of the bypass is attracting new investment to a town with a buoyant economy and a good standard of living. Selby has regained its excellent transport facilities making it easy to commute to other parts of the country.

BIBLIOGRAPHY

Acts of Parliament and Proclamations relating to East Riding of Yorkshire and Kingston upon Hull, 1529-1800, K.A MacMahon (ed), (University of Hull) 1961.

Anglian and Viking Yorkshire, Patricia Scott and D. Thornton (Leeds) 1986.

Anglo-Saxons, James Campbell (ed.) (Oxford) 1982.

Archery, Anecdotes of, A.E.Hargrave, 1845.

Battlefield Atlas of the English Civil War, Anthony Baker, (Surrey) 1986

Battlefield Walks in Yorkshire, David Clark, (Cheshire).

Battle of Marston Moor, 1644; Peter Newman, 2003.

Battle of Towton; A.W.Boardman, (Stroud) 1994

Black Death 1348-49, (Joseph Rowntree pamphlet, York) 1924

Black Death, Philip Zeigler, 1970

Britain and her Army 1509-1970, Correlli Barnett, (Harmondsworth) 1970

British Army, its origins, progress and equipment, Vol.1 Sir Sibbald Scott, 1868

Canal Selby, History and Bi-Centenary of, Pupils of Selby Grammar School, (Selby) 1978.

Castles of Cumbria, M.J.Jackson, (Carlisle) 1990

Cawood, the History of a Yorkshire Village, M.Bell (Cawood) 1987

Cawood, Wistow and Selby Light Railway, K.E.Hartley, (Leeds) 1973

Church Around the Corner, M.Cundiff, (Ketterring) 1987.

Cinemas of Selby, Bill Sutton, (Selby) 2001

Coming of Rome, John Wacher, 1979

Companion to British History, J.Gardiner and N.Wenborn (ed.) 1995

A History of Corunna House, Philip Milsom (Selby) 1997.

Deserted Villages, T.Rowley and J.Wood (Aylesbury) 1982

The Diary of Samuel Pepys, a Pepys Anthology, Robert and Linnet Latham (ed.) 2000.

Dictionary of National Biography, Vol X, Sidney Lee (ed.) 1908.

Directory of the County of York, Vol. 1. E.Baines, (Leeds) 1822.

Disease, Medicine and Society in England, 1550-1862, R. Porter, (Cambridge)

Early Yorkshire Charters Vols. 1-111, William Farrer, 1914.

East Yorkshire, A.N.Cooper, (Westborough Press).

East Yorkshire Railways, beginnings of, K.A. MacMahon, (East Yorkshire Local History Society) 1953.

English Social History, G.M.Trevelyan, 1944.

Exploring the River Ouse, Alison Waite, (Chorley) 1988

Fairfax, John Wilson, 1985

Feudal Kingdom of England 1042-1216, Frank Barlow, 1955.

Fifty Years of Selby; Patricia Scott and Fred Harland, Books One and Two. (Selby) 1988/89.

First Norman Abbey in Northern England, R.B.Dobson, Ampleforth Journal, 1969.

First Post, P.Davies and B.Maile, 1990.

Flax and Linen, Patricia Baines, (Princes Risborough) 1985.

Great and Close Siege of York, 1644, Peter Wenham, (York) 1970.

Great Medieval Houses of England and Wales, Vol. 1, Northern England, Anthony Emery, (Cambridge) 1996.

Hillam, A Village Remembered, Hillam Historians (Selby) 2004

History and Antiquities of the Parish of Hemingbrough, Thomas Burton, (York) 1888
History and Antiquities of Knottingley, C.Forrest (Hepworth) 1871
History and Antiquities of Selby, W.W.Morrell, (Selby) 1867
History of Drax, parts 1,11, John Hunter, (Drax) 1987
History of the English Speaking People, Vol.11. W.S.Churchill 1956
History of the Epidemics in Britain, Vols.1&2, C.Creighton, 1965.
History of Everyday Things in England, Vol. II, 1500-1799, Marjorie and C.H.B. Quennell, 1919.
History of Haddlesey, Rev.J.N.Worsfold, 1894.
History of Hull, E.Gillett and K.MacMahon, (Oxford) 1980.
History of the Merchant Navy. H.Moyse-Bartlett 1937
History of Selby and District ,parts 1,2; Patricia Scott and D.Thornton, (Leeds) 1986.
History of Sherburn and Cawood, W.Wheater, 1882.
History of Yorkshire, S.L.Rawnsby and F.B.Singleton (Chichester) 1960.
History of Yorkshire, Michael Pocock 1978
Humberside Medieval Pottery, C.Hayfield, 1985.
Hutchinson, Jonathan, Life and Letters, Herbert Hutchinson, 1946
Industrial Architecture of Yorkshire; Jane Hatcher, (Chichester) 1985.
In Search of the Dark Ages, Michael Wood, 1981.
Isle of Axholme, Topographical Account, Vols 1,11. W. Peck.
Knottingley, Sailing Ships and Mariners of, R.Gosney and R.Bowyer.
*Leeds Acts of Parliament, an Act for amending the Road from Selby to Leeds, Vol.1,*1820
Leeds; The Story of a City, D.Thornton, (Ayr) 2002.
Lion in the North; J.Prebble, (Harmondsworth) 1973.
Medieval English Pottery; B.Rockham, 1972.
Moated Sites of Yorkshire; H.E.J. le Patourel, 1973
Monastery and Society in the Late Middle Ages; J.H.Tillotson, (Suffolk 1988)
Monasticon Eboracense and the Ecclesiastical History of Yorkshire; John Burton, (York) 1758
Navigable Rivers, canals and railways throughout Britain; Historical Account; Joseph Priestley, 1831
Northern History, Vol.XV11, (Leeds) 1981.
Old Coaching Days in Yorkshire; T.Bradley (Leeds) 1889
Our Island Heritage, Vol.1, Readers' Digest, 1989.
Pelican History of England Roman Britain, I.A.Richmond, (Harmondsworth), 1955.
    English Society in the Middle Ages; D.M. Stenton, 1951
    England in the Late Middle Ages; A.R.Myers, 1952
    Tudor England; S.T.Bindoff, 1950
    England in the Eighteenth Century; J.H.Plumb, 1950.
Pilgrimage of Grace; G.Moorhouse, 2002
Plague, Population and English Economy, J.Hatcher, 1977.
Portrait of the Yorkshire Ouse, I Broadhead (Hale) 1982
Postal History of Goole, Howden and Selby; W.Sedgewick and R. Ward.
Prehistoric Britain; Christopher and Jacquetta Hawkes, (Harmondsworth) 1952.
Prehistoric England; Richard Cavendish, 1983
Prehistoric Yorkshire; Arthur Rastrick, 1976.
Roads and Canals, Transport Revolution in the 19th. Century; Richard Tames (Oxford) 1970.

Roads and Vehicles; Anthony Bird, 1969

Roman Roads in Britain; Ivan D. Margary, 1973

Rural Economy in Yorkshire in 1641. Surtees Society, Vol.33 (Durham) 1857.

Sailing Ships; Colin Munro, 1973.

Selby Abbey and Town; R.B.Dobson (Yorkshire) 1993.

Selby Abbey Church; A.Hutchinson, (Selby) 1948.

Selby Abbey in the Twentieth Century; T.H.Foster (Selby) 2001.

Selby Abbey, Past and Present; Canon Solloway, (Leeds) 1925.

Selby Abbey, the Story of; W.H.Scott (Selby) 1912.

Selby and the Aire and Calder Navigation, 1774-1826; B.F.Duckam (Journal of Transport History, Vol.7) 1965.

Selby/Hull Railways; S.Martin (Selby) 1990.

Selby Streets and Trade Directory, M.J.Curley 1959 and 1970.

Selby, the First Three Hundred Million Years; Henry Farrar 1987.

Selby United Reformed Church, 1809-1984; Charles Bryce (Selby) 1984.

Selby War Memorial Hospital, 1927-2002 Your Hospital; 1927 Committee, (Selby) 2002.

Selby Wesleyan Day School; C.R.Moody (Selby) 1982.

Slater's Directory of Yorkshire. 1887.

Smithson Tennant, 1761-1815; K.R.Webb, Journal of the Royal Institute of Chemistry 1861

Social History of England, Asa Briggs, 1984.

Some Account of the Late Smithson Tennant; J.Wishaw 1815.

South Yorkshire Travellers in 1724-1830; B.F.Duckham (Sheffield) 1967.

Sufferings of Early Quakers, 1652-1690; Joseph Besse, Facsimile of part of 1753 edition, (York) 1998.

Thomas Thwing-Trial for High Treason at York, Summer Assizes, 1680-81; 1681.

Trials of Arthur Thistlewood and Others, from Notes of a London Reporter, (Leeds) 1820.

Turnpikes and Canals; M.Johnston and C.Whitehead, (Hebden Bridge)

Upper Wharfedale; Harry Speight, 1900.

Victorian Histories of the Counties of England, Vol. II and III (Yorkshire)

West Riding of Yorkshire; Arthur Raistrick, 1970.

West Riding Session Book.

West Yorkshire; an Archaeological Survey to A.D. 1500, M.L.Faull and S.A.Moorhouse (ed) Vol III (Wakefield) 1981

Yesterday's Britain; Jonanthan Bastable (ed.) 1998.

York and the East Riding, J.J.Sheahan and T.W.Whellan, Vol.II, (Beverley) 1857.

Yorkshire Acts of Parliament; Turnpike from Doncaster to Selby. 1832

Yorkshire Archaeological Journals:

Vol.5 West Riding Sessions Rolls, Cripples and People with Passes; Fairless Barber 1879.

Vol.6 Rolls of the Collectors in the West Riding of the Lay-Subsidy, 1881

Vol.7 i *Civil War Proceedings in Yorkshire;*

  ii *The Book of Remarks of William Storr of Scalm Park 1678-1731;*

  Rev.W.Consitt Boulter. 1882

Vol.12 The Archictectural History of Selby Abbey; Charles C.Hodge, 1893.

Vol.15 Account Rolls of Selby Abbey 1397-8; 1900

Vol.29 Yorkshire and the Revolution of 1668; A.M.Evans.

Vol.38 *Two Fourteenth Century Effigies in Selby Abbey Church.* Miss A.W.Richardson 1955.

Vol.40 *Seven Archaeological Discoveries in Yorkshire, No.3; Human Skeletons, Riccall Landing.* Peter Wenham 1962

Vol.41 Medieval Pottery, P.Mayes, 1966.

Vol.44 The Abbot of Selby's Financial Statement for the Year ending Michaelmas 1338. G.S.Haslop 1972

*Vol.48 A Kitchener's Roll of the Early Fifteenth Century.*G.S.Haslop 1976

*Vol.52 The Defeat of John Belayse: Civil War in Yorkshire, January-April 1644.*P.R.Newman 1979

Vol.55 The Bishop Dyke and Huddleston Quarry. J.S.Miller and E.A.Gee. 1983.

Vol.64 Cawood: An Archiepiscopal Landscape. N.K.Blood and C.C.Taylor. 1992

Vol 66 Thomas Surbey's 1699 Survey of the Rivers Ouse and Humber. P.Hughes 1994

Yorkshire Archaeological Society Record Series.

Vol.10 The Coucher Book of Selby, Vols.1 and 2. Rev.J.T.Fowler (ed.), 1890

Vol.12 Yorkshire Inquisitions of the Reign of Henry lll and Edward 1,Vol 1. William Brown (ed.) *1891*

Vol.18 Royalist Composition Papers, compounding with Delinquents during the Commonwealth. John William Clay (ed.) Vol. 11, 1895

Vol.20 Royalist Composition Papers. John William Clay (ed) Vol.111, 1896.

Vol.44 Miscellanea: Extents of the Prebends of York (c1295) and Extent of Monk Friston, 1320 T.A.M. Bishop 1936.

Vol.47 Selby Wills; F.Collins (ed.) 1911

Vol 64 The Early Yorkshire Woollen Trade. John Lister (ed.) 1923.

Yorkshire from AD. 1000; David Hey, (Harlow) 1986

Yorkshire Ouse; Baron F.Duckham (Newton Abbot) 1967

Yorkshire Rivers, No.5, The Ouse. Th. Bradley (Leeds) 1891

Yorkshire Woollen Industries; H.Heaton (Oxford) 1965.

Documents and Reports

Riccall Skeletons, York Archaeological Trust, 2002.

Archaeological Watching Brief, Ousegate, Field Report No.35 Y.A.T. 1998.

Archaeological Evaluation of land, Ousegate; YAT. 2003.

Selby Local Board of Health Minutes, (1851-92) North Yorkshire County Council Records Office, Northallerton; DC/SBR MIC 1784

N.Y.C.C, Planning and Countryside Unit, Northallerton:

i) Borehole Analysis, Selby, Y.A.T. 1993.

ii) Desk Top Survey, Selby, Y.A.T. 2002.

iii) Archaeological Sample Excavations in Selby by MAP Archaeological Consultancy Ltd (Malton); 1993, 1994, 1996, 1997, 1998.

iv) An Archaeological Report of Work in Selby for Yorkshire Water; Alison Clarke, 1998.

v) A Watching Brief and Excavations for Selby District Council, Alison Clarke, 1990s.

Assessments/Disbursements-Poor, Churchwardens, Constables and Highway Surveyors, and Perambulations of the Parish 1734-1765;(Sel 50-56), Borthwick Institute of History, York.

Manuscript Copy of Selby Parish Registers, (Sel 328) Borthwick; 1579-1627
Ainsty Deanery Visitations, (RV1 A24) Borthwick.
Roall-Roman Fort i) Lower Aire-Calder Valley Survey, Interim Report 2, B.Yarwood and J.Marriott, 1992;
ii) Aerial Photographic Transcription and Analysis by D.Macleod, 1992; (English Heritage/Royal Commission for Historical Monuments in England, Swindon).
Manor of Selby, File of Surrenders, 1815: DDLO 22/1; Brynmor Jones Library,Hull.
Duties upon Houses, Windows or Lights within Selby Township, 1755; Yorkshire Archaeological Society, Leeds.
Chamberlain, Leonard: History of the Trust, 18th/19th. Century; East Yorkshire Archives, Beverley
Hospitals and Medical Services in Selby 19th/2Oth. Century Katherine Webb, York Health Archives, (York) 1993.
Leeds to Selby Railway, Report to the Committee of the Proposed Railway; James Walker 1829. John Goodchild's Collection, Wakefield.
Millgate Chapel Notes, 17th./ 20th. Century, John Goodchild's Collection, Wakefield.
Census, 1841, 1871, Selby Library.

Unpublished Works:

Royalist Army in Northern England, 1642-5; P.R.Newman, 2 Vols. D.Phil Thesis, University of York, 1978.
Some Aspects of Selby History, L.Atkinson, C.Buckle, M.Falkingham, V.Holmes and A.Tait, (Selby Grammar School, 1970s).

Newspapers, Magazines and Journals:

'Historical Notes' Patricia Scott, and *'Bygone Days'* Richard Moody, (Selby Times) 1980s onward.
Selby Newspaper Cuttings and Selby Town Records (Selby Library).
Articles from the Selby Times, Selby Chronicle, The Star, Yorkshie Evening Press, Yorkshire Post, York Herald and County Advertiser, The Times, Yorkshire Weekly Post, Yorkshire Life, Weekender Magazine.

Web Sites

http://users.ox.uk/peter/workhouse/Selby/Selby.html

INDEX